Seguin's

COMPUTER
Applications

for Microsoft® Office 365

2019 Edition

Denise Seguin

Fanshawe College, London, Ontario

PARADIGM
EDUCATION SOLUTIONS

St. Paul

Vice President, Content and Digital Solutions: Christine Hurney
Director of Content Development, Computer Technology: Cheryl Drivdahl
Developmental Editor: Jennifer Gehlhar
Director of Production: Timothy W. Larson
Production Editor: Carrie Rogers
Design and Production Specialist: Jack Ross
Interior Design: Jack Ross
Cover Design: Jack Ross
Page Layout: Jack Ross
Photo Researcher and Illustrator: Melora Pappas
Copy Editor: Penny Stuart
Proofreader: Eric Braem
Tester: Julia Basham and Janet Blum
Indexer: Terry Casey
Vice President, Director of Digital Products: Chuck Bratton
Digital Projects Manager: Tom Modl
Digital Solutions Manager: Gerry Yumul
Senior Director of Digital Products and Onboarding: Christopher Johnson
Supervisor of Digital Products and Onboarding: Ryan Isdahl
Vice President, Marketing: Lara Weber McLellan
Marketing and Communications Manager: Selena Hicks

Care has been taken to verify the accuracy of information presented in this book. However, the authors, editors, and publisher cannot accept responsibility for web, email, newsgroup, or chat room subject matter or content, or for consequences from the application of the information in this book, and make no warranty, expressed or implied, with respect to its content.

Trademarks: Microsoft is a trademark or registered trademark of Microsoft Corporation in the United States and/or other countries. Some of the product names and company names included in this book have been used for identification purposes only and may be trademarks or registered trade names of their respective manufacturers and sellers. The authors, editors, and publisher disclaim any affiliation, association, or connection with, or sponsorship or endorsement by, such owners.

Cover Photo Credit: © Shutterstock/vlastas
Interior Photo Credits: Following the index.

We have made every effort to trace the ownership of all copyrighted material and to secure permission from copyright holders. In the event of any question arising as to the use of any material, we will be pleased to make the necessary corrections in future printings.

ISBN 9780-76388-753-7 (print)
ISBN 978-0-76388-748-3 (digital)

© 2020 by Paradigm Publishing, LLC
875 Montreal Way
St. Paul, MN 55102
Email: CustomerService@ParadigmEducation.com
Website: ParadigmEducation.com

Printed in the United States of America

29 28 27 26 25 24 23 22 21 20   1 2 3 4 5 6 7 8 9 10

Brief Contents

Contents

Chapter 13
Creating a Table, Form, and Report in Access 305

Chapter 14
Integrating Word, Excel, PowerPoint, and Access Content 329

Chapter 15
Using Office Online and OneDrive........351

Glossary/Index 367

Preface

Course Overview

Today's students arrive in the classroom with more confidence in using technology than any generation before them. You have grown up with technology as a part of your life and the internet as a source of information, entertainment, and communication. Chances are you have used a word processor and a presentation program for several years to prepare materials for school projects. You may have learned your way around a computer application by trial and error. However, to be efficient and successful, you need to learn how to use software applications in a way that saves you time and makes the best use of the available feature set. To that end, *Seguin's COMPUTER Applications with Microsoft® Office 365*, 2019 Edition, provides the tools you need to succeed immediately in your academic and personal lives as well as prepare yourself for success in your future career. In this course, you will learn skills you can apply immediately to accomplishing projects and assignments for school and to organizing, scheduling, recording, planning, and budgeting for your personal needs. You will find the work done in this course to be relevant and useful, with the content presented in a straightforward approach.

Along with well-designed pedagogy, practice and problem solving will help you learn and apply computer topics and skills. Technology provides opportunities for interactive learning as well as excellent ways to quickly and accurately assess your performance. To this end, this course is supported by Cirrus, Paradigm Education Solution's web-based training and assessment learning management system.

Course Goals

Seguin's COMPUTER Applications offers instruction that will guide you to achieve entry-level competence with the latest editions of Microsoft Windows, web browsers, and the Microsoft Office productivity suite, including OneNote, Outlook, Word, Excel, PowerPoint, and Access. You will also be introduced to cloud computing alternatives to the traditional desktop suite. No prior experience with these software programs is required. Even those with some technological savvy can benefit from completing the course by learning new ways to perform tasks or reinforce skills. After completing this course, you will be able to:

- navigate the Windows operating system and manage files and folders.
- use web browsers such as Microsoft Edge, Google Chrome, and Mozilla Firefox to navigate and search the web, as well as download content to a PC or mobile device.
- use navigation, file management, commands, and features within the Microsoft Office suite that are standard across all applications.
- organize and manage class notes in OneNote.
- communicate and manage personal information in Outlook.
- create, edit, format, and enhance documents in Word.
- create, edit, analyze, format, and enhance workbooks in Excel.
- create, edit, format, and enhance slides and set up a slideshow in PowerPoint.
- create and edit tables, forms, queries, and reports in Access.
- integrate information among the applications within the Microsoft Office suite.
- use cloud computing technologies to create, edit, store, and share documents.

Reading time is minimized; you will learn just what you need to know to succeed within these programs. You will practice features with step-by-step instruction interspersed with text that explains why a feature is used or how the feature can be beneficial to you. You should work through each chapter at a PC or with a tablet, so that you can complete the steps as you learn.

Course Organization and Methodology

This course is divided into 15 chapters that are best completed in sequence; however, after assigning the essential skills learned in Chapters 1 through 5, your instructor may opt to assign Word, Excel, PowerPoint, Access, integration, and cloud computing technologies in the order of his or her choice.

Each chapter begins with a brief introduction to the chapter content and a list of learning objectives. Following the chapter opener, each chapter topic begins with a list of skills to be mastered. Each topic is presented in two or four pages. The topics were developed using features available in Microsoft Office 365. You may find that with your computer and version of Office, the appearance of the software and the steps needed to complete an activity vary slightly from what is presented in the courseware. A variety of marginal notes and other features expand or clarify the content. You will gain experience with topic features by working through hands-on exercises, which consist of step-by-step instructions and illustrative screen shots. At the end of each chapter, you will have a chance to review a summary of the chapter topics.

What Makes This Course Different from Others?

Many courses that teach computer applications were designed and organized for software that was in effect one or two decades ago. As software evolves and becomes more flexible and streamlined, so too should software courses. With this mandate, this course has been designed and organized with a fresh look at the skills a student should know to be successful in today's world. The author has chosen and placed in a logical sequence those skills that are considered essential for today's student. Consider this course a "software survival kit for school and life." Nothing more, nothing less!

Many of the student data files in this course are based on files created by students for projects or assignments in courses similar to those students may be enrolled in now. Students will open and manipulate real work completed by someone just like them. Other files include practical examples of documents that students can readily relate to their school and personal experiences.

This Course Is Green!

Instructions to print results have been intentionally omitted for all exercises and assessments. This approach is consistent with a green computing initiative to minimize wasteful printing for nongraded topics or assessment work and also provides instructors with maximum flexibility in designing their course structure.

Course Features

The following guide shows how this course uses a visual approach combined with hands-on activities to help you learn and master key skills and topics.

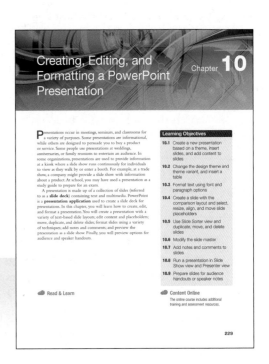

Chapter openers provide an overview of the software, give students a preview of the software features, and explain how the software is used in the workplace. The openers also provide a list of **learning objectives**, which align to each topic.

Chapter Elements

10.1 Creating a New Presentation and Inserting Slides

Begin creating a new presentation on the PowerPoint Start screen by choosing a template, theme, and variant on a theme, or by starting with a blank presentation. The first slide in a presentation is a **title slide** with a text **placeholder** for a title and a subtitle. A placeholder is a rectangular container on a slide that can hold text or other content. Each placeholder on a slide can be manipulated independently.

PowerPoint starts a new presentation with a title slide displayed in Normal view. In Normal view, the current slide displays in widescreen format in the **slide pane**. Numbered slide thumbnails display in the **slide thumbnails pane**. A notes pane at the bottom of the slide pane and a Comments pane at the right of the slide pane can be opened as needed.

① Start PowerPoint and then click the <u>More themes</u> hyperlink near the top right of the PowerPoint Start screen.

② Click the *Ion* theme in the New backstage area.

The New backstage area has a gallery of design themes. Click to preview a theme along with the theme variants. A **variant** is a different style and color scheme included in the theme family.

③ Click the last variant (orange color scheme), and then click the right-pointing arrow below the preview slide next to *More Images*.

Browse through the *More Images* slides to see a variety of content in the color scheme and view the theme or variant style and colors before making a selection.

④ Click the second variant (blue color scheme), and then click the right-pointing arrow below the preview slide to view the blue color scheme with a Title and Content layout depicting a chart.

Watch & Learn

Hands On Activity

- - - - - - - - skills

Create new presentation

Choose theme and theme variant

Insert slide

Edit text on slide

- - - - - - app tip

Double-click a theme to start a new presentation using the theme default style and color scheme.

Tutorial
Opening a Presentation Based on a Template

Topics are presented in two or four pages.

Skills learned in each topic are listed for review and reinforcement.

Step-by-step instructional text accompanied with frequent illustrative screen shots presents instructions for completing the tasks in simple, easy-to-follow steps.

Screen captures with step numbers provide visual confirmation and guidance.

App Tips extend or add to your knowledge of a feature.

Quick Steps briefly summarize the steps to complete major tasks, for quick reference and review.

Text to be typed is set in **magenta font** to stand out from the instructional text.

Oops! hints anticipate common challenges and provide solutions to help you succeed with the topic.

---

⑩ Select *5* in the *Number of columns* text box in the Insert Table dialog box and then type *2*.

⑪ Select *2* in the *Number of rows* text box, type *6*, and then click OK.

PowerPoint inserts a table on the slide with the colors in the theme variant.

⑫ With the insertion point positioned in the first cell in the table, type Type of Car and then press Tab or click in the second cell.

⑬ Type Cost.

⑭ Type the remaining entries in the table by pressing Tab to move to the next cell or by clicking in the next cell and then typing the text as follows:

Small size	$600
Medium size	$675
Large family sedan	$750
Minivan	$775
SUV	$825

Modifying a Table

The Table Tools Design and Table Tools Layout tabs provide options for modifying a table. These tools are the same table tools you learned in Word. Use the handles to enlarge or shrink the table size, or drag the border of a table to move it on the slide.

⑮ Drag the right-middle sizing handle to the left until the right border of the table ends approximately below the *c* in *Maintenance* in the title text, as shown in the image at right.

⑯ Click in any cell in the second column of the table.

⑰ Click the Table Tools Layout tab, click the Select button in the Table group, and then click *Select Column*.

⑱ Click the Center button in the Alignment group.

⑲ Click in any cell in the first column of the table, select the current entry in the *Width* text box in the Cell Size group, type 3.5, and then press Enter.

⑳ Drag the top border of the table to move it to the approximate location shown in the image at right.

㉑ Save the revised presentation using the same name (**CarMaintenance-YourName**). Leave the presentation open for the next topic.

- - - - quick steps

Change Theme
1. Click Design tab.
2. Click desired option in Themes gallery.
3. Click variant option.

Insert a Table on a Slide
1. Insert new slide.
2. Click Insert Table button in content place-holder.
3. Enter number of columns.
4. Enter number of rows.
5. Click OK.

- - - - - - Oops!

Pressed Tab after last entry and added a new row by mistake? Click the Undo button to remove the extra blank row.

Tutorial
Changing the Table Layout

- - - - - - Oops!

Table appears too small with first column wrapping text? You probably changed the width using the *Width* text box in the Table Size group instead of the Cell Size group. Use Undo and then try Step 19 again.

A **Topics Review** chart at the end of each chapter summarizes the main chapter content and key words learned.

Topics Review

Topic	Key Concepts
7.1 Inserting, Editing, and Labeling Images in a Document	Graphic elements assist with comprehension and/or add visual appeal to documents.
	Insert an image from a web resource or OneDrive using the **Online Pictures button** in the Illustrations group on the Insert tab.
	Click the **Layout Options button** to control how text wraps around the image and to change the position of the image on the page.
	Use the **Pictures button** to insert an image from a file stored on your computer or other storage medium.
	Edit the appearance of an image and/or add special effects using buttons on the Picture Tools Format tab.
	A caption is explanatory text above or below an image that is added using the **Insert Caption** feature on the References tab.
	Word automatically numbers images as Figures and can generate a Table of Figures automatically.
7.2 Adding Borders and Shading, and Inserting a Text Box	Add a border or **shading** to paragraphs to make text stand out on a page. Shading is color applied to the page behind the text.
	A page border surrounds the entire page and is added using the **Page Borders button** on the Design tab.
	Apply a border to selected text using the **Borders gallery** from the Borders button arrow in the Paragraph group on the Home tab.
	Shading is added using the Shading button arrow in the Paragraph group.
	A **pull quote** is a quote typed inside a text box.
	Insert text inside a box using the **Text Box button** in the Text group on the Insert tab.
7.3 Inserting a Table	A table is a grid of columns and rows in which you type text and is used when you want to arrange text side by side or in rows.
	A **table cell** is a rectangular-shaped box in the table grid that is the intersection of a column and a row. Text in the table is typed inside table cells.
	A **Quick Table** is a predesigned table with sample data, such as a calendar or a tabular list.
	Create a table by clicking a square in the table grid accessed from the Insert tab that represents the number of columns and rows or by entering the number of columns and rows in the Insert Table dialog box.
	Pressing Tab in the last table cell automatically adds a new row to the table.

continued…

5 Click the right-pointing arrow below the preview slide two more times to view other types of content with the blue color scheme.

6 With the Photo Layout preview displayed, click the Create button.

7 Compare your screen with the one shown in Figure 10.1.

Figure 10.1
A new PowerPoint presentation with Ion theme and blue color variant in the default Normal view is shown above. See Table 10.1 for a description of screen elements.

Table 10.1 PowerPoint Features

Feature	Description
Notes button	Button to turn on or turn off the notes pane at the bottom of the slide pane
Placeholders	Containers in which you type or edit text, or insert other content such as an image or audio clip
Slide pane	Pane that displays the active slide; add or edit content on a slide in this area
Slide thumbnails pane	Pane that displays numbered thumbnails of the slides in the presentation; navigate to, insert, delete, or duplicate a slide in this pane
Status bar	Bar that displays active slide number with total number of slides in the presentation and displays a message about an action in progress
View and Zoom buttons	These buttons change the display of the PowerPoint window. View buttons in order are: Normal, Slide Sorter, Reading View, and Slide Show. Zoom buttons enlarge or shrink the display of the active slide.

Quick Steps

Start a New Presentation
1. Start PowerPoint.
2. Click **More themes** hyperlink.
3. Click theme.
4. Click variant.
5. Click Create button.
Insert a Slide
Click New Slide button in Slides group.
OR
1. Click New Slide button arrow.
2. Click required slide layout.
Edit Text
1. Activate slide.
2. Select text or click in placeholder and move insertion point as needed.
3. Type new text or change text as required.

Tutorial
Exploring the PowerPoint Screen

Tables and **figures** organize information in a streamlined format to minimize your reading load.

Review & Assessment

Chapter Assessments allow you to put your new knowledge to work and demonstrate the kind of thinking and problem-solving needed in today's workplace. For each chapter you will find the following assessments.

An **Audio assessment** asks you to listen to instructions provided in an **Audio File** and then to compose the document, workbook, or presentation as instructed.

A **Mobile assessment** allows you to explore your new skills using mobile devices.

A **Jobs assessment** specifically challenges you to apply your skills to real-world job experiences.

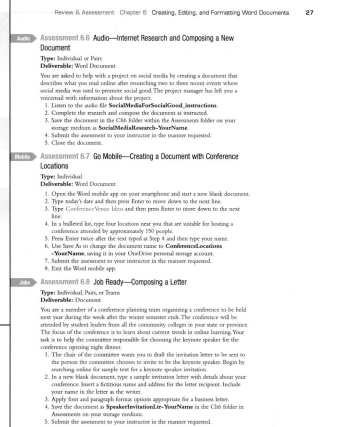

Audio Assessment 6.6 Audio—Internet Research and Composing a New Document

Type: Individual or Pairs
Deliverable: Word Document

You are asked to help with a project on social media by creating a document that describes what you read online after researching two to three recent events where social media was used to promote social good. The project manager has left you a voicemail with information about the project.
1. Listen to the audio file **SocialMediaForSocialGood_instructions**.
2. Complete the research and compose the document as instructed.
3. Save the document in the Ch6 folder within the Assessments folder on your storage medium as **SocialMediaResearch-YourName**.
4. Submit the assessment to your instructor in the manner requested.
5. Close the document.

Mobile Assessment 6.7 Go Mobile—Creating a Document with Conference Locations

Type: Individual
Deliverable: Word Document

1. Open the Word mobile app on your smartphone and start a new blank document.
2. Type today's date and then press Enter to move down to the next line.
3. Type Conference Venue Ideas and then press Enter to move down to the next line.
4. In a bulleted list, type four locations near you that are suitable for hosting a conference attended by approximately 150 people.
5. Press Enter twice after the text typed at Step 4 and then type your name.
6. Use Save As to change the document name to **ConferenceLocations -YourName**, saving it in your OneDrive personal storage account.
7. Submit the assessment to your instructor in the manner requested.
8. Exit the Word mobile app.

Jobs Assessment 6.8 Job Ready—Composing a Letter

Type: Individual, Pairs, or Teams
Deliverable: Document

You are a member of a conference planning team organizing a conference to be held next year during the week after the winter semester ends. The conference will be attended by student leaders from all the community colleges in your state or province. The focus of the conference is to learn about current trends in online learning. Your task is to help the committee responsible for choosing the keynote speaker for the conference opening night dinner.
1. The chair of the committee wants you to draft the invitation letter to be sent to the person the committee chooses to invite to be the keynote speaker. Begin by searching online for sample text for a keynote speaker invitation.
2. In a new blank document, type a sample invitation letter with details about your conference. Insert a fictitious name and address for the letter recipient. Include your name in the letter as the writer.
3. Apply font and paragraph format options appropriate for a business letter.
4. Save the document as **SpeakerInvitationLtr-YourName** in the Ch6 folder in Assessments on your storage medium.
5. Submit the assessment to your instructor in the manner requested.

Visual Assessment 6.5 Visual—Campus Flyer from Template

Type: Individual
Deliverable: Campus Flyer

1. Create a flyer for your school campus similar to the one shown in the Assessment 6.5 Campus Flyer below. Use a current date and a location suitable for concerts on or near your campus. Add current popular band names to the *FEATURING* section. Enter a fictitious web address and sponsor information. Make any other changes you think are necessary.
Note: Search for the template shown using the search phrase simple flyer in the New backstage area.
2. Save the flyer in the Ch6 folder within the Assessments folder on your storage medium as **CampusBandFlyer-YourName**.
3. Submit the assessment to your instructor in the manner requested.
4. Close the document.

Assessment 6.5 Campus Flyer

A **Visual assessment** challenges you to create a document similar to a model document. This type of assessment provides less step-by-step instruction than other assessments and thus requires attention to detail and creative problem solving. Some visual assessments will require internet research or creative writing.

The Cirrus Solution

Elevating student success and instructor efficiency

Powered by Paradigm, Cirrus is the next-generation learning solution for developing skills in Microsoft Office and computer concepts. Cirrus seamlessly delivers complete course content in a cloud-based learning environment that puts students on the fast-track to success. Students can access their content from any device anywhere, through a live internet connection. Cirrus is platform independent, ensuring that students get the same learning experience whether they are using PCs, Macs, or Chromebook computers. Cirrus provides access to all the *Seguin's COMPUTER Applications* content, delivered in a series of scheduled assignments that report to a grade book to track student progress and achievement.

Dynamic Training

Cirrus online versions of *Seguin's COMPUTER Application* course include interactive assignments to guide student learning.

Student Data Files for each section provide the files needed to complete each task. **Audio Files** needed for some assessments are also provided.

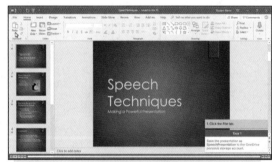

Watch and Learn Lessons show you how to perform the application topic tasks in a video, allow you to read the topic content, and include a short quiz that allows you to check your understanding of the content.

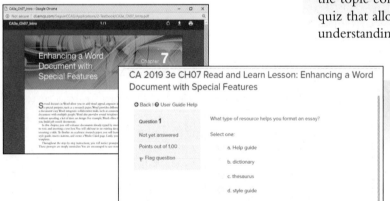

Read and Learn Lessons provide the chapter opening content to read and a short quiz allows you to check your understanding of the content.

Hands On Activities enable you to complete the Topic tasks in provided data files, compare your solutions against a model answer image, and submit your work for instructor review.

Tutorial Lessons provide interactive, guided training and measured practice.

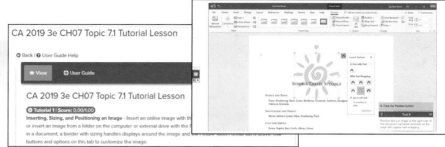

Interactive study tools, including a **Glossary** (including Key Terms, their definitions, and their location in the course), **Crossword Puzzle**, **Infographic** with quiz, and **Review Quizzes** (Multiple Choice, Completion, and Matching) give you an opportunity to help reinforce your understanding of the skills and topics in a fun, visual, game-like way.

Exercises and **Project Exams** provide opportunities for students to further develop and demonstrate topic skills. Exercises and Project Exams are completed live in the Office application and are automatically scored by Cirrus. Detailed feedback and how-to videos help students evaluate and improve their performance.

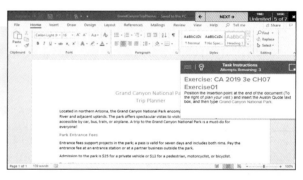

Skills Check Exams evaluate your ability to complete specific tasks. Skills Check Exams are completed live in the Office application and are automatically scored.

Multiple-choice **Chapter Exams** test your overall comprehension of the information learned in the chapters.

Student eBook

The Student eBook makes *Seguin's COMPUTER Applications* content available from any device (desktop, laptop, tablet, or smartphone) anywhere. The ebook is accessed through the Cirrus online course.

Instructor eResources

Cirrus tracks students' step-by-step interactions, giving instructors visibility into students' progress and missteps. With Exam Watch, instructors can remotely join a virtual, live, skills-based exam with students—a helpful option for struggling students who need one-to-one coaching, or for distance learners. In addition to these Cirrus-specific tools, other instructor materials are available. Accessed through Cirrus and visible only to instructors, the *Instructor eResources* for *Seguin's COMPUTER Applications* include the following materials:

- Planning resources, such as lesson plans, teaching hints, and sample course syllabi
- Delivery resources, such as activity answer keys and online images and templates
- Assessment resources, including live and annotated PDF model answers for topic work and review and assessment activities, rubrics for evaluating student work, a skills exam for each topic, and chapter-based exam files

Acknowledgments

The author and editors would like to thank the following individuals for their contributions to and feedback on the course: Julia Basham and Becky Jones; and Patti Ann Reynolds, Toni McBride, and Nicole Oke, Fanshawe College. A special thank you is extended to Michael Seguin for his contributions.

About the Author

Denise Seguin has served on the Faculty of Business at Fanshawe College of Applied Arts and Technology in London, Ontario, from 1986 until her retirement from full-time teaching in December 2012. She developed curriculum and taught a variety of office technology, software applications, and accounting courses to students in postsecondary Information Technology diploma programs and Continuing Education courses. Seguin served as Program Coordinator for Computer Systems Technician, Computer Systems Technology, Office Administration, and Law Clerk programs and was acting Chair of the School of Information Technology in 2001. Along with authoring *Seguin's COMPUTER Concepts*, First and Second Editions, and *Seguin's COMPUTER Applications with Microsoft® Office*, First and Second Editions, she has also authored Paradigm Education Solution's *Microsoft Outlook* and co-authored *Our Digital World, Benchmark Series Microsoft® Excel®, Benchmark Series Microsoft® Access®, Marquee Series Microsoft® Office*, and *Using Computers in the Medical Office*.

In 2007, Seguin earned her Masters in Business Administration specializing in Technology Management, choosing to take her degree at an online university. She has an appreciation for those who are juggling work and life responsibilities while furthering their education, and she has taken her online student experiences into account when designing instruction and assessment activities for this course.

Seguin's

COMPUTER
Applications

for Microsoft® Office 365

2019 Edition

Using Windows 10 and Managing Files

Windows 10 is the operating system (OS) software published by Microsoft Corporation. An OS provides the user interface that allows you to work with a computer or mobile device. The OS also manages all the hardware resources, routes data between devices and applications, and provides the tools for managing files and application software. Every computing device requires an OS; without one, your computer would not function. Think of the OS as the data and device manager that ensures data flows to and from each device and application. When you touch the screen, click the mouse, type words on a keyboard, or activate Cortana to say voice commands, the OS recognizes the input and sends the data to the application or device that needs it. If a piece of hardware is not working, the OS senses the problem and displays a message to you. For example, if a printer is not turned on, the OS communicates that the printer is offline. When you power on a computer or mobile device, the OS displays the user interface when the computer is ready.

Computers and mobile devices have an OS preloaded and ready to use. Some tasks require you to interact with the OS directly, such as when you launch an application, switch to another open window, and manage your files and folders. In this chapter, you will learn to navigate in Windows 10 and manage files on a storage medium.

Note: You will need a removable storage medium with enough storage space to download a copy of the student data files for this textbook.

Learning Objectives

1.1 Navigate Windows 10 using touch, a mouse, or a keyboard

1.2 Sign in to Windows 10, launch an app, and switch between apps

1.3 Use the search text box and minimize, maximize, close, and snap windows

1.4 Use icons in the notification area to view the status of a setting and view customization options for the notification area

1.5 Lock the screen, sign out, and shut down Windows 10

1.6 Use and customize the Start menu

1.7 Personalize the Lock screen, desktop background, and color scheme

1.8 Describe *file*, *folder*, *download*, and extract student data files

1.9 Browse files with File Explorer

1.10 Create new folders and copy files and folders

1.11 Move, rename, and delete files and folders and safely eject a USB flash drive

Read & Learn

Content Online

The online course includes additional training and assessment resources.

1.1 Using Touch, Mouse, and Keyboard Input to Navigate Windows 10

  Watch & Learn

Windows 10 is the latest edition of the Microsoft OS for personal computers (PCs) and mobile devices. The Windows 10 **user interface (UI)** uses icons and a Start menu to interact with users. The **Start menu** is a pop-up menu that displays when you click the **Start button** located at the bottom left corner. In the left pane of the Start menu are two columns. The first column has icons to change your account settings, display the Documents or Pictures folder, open the Settings app, or access Power options. In the top section of the second column are shortcuts to the most-used applications, followed by all of the applications installed on your PC in alphabetical order. The right pane contains tiles. A **tile** is a square or rectangle that, when clicked, starts an app or an application. An **app** is an application used on a smartphone, tablet, or PC that is designed usually for one purpose, to work on a touchscreen, to use less power than a desktop application, and to use fewer network resources. An **application**, which is more powerful than an app, is software used to get a task done with a wide range of functions and features. Applications make use of a full-size keyboard and a mouse, and they are designed for a larger screen and more powerful computing resources.

Windows 10 works with touchscreen input, mouse input, keyboard input, and voice recognition. In this topic, you will learn how to navigate the UI using touch gestures, the mouse, and the keyboard.

Using Touch to Navigate Windows 10

On a touchscreen, you perform actions using gestures. A **gesture** is an action or motion you perform with one or two fingers, a thumb, or a stylus. Table 1.1 on the next page explains the gestures used with the Windows interface.

On a touchscreen device with no attached keyboard, when a task requires typed characters, such as an email address, message text, or web address, the **touch keyboard** (Figure 1.1) is used. Tapping the area that requires typed input generally displays the touch keyboard. If the keyboard does not display when you need to type, tap the keyboard icon at the right end of the taskbar next to the date and time.

The touch keyboard is available in five layouts and two sizes. Tap the keyboard settings icon at the top left of the touch keyboard to choose an alternate keyboard layout or to make the keyboard narrower. Alternate keyboard layouts include a thumb keyboard, a miniature keyboard, a handwriting touchpad for writing with your finger or by using a stylus, and a full layout keyboard that provides access to the full range of keys on a standard keyboard (Figure 1.2 on the next page).

Skills

Describe Windows 10 touch gestures

Describe basic mouse actions

List common keyboard commands for Windows 10

Figure 1.1

The touch keyboard in lowercase mode is the default layout that appears when typed characters are expected.

Table 1.1 Windows Touch Gestures

Gesture	Description and Mouse Equivalent	What It Does	What It Looks Like
Tap or Double-tap	One finger touches the screen and immediately lifts off the screen once or twice in succession. **Mouse:** Click or double-click left mouse button.	• Launches an app or application • Follows a link • Performs a command or selection from a button or icon	
Press and hold	One finger touches the screen and stays in place for a few seconds. **Mouse:** Point or right-click.	• Shows a context menu • Shows pop-up information or details	
Slide	Move one or two fingers in the same direction. **Mouse:** Drag (may need to drag or scroll using scroll bars).	• Drags, pans, or scrolls through lists or pages	
Swipe	Move one finger in from the left or right a short distance. **Mouse:** Click the Notifications icon on the taskbar. **Mouse:** Click the Task View button on the taskbar.	• In from the right reveals the Action Center panel with Notifications and quick action tiles at the bottom • In from the left shows thumbnails of open windows so you can switch to another window	
Zoom Out	Two fingers touch the screen apart from each other and move closer together. **Mouse:** Ctrl + scroll mouse wheel toward you.	• Shrinks the size of text, an item, or tiles on the screen	
Zoom In	Two fingers touch the screen together and move farther apart. **Mouse:** Ctrl + scroll mouse wheel away from you.	• Expands the size of text, an item, or tiles on the screen	

Figure 1.2

The full Windows layout touch keyboard with access to letters, numbers, and special keys.

For some purposes, you still use a mouse and traditional keyboard with a touch-enabled device. For example, typing an essay for a school project is easier using a traditional keyboard, and doing precise graphics editing is easier with a mouse. Connect a universal serial bus (USB) or wireless mouse and/or keyboard for intensive work like this.

Using a Pointing Device to Navigate Windows 10

For traditional desktops or laptops, navigating the Windows user interface requires the use of a **mouse**, **trackball**, **touchpad**, or other pointing device. These devices are used to move and manipulate a **pointer** (displayed as ⬚) on the screen; however, the white arrow pointer can change appearance depending on the action being performed.

To operate the mouse, move the device up, down, right, or left on the desk surface to move the pointer on the screen in the corresponding direction. A scroll wheel on the top of the mouse can be used to move the screen up or down by rolling the finger upward or downward on the wheel. Left and right buttons on the top of the mouse are used to perform actions when the pointer is resting on an item. Table 1.2 provides a list and description of mouse actions.

•—————— app tip

If you run out of desk surface, lift the mouse up off the desk, place it back down, and then continue moving in the same direction to extend the mouse movement farther.

Table 1.2 Mouse Movements and Actions

Term or Action	Description
Point	Move the mouse in the direction required to rest the white arrow pointer on a button, icon, option, tab, link, or other screen item.
Click	Quickly tap the left mouse button once while the pointer is resting on a button, icon, option, tab, link, or other screen item.
Double-click	Quickly tap the left mouse button twice. On the desktop, an application is launched by double-clicking the application's icon.
Right-click	Quickly tap the right mouse button. Within a software application such as Word or Excel, a right-click causes a shortcut menu to appear. Shortcut menus in software applications are context-sensitive, meaning that the menu that appears varies depending on the item the pointer is resting upon when the right-click occurs.
Drag	Hold down the left mouse button, move the mouse up, down, left, or right, and then release the mouse button. Dragging is an action often used to move or resize an object.
Scroll	Use the scroll wheel on the mouse to scroll in a window. If the pointing device you are using does not include a scroll wheel, click the scroll arrows on a horizontal or vertical scroll bar at the right or bottom of a window, or drag the scroll box in the middle of the scroll bar up, down, left, or right.

With a trackball pointing device (Figure 1.3a), you roll your thumb or fingers over the ball to move the pointer on the screen. Buttons on the trackball operate like a mouse for performing actions. Some people prefer a trackball because it responds to smaller movements and the device stays stationary on the desk. A worker with a repetitive strain injury may switch to a trackball because the device is not moved on the desk to move the pointer.

To use a touchpad (Figure 1.3b), move your finger up, down, right, or left across the surface of the touchpad to move the pointer on the screen in the same direction. Tap the touchpad or a button below it to perform an action. Some touchpads support touch gestures.

a   b

Figure 1.3

(a) A trackball (the bright blue ball on the mouse shown) responds to smaller movements of the ball to position the pointer. (b) A touchpad lets you move the pointer using your finger.

Using a Keyboard to Navigate Windows 10

Some people like to use a **keyboard command** (also called a *keyboard shortcut*) to perform an action because it is fast and easy to use. The Start key (Figure 1.4) is positioned at the bottom left of a keyboard between the Ctrl or Function key (FN) and the Alt key. Many keyboard shortcuts use the Start key. For example, press the Start key at any time to bring up the Start menu. Useful keyboard commands are described in Table 1.3. If you prefer using keyboard commands, search online for articles that give other Windows 10 keyboard navigational commands.

Figure 1.4

Some keyboard commands listed in Table 1.3 use the Start key, which is found in the bottom row of the keyboard, left of the spacebar.

Note: Instructions in this textbook are written with mouse actions. If necessary, check with your instructor for the equivalent touchpad or other pointing device action. If you prefer to use touch gestures, refer to the gestures with mouse equivalent actions provided in Table 1.1 on page 5.

Table 1.3 Keyboard Commands or Shortcuts

Keyboard Shortcut	What It Does
Start key	Displays Start menu
Start key + a	Opens the Action Center panel at the right side of the screen
Start key + d	Returns to the desktop from an app or application window
Start key + e	Opens a File Explorer window
Start key + i	Opens the Settings app
Start key + l	Locks the screen
Start key + m	Minimizes all windows
Start key + q	Starts a search for apps, files, settings, and web links
Start key + Tab	Displays Task View to switch to another window
Alt + F4	Closes app, application, or other active window
Alt + Tab	Switches between open apps
Ctrl + D	Deletes selected folder(s) or file(s)
Up, Down, Left, or Right Arrow keys	Moves selection on Start menu to an app or application name, setting, folder name, or tile; pressing the Enter key launches the selection

app tip

To use a keyboard command, hold down the Start, Alt, or Ctrl key, press and release the letter or function key, and then release the Start, Alt, or Ctrl key.

1.2 Starting Windows 10 and Exploring Apps

If you are turning on your PC from a no-power state, the **Lock screen** shown in Figure 1.5 appears. The Lock screen also appears if you resume computer use after the system has gone into sleep mode. Depending on your PC or mobile device, turning on or resuming system use from sleep mode involves pressing the Power button or moving a mouse.

Each person using a computer with Windows will have a **user account**. A user account includes a username and a password or personal identification number (PIN). Windows stores settings information for each user account so that each person can customize options without conflicting with the settings for other people who use the same device. Microsoft offers two types of user accounts at sign-in: a Microsoft account or a local account.

Signing In with a Microsoft Account

To sign in to Windows using a phone number or an email address, set up the account as a **Microsoft account**. A Microsoft account allows you to download new apps from the Windows store, see live updates from messaging and social media services in tiles on the Start menu, and sync your Windows and browser settings online so that they are the same across all devices. To create a Microsoft account, open a browser, navigate to https://login.live.com, and then click <u>Create one!</u>

Signing In with a Local Account

If you prefer not to share Windows and browser settings on a PC or mobile device with other devices, set up an account as a **local account**. Automatic connections to messaging and social media services also do not work with a local account.

Note: The screen images in this textbook were made with a user signed in to Windows with a Microsoft account.

1. Turn on the computer or mobile device, or resume system use from sleep mode.

2. At the Lock screen (Figure 1.5), click anywhere on the screen or press any key on the keyboard to reveal the sign-in screen.

The Lock screen image can be changed. Your Lock screen may show a different image.

10:29
Friday, July 10

Icons show power and network connectivity status. Other notifications may also appear here.

Figure 1.5
The Windows 10 Lock screen displays landscape photos by default.

Watch & Learn

━━━━━━━━ Skills

Start and sign in to Windows 10

Launch an app

Switch apps

Tutorial
Signing In to and Out of Windows 10

━━━━━━━━ app tip

Touch user? When the Lock screen displays, swipe up from the bottom edge of the screen to reveal the sign-in screen.

3 Depending on the system, the next step will vary. Complete the sign in by following the instructions in 3a, 3b, or 3c that match the configuration of your device:

a. Type your password in the *Password* text box below your account name and press Enter or click the Submit button (right-pointing arrow).

b. Type your PIN in the text box below your account name, perform the touch gestures over your account's picture password, or perform another biometric sign-in, such as scanning your fingerprint.

A picture password uses an image from your Pictures library. You must perform three touch gestures over the image to sign in. A PIN code lets you sign in faster using a numeric code.

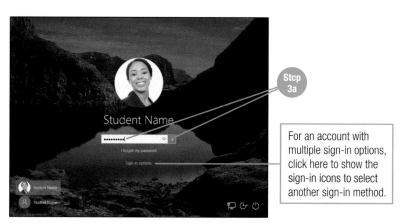

● – – – – – **app tip**

A PIN, picture password, or biometric authentication is set up in the Accounts category of the Settings app. You have to enroll in Windows Hello, which uses biometric authentication to unlock a device using facial recognition, an iris scan, or a fingerprint scan. Note that not all systems support these sign-in options.

c. If the active account is not your account, click the correct account name, picture, or silhouette icon at the bottom left of the sign-in screen, type your password in the *Password* text box, and then press Enter or click the Submit button (right-pointing arrow).

The Desktop

Once you are signed in, the desktop, similar to the one shown in Figure 1.6, appears. The **desktop** displays icons and buttons that are used to launch applications or open

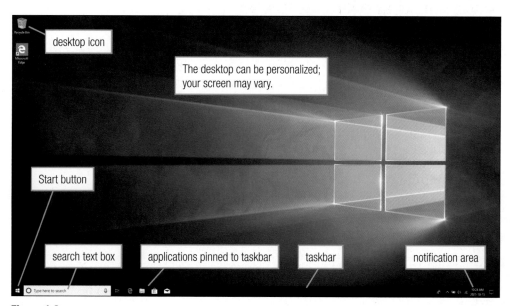

● – – – – – **app tip**

Signing in to Windows 10 on a tablet or other touchscreen device may convert the display to tablet mode, in which the Start screen displays tiles for common apps, a menu button, a power button, and a back button to navigate the UI.

Figure 1.6

The Windows 10 desktop displays a Start button, search text box, pinned icons, and a notification area on the taskbar along the bottom of the window. Icons on the desktop above the taskbar launch applications or open a window.

other windows and displays a taskbar at the bottom of the screen. The **taskbar** has the Start button, the search text box, icons to start applications, and the notification area. The **search text box** is used to locate applications, settings, files on your PC, or information online. The **notification area** at the right of the taskbar shows the current date and time and displays icons to view the status of system settings. When you sign in, Windows may open the Start menu on the desktop for you.

Launching an App

Built-in apps for Windows 10 include Photos, Maps, Mail, Calendar, Groove Music, and Movies & TV, to name a few. The Windows 10 family of apps is designed to look and operate consistently on all devices. To launch an app, click the Start button and then click the tile for the app in the right pane.

Note: If you are using a tablet with tablet mode active, swipe in from the right edge of the screen and tap the Tablet mode quick action tile to turn tablet mode off.

4 Click the Start button if the Start menu is not open. Click the Photos tile in the right pane on the Start menu to launch the Photos app. Messages or prompts may appear when you launch an app with information features or requesting permission to access your location. Close or navigate the prompts as desired.

The **Photos app** shows thumbnails of the photos stored in the Pictures library on a PC, tablet, or smartphone, and in OneDrive, grouped by date.

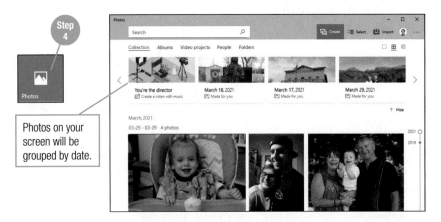

Step 4

Photos on your screen will be grouped by date.

5 Click the Start button and then click the Calendar tile in the right pane.

The **Calendar app** shows appointments and reminders for events stored in your Microsoft account. Birthday reminders for accounts connected to Facebook are shown in the calendar.

Step 5

The current month displays.

 Tutorials

Exploring the Windows 10 Desktop, Taskbar, and Start Menu

Opening and Closing Applications from the Start Menu

●------- Oops!

Can't find the Photos tile? Your Photos tile may be a different size or be live, which means the tile shows thumbnails of images instead of the tile shown here. If you still can't find it, type Photos in the search text box and then press Enter. If the Photos app or any other app in this topic or in topics that follow is not installed on your device, open any available app to practice the remaining steps.

⑥ Click the Store icon on the taskbar.

In the **Store app**, you can search for and download new apps for your PC or mobile device.

Switching Windows

You can switch between open apps by clicking the button on the taskbar for the app, by viewing open windows in Task View, or by using the keyboard shortcut Start key + Tab. Each application or other open window has a button on the taskbar. Pointing to a button on the taskbar displays a thumbnail above the button with a preview of the window and its active contents. The preview is helpful to select the correct window when you have multiple documents open in the same application.

⑦ Click the Photos button on the taskbar.

The Photos app moves to the foreground.

⑧ Click the Task View button on the taskbar.

⑨ Click the Calendar window.

The Timeline feature allows you to scroll down to view items opened in the past 30 days.

This section of Task View shows thumbnails of documents worked on in the past synced across all your devices. You can return with one click to a document, web page, picture, video, or other application.

Task View shows all open apps with large thumbnails so you can easily see the active contents in each window. Click the thumbnail for the app you want to display full-size. The **Timeline** feature in Task View displays along the right side of Task View. To view everything you have had open today, yesterday, and over the past 30 days, scroll down the Timeline scroll bar.

Click the magnifying glass at the top right of the scroll bar to open a search text box and type a name of a document or the name of an application. Windows filters the view to show results that match the search criterion.

quick steps

Start Windows 10 and Sign In
1. Turn on power or resume system from sleep mode.
2. Click anywhere on screen or press any key to remove Lock screen.
3. Type password and press Enter or click Submit button, type PIN, or perform other sign-in authentication.

Launch an App
Click Start button and then click desired tile in right pane at Start menu.

Switch Windows
Click desired button on taskbar.
OR
1. Click Task View on taskbar.
2. Click desired window.

Oops!

No Task View icon on taskbar? Right-click over the search text box or on an empty area of the taskbar and then click *Show Task View button*.

app tip

On a touchscreen, swipe in from the left edge of the screen to display Task View.

Tutorial
Moving between Open Windows

1.3 Using the Search Text Box and Working with Windows

The search text box is a quick way to start an app, launch an application, locate a file or setting, or find information online. Click in the search text box and start typing the first few letters of what you are looking for—app name, file name, or other topic. The search text box is the fastest way to locate help on anything in Windows 10. The search text box contains the dimmed text *Type here to search*.

1 Click in the search text box and then type al.

Watch the entries appear in the results list in two panes above the search text box. Each character you add in the search text box refines the list. Options appear grouped by categories such as *Best match* in the left pane, and Bing search results appear in the right pane. The options along the top filter the search results by Apps, Documents, Email, Web, or More.

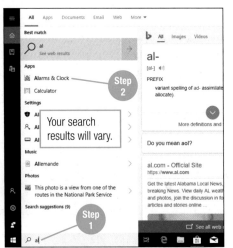

2 Click *Alarms & Clock* in the *Apps* section in the left pane of the results list.

You should now have four windows overlapping each other on your desktop.

Each app, application, setting, or other feature opens in a window, which allows you to view and work on multiple tasks at the same time. Each window contains standard features for moving, resizing, and closing a window so you can arrange items on your desktop to suit your work preferences. Figure 1.7 identifies the standard window features.

The Title bar shows the name for the window. Drag the window with the mouse positioned within the Title bar to move the window on the desktop.

Minimize button   Maximize button

Close button

Point to the edge of any side. When you see a double-headed arrow pointer, drag the mouse up, down, right, or left to resize the window larger or smaller.

Figure 1.7
Shown above is the Alarms & Clock window displaying standard features.

3 Click the Minimize button located on the Alarms & Clock Title bar.

The **Minimize button** is used to reduce the window to a button on the taskbar.

④ Click the Close button on the Calendar Title bar.

The **Close button** is used to close the window. In a window that contains an open document, the document is also closed, and you are prompted to save changes before closing if changes have been made since the last Save command.

⑤ Click the Maximize button on the Photos Title bar.

Clicking the **Maximize button** expands the window size to fill the entire desktop. At the same time, the Maximize button changes to the Restore Down button. Click the **Restore Down button** to return the window to its previous size.

⑥ Click the Restore Down button on the Photos Title bar.

⑦ Position the mouse pointer on the Photos Title bar and then drag the window up, down, left, or right a few inches to practice moving the window on the desktop.

⑧ Click the Alarms & Clock button on the taskbar to restore the window to the desktop.

The **Snap** feature in Windows lets you dock a window to one side of the screen without moving and then resizing the window manually. To "snap" a window to the left or right side of the screen, drag the Title bar of the current window to the left or right edge, releasing the mouse when you see the window outline fill the right or left half. Snap a window to one of four quadrants by dragging it to a corner. The **Snap Assist** feature pops up when a window is snapped, leaving part of the screen empty and other windows open. In the empty portion of the screen, Snap Assist shows thumbnails of the remaining windows. Click the thumbnail for the window you want to fill the remainder of the screen.

⑨ Drag the Alarms & Clock Title bar to the left edge of the screen until the outline of a window in the left half of the screen appears (drag off the left edge if necessary) and then release the mouse.

The Alarms & Clock window now fills the left half of the desktop, and Snap Assist shows you thumbnails for the Photos and Store windows in the empty space on the right.

⑩ Click the Photos window thumbnail.

The screen is now split in half, with the Alarms & Clock window in the left half and the Photos window in the right half.

⑪ Close the Photos, Alarms & Clock, and Store windows.

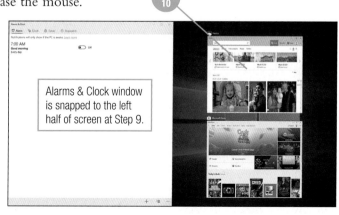

Alarms & Clock window is snapped to the left half of screen at Step 9.

1.4 Using the Notification Area

The notification area at the right end of the taskbar shows the current date and time, the Notifications icon that opens the **Action Center** panel, the Speaker icon used to adjust the volume, and the Network icon, which shows network connectivity. If additional icons are available but not visible, the Show hidden icons arrow is used to reveal other settings. Next to the Show hidden icons arrow is a People icon, which is used to pin contacts to the taskbar. A Power icon is included on devices that have a battery. Additional icons may appear depending on the installed applications. Use the notification area to view or manage the status of a setting or other feature.

Watch & Learn

---------- **Skills**

View system information in the notification area on the taskbar

View the Notifications & actions options in the System category of the Settings app

Tutorials

Adjusting the Sound Volume

Connecting to and Disconnecting from a Wireless Network

1 Click the current date and time in the notification area at the right end of the taskbar.

A calendar appears above the date and time displaying the current month. Change the month using the up- and down-pointing arrows. Appointments or reminders appear in the area below the calendar.

2 Click in an unused area on the desktop to hide the calendar.

3 Click the Speaker icon in the notification area.

The volume control slider opens. Take note of the current value for the volume level.

4 Drag the slider right to adjust the volume higher.

A chime sounds when you release the mouse at the new volume level.

5 Drag the slider left to restore the volume control to the original level.

6 Click in an unused area on the desktop to hide the volume control slider.

7 Click the Network icon in the notification area.

A list of Wi-Fi networks within range are shown, with the active network shaded blue. At the bottom of the panel are quick action tiles. A **quick action tile** is a shortcut to a setting. Clicking the quick action tile for a wireless network you are connected to turns the Wi-Fi connection off. Click the Airplane mode quick action tile to turn on the airplane mode setting, which turns off all wireless communications for your device. You use the Network panel to manage your network connectivity by disconnecting from your current Wi-Fi network or by connecting to another one. To connect to another Wi-Fi network, click the network name and then follow the prompts that appear.

8 Click in an unused area on the desktop to hide the Network panel.

●------- **Oops!**

Does your Network panel differ from the one shown here? If you are plugged into a network via a network cable, the icon shows as a screen with a network plug (▣), and the quick action tiles at the bottom of the panel shown here may not be visible if no Wi-Fi connection is active.

9 Click the Power icon in the notification area. Skip to Step 11 if you do not see a Power icon because you are using a PC that does not use a battery.

In the Power panel, the Battery settings link opens the Settings app with the Battery pane active, where you can adjust options that affect battery life.

10 Click in an unused area on the desktop to remove the Power panel.

11 Click the Notifications icon to open the Action Center panel.

In the top section of the Action Center panel, notifications appear from settings, apps, applications, and your connected accounts. For example, you will see messages regarding installed updates, new mail, or a birthday reminder from the Calendar app. At the bottom of the panel are rows of quick action tiles. The tiles shown vary depending on the type of device in use.

Your panel will vary with notifications specific to your device and account.

12 Click the All settings quick action tile in the Action Center panel to display the Settings window.

13 Click the System icon.

14 Click *Notifications & actions* in the left pane.

15 Scroll down and review the options for customizing Notifications.

16 Drag the switch slider left to turn a feature off or right to turn a feature on for an option that you would like to change, and then scroll back to the top of the page.

17 Click <u>Add or remove quick actions</u>.

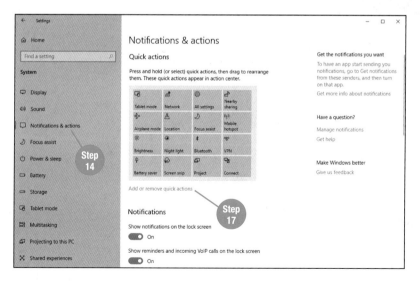

18 Review the options for quick action tiles and drag to slide a switch from On to Off or vice versa for any quick action that you would like to change.

19 Click the Back button (displays as a left-pointing arrow) to return to the previous screen.

20 Close the Settings app window.

1.5 Locking the Screen, Signing Out, and Shutting Down Windows 10

If you need to leave your PC or mobile device for a short period of time and do not want to close all the apps and documents, you can lock the device. Locking the system causes the Lock screen image to appear full screen so someone else cannot see your work. All your apps, applications, and documents are left open in the background, and you can resume work right away once you unlock the device with your password, PIN, picture password, or biometric authentication.

1. Click the Start button, type photos in the search text box and press Enter, or click the Photos tile to launch the Photos app.
2. Click the Start button.
3. Click the icon for your account at the top of the first column in the left pane.
4. Click *Lock*.

The Windows Lock screen appears with the current date and time and notifications, if any are available.

Step 4

Change account settings

Lock

Sign out

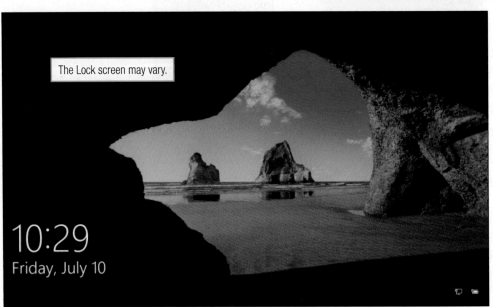

The Lock screen may vary.

10:29
Friday, July 10

5. Click anywhere on the Lock screen or press any key on the keyboard to display the sign-in screen.
6. Sign in with your account authentication credential.

Notice when you are back at the desktop that the Photos app remained open while the device was locked.

Signing Out of a Windows Session

When you are finished with a Windows session, you should **sign out** of the PC or mobile device. Signing out is also referred to as *logging off*. Signing out closes all apps, applications, and files. If a computer or mobile device is shared with other people, signing out is expected so that other users can sign in to their accounts. Signing out and locking also provide security for your device because someone would need to know your password, PIN, or picture password touch gestures to access applications or files.

Watch & Learn

Skills

Lock the Screen
Sign out of Windows 10
Shut down Windows 10

Tutorials

Locking the Screen
Signing Out of a Windows Session

app tip

If you have documents open with unsaved changes, Windows prompts you to save the documents before proceeding with the sign-out process.

7 If necessary, click the Start button.

8 Click the icon for your account at the top of the first column in the left pane, and then click *Sign out*.

Step 8

The Windows Lock screen appears; however, this time Windows closes the Photos app automatically.

9 Display the sign-in screen and sign in with your account authentication credential.

Notice the Photos app is not on the desktop because it was closed when you signed out of the previous Windows session.

Shutting Down the PC or Mobile Device

If you want to turn off the power to your computer or mobile device, perform a **shut down** command. Shutting down the system ensures that all Windows files are properly closed. The power turns off automatically when shut down is complete.

10 If necessary, click the Start button.

11 Click the Power icon at the bottom of the first column in the left pane.

Step 11   **Step 12**

Note: Check with your instructor before proceeding to Step 12, because some schools do not allow students to shut down computers. If necessary, click in an unused area on the desktop to remove the Start menu and proceed to the next topic.

12 Click *Shut down*. If someone else is signed in on the device you are shutting down, a message displays informing you the other user could lose unsaved work if you proceed (Figure 1.8). Click the Shut down anyway button to proceed with turning off the device, or click in an unused area on the desktop to remove the message and cancel the shutdown operation.

In a few seconds, the power will turn off. In some instances, system updates will be installed during a shutdown operation.

Figure 1.8

This warning message appears if you are about to power off a PC and someone else using the same computer has not signed out. Proceeding to shut down may cause her or him to lose changes that were not saved.

13 Wait a moment or two and then press the power button to turn the PC back on.

14 When the Lock screen appears, display the sign-in screen and then sign back in to Windows.

quick steps

Lock Device
1. Click Start button.
2. Click account icon.
3. Click *Lock*.

Sign Out of Windows
1. Click Start button.
2. Click account icon.
3. Click *Sign out*.

Shut Down PC or Mobile Device
1. Click Start button.
2. Click Power icon.
3. Click *Shut down*.

Tutorial

Shutting Down the PC or Mobile Device

app tip

The Restart command in the Power menu is often used to reset a PC when issues are occurring that are preventing normal operations. Restart is also called a *warm boot*.

1.6 Using and Customizing the Start Menu

The Start menu can be customized to suit your preferences by adding or removing tiles, rearranging tiles, resizing a tile, and turning a live tile on or off to enable or stop notifications or other content from appearing on the tile.

Note: In some school computer labs, the ability to change Windows settings is disabled. If necessary, complete this topic and the next topic on a home computer.

1. Double-click the Recycle Bin icon on the desktop to open the Recycle Bin window.

2. Click the Start button, and then click the Settings icon (first icon above the Power icon) to open the Settings app.

3. Click the Start button, scroll down the list of applications, and then click *Money* to launch the Money app. Choose another app if you do not have the Money app installed.

4. Click in the search text box, type calc, and then press Enter to launch the Calculator app.

5. Close the Calculator, Money, Settings, and Recycle Bin windows.

The methods you just practiced to start apps and open a window included the following: double-clicking an icon on the desktop, clicking an option in the left pane on the Start menu, clicking a tile in the right pane on the Start menu, and typing the first few characters in the search text box. The method you decide to use most often is a personal preference. You will develop your own style for using the Start menu and desktop interface as you gain experience.

Resizing the Start Menu

You can make the Start menu wider or taller by dragging the top of the Start menu up or the right border right. Drag the top border down or right border left to make the Start menu shorter or narrower.

6. Click the Start button, point at the right border of the Start menu, and then drag right when the pointer changes to a right-and-left-pointing arrow to make the menu wider. If your menu is already at the maximum width, drag the border left to make the menu narrower.

7. With the Start menu still open, point at the top border and then drag up when the pointer changes to an up-and-down-pointing arrow to make the menu taller.

Watch & Learn

skills

Navigate the Start menu

Resize the Start menu

Pin/unpin a tile to/from the Start menu

Move a tile

Resize a tile

Turn on and off live updates

app tip

Right-click the Start button to open the Quick Access menu, which provides access to advanced system tools, such as Device Manager, Computer Management, and Task Manager, to name a few.

Tutorials

Using the Start Menu

Resizing the Start Menu

Pinning and Unpinning Tiles to and from the Start Menu

Right-click a tile to reveal the shortcut menu with the options *Unpin from Start*, *Resize*, and *More*. The More menu is used to access the options *Turn Live Tile on* or *Turn Live Tile off* (depending on its current state), *Pin to taskbar*, *App settings*, *Rate and review*, and *Share*. Click **Unpin from Start** to remove the tile from the Start menu. A tile is added to the Start menu by right-clicking the app or application name in the application list on the Start menu, and then clicking **Pin to Start**. The shortcut menu offers more or fewer choices depending on the app or application name that you right-click on the Start menu.

8 With the Start menu open, right-click the Photos tile and then click *Unpin from Start* on the shortcut menu.

The tile is removed, and the Start menu remains open.

9 Scroll down the list of applications in the left pane, and then right-click *Photos*.

10 Click *Pin to Start* on the shortcut menu.

The Photos tile is added back to the Start menu, and the Start menu remains open. Notice that the tile is not added back to the same location from which it originated.

Rearranging Tiles

Tiles can be moved to a new location on the Start menu by dragging the tile to the desired location.

11 Drag the Photos tile back to its original location in the right pane on the Start menu.

As you drag a tile around on the Start menu, the tiles are dimmed, and you will notice other tiles shifting around to make room for the tile.

Resizing a Tile and Turning Live Updates Off or On

Tiles are either square or rectangular in shape and can be sized Small, Medium, Wide, or Large using the *Resize* option on the shortcut menu. Some tiles do not offer all size options. Some tiles display live updates, with notifications, headlines, or pictures displayed on the tile. Change the live update status using the **Turn Live Tile off** or **Turn Live Tile on** option on the shortcut menu.

12 With the Start menu open, right-click the Calendar tile, point to *Resize*, and then click *Large*.

13 Right-click the Calendar tile, point to *Resize*, and then click *Medium*. If necessary, drag the Mail or another tile back upward to fill in the space next to the Calendar tile.

14 Right-click the Mail tile, point to *More*, and then click *Turn Live Tile off*.

15 Right-click the Mail tile, point to *More*, and then click *Turn Live Tile on*.

16 Resize the Start menu back to its original height and width, if desired.

17 Rearrange tiles or make other changes as needed to restore the Start menu to its original settings. Click on an unused area of the desktop to close the Start menu.

● ---- quick steps

Remove a Tile from the Start Menu
1. Right-click tile.
2. Click *Unpin from Start.*

Add a Tile to the Start Menu
1. Click Start button.
2. Scroll down left pane list to locate desired app or application name.
3. Right-click app or application name.
4. Click *Pin to Start.*

Rearrange Tiles
Drag tile to desired location.

Resize a Tile
1. Right-click tile.
2. Point to *Resize.*
3. Click desired size.

Turn Off/On Live Updates
1. Right-click tile, then point to *More.*
2. Click *Turn Live Tile off* or *Turn Live Tile on.*

☁ **Tutorials**

Pinning and Unpinning Tiles to and from the Start Menu

Rearranging Tiles

Resizing a Tile and Turning Live Updates Off or On

1.7 Personalizing the Lock Screen and the Desktop

Most people like to put a personal stamp on their device. In Windows 10, you can personalize the Lock screen by changing the picture that displays and the apps that provide notifications when the screen locks. The desktop background can be changed to another image, and a different color can be chosen for tiles and window accents. A theme changes the background image, color, and sound scheme in one step. The Start menu by default shows the most used and recently added apps and applications in the left pane. You can turn one or both of these categories off. Open the Settings app and click *Personalization* to make the changes described.

1 Click the Start button and then click the Settings icon.

2 Click *Personalization* in the Settings window.

3 Click *Lock screen* in the left pane.

The current Lock screen image is shown above five thumbnails for other background images on the Lock screen pane. Click a thumbnail to preview the image or click the Browse button to choose an image on your computer to use as the Lock screen image. You can also opt to show a slide show for the Lock screen by changing the *Background* option from *Picture* to *Slideshow*.

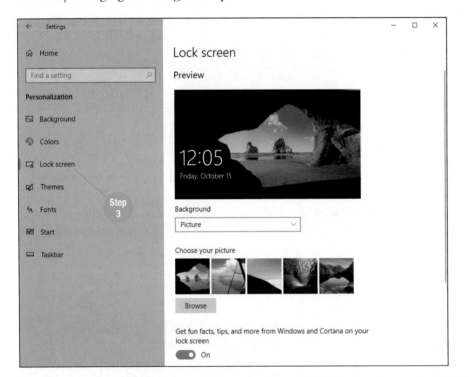

4 Click one of the five background thumbnails below the current Lock screen image. You determine the background image you want to view.

The app buttons below the background thumbnails control which apps give notifications on the Lock screen image.

5 If necessary, scroll down to view the *Choose apps to show quick status* section, click the first button with a plus symbol and then click *Weather*.

The Weather app will now provide notifications when the screen is locked.

6 Click the *Background* option in the left pane.

7 Click one of the five background thumbnails in the *Choose your picture* section. You determine which picture you want for your background. If the *Choose your picture* thumbnails are not visible, click the *Background* option box arrow and then click *Picture*.

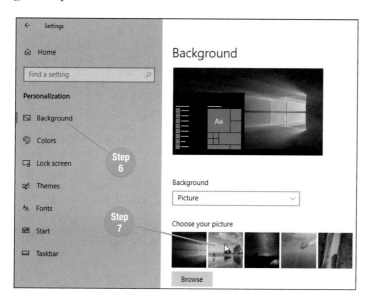

8 Click *Colors* in the left pane.

9 Click a color square in the *Windows colors* section and then close the app window. You determine the color you want to use for tiles and window accents.

The new background image is shown on the desktop.

10 Click the Start button and look at the new accent color used on tiles.

11 Lock the screen.

The picture you chose at Step 4 appears as the new Lock screen image.

12 Sign back in to unlock the system.

13 Open the Settings app and repeat Step 2 through Step 9 to restore the Lock screen, background, and color scheme to their original settings. At Step 5, scroll up the list and click *None* on the Weather button to remove the app from the Lock screen.

14 Close the Settings window.

1.8 Understanding Files and Folders and Downloading and Extracting Data Files

A **file** is a document, spreadsheet, presentation, photo, or any other data that you create and save in digital format. Files are also videos and music that you play on a device. Each file has a unique **file name**, which is a series of characters you assign to the file when you save it that allows you to identify and retrieve the file later.

A system of organizing files so that you can find and retrieve a specific document or photo when you need it is necessary. Folders are created on a storage device to organize electronic files. A **folder** is a name assigned to a placeholder or container in which you store a group of related files. Think of a folder on the computer in the same way you consider a paper file folder in a desk drawer in your home. You might have one file folder for your household bills and another file folder for your school documents. Separating documents into file folders makes it easy to put a document away when you are done with it and to locate the document when you need it again. In Figure 1.9, files and folders are shown to help you understand how digital data is organized on a storage device.

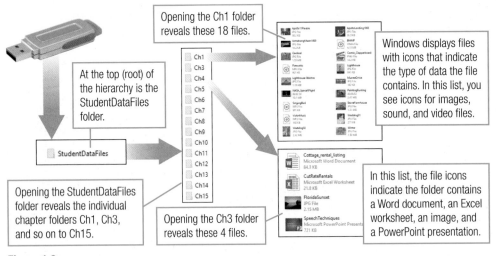

Figure 1.9
Digital data is stored in files, which are organized into folders.

To complete the tasks in the rest of this textbook, a set of student data files must be copied to a USB flash drive or other storage medium. Check with your instructor for the storage medium to use for your course. For example, your instructor may prefer that you save files to a network folder at your school.

The student data files are copied from the Cirrus course. The files are packaged so that you need to download only one file, called an *archive file* or a ZIP file. A **ZIP file** assembles and compresses a group of files under one name that looks like a folder name with a .zip file extension. The files are compressed so that the ZIP file size is as small as possible, meaning the file will copy faster over a network. A ZIP file should be uncompressed before the files stored within it are used so that each file is restored to its original size and put back in the folder from which the file originated. To restore the files within a ZIP file to their original size and folder structure, you perform a process called *extracting*.

Note: You will need a USB flash drive to complete the steps in this topic and the next three topics. Check with your instructor for alternative instructions if he or she prefers that you save files somewhere else, such as in a network folder on a school server.

Watch & Learn

— — — — — — — skills

Define *file*, *file name*, and *folder*

Download and extract student data files to a USB flash drive

Tutorials
Creating a Compressed Archive (ZIP) File

Downloading and Extracting Student Data Files

— — — — — — app tip

You can recognize a ZIP file in a file list because Windows displays the icon as a file folder with a zipper.

1. Insert a USB flash drive into an available USB port on your PC. Skip this step if you are saving files to another storage medium.

2. Go to your Cirrus course online and navigate to the course resources.

3. Click Student Data Files, and on the next page, click https://CA3.ParadigmEducation.com/StudentDataFiles.

Student Data Files
Click https://CA3.ParadigmEducation.com/StudentDataFiles link to open resource.

Step 3

4. If the files do not start downloading automatically, copy the hyperlink and paste it in the address bar.

The ZIP archive file will copy to the Downloads folder. The download will take a few moments depending on the speed of your network connection. Watch the progress of the download at the bottom of the browser window.

5. Click the button at the bottom of the browser for the StudentDataFiles ZIP folder when the message displays that StudentDataFiles.zip finished downloading. A File Explorer window opens. The Extract Compressed Folder Tools tab appears because the file opened is a ZIP archive file.

File Explorer is the utility used to browse files and folders on storage devices and perform file management routines. You will learn more about File Explorer in the next three topics.

6. If necessary, click the Extract Compressed Folder Tools tab.

7. Click the Extract all button.

8. Click the Browse button in the Extract Compressed (Zipped) Folders dialog box.

9. Click your USB flash drive in the left pane of the Select a destination dialog box, and then click the Select Folder button.

Your drive letter may vary.

10. Click the Extract button in the Extract Compressed (Zipped) Folders dialog box.

A progress message displays the status of the extraction. When finished, a new File Explorer window opens with the StudentDataFiles folder shown.

progress message during extraction

11. Close all open windows, including the OneDrive browser window.

● - - - - **quick steps**

Download and Extract Student Data Files
1. Navigate to the Cirrus course.
2. Click Student Data Files and then click https://CA3.ParadigmEducation.com/StudentDataFiles.
3. If necessary, copy and paste the hyperlink in the address bar.
4. Click file button to open File Explorer.
5. If necessary, click Compressed Folder Tools Extract tab.
6. Click Extract all button.
7. Click Browse button.
8. Click USB flash drive, then Select Folder.
9. Click Extract button.

● - - - - - - - **Oops!**

A window other than File Explorer opens at Step 5? Another ZIP archive utility installed on your device (such as 7-Zip), may open the downloaded item in the archive application. In that case, close the window and click the File Explorer icon on the taskbar. Click *Downloads* in the left pane. Right-click StudentDataFiles.zip in the right pane, point to *Open with*, click *Windows Explorer*, and then proceed to Step 7.

1.9 Browsing Files with File Explorer

To view or manage the files on a storage device, open a File Explorer window by clicking the File Explorer button on the taskbar. In File Explorer, you perform file maintenance tasks, such as creating new folders to organize files, renaming files, copying files, moving files, and deleting files. To begin, you will learn how to navigate the File Explorer window shown in Figure 1.10.

1 Click the File Explorer button on the taskbar.

File Explorer is divided into two panes: the Navigation pane (left pane) displays the list of places associated with the device, and Content pane (right pane) displays files and folders stored on the device or folder selected in the Navigation pane. File Explorer opens by default in a view called **Quick access**, which by default shows a list of frequently used and recently used files, as well as the contents stored in three places: Downloads, Documents, and Pictures.

Watch & Learn

● ─ ─ ─ ─ ─ ─ **Skills**

Identify features in a File Explorer window

Browse files on a device using File Explorer

Tutorial

Navigating between Local Volumes and Folders in File Explorer

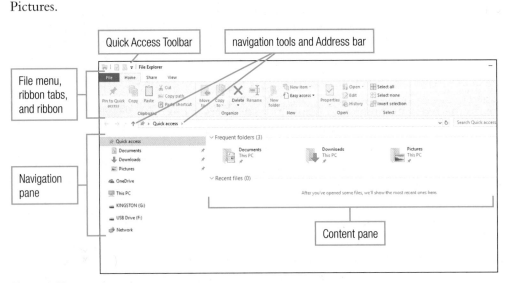

Figure 1.10

Shown here is the File Explorer window.

2 Click This PC in the Navigation pane.

The This PC window displays all the available storage options on the computer.

Each storage device is identified with an icon, a drive letter, and the storage capacity.

Your Content pane may vary depending on the installed storage devices.

● ─ ─ ─ ─ ─ ─ **app tip**

You can set File Explorer to always open with This PC active instead of the Quick access view. To do this, right-click Quick access in the Navigation pane, click *Options*, change the *Open File Explorer* option to *This PC*, and then click OK.

③ If necessary, insert your USB flash drive into an available USB port. If a new window opens when you insert the USB flash drive, close the window.

④ Double-click the icon representing your USB flash drive in the *Devices and drives* section to view the contents in the Content pane.

The Content pane shows the name of the folder you extracted from the ZIP file in the previous topic. Your Content pane may show additional files if you did not use an empty USB flash drive.

quick steps

Browse Files in File Explorer
1. Click File Explorer icon on taskbar.
2. If necessary, insert a removable storage medium such as a USB flash drive.
3. Click desired location or device in Navigation pane, *or* double-click a folder or device name in Content pane.

⑤ Double-click the folder *StudentDataFiles*.

A list of folders stored within the StudentDataFiles folder appears. A folder within another folder is sometimes referred to as a **subfolder**.

⑥ Double-click the folder *Ch1*.

A list of files stored in the Ch1 subfolder appears in the Content pane.

⑦ Click the View tab.

⑧ Click the *Tiles* option in the Layout group.

Use the Layout options to view files in the Content pane as small, medium, large, or extra large icons; as a list format with or without file details, such as the date and time the file was created or last updated and the file size; as a list with the file type and file properties such as author (Content); or as tiles (shown below).

app tip

Double-clicking a file name opens the application associated with the file and automatically opens/plays the document, image, video, or sound.

Your list will vary if this check box has a check mark in it. File extensions add a period and three or four characters after the file name. The extension indicates the type of file. For example, *.png*, *.jpg*, and *.jpeg* all indicate image files.

⑨ Click Desktop in the Navigation pane.

Browse content in File Explorer by clicking names in the Navigation pane, or by double-clicking device or folder names in the Content pane.

⑩ Close the File Explorer window.

Note: Leave the USB flash drive in the device for the remaining topics.

1.10 Creating Folders and Copying Files and Folders

As you work with software applications, such as Word or Excel, you will create many files that are documents or spreadsheets. You may also download files from a digital camera or a website and receive files from email or text messages. Storing the files in an organized manner with recognizable names will allow you to easily locate the files later. If you want to have folders created in advance of creating files, you need to have an organizational structure already in place. From time to time, you also need to rename, copy, move, or delete files and folders to maintain a storage medium in good order.

Creating a Folder

Creating a folder on a computer is like labeling a file folder in your filing cabinet. The title provides a brief description of the type of documents that will be stored inside the file folder. On the computer, in File Explorer, click the **New folder button** in the New group on the Home tab, and then type a name for the folder to set up the electronic equivalent of a paper filing system.

① Click the File Explorer icon on the taskbar.

② Click This PC in the Navigation pane.

③ Double-click the icon representing your USB flash drive.

④ If necessary, click the Home tab to display the ribbon interface.

The **ribbon** provides the buttons you need to perform file management tasks. Buttons are organized into the tabs Home, Share, View, and Manage. Within each tab, buttons are further organized into groups, such as Clipboard, Organize, New, Open, and Select (on the Home tab).

⑤ Click the New folder button in the New group.

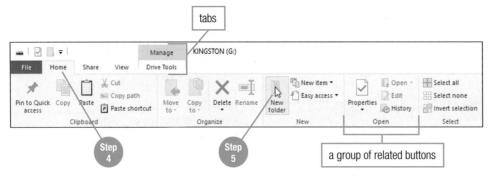

tabs

Step 4

Step 5

a group of related buttons

⑥ Type ComputerCourse and then press Enter.

Watch & Learn

------- Skills

Create a folder and sub-folder

Copy files and folders

Tutorial

Creating and Renaming a File or Folder

------- app tip

Tabs and/or buttons on the ribbon change and become available or unavailable depending on what is selected in the window.

------- app tip

In the folder structure you are creating, no spaces between words are used. Windows allows the use of spaces; however, an industry best practice is to avoid spaces in folder names.

⑦ Click the View tab and then click the *List* option in the Layout group.

List view displays names with small icons representing each file or folder and without details such as the date or time the file or folder was created or modified, the file type, or the file size. Each folder can have a different view.

⑧ Click the Home tab. If the ribbon is not currently expanded, a down-pointing arrow (Expand the Ribbon icon) displays below the Close button near the top right of the window. Click the down-pointing arrow to expand the ribbon; otherwise, proceed to Step 9.

The down-pointing arrow expands the ribbon permanently in the window. Once it has been clicked, it displays as an up-pointing arrow (like a caret ^ symbol), which is the Minimize the Ribbon icon.

⑨ Double-click the *ComputerCourse* folder in the Content pane.

You have now opened the ComputerCourse folder. File management tasks performed next will occur inside this folder.

⑩ Click the New folder button, type ChapterTopicsWork, and then press Enter.

ChapterTopicsWork is a folder within a folder, sometimes called a *subfolder*.

⑪ Click the New folder button, type Assessments, and then press Enter.

You now have two folders (or subfolders) within the ComputerCourse folder.

⑫ Click the Up arrow button on the Address bar.

Notice you now see only the ComputerCourse folder and the StudentDataFiles folder. The two folders created in Steps 10 and 11 are no longer visible because they are *inside* the ComputerCourse folder.

After clicking the Up arrow, the Address bar shows that you moved the display up one level in the folder hierarchy.

Copying Files and Folders

Copying a file or folder from one storage medium to another makes an exact copy of a document, spreadsheet, presentation, image, video, music file, or other object. Copying is one way to make a backup of an important file on another storage medium. Use the **Copy button** and the **Paste button** in the Clipboard group on the Home tab to copy a selected file or folder.

 Tutorial
Moving and Copying Using Copy and Paste

13 Click to select the StudentDataFiles folder.

Before you can copy, you must first select a file or folder—a single-click selects a file. A selected file or folder displays with a blue background in the Content pane. On touchscreen devices, a check box also displays next to folder and file names; a check mark in the check box indicates the file is selected.

14 Click the Copy button in the Clipboard group on the Home tab.

15 Double-click the folder *ComputerCourse* in the Content pane.

16 Click the Paste button in the Clipboard group.

 app tip
Ctrl + C is the universal keyboard shortcut to Copy.

 app tip
Ctrl + V is the universal keyboard shortcut to Paste.

This step is copying all the student data files and placing the copy of the folder and all its contents in the ComputerCourse folder. As the copying takes place, Windows displays a progress message. When the message disappears, the copy is complete.

Before you paste files, you first navigate to the storage medium and folder into which you want the files copied.

The folder StudentDataFiles and all the subfolders and files contained within will be copied to the ComputerCourse folder when you click the Paste button.

copy-progress message box

17 Double-click the StudentDataFiles folder name.

18 Double-click the *Ch1* folder name.

In the next steps, you will copy individual files to another folder.

19 Click the View tab and then click the *List* option in the Layout group. Skip this step if List view is already active.

20 Click **Lighthouse**, hold down the Shift key, and then click **Winter**.

This action selects all the files, starting with **Lighthouse** and ending with **Winter**. Holding down the Shift key while clicking a file name instructs Windows to select all files from the file name selected first to the file name selected second.

Another way to select multiple files is to hold down the Ctrl key while clicking a file name. Use the Ctrl key if you do not want all the files in between two selected files to be selected. In other words, Ctrl + click is used to select multiple files that are not next to each other.

21 Click the Home tab.

22 Click the Copy button.

23 Click *ComputerCourse* in the Address bar.

Clicking a device or folder name in the Address bar is another way to navigate to devices or folders.

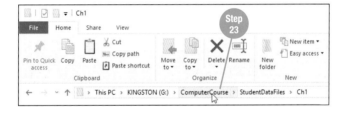

24 Double-click the folder *ChapterTopicsWork* in the Content pane.

25 Click the Paste button.

The selected files are copied into the ChapterTopicsWork folder.

26 Click the View tab and then click *List*.

27 Click the Close button to close the File Explorer window.

Quick Steps

Copy Files or Folders
1. Open File Explorer.
2. Navigate to source data storage medium and folder.
3. Select file(s) or folder(s) to be copied.
4. If necessary, click Home tab.
5. Click Copy button.
6. Navigate to destination storage medium and folder.
7. Click Paste button.

1.11 Moving, Renaming, and Deleting Files and Folders and Ejecting a USB Flash Drive

File Explorer is also used to move, rename, and delete files and folders. Sometimes you will copy a file or save a file in a folder and later decide you want to move it elsewhere. You may also assign a file name to a file or folder and later decide you want to change the name. Files or folders no longer needed can be deleted to clean up the disk. When you are finished using a USB flash drive, you should properly eject the drive to avoid problems that can occur when files are not properly closed.

Moving Files

Files are moved using a process similar to copying. Begin by selecting files and clicking the **Cut button** in the Clipboard group on the Home tab in File Explorer. Navigate to the destination location and click the Paste button. When files are cut they are removed from the source location.

1. Right-click the Start button and then click the *File Explorer* option.

2. Click This PC in the Navigation pane and then double-click the icon for your USB flash drive in the *Devices and drives* section.

3. Double-click *ComputerCourse* in the Content pane.

4. Double-click *ChapterTopicsWork* in the Content pane.

Assume that you decide that the files copied from the StudentDataFiles Ch1 folder in the last topic should be stored inside a folder within ChapterTopicsWork.

5. Click the New folder button in the New group on the Home tab, type Ch1, and then press Enter.

6. Click **Lighthouse**, hold down the Shift key, and then click **Winter**.

7. Click the Cut button in the Clipboard group.

8. Double-click *Ch1*.

9. Click the Paste button in the Clipboard group.

The files are removed from the ChapterTopicsWork folder and placed within the Ch1 folder.

The Address bar shows the destination folder is Ch1 within ChapterTopicsWork.

Watch & Learn

- - - - - - - - Skills

Move a file or folder
Rename a file or folder
Delete a file or folder
Empty the Recycle Bin
Eject a USB flash drive

Tutorial

Moving Files

- - - - - - app tip

Ctrl + X is the universal keyboard shortcut to Cut.

10 Click the Back button to return to the previous list.

Notice the files are no longer in the ChapterTopicsWork folder.

11 Click the Forward button (right-pointing arrow next to Back button) to return to the Ch1 folder.

Renaming Files and Folders

At times you will receive a file from someone else and decide you want to rename the file to something more meaningful to you, or you may decide upon a new name for a file or folder after the file or folder was created. Change the name of a file or folder with the **Rename button** in the Organize group on the Home tab.

12 Click the View tab and then click the *Extra large icons* option in the Layout group.

13 If necessary, scroll down the Content pane to view the contents shown for each file in the folder.

14 Click to select the file ***Winter***.

Assume a friend sent you this image of a weeping birch tree laden with snow in a winter scene. You decide to rename the image.

15 Click the Home tab and then click the Rename button in the Organize group.

16 Type BirchTreeInWinter and then press Enter.

17 Click to select the file ***ViolinMusic***.

Assume this file is the song "Danny Boy" played on a violin and recorded by you as you heard the song at an outdoor event.

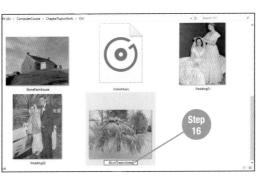

•–––– quick steps

Move Files or Folders
1. Open File Explorer.
2. Navigate to source data storage medium and folder.
3. Select files or folder to be moved.
4. If necessary, click Home tab.
5. Click Cut button.
6. Navigate to destination storage medium and folder.
7. Click Paste button.

Rename Files or Folders
1. Open File Explorer.
2. Navigate to data storage medium and folder.
3. Select file to be renamed.
4. If necessary, click Home tab.
5. Click Rename button.
6. Type new name and press Enter.

Tutorial

Renaming Files and Folders

18 Click the Rename button, type DannyBoyViolin, and then press Enter.

19 Click *ComputerCourse* in the Address bar.

You can rename a folder as well as a file.

20 If necessary, click to select the folder named *ChapterTopicsWork*.

21 Click the Rename button, type CompletedTopics, and then press Enter.

Deleting Files and Folders

Delete files or folders when you no longer need to keep them. You should also delete files or folders if you have copied them to a removable storage medium for archive purposes and want to free up space on the local disk. In File Explorer, select the files or folders to be deleted and then click the **Delete button** in the Organize group on the Home tab. Files and folders deleted from the local hard disk are moved to the Recycle Bin. While it is in the Recycle Bin, you can restore the file to its original location if you deleted the file in error. Files deleted from a USB flash drive are not sent to the Recycle Bin; therefore, exercise caution when deleting a file from a USB flash drive.

22 Double-click *CompletedTopics* and then double-click *Ch1*.

23 Click *Lighthouse*, hold down the left mouse button, and then drag the file to Documents in the Navigation pane.

Dragging a file from a folder on one storage medium to a location on another storage medium copies the file.

24 Click Documents in the Navigation pane.

25 Click *Lighthouse* and then click the Delete button in the Organize group (click the top of the button—not the down-pointing arrow).

26 Click This PC in the Navigation pane and then double-click the icon for your USB flash drive in the *Devices and drives* section.

Your list will vary. Locate and click to select the file *Lighthouse* in your Documents folder.

━━━━━━ app tip

Dragging a file or folder on the same storage medium moves the file. To be sure of the operation you want to perform, drag a file or folder to another location using the right mouse button. When you release the mouse, a shortcut menu appears. Choose the Copy or Move option on the menu.

☁ **Tutorial**
Deleting Files and Using the Recycle Bin

27 Double-click *ComputerCourse*, double-click *CompletedTopics*, and then double-click *Ch1*.

28 Click *SingingBird* and then click the Delete button.

29 Click the Yes button in the Delete File message box that appears.

The confirmation message appears when you delete a file from a USB flash drive because the files are permanently deleted, not sent to the Recycle Bin from which the file could be restored.

30 Close the File Explorer window.

31 Double-click the Recycle Bin icon on the desktop.

32 Click the Empty Recycle Bin button in the Manage group on the Manage Recycle Bin Tools tab.

33 Click the Yes button to permanently delete the file in the Delete File message box.

34 Close the Recycle Bin window.

The file deleted in Step 25 was moved here.

When you are finished with a USB flash drive, you should always use the **Safely Remove Hardware and Eject Media** feature before pulling the drive out of the USB port. This ensures all files are properly closed to avoid data corruption.

35 Click the Show hidden icons arrow in the notification area (up-pointing arrow like caret ^ symbol) on the taskbar and then click the Safely Remove Hardware and Eject Media icon.

36 Click the *Eject* option in the pop-up menu. Your menu may show *Eject USB Flash Drive*, *Eject Storage Media*, or some other label after *Eject*, depending on the device. If more than one USB flash drive appears in the list, click to select the correct drive before ejecting the drive.

37 Remove your USB flash drive from the computer when the message appears that it is safe to do so.

A message appears when the USB device can be safely removed.

Topics Review

Topic	Key Concepts and Key Terms
1.1 Using Touch, Mouse, and Keyboard Input to Navigate Windows 10	**Windows 10** is the operating system from Microsoft. The **user interface (UI)** is a desktop that includes icons, a **Start menu** accessed from the **Start button**, and a taskbar along the bottom of the screen.
	A **tile** is a square or rectangle on the Start menu used to launch an app, application, or other feature.
	An **app** is a small application designed for a smartphone, tablet, or PC with touchscreen input and is mainly for one task.
	An **application** is a more complex program that does more tasks than an app, uses full-size keyboards, uses a mouse, and requires more extensive hardware resources.
	A **gesture** is an action, such as a tap or swipe motion, that you perform with your finger or stylus on a touch-enabled device.
	The **touch keyboard** appears on-screen when typed characters are expected, such as in text messages.
	A **mouse**, **trackball**, **touchpad**, or other pointing device is used to move the white arrow **pointer** on the screen and perform mouse actions, such as click or double-click. A trackball has a ball that you roll your thumb or fingers over to move the pointer. A touchpad on a laptop lets you move your finger over the surface to move the pointer.
	Pressing the Start key brings up the Start menu.
	A **keyboard command** involves pressing the Start key, Ctrl, Alt, or a function key with a letter to perform an action.
1.2 Starting Windows 10 and Exploring Apps	The **Lock screen** appears when you start Windows or resume system use from sleep mode.
	A **user account** is a username with a password, PIN, or other authentication method used to sign in to Windows.
	Signing in to Windows using a **Microsoft account** (a phone number or email address) means that your settings are stored online and synced with other devices.
	Signing in with a **local account** means that your settings are not shared with other devices, and you do not see live updates on some of the tiles on the Start menu.
	Once signed in, the **desktop** appears and the Start menu opens. The desktop has icons to launch applications and a **taskbar** along the bottom of the screen.
	On the taskbar, the Start button, **search text box**, and icons are pinned to quickly start apps or applications. The **notification area** at the right end has icons to show system status.
	The **Photos app** shows images stored on the local PC and from OneDrive.
	The **Calendar app** is used to enter appointments or events.
	Use the **Store app** to search for and download new apps.
	Switch between apps using the app button on the taskbar or by displaying **Task View** using the Task View button on the taskbar to click the desired thumbnail.
	The **Timeline** feature in Task View shows what you have opened today, yesterday, and further back up to 30 days.

continued…

Topic	Key Concepts and Key Terms
1.3 Using the Search Text Box and Working with Windows	Click in the search text box, type the first few letters of what you are looking for, and then click the item in the search results.
	The **Minimize button** reduces a window to a button on the taskbar.
	Click the **Close button** to close a window and any content within the window.
	The **Maximize button** expands a window size to fill the entire desktop.
	The Maximize button changes to the **Restore Down button** when a window is maximized. Use Restore Down to return the window to its previous size.
	The **Snap** feature lets you dock a window to the left or right half of the window, or to one of four quadrants by dragging the window left, right, or to a corner.
	Snap Assist shows thumbnails of open windows when you snap a window and leave part of the screen empty. Click one of the thumbnails to fill the empty part of the screen with another window.
1.4 Using the Notification Area	Click the current date and time at the right end of the taskbar to view a pop-up calendar.
	Click the Notifications icon to open the **Action Center** panel where you can view system messages or access several quick action tiles for managing settings.
	Click the Speaker icon to adjust the volume.
	Click the Network icon to manage network connectivity.
	A **quick action tile** displays in Notification panels and is used to turn on or turn off a setting or open a setting window.
	The Power icon displays the battery status and a link to manage battery settings.
1.5 Locking the Screen, Signing Out, and Shutting Down Windows 10	Lock the device if you need to leave your PC or mobile device for a short period of time by clicking Start, your account name, and then Lock.
	Locking leaves all documents and apps open but unavailable to anyone but yourself.
	Click Start, your account name, and then **sign out** to close all apps and documents (also referred to as *logging off*).
	Perform a **shut down** command if you want to turn off the power to the computer.
	The *Shut down* option is accessed from the Power option on the Start menu.
1.6 Using and Customizing the Start Menu	Apps or applications can be started by double-clicking an icon on the desktop, by clicking a tile on the Start menu, by scrolling the list in the left pane on the Start menu, or by typing the first few letters of the name in the search text box.
	Resize the Start menu by dragging the right border or the top border left, right, up, or down as desired.
	Right-click a tile and click **Unpin from Start** to remove the tile from the Start menu; locate an app or application in the list on the Start menu, right-click the name, and click **Pin to Start** to add a tile for the software to the Start menu.
	Move tiles to a new location on the Start menu by dragging the tile.
	Tiles are either square or rectangular in shape and can be resized larger or smaller.
	The **Turn Live Tile off** command stops a tile from displaying notifications or status updates; use **Turn Live Tile on** to restore the tile's notifications.

continued…

Topic	Key Concepts and Key Terms
1.7 Personalizing the Lock Screen and the Desktop	Click the Start button, click Settings, then click *Personalization* in the Settings app to personalize the Lock screen and desktop options.
	You can choose from five other pictures for the Lock screen or browse to a picture on your PC or mobile device. You can also change the apps that display notifications on the Lock screen.
	Change the desktop background image and/or the color scheme in the Settings app using the Background and Colors categories.
1.8 Understanding Files and Folders and Downloading and Extracting Data Files	A **file** is any document, spreadsheet, picture, or other text or image saved as digital data.
	When you create a file, you assign a unique **file name** that allows you to identify and retrieve the file.
	A **folder** is a name assigned to a placeholder where a group of related files are stored.
	A group of files and folders can be compressed and saved as a **ZIP file**, which bundles everything together in one file with a .zip file extension.
	When you open a ZIP file, a window opens with the Extract all button used to restore the files and folders from the zipped package, allowing you to use them in their original state and folder structure.
	File Explorer is the Windows utility used to browse files and perform file management tasks.
1.9 Browsing Files with File Explorer	File Explorer opens in **Quick access** view, which shows frequently used and recently used files.
	The left pane in File Explorer is the Navigation pane, and the right pane is the Content pane.
	Click This PC in the Navigation pane to view all the available storage devices.
	To browse content, click names in the Navigation pane or double click names in the Content pane.
	Use options in the Layout group on the View tab to change the Content pane display of files.
	A folder created within another folder is sometimes called a **subfolder**.
1.10 Creating Folders and Copying Files and Folders	Click the **New folder button** in the New group on the Home tab in File Explorer to create a new folder.
	The **ribbon** in File Explorer provides buttons organized into tabs and groups. Buttons are used to carry out file management tasks.
	Copying a file or folder makes an exact duplicate of a document, spreadsheet, presentation, image, video, music file, or other object in another folder and/or storage medium.
	Begin a copy task by first selecting the file or folder to be copied and then use the **Copy button** and the **Paste button** in the Clipboard group on the Home tab.
1.11 Moving, Renaming, and Deleting Files and Folders and Ejecting a USB Flash Drive	Files are moved by selecting the files or folders, clicking the **Cut button** in the Clipboard group on the Home tab, navigating to the new destination drive and/or folder, and clicking the Paste button.
	Click the **Rename button** in the Organize group on the Home tab, type a new name, and then press Enter to change the name of the selected file or folder.
	Select files or folders no longer needed; then click the **Delete button** in the Organize group on the Home tab.
	Files deleted from a hard disk drive are sent to the Recycle Bin and remain there until the Recycle Bin is emptied.
	Files deleted from a USB flash drive are not sent to the Recycle Bin.
	Open the Recycle Bin from the desktop to view files deleted from the hard disk drive.
	Emptying the Recycle Bin permanently deletes the files or folders.
	Eject a USB flash drive using the **Safely Remove Hardware and Eject Media** icon in the notification area on the taskbar. Click the Show hidden icons arrow to locate invisible icons.

Topics Review

Navigating and Searching the Web

For many people reading this textbook, the internet is part of daily life, used to search for information, connect with friends and relatives, watch videos, listen to music, play games, or shop. Mobile devices, such as tablets and smartphones, are used to browse the web anywhere they happen to be via cellular or Wi-Fi connections. According to Statista (a market and consumer data company), 52 percent of website visits originated on a mobile device in 2018. In the workplace, being able to effectively navigate and search the web is a requirement for all workers.

In this chapter, you will learn definitions for internet terminology and learn how to navigate the web using the two most popular web browsers. You will also learn how to use search tools to find and print information, view multiple websites in a browsing session, bookmark web pages you visit often, and copy an object from a website to your computer.

Note: *No student data files are required to complete this chapter.*

Learning Objectives

2.1 Define *internet*, *World Wide Web*, *web browser*, *web page*, *hyperlink*, and *web address*

2.2 Navigate the web using Microsoft Edge, use tabs to view multiple websites, and add a page to the Favorites list

2.3 Navigate the web using Chrome, use tabs to view multiple websites, bookmark a page, and use the Find bar

2.4 Use a search engine website to find information, refine a search using advanced search tools, and print a web page

2.5 Download a picture from a web page

Read & Learn

Content Online

The online course includes additional training and assessment resources.

2.1 Introduction to the Internet and the World Wide Web

🌥 **Watch & Learn**

●———————— skills

Define *internet*

Define *World Wide Web*

Explain *web browser,* *web page,* and *hyperlink*

Describe *web address*

The **internet**, or **net**, is a global network that links other networks such as individuals, businesses, schools, government departments, nonprofit organizations, and research institutions. The worldwide system of interconnected high-speed communications and network equipment, computing devices, and communication protocols to send and receive data is known as the *internet*. When you want to look up flight times on the internet, the request sent from your device must travel via communications media, communications equipment, and computers owned by a telephone, cable, or satellite company to reach the airline web server.

The World Wide Web

The collection of electronic documents circulated on the internet in the form of web pages make up the **World Wide Web**, or **web**. A **web page** is a document that contains text and multimedia content, such as images, video, sound, and animation. Web pages also contain hyperlinks. A **hyperlink**, also called a **link**, is text, an image, or an icon on a web page that moves you to another related page when clicked. Web pages are stored in a format that is read and interpreted for display within a **web browser**, which is application software used to view web pages. A website is a collection of related web pages for one organization or individual. For example, the collection of web pages linked to the main page for your school make up your school's website. All the web pages and resources such as photos, videos, sounds, and animations that make the website work are stored on a computer called a *web server*. Web servers are connected to the internet continuously.

You connect your PC or mobile device to the internet by subscribing to internet service through an **internet service provider (ISP)**, a company that provides access to internet infrastructure for a fee. The ISP will provide you with the equipment needed to connect to its network, as well as instructions for installing and setting up the equipment to work with your computer and other mobile devices. Once your account and equipment are set up, you can start browsing the web using a browser, such as Microsoft Edge or Google Chrome.

Web Addresses

Similar to your postal address, each web page has a unique text-based **web address** that is used to navigate to the page. A web address is also called a **uniform resource locator (URL)**. One way to navigate the web is to type a web address into the **Address bar** of a web browser. For example, to view the main web page for the publisher of this textbook, you would use the web address https://ParadigmEducation .com. If *http* or *https* (*s* indicates a secure connection that encrypts data) is left out when typing a web address, the browser still finds the web page by assuming *http* or *https*. For this reason, many people often go to a page by typing only the portion of the address after *http://*. To illustrate all of this, the parts of the web address (URL) https://www. nasa.gov/topics/moon-to-mars/index.html shown in Figure 2.1 on the next page are explained in Table 2.1.

Although you navigate to a web page using a friendly text-based address, the real address for the computing device that stores the web page is called an **internet protocol (IP) address**. An IP address is either four groups of numbers 0 to 255 separated by periods (called *IPv4*), or eight groups of characters (0 to 9 or *a* to *f*) separated by colons (called *IPv6*). A server called a Domain Name System (DNS) server, owned by a business or ISP, maintains a directory that references the IP address to the web address. When you type a web address into the browser, a DNS server locates the IP address to transmit the data to the correct computer.

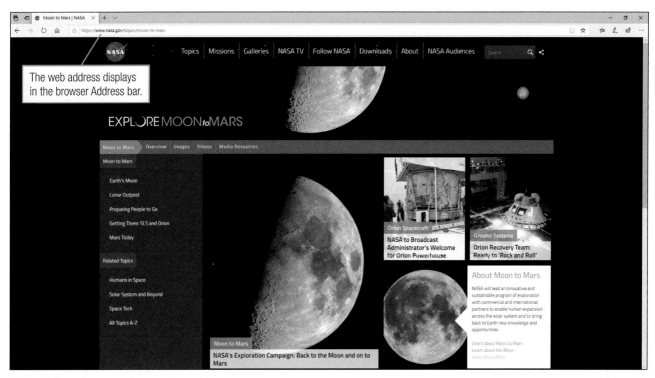

The web address displays in the browser Address bar.

Figure 2.1

A web page from NASA is shown in the Microsoft Edge browser window. Your page may look different if NASA has updated the page since publication.

Table 2.1 The Parts of the Web Address (URL) https://www.nasa.gov/topics/moon-to-mars/index.html

Part of URL	What It Means	Examples
https://	Hypertext Transfer Protocol Secure. A set of rules for transmitting data in encrypted format over the internet. *Https* is used for exchanging data in online transactions. Other websites (like nasa.gov) are starting to use the protocol to protect data on their websites and to authenticate their websites for the general public. Other protocols used are http (to transfer data without encryption) and ftp (to transfer a file).	http ftp https
www.nasa.gov	Domain name. A text-based address for the web server that stores the web page. The last three letters are the extension and generally tell you the type of organization; e.g., nasa.gov is a government website. Some domain names end with a two-character country code, such as eBay.ca for the Canadian auction site eBay. Using *www* in a domain name is becoming less common. In the *Examples* column are five domain names to show a sampling of a variety of extensions. Other extensions, such as *.net, .biz, .legal,* and *.realtor* are also used. Extensions are either restricted or urestricted. A restricted extension means that registration of a domain that uses the extension has to meet specific criteria. For example, only accredited educational institutions can register for a domain with the extension *.edu.* An unrestricted extension, like *.com*, can be registered by anyone.	www.google.com (Google) www.harvard.edu (Harvard University) www.navy.mil (US Navy) www.linux.org (Linux open-source community) driftaway.coffee (Driftaway coffee bean subscription service)
/topics/moon-to-mars/	Folder path to the web page. The forward slash (/) and text after the slash are the folder names on the web server where the page is stored.	Folder path names will vary.
index.html	Web page file name. The file name extension indicates the language used to create the web page. *Html* stands for *Hypertext Markup Language*, which uses tags to describe content.	File names will vary.

Many times when you go to the web to look for information, you do not know the web addresses for the pages you need. In this case, search tools help you find web pages. You will learn to find web pages using search tools in Topic 2.4.

2.2 Navigating the Web Using Microsoft Edge

Microsoft Edge is the web browser included with Windows 10. The browser replaced the Internet Explorer web browser included with earlier Windows versions. Similar to the Windows apps you learned about in Chapter 1, where an app looks and feels the same on all devices, Microsoft Edge is the browser for all Windows 10 devices, including tablets. A mobile app for Microsoft Edge is also available for Android and Apple smartphones.

When you launch the web browser, the Start page displays with news and information feeds unless the browser has been customized to display another page. For example, many schools customize browsers to first display the student portal. Microsoft Edge is designed to be a fast and secure browser, with a clean, distraction-free interface. Reading view strips away the sidebars and navigation on a web page to show only the main content on a page. The Reading view icon on the Address bar is active for a page that can be viewed without the navigation items. Microsoft Edge also has tools to annotate a web page with markup, highlights, handwriting, or typed notes, saving the page as a web note for reading in the Reading list, a OneNote notebook, or shared via email.

Watch & Learn

Skills

Navigate the web using Microsoft Edge
Use Reading view
View multiple websites within the same window
Add a page to Favorites

Tutorial
Getting Started with the Microsoft Edge Browser

Starting Microsoft Edge and Displaying a Web Page

1 Click the Microsoft Edge icon on the taskbar.

The Microsoft Edge browser window displays the Start page shown in Figure 2.2 unless the browser has been customized to display another page.

2 Click the Address bar (contains the dimmed text *Search or enter web address*), type nps.gov/grca, and then press Enter. If a message box appears asking you to sign up for national park news, close the message using the × at the top right corner. Review the layout and tools in the Microsoft Edge window shown in Figure 2.3 on the next page.

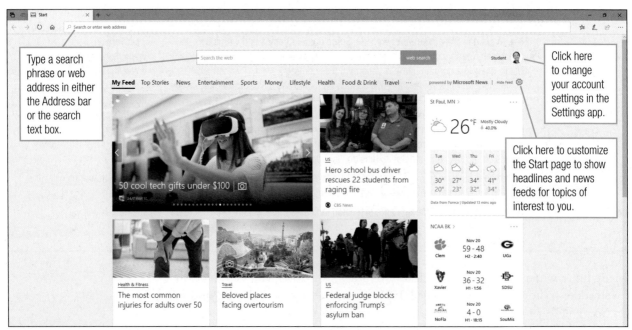

Figure 2.2
The Microsoft Edge Start page is displayed. The Start page provides hyperlinks to business, entertainment, health, and finance news and current weather forecast and sports scores.

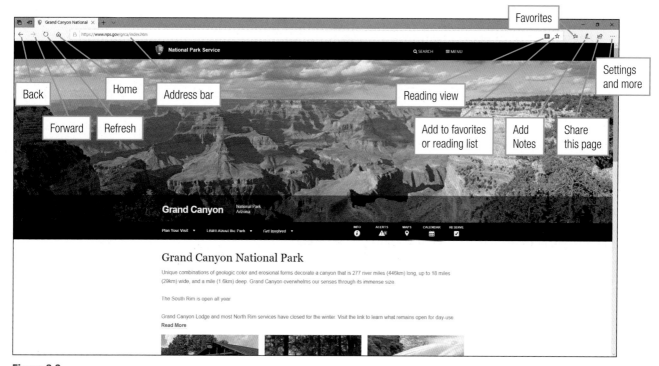

Figure 2.3

The National Park Service Grand Canyon web page is shown in the Microsoft Edge browser window.

(3) Click <u>MENU</u> near the top right of the web page.

(4) Click <u>About Us</u>.

(5) Click <u>News</u>.

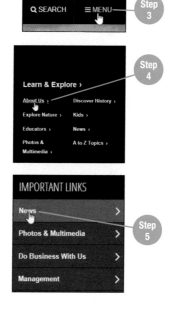

Navigating web pages involves clicking links to move from one page to another on a website or to a web page stored on another website. Click **Back** to return to the previous page viewed, or click **Forward** to move forward one web page viewed. To display a different web page, click the Address bar to select the current entry (or drag to select the current text in the Address bar), type the web address, and then press Enter.

(6) Click in the Address bar or drag to select the existing web address, type loc.gov, and then press Enter. If a message box appears asking you to support the Library of Congress, close the message.

The Library of Congress web page appears. The starting page for a website is called the **home page**.

(7) Click the icon with three bars at the top right of the page.

A button or icon with three bars is called a *hamburger button* because it resembles a hamburger patty between a top and bottom bun. The hamburger button indicates a menu.

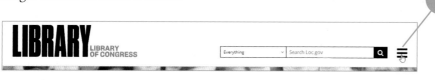

8 Click Visit.

9 Click Back to return to the Library of Congress home page (move back one web page).

10 Click Forward to return to the Visiting the Library page (move forward one web page).

11 Click Guidelines & Tips.

12 Click Reading view on the toolbar.

The page reformats within Microsoft Edge to remove all the sidebars and navigational items and show the text in a distraction-free reading layout. Some web pages cannot be reformatted in Reading view. A web page that is not available in Reading view displays a dimmed Reading view icon on the toolbar.

13 Scroll right to view the second screen in Reading view.

14 Click Reading view on the toolbar to turn off the view.

15 Click in the Address bar or drag to select the existing web address, type nasa.gov/topics/history, and then press Enter.

16 Scroll down and click a link to a story that interests you. Read the story using Reading view, if the view is available.

17 If necessary, turn off Reading view and then click Back to return to the NASA History page.

Displaying Multiple Web Pages and Adding a Page to Favorites List

Open multiple web pages within the same Microsoft Edge window by displaying each page in its own tab. Click **New tab** (displays as a plus symbol) to open a new page in the window. Switch between web pages by clicking the tab for the page you want to view. This is called **tabbed browsing**. The web address for a page you visit frequently can be saved to the **Favorites** list by displaying the page and then using the star on the toolbar to add the page to Favorites.

18 Click New tab (plus symbol) next to the tab for the NASA History page at the top of the window.

19 Type flickr.com/commons in the Address bar on the new tab and then press Enter.

☁ **Tutorial**

Using Tabbed Browsing

The Commons contains public photography archives. Images in The Commons have no known copyright restrictions. The next time you need a photo for a project, consider sourcing an image from this website.

20 Click the NASA History page tab to change the web page displayed in the window.

Step 20

When the pointer is resting on a tab, a thumbnail of the web page appears.

21 Click the Close tab icon (displays × on tab) on the NASA History tab.

22 With The Commons page displayed in the window, click the star at the right end of the Address bar.

23 Click the Add button to accept the default option to save the page in Favorites.

The page will now display in the Favorites list with the name Flickr: The Commons. The star turns gold for a page that is added to the Favorites list.

24 Click Favorites to open the Favorites panel at the right side of the window.

Display the Favorites panel to view the Favorites list, Reading list, History list, or Downloads list.

Step 22

Step 23

Step 24

25 Click *Favorites* in the left pane of the panel to view the Favorites list, if another list is currently active.

26 Click Favorites to close the panel.

27 Close the Microsoft Edge window.

Step 25

Step 26

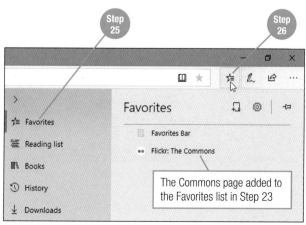

The Commons page added to the Favorites list in Step 23

2.3 Navigating the Web Using Chrome

☁ **Watch & Learn**

●━━━━━━ skills

Navigate the web using Chrome

View multiple websites within the same window

Bookmark a page

Use the Find bar

●━━━━━ go online

**https://CA3
.ParadigmEducation
.com/Chrome**

Go here to download and install Chrome on your PC or mobile device.

Chrome is a web browser for PCs and mobile devices from Google. In 2018, StatCounter (a company that measures web traffic) reported that Chrome was the browser of choice for almost 50 percent of people within the United States and Canada. Since the release of Chrome in 2008, the browser has gained a significant following due to its fast page loading and direct searching capability from the Address bar using the Google search engine.

Starting Chrome and Displaying a Web Page

1 Click the Chrome icon on the taskbar or double-click the icon on the desktop, and then review the layout and tools in the Chrome window shown in Figure 2.4.

If Chrome is not currently set as the default browser, you may be prompted with a message bar below the Address bar to set it as the default browser.

2 With the insertion point positioned in the Address bar, type techmeme.com and then press Enter.

Techmeme is a technology news site that posts each day the top news headlines from the technology industry.

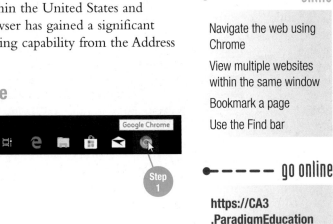

New tab | search text box | Bookmark this page

Address bar | Chrome menu

Google

Shortcuts to sites you visit the most appear here. Click the Add shortcut icon to add a page to this area.

Figure 2.4

The Google search engine is the default search engine used for new search requests in the Chrome browser. Chrome is regularly updated—your image may vary from the one shown here.

③ Click a link to a technology story that interests you on the Techmeme page.

Techmeme is a content aggregator—a company that searches, collects, and organizes content in one place. Clicking a link to a story on the Techmeme page takes you to another website.

④ Click Back to return to the Techmeme page.

Step 4

Your web address will vary depending on the story you clicked in Step 3.

☁ **Tutorials**

Starting Chrome and Displaying a Web Page

Displaying Multiple Web Pages and Bookmarking Pages

Displaying Multiple Web Pages and Bookmarking Pages

Similar to Microsoft Edge, Chrome uses tabbed browsing to display more than one web page within the same browser window. Open a new tab and navigate to a web address to browse a new site without closing the existing web page. Chrome displays a page name at the top of the tab along with a close control. Web pages you visit frequently can be bookmarked by clicking the white star at the end of the Address bar (displays the ScreenTip *Bookmark this page*).

⑤ With techmeme.com the active web page, click the white star at the end of the Address bar.

The white star changes to blue, and the Bookmark dialog box appears.

⑥ Click Done to close the Bookmark dialog box.

Step 6

● ─ ─ ─ ─ ─ **app tip**

By default, bookmarks are added to the Bookmarks bar, which is docked below the Address bar when the bar is turned on.

The **Bookmarks bar** displays below the Address bar. The Booksmarks bar is turned off or on using the **Chrome menu** (three vertical dots) near the top right of the window. You will practice showing the Booksmarks bar in the next step.

⑦ Click the Chrome menu (three vertical dots with the ScreenTip *Customize and control Google Chrome*) and then point to *Bookmarks*. A check mark next to *Show bookmarks* bar means that the bar is turned on. In that case, click in a blank area away from the menu to close the menu; otherwise, click *Show bookmarks bar* to turn the bar on.

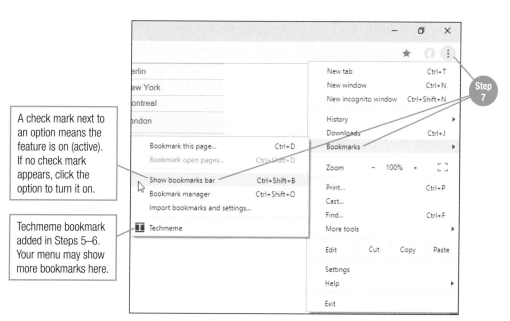

A check mark next to an option means the feature is on (active). If no check mark appears, click the option to turn it on.

Techmeme bookmark added in Steps 5–6. Your menu may show more bookmarks here.

8 Click New tab (plus symbol) next to the Techmeme tab to open a new page.

9 Type youtube.com and then press Enter.

10 Click the white star and then click Done to add youtube.com to the Bookmarks bar.

The Bookmarks bar with the two bookmarks added in this topic appears below the Address bar. Your bar may show more bookmarks.

Searching the Web from the Address Bar

 Tutorial

Searching the Web from the Address Bar

Web browsers like Microsoft Edge and Chrome allow you to type a search phrase in the Address bar. In Chrome, search results from Google appear in the window. The default search engine can be changed if you prefer to use another search engine website, such as bing.com. To change the default search engine, click the Chrome menu, click *Settings*, and then change the *Search engine used in the address bar* option by clicking the down-pointing arrow next to the current search engine (such as Google) in the *Search engine* section. Close the Settings tab when finished.

11 Click New tab next to the YouTube tab, type seven wonders of the world, and then press Enter.

Notice that as you type, searches that match your entry appear in a drop-down list below the Address bar. If one of the searches is what you are looking for, click the entry in the list.

12 Click the Images hyperlink below the Address bar to filter search results to display images only.

13 Scroll down a few screens to view images, and then scroll back to the top of the page and click the All hyperlink below the Address bar.

14 Click in the Address bar or drag to select the current web address, type great wall of china, and then press Enter.

(15) Click <u>Great Wall of China - Wikipedia</u>, then scroll down to review the *Wikipedia* page about the Great Wall of China.

(16) Scroll back up to the top of the *Wikipedia* page.

Finding Text on a Page

Use the **Find bar** to locate a specific word or phrase on a web page. The Find bar is turned on from the Chrome menu. Using the Find bar is helpful when viewing a long story or article and you need to locate a reference that you know exists in the text.

(17) Click the Chrome menu and then click *Find*.

The Find bar opens at the right side of the window, below the Address bar, with the insertion point positioned in the Find bar search text box.

(18) Type first emperor in the Find bar search text box.

The currently selected match is shaded with an orange background on the page, and the number of matches found on the web page displays in the Find bar next to the search text box. Additional matches below the current selection are shaded yellow (scroll to see the yellow highlights).

(19) Click Next (down-pointing arrow) on the Find bar to scroll the page to the next occurrence of *first emperor*.

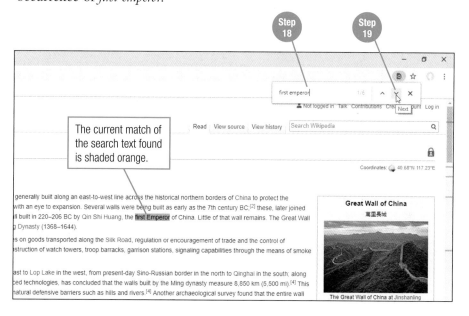

The current match of the search text found is shaded orange.

(20) Continue clicking Next until you have seen all occurrences.

(21) Click Close (displays ×) on the Find bar to remove the bar from the screen.

(22) Close the Chrome window.

quick steps

Start Chrome
Click Chrome icon on the taskbar or double-click the icon on the desktop.

Display a Web Page
Click in Address bar, type web address, and then press Enter.

Display Multiple Web Pages
1. Click New tab.
2. Type web address for new web page.
3. Press Enter.

Bookmark a Web Page
1. Display desired web page.
2. Click white star.
3. Click Done.

Find Text on a Web Page
1. Click Chrome menu.
2. Click *Find*.
3. Type text to find.
4. Click Next for each occurrence.

Tutorial

Finding Text on a Page

app tip

In Microsoft Edge, the Find bar is accessed by clicking Settings and more, then *Find on page*.

app tip

Ctrl + F is the universal keyboard shortcut for the Find command in any browser or application.

2.4 Searching for Information and Printing Web Pages

A **search engine** is managed by a company that indexes web pages by keywords and provides a search tool with which you can search their indexes to find web pages. To create indexes, search engines use software called a **spider**, or **crawler**, that reads web pages and other information supplied by the website owner to generate index entries. Search engines also provide advanced tools, which you can use to narrow search results.

Using a Search Engine to Locate Information on the Web

Several search engines are available, with Google and Bing the two leading companies; however, consider searching the web using other search engines, such as Dogpile, Ask, and DuckDuckGo, because you get different results from each company. Spider and crawler application capabilities and timing for indexing create differences in search results among companies. Depending on the information you are seeking, performing a search in more than one search engine is a good idea.

① Click the Microsoft Edge icon on the taskbar.

By default, Microsoft Edge performs searches using Bing, the search engine from Microsoft.

② With the insertion point positioned in the search text box (which displays the dimmed text *Search the web*) on the Start page, type cover letter examples and then press Enter or click the web search button.

Notice that as you type, Bing provides search suggestions in a drop-down list as soon as you begin typing. Click a search suggestion in the list if you see a close match.

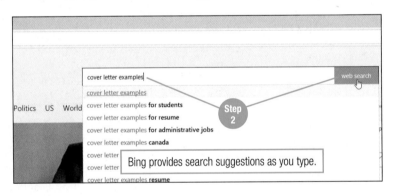

Bing provides search suggestions as you type.

③ Scroll down the search results page and click a link to a page that interests you.

Your results will vary. Choose a page that interests you.

④ Read a few paragraphs about cover letters at the page you selected.

Watch & Learn

———————— skills

Use search tools to find information on the web

Narrow search results by applying advanced search options

Print a web page, including selected pages only

Tutorial

Using Search Engines to Find Content

●————— go online

https://CA3 .ParadigmEducation .com/Dogpile
Go here to search using a metasearch search engine. A metasearch search engine sends the search phrase to other search engines and displays one list of search results from the wider group.

⑤ Click Back to return to the search results list.

⑥ Click in the Address bar or drag to select the current web address in the Address bar, type duckduckgo.com, and then press Enter.

Many people who want to browse the web in private like to use DuckDuckGo. While most search engines collect your search data to show you personalized results and ads, DuckDuckGo does not track your activity and does not personalize search results.

⑦ With the insertion point positioned in the search text box, type cover letter examples and then press Enter or click the search button (magnifying glass).

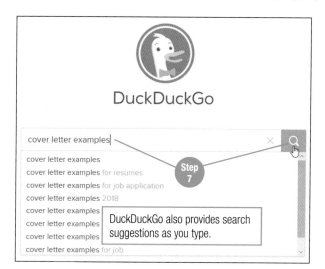

DuckDuckGo also provides search suggestions as you type.

● ─ ─ ─ ─ ─ app tip

Click a category, such as Images, Videos, Maps, or News, on a search engine website to restrict search results to a specific type of content.

⑧ Scroll down the search results page. Notice that some links are to the same web pages that you saw in the Bing search results; however, the same page may be in a different location in the search results list, or you may notice new links that were not shown by Bing.

Using Advanced Search Options

In both the Bing and DuckDuckGo "cover letter examples" search results, thousands of links were located and shown on the results pages. To help you narrow a list by specifying additional criteria, search engines provide advanced search tools or filters. Each search engine provides different tools. Explore the options at the search engine you prefer, or look for a help link that provides information on how to use advanced search tools.

☁ **Tutorial**

Using Advanced Search Options

⑨ Click in the Address bar or drag to select the current web address, type google.com, and then press Enter.

⑩ With the insertion point positioned in the search text box, type cover letter examples and then press Enter.

⑪ Click Settings (below search text box), and then click Advanced search in the drop-down list.

12 Click in the *site or domain* text box and then type edu. (You may need to scroll down the screen to locate the *site or domain* option.)

A .edu domain is restricted to US-accredited postsecondary institutions.

13 Click the Advanced Search button near the bottom of the Advanced Search page.

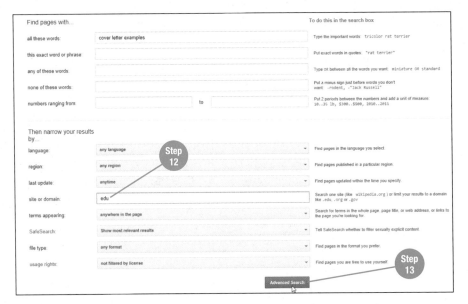

14 Click Tools below the search text box, click Any time, and then click Past month.

The search results list is now significantly reduced from the millions in the prior results list.

15 Scroll down the search results page and then click a link to a page that interests you. Notice that all URLs are .edu domains and all dates are within the past month.

Printing a Web Page

Printing a web page can sometimes be frustrating, because web pages are designed for optimal screen viewing (not printing). Many times you may print a web page only to discard a second or third page that you did not need, or the content printed did not fit the width of the paper and the printout was unusable.

16 Click in the Address bar or select the current web address, type https://www.rollins.edu/career-life -planning/documents/samples-cover-letter.pdf and then press Enter.

The web address provides four sample cover letters in the portable document format (PDF), suitable for printing. Assume you decide to print two of the example letters for later use when you are looking for a job.

17 Click Settings and more (three dots) and then click *Print*.

☁ **Tutorial**

Printing a Web Page

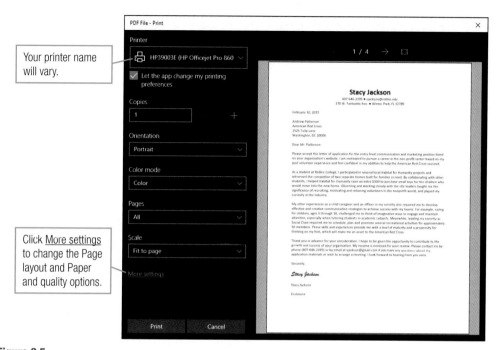

Your printer name will vary.

Click More settings to change the Page layout and Paper and quality options.

Figure 2.5

The Print dialog box in Microsoft Edge.

Page 1 in the printout (first cover letter example) is previewed in the Print dialog box shown in Figure 2.5. The Next page arrow (right-pointing arrow above the preview area) is used to navigate through all the pages that will print. Option boxes are available to change the destination printer, number of copies, page orientation, color mode, pages to print, and scale. The options available vary depending on the page selected for printing. For example, since this is a PDF page, options to change the margins and header/footer are omitted.

18   Click the Next page arrow (right-pointing arrow) above the preview page to view the second page that will be printed.

19   Click the Next page arrow two more times to view the remaining letters.

Assume you decide to print only the first and third letters.

20   Click the *Pages* option box (by default it displays *All* or *All pages*) and then click *Page range*.

21   Click in the *Range* text box and then type 1,3.

In the dialog box, the red text displayed above the *Range* text box illustrates acceptable ways to enter a print range.

22   Click the Print button, or if you are not connected to a printer, click the Cancel button to close the Print dialog box.

Only pages 1 and 3 of the web page print. Avoid wasting paper by previewing a web page before printing to make sure you only print the pages that you intend to use.

23   Close the Microsoft Edge window. Click *Close all* if prompted to close all tabs.

2.5 Downloading Content from a Web Page

Copying an image, audio clip, video clip, or music file (such as MP3) from a web page to your PC or mobile device is referred to as **downloading** content. Most content is protected by copyright law from being used by someone without permission. Before you download content, check the website for restrictions against copying information. Look for a contact link and request permission from the website owner to use the content if no restrictions are shown. When you include work created by someone else in an academic aasignment or in any other publication created by you, always provide a citation for the source of that work. Some authors will request that you provide a link to the page where the original work resides.

Saving an Image from a Web Page

Saving content from a web page generally involves right-clicking an object to display a context menu with a save option. In most cases, a file for an image, video clip, or audio clip is saved to the Downloads folder on the local device.

1 Click the Microsoft Edge icon on the taskbar.

Assume you want to find an image from the Grand Canyon for a project. You decide to use the Flickr: The Commons page to find an image in the public domain that can be used without copyright restrictions.

2 Click Favorites.

3 Click Favorites in the left pane if the Favorites list is not currently shown.

4 Click *Flickr: The Commons* in the Favorites list (you added this link to the Favorites list in Topic 2.2).

5 If necessary, scroll down to the section titled *A Commons Sampler*.

6 Click in the *Search The Commons* text box, type grand canyon, and then press Enter or click the Search button.

7 Scroll down and view the images in the search results page.

8 Click an image that you like and want to save.

9 On the next page, scroll down and read the information below the photograph. Look for entries about copyright restrictions. The entry *Unrestricted* means you are free to copy and use the image.

10 If necessary, scroll back up the page to the image preview.

11 Click the <u>Download this photo</u> icon (the down-pointing arrow above a bar) at the bottom right of the image preview area and then click <u>Medium</u> in the pop-up list. Note that the dimensions for each size option will vary depending on the image that is currently selected.

12 Click the Save button in the message bar that appears at the bottom of the window, then click Close (✕) when the message displays that the image finished downloading.

13 Click in the Address bar to select the current web address, type facebook .com/GrandCanyonNationalPark, and then press Enter. You may be prompted to sign in to Facebook to view the page. If necessary, skip to Step 18 if you cannot view the Facebook page.

The timeline pictures will vary. Choose any picture you want to save.

Step 14

14 Scroll down the timeline to a picture that you would like to save, and then click on the picture to view it in a larger window.

15 Right-click the picture and then click *Save picture as.* (You may need to right-click in the center of the image to get the menu shown at the right.)

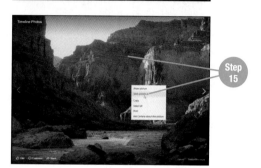

Step 15

16 In the Save As dialog box, click Downloads in the Navigation pane, select the current text in the *File name* text box, type GrandCanyon, and then click Save.

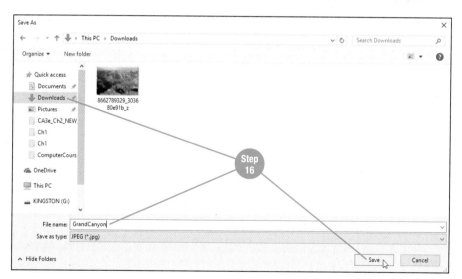

17 Close the Microsoft Edge window. Click Close all if prompted to close all tabs.

18 Click the File Explorer icon on the taskbar.

19 Click Downloads in the Navigation pane.

You will see the two downloaded pictures in the Content pane.

20 Double-click each image you downloaded to view the image in the Photos app or other image viewing window, and then close the window.

21 Close File Explorer.

Topics Review

Topic	Key Concepts
2.1 Introduction to the Internet and the World Wide Web	The **internet**, or **net**, is the infrastructure of interconnected communications equipment, network equipment, and computing devices that represents the global network linking individuals and organizations.
	All the web pages circulated on the internet form the **World Wide Web**, or **web**.
	A document stored on a web server that contains text and multimedia is called a **web page**.
	Text, an object, or icon on a web page can be a **hyperlink**, or **link**, that moves you from one page to another when clicked.
	A **web browser** is software, such as Microsoft Edge or Google Chrome, that is used to view web pages.
	An **internet service provider (ISP)** is a company that provides internet service to individuals and businesses for a fee.
	A **web address** is a unique text-based address, also called a **uniform resource locator (URL)**, that identifies each web page on the internet.
	One way to display a web page in a browser is to type the web address in the browser's **Address bar**, located at the top of the window.
	Every device connected to the internet is given a unique **internet protocol (IP) address**, which is either four groups of numbers 0 to 255, or eight groups of characters 0 to 9 or *a* to *f*. A Domain Name System (DNS) server looks up in a directory the associated IP address for a requested web address.
	A web address is made up of parts that define the protocol, domain, folder(s), and file name for the web page.
2.2 Navigating the Web Using Edge	**Microsoft Edge** is the web browser included with Windows 10.
	Start Microsoft Edge by clicking the Microsoft Edge icon on the taskbar.
	To display a web page, type the web address (URL) in the Address bar and then press Enter.
	Click **Back** to move back one page; click **Forward** to move forward one page.
	The first page that displays for a website is called the **home page**.
	Display a web page in Reading view to read the page content without the sidebars and navigational items.
	Click **New tab** (plus symbol) to open a new page in the window.
	Tabbed browsing means you have more than one web page open in a window. Each web page has a tab that you click to switch from viewing one page to another page.
	Display a web page, click the star at the right end of the Address bar, and then click the Add button to save a page to the **Favorites** list.
	Click **Favorites** to show Favorites, Reading list, History, and Downloads in a panel at the right side of the window.
2.3 Navigating the Web Using Chrome	**Chrome** is a web browser from Google for PCs and mobile devices.
	Start Chrome by clicking the Chrome icon on the taskbar or by double-clicking the Chrome icon on the desktop.
	Display a web page by typing a web address or search phrase in the Address bar.
	Click the white star to bookmark the current web page on the **Bookmarks bar**.
	Click the **Chrome menu** to turn on or turn off the display of the Bookmarks bar that docks below the Address bar.
	Open the **Find bar** from the Chrome menu to locate all occurrences of a word or phrase on the current web page.

continued...

Topic	Key Concepts
2.4 Searching for Information and Printing Web Pages	A search tool to find indexed pages is called a **search engine**. A company indexes web pages by keywords using software called a **spider**, or a **crawler**.
	Consider searching for information by using more than one search engine because you will get different results from each due to differences in spider and crawler software and timing differentials.
	To find information using a search engine, launch a web browser, type the web address for the desired search engine, type a search word or phrase in the search text box, and then press Enter.
	Each search engine provides tools for advanced searching, which narrows the search results list. For example, at Google, the Advanced Search page provides options to include or exclude words in the search and restrict search results to types of domains, file formats, a country, or a language.
	Print a web page by accessing the Print option from a menu in the browser (in Microsoft Edge, click Settings and more, and then click *Print*).
	In the preview area of the Print dialog box, preview each page to avoid unnecessary printing of pages that are wasteful.
2.5 Downloading Content from a Web Page	Saving a copy of an image, audio clip, video clip, or music file from a web page to your PC or mobile device is called **downloading**.
	Some websites, such as flickr.com, provide a download tool that facilitates downloading an image on their website to the Downloads folder.
	If no download tool is on the web page, saving content generally involves right-clicking the object and selecting a save option on the shortcut menu.

 Topics Review

Exploring Office 2019 Essentials

Office 2019 is a suite of software applications that includes the applications Word, Excel, PowerPoint, Access, and Outlook. The suite is available in various editions that package the applications in collections geared toward a home, business, or student customer using the software under a one-time purchase for a PC installation, or a subscription installation called Office 365. The Office Professional 2019 edition for a PC installation and the Office 365 Home subscription include all the applications used in this textbook.

One reason the Office suite is popular is because several features or elements are common to all the applications. Once you learn your way around one of the applications in the suite, another application looks and operates similarly, making the learning process faster and easier.

In this chapter, you will navigate the Office 2019 interface and perform file-related tasks or routines common to all the applications. You will customize the Quick Access Toolbar and choose options using multiple methods. You will also save and open files to and from OneDrive, an online file storage option.

Learning Objectives

3.1 Start an Office application, identify common features, and explore the ribbon

3.2 Open, save, print, export, close, and start new documents in the backstage area

3.3 Customize and use the Quick Access Toolbar

3.4 Select text and objects, perform commands using the ribbon and Mini toolbar, and select options in a dialog box

3.5 Copy and paste using buttons in the Clipboard and format an object using a task pane

3.6 Use the Tell Me feature and the Help task pane to find options and help resources

3.7 Save files to and open files from OneDrive, navigate longer documents, and use Undo

3.8 Change the Zoom setting and screen resolution

Read & Learn

Content Online

The online course includes additional training and assessment resources.

3.1 Starting and Switching Applications, Starting a New Presentation, and Exploring the Ribbon

Watch & Learn

●————— Skills

Start an Office application

Switch between applications

Start a new presentation

Explore the ribbon

Word, Excel, PowerPoint, and Access begin on a Start screen and share some common features and elements. An application can be started using an icon on the desktop, from a tile or application name on the Start menu, or by using the search text box on the taskbar.

Office 2019 Editions

The Office 2019 suite is packaged in a variety of application bundles (called *editions*) as one-time purchased software. Table 3.1 lists three of these editions. The suite is also available through a monthly or annual subscription as Office 365. **Office 365** includes Word, Excel, PowerPoint, Outlook, Publisher, and Access, along with Skype calling minutes, additional OneDrive storage, and technical support from Microsoft. Other advantages to an Office 365 subscription are the suite is accessible for up to six users and updates to the software are automatically pushed to each installation.

Microsoft also offers a special edition of Office 365 for students called Office 365 University, available only to verified students and faculty of postsecondary institutions. Other editions for installation on a Mac computer and collections of software and services geared toward business environments are available.

Table 3.1 Office 2019 One-Time Purchase Editions

Edition	What It Includes
Office Home and Student 2019	Word, Excel, and PowerPoint
Office Home and Business 2019	Word, Excel, PowerPoint, and Outlook
Office Professional 2019	Word, Excel, PowerPoint, Access, Publisher, and Outlook

Office 2019 System Requirements

Table 3.2 provides the standard system requirements for installing Office 2019. Generally, if the PC can successfully run Windows 10, then Office 2019 will also work on the same hardware, provided there is enough free disk space for the application software files.

Table 3.2 Office 2019 System Requirements

Hardware Component	Requirement
Processor	1 gigahertz (GHz) or faster processor
Memory	2 gigabytes (GB) of RAM Mac computer requires 4 GB RAM
Disk space	3 GB available free space Mac computer requires 6.0 GB available disk space
Operating system	Windows 10 Mac computer requires Mac OS X 10.10 or newer
Display setting	1024 x 768 screen resolution or higher (PC) 1280 x 800 screen resolution or higher (Mac)
Browser	Current versions of Edge, Chrome, Firefox, or Safari

Starting an Application in the Office 2019 Suite

To start an application in the Office 2019 suite, double-click the application icon on the desktop or click the Start button and then click the application tile in the right pane on the Start menu. If a tile for the application is not on the Start menu, scroll down the list of application names in the left pane on the Start menu and then click the application name.

A quick way to find and start an application is to type the application name in the search text box on the taskbar and then click the name in the search results list. In many instances, you will see the desired application name appear in the search results list after typing only the first few letters in the name.

Tutorial
Opening a Blank Document

1. Click in the search text box on the taskbar, type word, and then click *Word* in the right pane. Close any message or task pane that may appear about new features.

   Word 2019 is the application used to create, edit, and format text-based documents. When you start Word, the Start screen appears. The **Start screen** for Office applications shows the *Recent* option list used to open a document worked on recently.

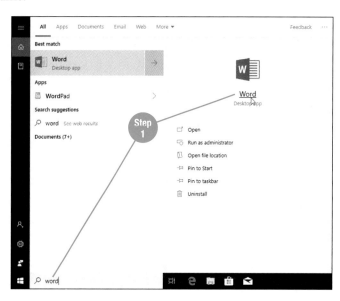

2. Click the Maximize button ☐ near the top right of the window if Word does not fill the screen. Skip this step if you see the Restore Down button ☐ since the window is already maximized.

3. Compare your screen with the Word Start screen shown in Figure 3.1.

4. Click the Start button and then click the Excel tile in the right pane on the Start menu. If an Excel tile is not available, scroll down the application list in the left pane, and then click *Excel*. Click the Maximize button if the Excel window does not fill the screen.

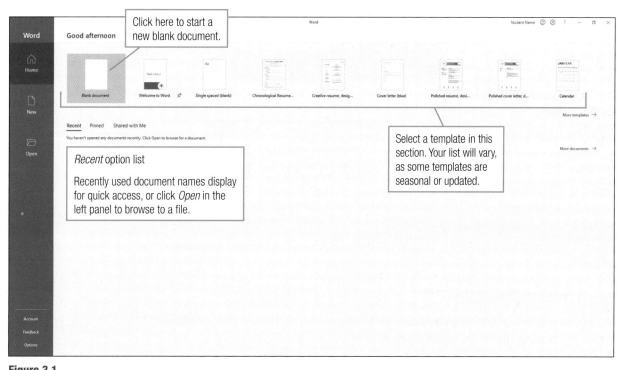

Click here to start a new blank document.

Select a template in this section. Your list will vary, as some templates are seasonal or updated.

Recent option list
Recently used document names display for quick access, or click *Open* in the left panel to browse to a file.

Figure 3.1
Word 2019 opens with the Word Start screen shown above.

Use **Excel 2019** when your focus is on entering, calculating, formatting, and analyzing numerical data.

⑤ Compare the Excel Start screen with the Word Start screen shown in Figure 3.1 on the previous page.

Each Office application offers templates in the template gallery on the Start screen. A template is a preformatted document, worksheet, presentation, or database. Click a thumbnail to preview a larger picture of the template. The first thumbnail is used to start a new blank document, workbook, presentation, or database.

⑥ Start PowerPoint by typing powerpoint in the search text box and then pressing Enter or by using the Start menu. If necessary, maximize the window.

Create slides for an oral or kiosk-style presentation that includes text, images, sound, video, or other multimedia in **PowerPoint 2019**.

⑦ Compare the PowerPoint Start screen with the Word Start screen shown in Figure 3.1.

⑧ Start Access using any method described in Step 1 or Step 4. If necessary, maximize the window and then compare the Access Start screen with the Word Start screen shown in Figure 3.1.

Access 2019 is a database application in which you organize, store, and manage related data, such as information about customers or products.

app tip

Each Office application has its own color scheme. Word is blue, Excel is green, PowerPoint is orange, and Access is maroon.

Switching between Office Applications

As learned in Chapter 1, you switch to another open application by clicking the application button on the taskbar. Point to a button on the taskbar to see a thumbnail appear above the button with a preview of the open document. If more than one document is open, the thumbnails make it easy to switch to the correct window.

⑨ Point to the Excel button on the taskbar to preview the thumbnail of the Excel Start screen and then click the button to switch to the Excel window.

⑩ Click the Access button on the taskbar to switch to the Access window.

⑪ Click the Close button (✕) at the upper right corner of the Access window.

⑫ Click the Close button to close Excel.

⑬ You should now see the PowerPoint window. If PowerPoint is not the active window, click the PowerPoint button on the taskbar.

Starting a New Presentation

For any application in the Office suite, start a new document, workbook, presentation, or database by clicking the thumbnail for the new blank document, workbook, presentation, or database in the Templates gallery on the Start screen.

14 Click *Blank Presentation* on the PowerPoint Start screen.

Exploring the Ribbon

The ribbon appears along the top of each Office application. Buttons within the ribbon are used to access commands and features within the application. The ribbon is split into individual tabs, with each tab divided into groups of related buttons, as shown in Figure 3.2. Word, Excel, PowerPoint, and Access all have the File and Home tabs as the first two tabs in the ribbon. The File tab is used to perform document-level routines, such as saving, printing, and exporting. This tab is explored in the next topic. The Home tab contains the most frequently-used features in each application, such as formatting and editing buttons.

This is the active tab. Click a tab name to change the active tab.

Your background design may vary.

Ribbon Display Options button

The Font group organizes related buttons into one part of the ribbon.

Figure 3.2
The PowerPoint ribbon appears along the top of the application window, as it does for all Office applications.

Clicking the **Ribbon Display Options button** near the top right of the window displays a drop-down menu to change the ribbon display from *Show Tabs and Commands* to *Show Tabs*, which hides the command buttons until you click a tab, or *Auto-hide Ribbon*, to display the ribbon only when you click along the top of the window.

15 Click the Insert tab to view the groups and buttons on the Insert tab ribbon for PowerPoint.

16 Click the Word button on the taskbar and then click *Blank document* on the Start screen to start a new Word document.

17 Click the Insert tab to view the groups and buttons on the Word Insert tab ribbon.

18 Click the Design tab in Word and then review the buttons on the Word Design tab ribbon.

19 Switch to PowerPoint and then click the Design tab.

20 Spend a few moments exploring the other tabs on the PowerPoint ribbon and then close PowerPoint.

21 Spend a few moments exploring the other tabs on the Word ribbon and then close Word.

3.2 Using the Backstage Area to Manage Documents

The File tab opens the **backstage area** in the Office applications. The backstage area is where you find file management options, such as *Open*, *Save*, *Save As*, *Print*, *Share*, *Export*, and *Close*. You also go to the backstage area within an application to start a new document. Other tasks performed in the backstage area include displaying information about a document, protecting a document, and managing the document properties and versions.

Each application in the Office suite provides options that can be personalized in the Options dialog box accessed from the left panel in the backstage area. Your Microsoft account and/or connected services and the background or theme for all the Office applications are managed in the Account backstage area.

Note: If necessary, insert your storage medium into an empty port before starting this topic. Close the File Explorer window if it opens after you insert a removable drive.

1. Start Word.
2. On the Word Start screen, click *Open* in the left panel.
3. Click the *Browse* option.
4. If necessary, scroll down the list of places in the Navigation pane in the Open dialog box until you can see the entry for your storage medium.
5. Click the entry in the Navigation pane for your storage medium.
6. Double-click *StudentDataFiles* in the Content pane.
7. Double-click *Ch3*.

The Word document **Cottage_rental_listing** is displayed in the Content pane. Within an Office application, the Open dialog box by default shows only file types that the active application can read.

8. Double-click ***Cottage_rental_listing***.

Word document file names have a file extension *.docx*. Your system may be set to show the file extensions. In the next steps, you will use the Save As command to save a copy of the document in another folder.

9. If a yellow message bar displays indicating the document is shown in Protected view, click the Enable Editing button to turn off Protected view.

As a precaution, documents open in Protected view whenever the file originates from an online source, such as by downloading the file from a website or from a saved email attachment.

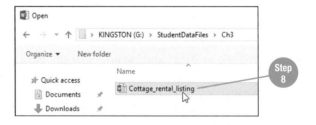

10. Click the File tab to display the backstage area.

When a document is open, the backstage area displays the Info panel with document properties for the active file and buttons to protect, inspect, and manage versions of the document.

Watch & Learn

-------- Skills

Open, Save As, Print, and Close a document

Export a document as a PDF file

●------- app tip

The *Recent* option list on the Start screen displays by default the last 50 documents opened. If the file you want is in the *Recent* option list, click the file name to open the document.

Tutorial

Opening a Document from the Recent Option List

11 Click *Save As* in the left panel.

The Save As command is used to save a copy of a document in another location or to save a copy of the document in the same location but with a different file name.

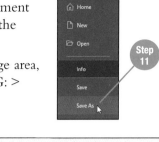

12 With *This PC* already selected in the Save As backstage area, click the Up arrow next to the current file location G: > *StudentDataFiles* > Ch3 in the right panel.

13 Click the Up arrow a second time.

14 Click the *ComputerCourse* folder name in the right panel.

15 Click the *CompletedTopics* folder name in the right panel and then click the <u>More options</u> hyperlink above the folder list.

16 In the Save As dialog box, click the New folder button on the Command bar, type Ch3, and then press Enter.

17 Double-click *Ch3*.

18 Click in the *File name* text box or drag to select the current file name, type CottageListing-YourName, and then press Enter or click the Save button.

quick steps

Open a Document
1. On Word Start screen, click *Open* in the left panel.
2. Click *Browse*.
3. Navigate to drive and folder and then double-click file name.

Use Save As to Save a Copy of a Document
1. Click File tab.
2. Click *Save As*.
3. Navigate to desired location using folder names in right panel or by clicking Browse option.
4. If necessary, change file name.
5. Click Save.

Tutorials

Managing Documents

Managing Folders

19 Click in the document next to *List Date:* below the address *3587 Bluewater Road* (in the second column of the table) and then type the current date.

20 Click next to *Assigned Agent:* below the date (in the second column of the table) and then type your name.

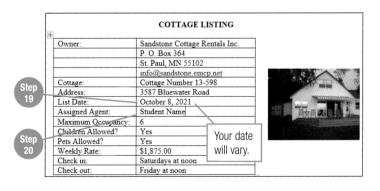

Oops!

Typing mistake? Press Backspace to delete what you have typed if you make an error and then retype the text. You can also drag across text and then press Delete.

Printing a Document

Display the Print backstage area when you want to preview and print a document. Before printing, review the document in the **Print Preview** panel of the backstage area shown in Step 23. The bottom of the Print Preview panel shows the number of pages needed to print the document, and navigation buttons are included to move to the next page and previous page in a multipage document.

In the Print panel, choose the printer at which to print the document in the *Printer* section, and modify the print settings and page layout options in the *Settings* section. When you are ready to print, click the Print button.

21 Click the File tab and then click *Print*.

22 Examine the document in the Print Preview panel, check the name of the default printer, and review the default options in the *Settings* section.

When print settings are changed, the options are stored with the document, so you do not need to change them again the next time you want to print.

23 Click the Print button to print the document.

The document is sent to the printer, and the backstage area closes.

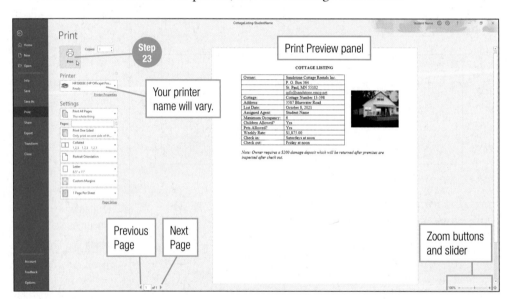

Exporting a Document as a PDF File

Many people exchange documents as Portable Document Format (PDF) files via email or websites. A **PDF document** is a document saved in an open standard for exchanging files as electronic documents. The standard was developed by Adobe Systems. A PDF document can be viewed in any web browser.

The advantage of a PDF file is that the document looks and prints as it would in the application in which it was created but without having to open or install the source application. Export a Word document as a PDF if you need to send a document to someone who does not have Word installed on his or her computer.

24 Click the File tab and then click *Export*.

25 With *Create PDF/XPS Document* selected in the Export backstage area, click the Create PDF/XPS button.

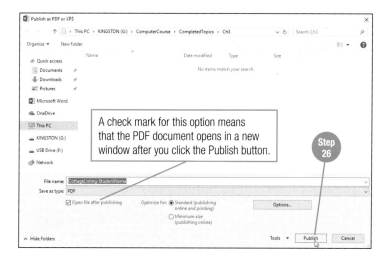

26 Click the Publish button in the Publish as PDF or XPS dialog box.

By default, the PDF is created in the same drive and folder in which the Word document resides and with the same file name but with the file extension *.pdf*. The same name can be used for both the Word document and the PDF document because PDF files have a file extension different than a Word document.

A check mark for this option means that the PDF document opens in a new window after you click the Publish button.

27 The published PDF document opens in a reader app, such as Windows Reader or Adobe Reader, or in a browser window. If no application is associated with PDF documents, a message box similar to the one shown at the right opens with the prompt *How do you want to open this file?* In that case, click the OK button to open the PDF document in the selected option, *Microsoft Edge*.

28 Close the window in which the PDF document opened to return to Word.

29 Click the File tab and then click *Close*.

30 Click the Save button when prompted in the message box asking if you want to save your changes. Leave Word open for the next topic.

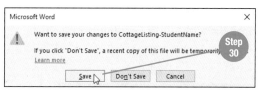

Close a document when you are finished editing, saving, printing, and publishing. A blank window displays when no documents are open.

quick steps

Print a Document
1. Click File tab.
2. Click *Print*.
3. Preview and/or change options as necessary.
4. Click Print.

Export as PDF
1. Click File tab.
2. Click *Export*.
3. Click Create PDF/XPS.
4. Click Publish.

Oops!

PDF does not open in a reader app or browser window? The default settings on your PC or mobile device may differ and the option may be turned off. In that case, skip Steps 27 and 28.

Tutorial

Closing a Document and Closing Word

3.3 Customizing and Using the Quick Access Toolbar

The **Quick Access Toolbar** is at the upper left corner of each Office application window. With the default installation, the Quick Access Toolbar has the AutoSave option turned off and buttons to Save, Undo, and Repeat (which changes to Redo after Undo has been used). A touchscreen device includes a fourth button—the Touch/Mouse Mode button—that is used to optimize the spacing between commands for the mouse or for touch. Most people customize the toolbar by adding buttons that are used often.

To add a button to the Quick Access Toolbar, click the Customize Quick Access Toolbar button at the end of the toolbar (displays as a down-pointing arrow with a bar above) and then click the desired button in the drop-down list.

Note: Skip this topic if the Quick Access Toolbar on the computer you are using already displays the New, Open, Quick Print, and Print Preview and Print buttons in Word, PowerPoint, and Excel. Skip any steps in which a drop-down list option already displays with a check mark, which means the button is already on the toolbar.

Watch & Learn

Hands On Activity

------- **Skills**

Add buttons to the Quick Access Toolbar

Use buttons on the Quick Access Toolbar to perform commands

1. With a blank Word document, click the Customize Quick Access Toolbar button.

2. Click *New* in the drop-down list.

Options displayed with a check mark are already added to the toolbar. Buttons added to the Quick Access Toolbar are placed at the end of the toolbar.

3. Click the Customize Quick Access Toolbar button.

4. Click *Open* in the drop-down list.

5. Click the Customize Quick Access Toolbar button.

6. Click *Quick Print* in the drop-down list.

7. Click the Customize Quick Access Toolbar button.

8. Click *Print Preview and Print* in the drop-down list.

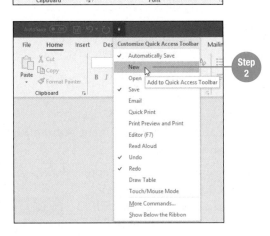

------ **app tip**

Clicking a check-marked option removes the button from the Quick Access Toolbar.

------ **app tip**

Right-click any button on the ribbon and then click *Add to Quick Access Toolbar* to add the button.

| Touch-enabled devices also show a Touch/Mouse Mode button. | | Quick Access Toolbar after buttons added in Steps 1–8 |

9. Click the Open button on the Quick Access Toolbar.

The Open backstage area opens with the *Recent* option list in the right panel.

Step 9

10 Click the file **CottageListing-StudentName** in the *Recent* option list.

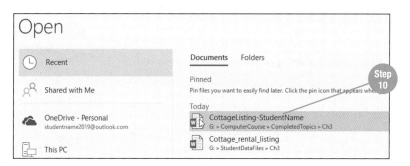

11 Click the Print Preview and Print button on the Quick Access Toolbar. The Print backstage area opens.

12 Click the Back button (left-pointing arrow inside circle) to return to the document without printing.

13 Start PowerPoint.

14 Click *Blank Presentation* on the PowerPoint Start screen.

Notice the customized Word Quick Access Toolbar does not carry over to other Office applications.

15 Customize the Quick Access Toolbar in PowerPoint by adding the New, Open, Quick Print, and Print Preview and Print buttons.

16 Close PowerPoint.

17 Start Excel and then click *Blank Workbook* on the Excel Start screen.

18 Customize the Excel Quick Access Toolbar to add the New, Open, Quick Print, and Print Preview and Print buttons.

19 Close Excel.

20 In the Word document, click the File tab and then click *Close*.

21 Click the New button on the Quick Access Toolbar.

A new blank document window opens. Leave this document open for the next topic.

3.4 Selecting Text or Objects, Using the Ribbon and Mini Toolbar, and Selecting Options in Dialog Boxes

Watch & Learn

Hands On Activity

●------- skills

Select text and objects

Perform commands using the ribbon and Mini toolbar

Display a task pane and dialog box

Choose options in a dialog box

Creating a document, worksheet, presentation, or database involves working with the ribbon to select options or perform commands. Some options involve using a button, list box, or gallery, and some commands cause a task pane or dialog box to open in which you select options.

In many instances, before you choose an option from the ribbon, you first select text or an object as the target for the action. Select text by clicking within a word, paragraph, cell, or placeholder or by dragging across the text you want to select. Select an object, such as an image or other graphic, by clicking on the object.

Selected objects display with a series of selection handles. A **selection handle** is a circle at the middle and/or corners of an object, or at the beginning and end of text on a touch-enabled device. Selection handles are used to manipulate the object or to define the selection area on a touch-enabled device. Table 3.3 provides instructions for selecting text using a mouse or touch and for selecting an object.

Table 3.3 Selecting Text and Objects Using the Mouse and Touch

Selecting Text Using a Mouse	Selecting Text Using Touch	Selecting Objects

1. Point at the beginning of the text or cell to be selected.
 	
   The pointer displays as ⌶, called an *I-beam* in Word and PowerPoint, or as ⇧, called a *cell pointer* in Excel.
2. Hold down the left mouse button and drag to the end of the text or cells to be selected.
3. Release the mouse button.
 	
   In some cases, a Mini toolbar displays when you release the mouse after selecting text.
 	
Mini toolbar
	1. Tap at the beginning of the text to be selected. A selection handle appears below the text (displays as an empty circle).
	
	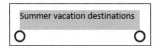
	
	   selection handle
	
	2. Slide the selection handle right to move the insertion point to edit text. Alternatively, double-tap at the beginning of the text to select the first word and show a second selection handle, then slide the right selection handle to extend the selection.
	
	Summer vacation destinations
	
	3. After releasing your finger, you can slide the left or right selection handle to redefine the area, if necessary.
	4. To display the Mini toolbar, press and hold inside the selected text area. The toolbar appears when you release your finger and displays already optimized for touch.
	
	Mini toolbar
		1. Click anywhere on the object.
		
		   Selection handles appear at the ends, corners, and middle (depending on width and height) of each side of the object.
		
		   A Layout Options button also appears next to a selected object with options for aligning and moving the object with surrounding text.
		
		Layout Options button for selected object

1 In a blank Word document, type Summer vacation destinations and then press Enter.

2 Type Explore the beaches of Florida and experience the Florida sunset with friends or family. and then press Enter.

3 Select the title *Summer vacation destinations* to display the Mini toolbar.

The **Mini toolbar** appears near text after text is selected or with the shortcut menu when you right-click a selection. The toolbar contains frequently-used formatting commands for quicker access within the work area than using the ribbon.

If necessary, refer to the instructions in Table 3.3 for selecting text using the mouse or touch.

4 Click the Bold button on the Mini toolbar.

5 Click in the blank line below the sentence that begins with *Explore* to deselect the title.

6 Click the Insert tab.

7 Click the Pictures button in the Illustrations group.

This opens the Insert Picture dialog box.

8 If necessary, scroll down the list of places in the Navigation pane. Click the entry in the Navigation pane for your storage medium.

9 Double-click *StudentDataFiles*, double-click *Ch3*, and then double-click **FloridaSunset.jpg**.

The FloridaSunset image is inserted in the document and is automatically selected.

10 Drag the selection handle at the lower right corner of the image until the image is resized to the approximate height and width shown below.

The mouse pointer changes shape to a double-headed diagonal arrow (⬉) when you point at the lower right corner of the image. Drag upward and to the left when you see this icon. The pointer changes shape to a crosshairs—a large, thin, black cross (+)—while you drag the mouse. When you release the mouse, the selection handles reappear.

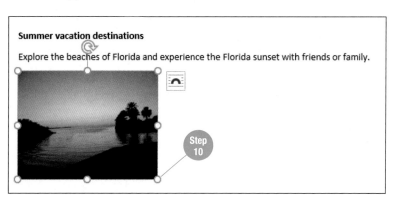

quick steps

Select Text or an Object
Click or drag in word, paragraph, cell, or place-holder, or click on the object.

Format Text Using the Mini Toolbar
1. Select text.
2. Click desired button on Mini toolbar.

app tip

All the buttons available on the Mini toolbar are also available on the ribbon.

Tutorials

Applying Font Formatting Using the Mini Toolbar

Selecting, Replacing, and Deleting Text

Oops!

No selection handles? If you click away from the object, the selection handles disappear. Click on the image to redisplay the selection handles.

11 Click the Save button on the Quick Access Toolbar.

12 With the *Recent* option selected, click the Ch3 folder name associated with your storage medium and the folders » ComputerCourse » CompletedTopics.

13 Click in the *File name* text box (displays the dimmed text *Enter file name here*), type VacationDestinations-YourName, and then press Enter or click the Save button.

●------ **app tip**

The first time a document is saved, the Save As backstage area appears so the document can be assigned a file name. Once the document is named, clicking Save on the Quick Access Toolbar saves changes using the existing name and storage location.

Working with Objects, Contextual Tabs, and Dialog Boxes

An **object** is an image, shape, chart, or other item that can be manipulated separately from text or other objects around it. When an object is selected, a contextual ribbon tab appears. More than one contextual tab may appear. A **contextual tab** contains commands or options that are related to the type of object that is currently selected.

Some buttons in the ribbon display a drop-down gallery. A **gallery** displays visual representations of options for the selected item in a drop-down list or grid. Pointing to an option in a gallery displays a **live preview** of the text or object if the option is applied. Live previews let you see how formatting will look before applying an option. Use live preview to try out a few format options before making a choice, or click on the screen away from the list to leave the existing formatting intact.

14 With the image still selected, click the Picture Tools Format tab if the tab is not the active tab and then click the Corrections button in the Adjust group.

15 Point to the third option in the last row in the Corrections gallery. Notice the colors in the image deepen to show a more vibrant sunset when you point to the option.

16 Click the third option in the last row in the Corrections gallery to apply the *Brightness: 0% (Normal) Contrast: +40%* correction.

●------- **Oops!**

Picture Tools Format tab not visible? This tab appears only when a picture is selected. Click on the picture to display the contextual tab.

Some ribbon groups have a small button at the lower right corner of the group that is a diagonal downward-pointing arrow (⌐). This button is called a **dialog box launcher**. Clicking the button causes a task pane or a dialog box to appear. A **task pane** appears at the left or right side of the window, whereas a **dialog box** opens in a separate window above (or, from the viewer's perspective, in front of) the document. Task panes and dialog boxes contain more options as buttons, lists, sliders, check boxes, text boxes, and option buttons.

quick steps

Display the Contextual Tab(s)
Click to select object.

Display a Task Pane or Dialog Box
Click dialog box launcher at bottom right of group on ribbon.

17 Click the dialog box launcher at the lower right corner of the Picture Styles group.

The Format Picture task pane opens at the right. You will work in a task pane in the next topic.

18 Click the Close button (×) at the upper right corner of the Format Picture task pane to close the pane.

19 Click the dialog box launcher at the lower right corner of the Size group.

The Layout dialog box opens with the Size tab active.

20 Select the current value in the *Absolute* text box in the *Width* section and then type 3.

21 Click the Text Wrapping tab and then click the *Square* option in the *Wrapping style* section.

22 Click OK.

23 With the picture still selected, position the pointer on top of the picture and then drag the picture up to the top of the document, releasing it when the green horizontal and vertical alignment guides show the picture aligned at the top and left margins.

An **alignment guide** is a colored horizontal or vertical line that appears when you are moving an object to help you align and place the object within the document boundaries or in relation to surrounding text or other nearby objects.

Oops!

Measurement displays with *cm*? In Canada, Office installs with the metric measurement system. In Step 20, type 3 in or change to inches in the Options dialog box (accessed from the File tab). Click *Advanced* in the left pane, scroll down to the *Display* section, and then change the *Show measurements in units of* option.

24 Click the Save button on the Quick Access Toolbar. Leave the document open for the next topic.

Because the document has already been saved once, the Save button saves the changes using the existing file name and location.

Tutorial

Applying Font Formatting Using the Font Dialog Box

Alignment guides show the picture is aligned at the upper left margin.

3.5 Using the Office Clipboard and Formatting Using a Task Pane

☁ **Watch & Learn**

●——————— skills

Copy and paste text and an object

Copy and paste formatting options using Format Painter

Use a task pane to format a selected object

The Clipboard group is standardized across Office applications. The buttons in the Clipboard group are Cut, Copy, Paste, and Format Painter. You used Cut, Copy, and Paste in Chapter 1 when you learned how to move and copy files and folders. Cut, Copy, and Paste are also used to move or copy text or objects.

Format Painter is used to copy formatting options from selected text or an object to other text or another object.

1. With the **VacationDestinations-YourName** document still open, start PowerPoint and then click *Blank Presentation*.

2. Click anywhere on *Click to add title* on the blank slide and then type Florida Sunset.

3. Click the Word button on the taskbar.

4. Select the sentence that begins with *Explore* below the title and then click the Copy button in the Clipboard group on the Home tab.

5. Click the PowerPoint button on the taskbar to switch to PowerPoint and then click anywhere on *Click to add subtitle* on the slide to place an insertion point.

6. Click the top part of the Paste button in the Clipboard group. Do *not* click the down-pointing arrow on the button.

●—————— app tip

Some buttons on the ribbon have two parts. Clicking the top or left of the button causes the default action to occur. Clicking the bottom or right of the button (arrow) displays a list of options to modify the action that occurs.

The selected text that was copied from Word is pasted on the slide in PowerPoint. Notice also the Paste Options button that appears below the pasted text.

7 Click the Paste Options button to display the Paste Options gallery.

Paste options vary depending on the pasted text or object. Buttons in the gallery allow you to change the appearance or behavior of the pasted text or object in the destination location.

8 Click the Word button on the taskbar to switch to Word.

9 Click on the image to select it, click the Copy button, click the PowerPoint button on the taskbar, and then click the Paste button. (Remember not to click the down-pointing arrow on the Paste button.)

The pasted image is dropped onto the slide overlapping the text.

10 Click the Paste Options button. Notice that the paste options for a picture are different than the paste options for text.

11 Click on white space away from the image to remove the Paste Options gallery.

12 If necessary, click to select the image object.

13 Drag the selected image below the text. Release the image when the orange guide shows the image is aligned with the middle of the text placeholders.

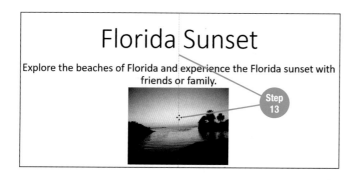

14 Click the Save button on the Quick Access Toolbar.

●----- **Quick Steps**

Copy and Paste Text or an Object
1. Select text or object.
2. Click Copy button.
3. Navigate to destination document or location within current document.
4. Click Paste button.

☁ **Tutorials**

Cutting, Copying, and Pasting Text

Using Paste Options

●------- **app tip**

Paste options are helpful if different formatting exists between the source or destination documents, and you want to control which formatting is applied to the pasted text or object.

15 In the Save As backstage area, click *This PC* and then click *Browse*.

16 Navigate to the Ch3 subfolder in the folders › ComputerCourse
    › CompletedTopics on your storage medium.

17 Select the current text in the *File name* text box, type FloridaVacation-YourName,
    and then press Enter or click the Save button.

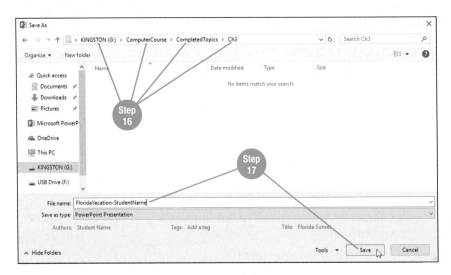

Using Format Painter to Copy Formatting Options

Sometimes instead of copying text or an object, you want to copy formatting options.
Format Painter copies to the Clipboard the formatting attributes for selected text or
an object.

Click the Format Painter button to do a one-time copy of formatting options or
double-click the button if you want to paste the formatting options multiple times.
Double-clicking the Format Painter button turns the feature on until you click the
button again to turn the feature off. A button that operates in an on or off state is
called a **toggle button**.

18 Select the first occurrence of the word
    Florida in the subtitle on the slide.

19 Click the *Font Color* option box arrow
    (down-pointing arrow at the right of
    the Font Color button) in the Font
    group on the Home tab.

20 Click the *Purple* square (the last square
    in the *Standard Colors* section).

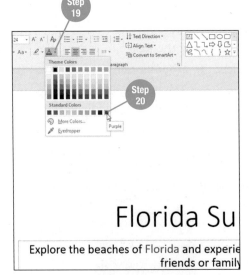

☁ **Tutorials**

Applying Font
Formatting Using the
Font Group

Formatting with
Format Painter

21 With the text still selected, click the Italic button in the Font group on the Home tab.

22 With the text still selected, click the Format Painter button in the Clipboard group.

Step 21

23 Drag the mouse pointer with the paintbrush icon across the second occurrence of the word *Florida* in the subtitle.

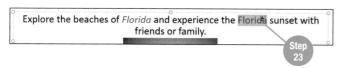

Explore the beaches of *Florida* and experience the Florida sunset with friends or family.

Step 23

Step 22

24 Click on white space away from the selected text to deselect the text.

25 Click the Save button on the Quick Access Toolbar.

26 Click on the image to select it and display the contextual tab.

27 Click the Picture Tools Format tab.

Step 27

28 Click the *Drop Shadow Rectangle* option in the Picture Styles gallery (fourth picture style option).

Drop Shadow Rectangle

Step 28

29 With the image still selected, click the Home tab, click the Format Painter button, and then click the title text *Florida Sunset* at the top of the slide.

30 With the Florida Sunset placeholder selected, click the dialog box launcher in the Drawing group on the Home tab to open the Format Shape task pane at the right side of the window.

31 Click the Size & Properties tab (last option) in the Format Shape task pane.

32 Click *Text Box* to reveal the options.

33 Click the *Vertical alignment* option box arrow (down-pointing arrow at the right of *Bottom*) and then click *Middle*.

34 Close the Format Shape task pane.

35 Save and then close PowerPoint. Leave the Word document open for the next topic.

title aligned in the middle of the placeholder vertically at Steps 31–34

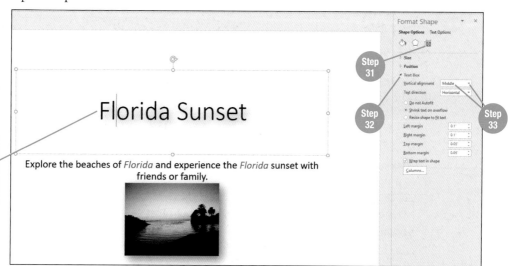

Florida Sunset

Explore the beaches of *Florida* and experience the *Florida* sunset with friends or family.

3.6 Using the Tell Me Feature and Help Task Pane

Watch & Learn

A text box to the right of the Help tab on the ribbon containing the dimmed text *Search* is the **Tell Me** feature in Office 2019. Use the search text box to type an option and quickly access the command or feature directly from the *Tell Me* text box instead of navigating the ribbon tabs. You can also use the *Tell Me* text box to type a word or phrase and search resources in a Help task pane to learn how to use an option or feature. The **Smart Lookup** option in the Tell Me drop-down list opens a task pane at the right side of the window that lets you see a definition of the term or explore web resources related to the term.

━━━━━━━ skills

Use Tell Me to locate an option

Use Tell Me to look up a definition

Use Help task pane to find information

1. With the **VacationDestinations-YourName** document still open, click to place the insertion point after the period in the sentence below the document title, press Enter, and then type Visit https://CA3.ParadigmEducation.com /FloridaTours for information on our Florida vacation packages.

2. Press Enter and then type Our exclusive Got2GoSunset package is our most popular booking.

3. Click to place the insertion point after the last *t* in *Got2GoSunset*.

   Assume that Got2GoSunset is a trademarked name and you want to insert the trademark sign but do not know where the symbol feature is located.

4. Click in the search text box at the right of the Help tab on the ribbon and then type insert trademark symbol.

5. Click *Insert a Symbol* in the drop-down list and then click the trademark symbol ™ in the Symbol palette that appears.

Your symbol palette may show different symbols and/or these symbols in a different order. The palette updates as symbols are used.

Tutorials

Using the Tell Me Feature

Using the Help Feature

trademark sign inserted at Step 5

6. Click in the search text box and then type watermark.

7. Click *Smart Lookup on "watermark"*.

The Smart Lookup task pane opens at the right side of the window. On the Explore tab of the task pane are web links to resources related to watermark. On the Define tab, you can view a definition of the word *watermark*.

8. Click the Turn on button in the Smart Lookup task pane if a message displays to turn on intelligent services to let Office get web results for your highlighted text. Skip this step if no message about intelligent services displays in the task pane.

9. Click the Define tab in the Smart Lookup task pane and then read the definition for the word *Watermark* in the pane.

10. Close the Smart Lookup task pane.

11. Click the Help tab and then click the Help button in the Help group.

A Help task pane opens at the right side of the window.

12. If necessary, click in the search text box in the Help task pane, type watermark, and then press Enter or click the search icon (magnifying glass).

13. Click the hyperlink to the Add a watermark help topic that displays in the Help task pane below the search text box.

14. Read the steps for adding a watermark in the Help task pane and then close the Help task pane.

You can continue searching for other help information by typing a keyword or phrase in the search text box, or continue clicking hyperlinks in help topics displayed in the task pane.

15. Click in the search text box, type watermark, click *Watermark* in the drop-down list, and then click *SAMPLE 1* in the Watermark gallery.

16. View the SAMPLE watermark added to the document background, click the Save button on the Quick Access Toolbar, and then close the Word window. Click *No* when prompted to save the copied item.

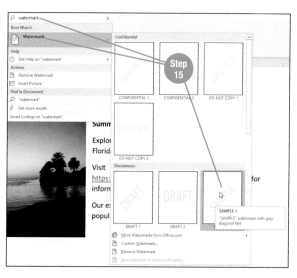

3.7 Using OneDrive for Storage, Scrolling in Documents, and Using Undo

Watch & Learn

OneDrive is secure online storage available to individuals signed in with a Microsoft account (often referred to as *cloud storage*). You can save files to and open files from OneDrive, giving you the ability to access the files from any internet-connected device.

When working with longer documents, you will need to scroll the display or change the Zoom setting to see more or less text in the window. You will learn how to use the Zoom feature in the next topic. Undo reverses an action and is used often to restore a document when you make a mistake.

Note: To complete this topic, you need to be signed in with a Microsoft account. If you do not have a Microsoft account, skip the OneDrive section in Steps 2 to 19 and proceed to Step 20 after opening the presentation.

- - - - - - - skills

Save and open files to and from OneDrive

Navigate in longer documents

Use Undo

1 Start PowerPoint and then open the presentation **SpeechTechniques** from the Ch3 subfolder within the StudentDataFiles folder on your storage medium. If a yellow message bar displays indicating the presentation is open in Protected view, click the Enable Editing button to remove Protected view.

2 Click the File tab and then click *Save As*.

3 Click the *OneDrive - Personal* option in the Save As backstage area.

4 Click the <u>More options</u> hyperlink in the right panel.

Tutorial
Using OneDrive for Storage

5 With the text in the *File name* text box in the Save As dialog box selected, type SpeechPres-YourName and then click the Save button. When the save is complete, if a message displays below the Quick Access Toolbar that AutoSave is On, click the Got it button to dismiss the message.

If you decide to use OneDrive for saving work, you should use folders to organize files. In the next steps, you will save the presentation to OneDrive a second time by creating a folder as you save the file.

6 Click the File tab and then click the *Save a Copy* option.

7 With your OneDrive account already selected in the Save As backstage area, click the *Browse* option.

8 In the Save As dialog box, click the New folder button on the Command bar.

Notice that the file saved in Step 5 appears in the Content pane.

9 Type CompletedTopics and then press Enter.

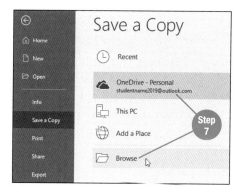

quick steps

Save a File to OneDrive
1. Click File tab.
2. Click *Save As*.
3. Click OneDrive account name.
4. Click folder in right panel or click More options hyperlink.
5. If necessary, navigate to desired folder in Save As dialog box.
6. Type name for file in *File name* text box.
7. Click Save.

10 Double-click *CompletedTopics*.

11 Click the New folder button on the Command bar, type Ch3, and then press Enter.

12 Double-click *Ch3*.

13 Click the Save button to save the presentation using the same name as before.

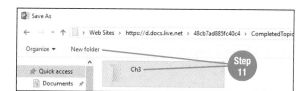

app tip

You may notice a one- or two-second delay when navigating folders in the Open or Save As dialog box when working on OneDrive. When that happens, wait a few seconds for the screen to update—do not click options or commands a second time.

You now have two copies of the presentation saved on OneDrive.

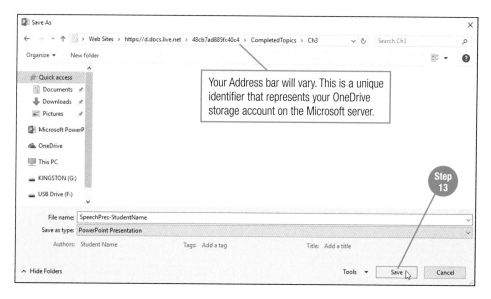

Your Address bar will vary. This is a unique identifier that represents your OneDrive storage account on the Microsoft server.

14 Click the File tab and then click *Close*.

Depending on the speed of your internet connection, you may notice an Uploading to OneDrive message box while the file is uploaded to your OneDrive account.

15 Click the Open button on the Quick Access Toolbar.

Because you just closed the presentation, you will notice the presentation appears twice in the *Recent* list in the right panel. Notice that your OneDrive account is associated with each of these entries. You could reopen the presentation from OneDrive using the *Recent* list; however, in the next steps, you will use Browse to practice opening a file from OneDrive in case a file you need is not in the *Recent* list for the Office application.

16 Click *Browse* in the Open backstage area.

You will notice the file you want to reopen is already in the Content pane because the Quick Access feature shows recently opened presentations; however, you will practice navigating in case you ever need a file that has not been recently opened.

Your *Recent* list may vary below the first three entries that are related to this topic.

17 Click *OneDrive* in the Navigation pane.

18 In the Content pane, double-click the folders *Completed Topics* and *Ch3*.

19 Double-click **SpeechPres-YourName** in the Content pane.

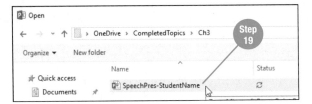

Using the Scroll Bars

Larger files with content beyond the current view display in the application window with a horizontal and/or vertical scroll bar. A **scroll bar** has arrow buttons at the top and bottom or left and right ends used to scroll up, down, left, or right. A **scroll box** in the scroll bar between the two arrow buttons is also used to scroll by dragging the box up or down, or left or right. PowerPoint also has two buttons at the bottom of the vertical scroll bar that are used to navigate to the next or previous slide.

20 Click the Next Slide button at the bottom of the vertical scroll bar to view the second slide in the presentation.

㉑ Click the Next Slide button two more times to move to Slide 4.

㉒ Click the up arrow button at the top of the vertical scroll bar repeatedly until you are returned to the first slide.

㉓ Drag the scroll box at the top of the vertical scroll bar downward until you reach the end of the slides.

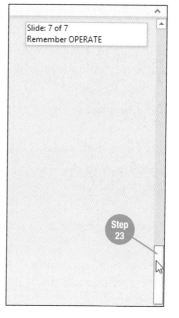

As you drag the scroll box downward, a ScreenTip displays the slide numbers and titles for the slides so you know when to release the mouse.

㉔ Press Ctrl + Home.

Ctrl + Home is the universal keyboard shortcut for returning to the beginning of a file.

㉕ Press Ctrl + End.

Ctrl + End is the universal keyboard shortcut for navigating to the end of a file.

Using Undo

The **Undo** command in all Office applications can be used to restore a document, presentation, worksheet, or Access object to its state before the last action that was performed. If you make a change to a file and do not like the results, immediately click the Undo button on the Quick Access Toolbar. Some actions, such as Save, cannot be reversed with Undo.

㉖ Navigate to the first slide in the presentation.

㉗ Select the title text *Speech Techniques*.

㉘ Click the Bold button on the Mini toolbar or in the Font group on the Home tab.

㉙ With the text still selected, click the Underline button on the Mini toolbar or in the Font group on the Home tab.

㉚ Click on any part of the slide away from the selected text to deselect the title text.

㉛ Click the Undo button on the Quick Access Toolbar. Do *not* click the down-pointing arrow on the button.

The underline is removed from the title text, and the text is selected.

㉜ Click the Undo button a second time to remove the bold formatting.

㉝ Click on the slide away from the selected text to deselect the text and then click the Save button on the Quick Access Toolbar.

㉞ Close the presentation and then close PowerPoint.

●━━━━ quick steps

Scroll within a File
Click arrow button for desired direction to scroll in horizontal or vertical scroll bar, or drag scroll box in horizontal or vertical scroll bar.

Use Undo
Click Undo button on the Quick Access Toolbar.

☁ Tutorials
Scrolling
Using Undo and Redo

●━━━━━ app tip

Undo stores multiple actions. To undo an action that was not the last action performed, click the Undo option box arrow and then click the desired action in the drop-down list.

●━━━━━ app tip

Use the Redo button on the Quick Access Toolbar if you change your mind after using Undo and want the action reapplied to the document.

3.8 Changing the Zoom Option and Screen Resolution

🌥 **Watch & Learn**

Word, Excel, and PowerPoint display a **Zoom slider** bar near the bottom right corner of the window. Using the slider, you can zoom out or zoom in to view more or less of a document, worksheet, slide, or presentation. At each end of the slider bar is a **Zoom In** (plus symbol) and a **Zoom Out** (minus symbol) control that increases or decreases the magnification by 10 percent on each click.

●————— Skills

Change the Zoom setting

View the screen resolution and change the setting if possible to match textbook illustrations

1 Start Excel and then open the workbook **CutRateRentals** in the Ch3 folder in StudentDataFiles. Click the Enable Editing button if a yellow message bar displays indicating the worksheet is opened in Protected view.

Notice the current Zoom setting near the bottom right corner of the Excel window, which is 100 percent if the setting is at the default option.

2 Click the Zoom In control (displays as a plus symbol).

3 Click the Zoom In control two more times.

The worksheet is now much larger in the display area with the magnification increased 30 percent.

4 Click the Zoom Out control (displays as a minus symbol).

5 Drag the Zoom slider left or right and watch magnification of the worksheet decrease or increase as you move the slider.

6 Drag the Zoom slider to the middle of the slider bar to change the zoom to 100 percent.

7 Click *100%* at the right of the Zoom In control.

●————— Oops!

Having trouble using the Zoom slider on a touch device? Tap the controls or the percentage number to open the Zoom dialog box (Steps 7–8), or use the Zoom buttons on the View tab on the ribbon.

This opens the Zoom dialog box, where you can choose a predefined magnification, type a custom percentage value, or choose the *Fit selection* option to fit a group of selected cells to the window.

8 Click *75%* and then press Enter or click OK.

9 Click the View tab and then click the 100% button in the Zoom group.

Zoom In, Zoom Out, the Zoom slider, and the Zoom dialog box function the same in Word and PowerPoint.

Viewing and Changing Screen Resolution

The ribbon on your computer may show fewer or more buttons than the illustrations in this textbook, or some buttons may show icons only (no labels). The appearance of the ribbon is affected by the screen resolution (Figure 3.3 on the next page). **Screen resolution** refers to the number of picture elements, called *pixels*, that form the image

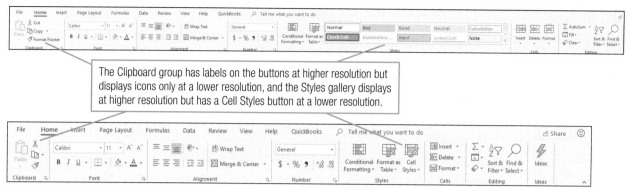

The Clipboard group has labels on the buttons at higher resolution but displays icons only at a lower resolution, and the Styles gallery displays at higher resolution but has a Cell Styles button at a lower resolution.

Figure 3.3

Shown is the Excel Home tab at 1920 x 1080 pixels (top) and at 1280 x 1024 pixels (bottom).

on the display. A pixel is a square with color values. Millions of pixels are used to render display images. Resolution is expressed as the number of horizontal pixels by the number of vertical pixels.

Note: Check with your instructor before proceeding onward. Some schools do not allow the display properties to be changed. If necessary, perform Steps 10–17 on your home PC.

⑩ Minimize the Excel window to display the desktop.

⑪ Right-click a blank area on the desktop and then click *Display settings*.

⑫ If the current setting for *Resolution* is *1920 x 1080*, skip to Step 14; otherwise, click the *Resolution* option box arrow and then click *1920 x 1080* if the option is available; otherwise, use the resolution option that displays with *(Recommended)*.

⑬ Click the Keep changes button.

Change Zoom Magnification

Click Zoom In or Zoom Out button or drag Zoom slider to desired setting.

OR

1. Click zoom percentage.
2. Select desired zoom option in Zoom dialog box.
3. Click OK.

quick steps

Change Zoom Magnification

Click Zoom In or Zoom Out button or drag Zoom slider to desired setting.

OR

1. Click zoom percentage.
2. Select desired zoom option in Zoom dialog box.
3. Click OK.

app tip

Screen resolution is an operating system setting. A higher resolution uses more pixels and means the image quality is sharper or clearer. It also means more content can be displayed in the viewing area.

⑭ Close the Settings app window.

⑮ Click the Excel button on the taskbar to view the Excel window at the new screen resolution.

⑯ If you changed your screen resolution, examine the screen to see if you like the new setting. If the interface is not of good quality, repeat Steps 10 to 14 to restore the resolution option to its original setting. The setting that displays with *(Recommended)* is usually the best choice for your device.

You do not need to change the screen resolution to the same setting used for the images in this textbook. Just be aware that some illustrations may not match exactly what is on your display if your resolution is at a different setting.

⑰ Close the **CutRateRentals** worksheet and then close Excel.

Tutorial

Changing the Zoom

Topics Review

Topic	Key Concepts
3.1 Starting and Switching Applications, Starting a New Presentation, and Exploring the Ribbon	The Office suite is sold as a one-time purchase edition or as a subscription plan called **Office 365**.
	Word 2019 is the application used for text-based documents.
	An Office application starts with the **Start screen**, which shows a list of recently opened files and a templates gallery.
	Excel 2019 is used when the focus is on working with numeric data.
	Create slides for an oral or kiosk-style presentation using **PowerPoint 2019**.
	Access 2019 is a database application used to organize, store, and maintain related data, such as information about customers or products.
	All applications display the ribbon along the top of the window, which contains buttons divided into tabs as well as groups for commands and features within the software.
	The **Ribbon Display Options button** lets you control whether the ribbon shows tabs only, tabs with commands, or no ribbon.
3.2 Using the Backstage Area to Manage Documents	The **backstage area**, accessed from the File tab on the ribbon, is where you perform document-level routines, such as *Open*, *Save*, *Save As*, *Print*, *Share*, *Export*, and *Close*.
	Use the *Open* option on the Word Start screen to navigate to a document not in the *Recent* option list.
	Use the *Save As* option to save a copy of a document in another location or in the same location but with a different file name.
	Use the Print backstage area to preview a document in the **Print Preview** panel to see how the document will look with the current print settings before printing.
	A **PDF document** (Portable Document Format) is a document saved in an open standard for exchanging electronic documents that opens as it would appear if printed.
	Use the *Export* option in the backstage area to publish a Word document in PDF format.
3.3 Customizing and Using the Quick Access Toolbar	The **Quick Access Toolbar** at the top left of each application window contains buttons for frequently used commands. The toolbar can be customized for each application.
	Add to or remove buttons from the Quick Access Toolbar by clicking the Customize Quick Access Toolbar button and then clicking the desired option in the drop-down list.
3.4 Selecting Text or Objects, Using the Ribbon and Mini Toolbar, and Selecting Objects in Dialog Boxes	Each circle at the middle and/or corners of a selected object is called a **selection handle**.
	The **Mini toolbar** appears near selected text or with the shortcut menu containing buttons for formatting the selected text or object.
	Dragging a selection handle resizes a picture, shape, chart, or other item referred to as an **object**.
	A **contextual tab** appears when an object is selected with command buttons related to the object.
	A **gallery** is a drop-down list or grid with visual representations of options. A **live preview** shows the text or object as it would look if the option on which the mouse is resting is applied.
	At the lower right of a group on the ribbon is a **dialog box launcher** that displays a task pane or **dialog box** when clicked.
	Dialog boxes and task panes provide additional options for the related ribbon group as buttons, lists, sliders, check boxes, text boxes, and option buttons. A **task pane** opens at the left or right side of the document window, whereas a dialog box opens in a separate window on top of the document text.
	A colored horizontal or vertical line called an **alignment guide** appears when moving an object to help you place and align the object with text, margins, or other nearby objects.

continued...

Topic	Key Concepts
3.5 Using the Office Clipboard and Formatting Using a Task Pane	The Clipboard group on the ribbon is standardized across all Office applications.
	Use Cut, Copy, and Paste buttons to move or copy text or objects.
	A Paste Options button appears when you paste text or an object with options for modifying the paste action.
	The **Format Painter** button in the Clipboard group is used to copy formatting options from selected text or an object to other text or object(s).
	A button, such as the Format Painter button, that operates in an on or off state is called a **toggle button**.
3.6 Using the Tell Me Feature and Help Task Pane	Click in the **Tell Me** text box that displays *Tell me what you want to do* and then type a term or option to locate the option directly from the Tell Me list or to look up other resources about the feature in a task pane.
	Click the **Smart Lookup** option in the Tell Me drop-down list to open a task pane with web links and definitions for the term.
	Click the Help tab on the ribbon and then click the Help button to open the Help task pane to find information about Office features.
3.7 Using OneDrive for Storage, Scrolling in Documents, and Using Undo	**OneDrive** is cloud storage where you can save files that can be accessed from any other internet-connected device by selecting your OneDrive account in the Open and Save As backstage areas.
	A horizontal or vertical bar called a **scroll bar** with arrow buttons and a **scroll box** is used to navigate documents, workbooks, presentations, or database tables that do not fit in the window.
	The **Undo** feature is used to reverse an action performed, restoring a document to its previous state.
3.8 Changing the Zoom Option and Screen Resolution	Use the **Zoom In**, **Zoom Out**, **Zoom slider**, and Zoom dialog box in Word, Excel, and PowerPoint to increase or decrease the magnification setting.
	Screen resolution refers to the number of horizontal and vertical pixels (squares with color values) used to render the display image. Millions of pixels are used for generating an image.
	The **screen resolution** setting for your PC or mobile device affects the display of the ribbon. Change the screen resolution using the *Display settings* option on the desktop shortcut menu.

Topics Review

Using OneNote for Windows 10

OneNote is a note-taking application referred to as a *digital notebook*. OneNote is like an electronic binder with notes organized by dividers. Note-taking software can store, organize, search, and share notes of any type, including typed notes, handwritten notes, web pages, images, documents, presentations, worksheets, messages, appointments, contacts, and more. A OneNote notebook can collect everything you want to keep track of for a subject or topic in one place.

OneNote notebooks are stored on OneDrive so that you can access the notes from any internet-connected device. Another advantage to storing a notebook on OneDrive is that you can share it with others and allow each participant to edit notes. For group projects, OneNote is used to collaborate and share ideas, research, and content.

OneNote was originally available as a desktop application bundled with the Office suite with Word, Excel, PowerPoint, and Outlook. With the release of Office 2019, Microsoft converted OneNote to an app that is included with Windows 10.

In this chapter, you will learn how to use the OneNote app for Windows 10 to add sections, pages, and content to the default OneNote notebook. You'll also learn how to tag notes, create a new notebook, and share a notebook with others.

If the OneNote app is not on your Windows 10 device, download and install the app from the Windows Store before starting this chapter. If you are using Windows 7, you will need to use OneNote Online. Go to https://www.onenote.com and sign in with your Microsoft account. Windows apps can be updated at any time, and the screens shown and instructions provided may vary.

Read & Learn

Learning Objectives

4.1 Add a section and a page in a notebook

4.2 Add a note, apply color to a note, and add web content

4.3 Insert an image, a document, and embed a PDF copy of a presentation into a notebook

4.4 Tag a note and search tags

4.5 Search notes

4.6 Create a new notebook and share a notebook

Content Online

The online course includes additional training and assessment resources.

4.1 Adding Sections and Pages in a Notebook

☁ **Watch & Learn**

●───────── skills

Add a section
Add a page

OneNote is the note-taking app automatically included on a Windows 10 PC. The app is also available for download from the Apple or Google app stores for use on Mac or Android devices. A **OneNote notebook** is organized into sections, which are accessed by tabs. Think of a section like a divider you would use in a binder to organize notes by subject, topic, or category. Within each section you add pages. Notes and other content are added on a page. You can add as many sections and pages as you like to organize a notebook. Content can be placed anywhere on a page in a section.

1 Click the Start button and then click the OneNote tile or scroll down the list of applications in the left pane and then click *OneNote*. If necessary (for example, if this is the first time you have started OneNote), click the Get Started button. By default, OneNote opens automatically signed in with the Microsoft account associated with Windows 10. If an introduction screen appears, click *Skip*, or if a *What's New in OneNote* box appears, click the option to dismiss the message box.

The OneNote window (Figure 4.1) appears with a notebook open. By default a personal notebook for your Microsoft account is created and opened. The notebook is stored on OneDrive. The OneNote app works with notebooks stored on OneDrive.

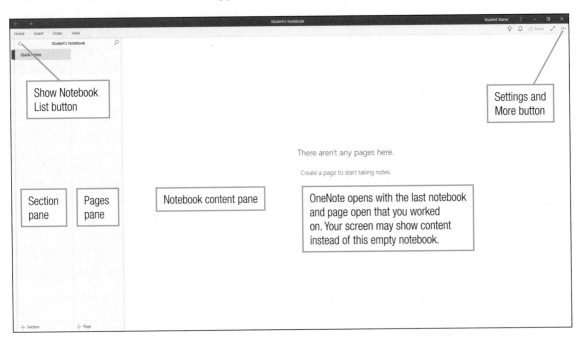

Figure 4.1

The OneNote window is shown with a notebook open and the Quick Notes tab active. If this is the first time you have used OneNote, the personal notebook is empty as shown here.

A section is like a divider in a binder. Sections organize content by category, topic, or subject. Each section can hold multiple pages. To create a new section in a notebook, click the **Section button** at the bottom of the Section pane, type a name for the section, and then press Enter. For each new section created, a blank page opens with an insertion point in the page title area. Type a title for the page and then press Enter.

Click the **Page button** at the bottom of the Page pane to add a new page within the active section. Type a title for the page and then press Enter. Starting to work with a digital notebook is like getting a new binder for a project and putting dividers and blank pages into it. You can add new sections and pages as you go along, but creating a few sections and pages lets you get started.

② Click the Section button (bottom of Section pane).

Step 2

A new tab is added to the notebook with a section name added by default and with the default text selected. Type a name for the section and press Enter. In a digital notebook to keep track of school content, one way to organize the notebook is to create a section for each course.

③ Type Computers and then press Enter.

④ Click above the dimmed line in the in the page title area in the Notebook content pane, type Web Info and then press Enter.

Step 3

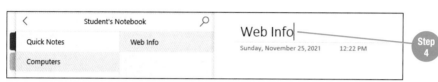

Step 4

⑤ Click the Page button (bottom of Pages pane).

Step 5

⑥ Type Images as the page title and then press Enter.

⑦ Click the Page button.

⑧ Type Presentations as the page title and then press Enter.

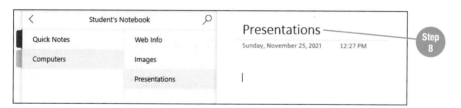

Step 8

⑨ Click the Section button, type Law, and then press Enter.

⑩ Click in the page title area, type Family Law, and then press Enter.

⑪ Click the Section button, type English, and then press Enter.

⑫ Click in the page title area, type Assignments, and then press Enter.

To add a new page to an existing section, first make the desired section active by clicking the section tab, and then use the Page button to add a page.

⑬ Click the Law tab to make Law the active section.

⑭ Click the Page button.

⑮ Type Civil Law and then press Enter.

Leave OneNote open for the next topic.

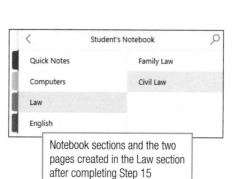

Notebook sections and the two pages created in the Law section after completing Step 15

4.2 Adding Notes to Pages and Inserting Web Content

Watch & Learn

To add a note to a page, make the page active and start typing to add text at the location of the insertion point. If you don't see an insertion point, click on the page. Click to start typing a new note anywhere on the current page. OneNote content is placed inside a box referred to as a **note container**. A selection handle, which can be used to select text that you want to format, appears on the left side of the note container when the pointer is resting on the note text. A four-headed white arrow pointer appears when you point to the top gray bar on the note container. To move a note somewhere else on the page, drag the note container when you see the four-headed white arrow.

1. With OneNote open and the Civil Law page active, click the English tab in the Section pane.

2. With Assignments the active page and an insertion point positioned below the page title, type Reflection paper due by end of week four.

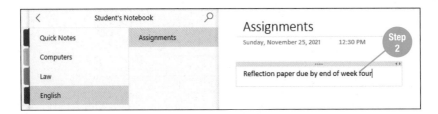

------- Skills

Add a note to a page

Apply highlight color to text in a note

Add a web link in a note

Copy and paste web content into OneNote

3. Click beyond the right edge of the first note container on the same page and then type Child literature assignment is a group presentation.

4. Point to the gray bar along the top of the note container. When you see the four-headed white arrow pointer, drag the note container to the top of the page below the first note as shown in the image at the right.

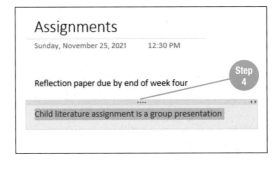

------- app tip

If you have a touch-enabled device, you can handwrite notes or draw illustrations. Options on the Draw tab let you change ink color and convert ink to text or ink to a shape. The Math option recognizes and solves equations in a Math pane.

Tutorial
Adding Content to a Page in OneNote

5. Click to place an insertion point within the note text in the first note container.

A selection handle appears left of the note container. You can use the selection handle to select text, or drag across text you want to select to apply a formatting option.

6. Point to the selection handle that appears ( ) at the left of the note container for the first note and click when you see the mouse pointer change to the four-headed white arrow pointer.

The text *Reflection paper due by end of week four* is selected. A Highlight tool is used to apply color highlighting to notes just as you would use a highlighter to highlight important points while reading a textbook. Click the **Highlight button** to apply the default yellow highlighting to the selected text, or use the down-pointing arrow on the button to choose a different highlight color.

------- app tip

To delete a note, select the note text using the selection handle or the gray bar at the top of the note container and then press the Delete key on the keyboard.

7 Click the Home tab if the ribbon is not currently visible and then click the Highlight button. Do not click the down-pointing arrow on the button.

●----- quick steps

Add a Note to a Page
1. Click at desired location on page.
2. Type note text.
3. Click in blank space outside note container.

Tutorial

Inserting a Link in a OneNote Page

One reason people like to use OneNote is that the app can be used as a receptacle for organizing information found online that you want to keep for later use. In the next steps, you will add a web link in a note and copy and paste content found on a web page into OneNote.

8 Click the Computers tab in the Section pane and then click the Web Info page in the Page pane.

9 With an insertion point active below the Web Info page title, type https://twitter .com/Techmeme and then press Enter twice.

OneNote automatically formats web addresses as hyperlinks.

10 Type Techmeme provides daily summaries of leading technology stories and tweets headlines with links throughout the day. and then click in a blank area away from the note container.

11 Move the mouse pointer over https://twitter.com/Techmeme and click the hyperlink to view the Twitter page in Microsoft Edge or other browser window.

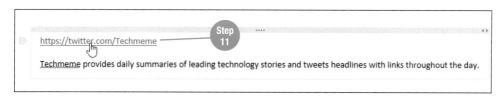

12 Scroll down to view the latest tweets by Techmeme.

13 Click in the Address bar in the browser window to select the web address or drag to select the web address, type https://en.wikipedia.org/wiki/Tim_Berners-Lee, and then press Enter.

Use the standard copy and paste tools to select and copy text from a web page and paste into a notebook. When you paste text copied from a web page, OneNote automatically includes the source URL below the pasted text.

14 Select the first three paragraphs of text below the title "Tim Berners-Lee" on the Wikipedia page and then press Ctrl + C.

Recall from Chapter 1 that the universal shortcut keys for copy and paste are Ctrl + C (copy) and Ctrl + V (paste).

15 Close the browser window to return to OneNote.

16 Click on the Web Info page away from the existing note container to start a new note and then press Ctrl + V to insert the copied text from the Wikipedia page.

17 Move the note container below the first note, if necessary. Leave OneNote open for the next topic.

4.3 Inserting Files into a Notebook

Images, documents, presentations, workbooks, contacts, email messages, appointment details, and more can be added to a notebook as a link to the source content or as a PDF copy of the content. Some people use a OneNote notebook as a repository to collect all the data related to a course, subject, or other topic. The advantage to assembling content in one place is that you no longer need to keep track of web links or web pages separately from documents and other notes for a subject or project.

Items are inserted into OneNote using buttons on the Insert tab. A document can be inserted as an attachment that links to the source file, or a PDF printout of the content can be embedded into the notebook. Once inserted, you can add annotations with your own notes.

1. With OneNote open and the Web Info page active, click the Images page in the Computers section.

2. Click the Insert tab, click the Pictures button, and then click *From File*.

3. In the Open dialog box, navigate to the Ch4 folder in StudentDataFiles on your storage medium.

4. Double-click *AnalogCptr_1950s*.

5. With an insertion point positioned in the note container below the image, type Analog computer from the 1950s.

6. Click the Page button, type Documents, and then press Enter.

7. Click the File button on the Insert tab.

8. In the Open dialog box with the Ch4 folder in StudentDataFiles active, double-click the Word document *Tech_Wk1_SocialMedia*.

9. With an insertion point positioned in the note container below the Word document icon and file name, type Week 1 Assignment and then click on the page away from the note container.

Analog computer from the 1950s

A link to the source document is inserted in the note. The document can be opened from OneNote by double-clicking the Word document icon.

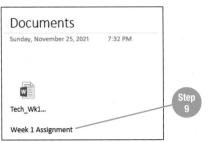

Documents
Sunday, November 25, 2021   7:32 PM

Tech_Wk1...

Week 1 Assignment

Watch & Learn

━ ━ ━ ━ ━ ━ ━ **skills**

Insert an image

Insert a link to a document

Embed a copy of a presentation

Tutorials

Inserting Files into a Notebook

Inserting a Picture in a OneNote Page

━ ● ━ ━ ━ ━ ━ **app tip**

You can also drag and drop an image onto a OneNote page from a File Explorer window.

● ━ ━ ━ ━ ━ **app tip**

Use the Audio button on the Insert tab to have OneNote create a file by recording audio. Use this option to record a lecture in class or an interview as long as you are sitting close enough for the microphone on your device to pick up the voice. You could also use this at home to create audio notes rather than typing note text.

⑩ Double-click the document icon.

Word opens and the document linked to the OneNote page is opened in Protected view.

⑪ Scroll down to review the Word document and then close Word.

⑫ Click Presentations in the Page pane.

⑬ Click the PDF button on the Insert tab.

⑭ In the Open dialog box, navigate to the Ch4 folder in StudentDataFiles on your storage medium.

⑮ Double-click the PDF file *Tech_Wk1*.

Use the **Insert Printout from PDF** option to embed a copy of content on the current page that has been saved in PDF format. This option allows you to add your own notes with the content. For example, you can save a PowerPoint presentation with lecture notes for a class as a PDF file to embed the slides in OneNote. Once the slides are inserted, type your own notes directly on or next to a slide.

⑯ Scroll up to the top of the Presentations page. Notice that an icon with a link to the source file is included above the embedded slides.

⑰ Scroll down to the last slide on the page.

⑱ Double-click to start a new note on the slide below the last bulleted list entry and then type Jasmine described using an app that let her use virtual reality to visit the Great Wall of China! She talked about using virtual reality to visit places all over the world.

⑲ Select the text in the note container, click the Home tab, click the *Font Size* option arrow and then click *12*.

⑳ Click the Highlight button to apply yellow highlight to the text. Leave OneNote open for the next topic.

4.4 Tagging Notes

A **tag** is a category assigned to a note. The tag allows you to identify the note later as an item flagged for a to-do list, as important, as a question, as critical content, as a contact, as an address, or as a phone number. OneNote includes a **Tag This Note button** on the Home tab with predefined tags in a drop-down list. Use the Create New Tag option to open the Create a Tag pane at the right side of the window to create your own tag.

1. With OneNote open and the Presentations page active with the last slide visible in the embedded presentation, double-click next to the slide title *REFLECTION BLOG* to start a new note.

2. Type Blog post due by Friday.

3. Click at the beginning of the note text *Blog post due by Friday* in the note container, click the Tag This Note button on the Home tab, and then click *To Do*.

OneNote inserts a check box left of the insertion point. The To-Do tag check box is interactive. When you complete the task, click the check box to insert a check mark to mark the activity completed.

4. Click the Web Info page in the Page pane.

5. Double-click in white space near the top of the page next to the content pasted from Wikipedia to place an insertion point.

6. Click the Tag This Note button, and then click *Important*.

A gold star tag is inserted inside a new note container on the page.

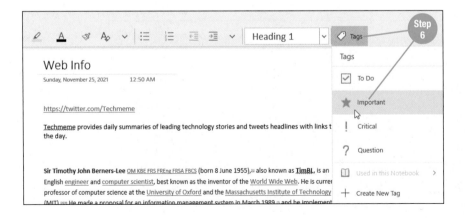

⑦ Type Use this information in Assignment 1. If necessary, drag the top gray bar to move the note container to the right side of the page as shown in the image below if it overlaps other text.

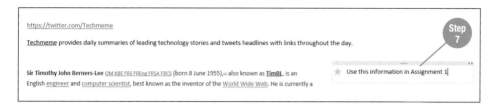

⑧ Click the Images page in the Page pane.

⑨ Click at the beginning of the caption text below the photo of the analog computer to place an insertion point, click the Tag This Note button, and then click *Question*.

A purple question mark appears next to the caption text as shown in the image below.

⑩ Click the Documents page in the Page pane.

⑪ Click to place an insertion point at the beginning of the text *Week 1 Assignment* in the note container, click the Tag This Note button, and then click *To Do*.

⑫ Click the English tab in the Section pane.

⑬ Click to place an insertion point at the beginning of the text *Reflection paper due by end of week four*, click the Tag This Note button, and then click *Critical*.

The Critical tag inserts a red exclamation mark next to the note text.

4.5 Searching Notes and Tags

Watch & Learn

------ **skills**

Search notes
Close a notebook

An advantage to using an electronic versus a paper-based notebook is the ability to search all notebook pages for a keyword or phrase and instantly locate each occurrence. You can also search notebooks by a tag, such as the To-Do tag, to locate tagged notes. Click the magnifying glass icon next to the notebook name above the Page pane to open the search pane and then type the search keyword or phrase in the search text box, or click the tag you want to locate. OneNote begins displaying matches to the search text as you type. Matches are highlighted on the active page and other pages and in the search results list on the Pages tab or the Tags tab. Click the Pages tab or the Tags tab and then click an entry in the search results list to display the page where the text or tag appears. Click the Close button (displays as ×) to close the Search pane when finished.

Tutorial

Searching Notes

1. With OneNote open, click the Law tab in the Section pane. If necessary, click to place an insertion point below the Family Law page title.

2. Click the Insert tab and then click the PDF button.

3. Double-click *FamilyAndLawAssgnt*. If you don't see the document, navigate to the Ch4 folder in StudentDataFiles on your storage medium.

4. With an insertion point below the embedded PDF printout, type Draft copy of first assignment, and then click in white space away from the note container.

5. Click the Search icon.

6. Type Berners-Lee in the search text box and then press Enter.

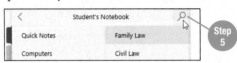

7. If necessary, click the Pages tab below the search text box and then click the Web Info page in the search results list to display the page and view the highlighted text entries.

Sir Timothy John **Berners-Lee** OM KBE FRS FREng FRSA FBCS (born 8 June 1955), also known as **TimBL**, is an English engineer and computer scientist, best known as the inventor of the World Wide Web. He is currently a professor of Computer Science at the University of Oxford and at Massachusetts Institute of Technology (MIT). He made a proposal for an information management system in March 1989, and he implemented the first successful communication between a Hypertext Transfer Protocol (HTTP) client and server via the internet in mid-November the same year.

Berners-Lee is the director of the World Wide Web Consortium (W3C), which oversees the continued development of the Web. He is also the founder of the World Wide Web Foundation and is a senior researcher and holder of the 3Com founders chair at the MIT Computer Science and Artificial Intelligence Laboratory (CSAIL). He is a director of the Web Science Research Initiative (WSRI), and a member of the advisory board of the MIT Center for Collective Intelligence. In 2011, he was named as a member of the board of trustees of the Ford Foundation. He is a founder and president of the Open Data Institute.

In 2004, **Berners-Lee** was knighted by Queen Elizabeth II for his pioneering work. In April 2009, he was elected a foreign associate of the United States National Academy of Sciences. Named in *Time* magazine's list of the 100 Most Important People of the 20th century, **Berners-Lee** has received a number of other ... "Inventor of the World Wide Web" during the 2012 ...eared in person, working with a vintage NeXT ...ed "This is for everyone", which instantly was spelled ...eople in the audience. **Berners-Lee** received the 2016 ...first web browser, and the fundamental protocols and algorithms allowing the Web to scale".

From <https://en.wikipedia.org/wiki/Tim Berners-Lee>

> OneNote highlights matches to the searched text on each page in the search results list.

Step 5

Step 6

Step 7

8   Select *Berners-Lee* in the search text box, type analog, and then press Enter.

9   Click *Images* on the Pages tab in the search results list to display the page with the photo of the analog computer.

10   Select *analog* in the search text box, type blog, and then press Enter.

11   Click *Presentations* on the Pages tab in the search results list to display the page with the embedded presentation and, if necessary, scroll down to the last slide with the blog note text.

12   Select *blog* in the search text box, type assign, and then press Enter

13   Click *Assignments* on the Pages tab in the search results list.

quick steps

Search Notes
1. Click Search icon (magnifying glass).
2. Type search keyword or phrase.
3. Click pages in search results list.
4. Click Close button when finished.

In this search, multiple pages have matches to the search text. Notice the search text is matched to part of the word *Assignments* in a page name as well as text in notes on the page. Typing a partial word is helpful if you think you may have notes with inconsistent spellings or forms of a word.

app tip

To search for a tag, delete search text in the search text box and click the tag you want to locate in the drop-down list that appears. The Tags tab becomes active automatically in the search results list with pages that contain the tag.

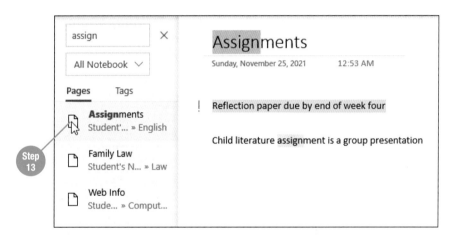

14   Click each of the pages in the search results list to view the matches to the search text.

By default, all notebooks are searched. Use the down-pointing arrow next to *All Notebooks* below the search text box to narrow the search scope to *Current Notebook*, *Current Section*, or *Current Page*.

15   Click the down-pointing arrow next to *All Notebooks* below the search text box.

16   Click *Current Section: Computers*.

Notice the search results list now displays two pages instead of four.

17   Click the Close button (displays as ✕) next to the search text box to close the Search pane and restore the Section pane and Page pane. Leave OneNote open for the next topic.

4.6 Creating a New Notebook and Sharing a Notebook

Some people like to organize all their notes for all purposes within one notebook (the default notebook file), using sections and pages to create an organizational structure. Others prefer to create separate notebooks to organize notes. For example, you may want to maintain separate notebooks for home, work, and school items. To create a new notebook, display the Notebooks list using the **Show Notebook List button**, click the **Notebook button** at the bottom of the Notebook pane, type a name for the new notebook, and then click the Create Notebook button.

A shared notebook is used to collaborate with others when working on a group project at school or work. You may also want to share a notebook with family members or friends to share ideas for an event or trip. In a shared notebook, members of the group can each post research, links, images, ideas, or other notes in one place. Click the **Share button** to open the Share pane and send an email invitation to each participant.

Note: Check with your instructor for the name of the classmate with whom you will share the notebook created in this topic. In Step 12, you will need the Microsoft account email address for the classmate. If necessary, you can practice sharing the notebook with a friend or relative.

☁ Watch & Learn

●------- Skills

Create a new notebook

Share a notebook

☁ Tutorial

Emailing a Link to OneNote Content

1   With OneNote open, click the Show Notebooks List button (left-pointing arrow next to the notebook name below the ribbon).

2   Click the Notebook button at the bottom of the Notebook pane.

3   With the insertion point positioned in the *Notebook name* text box in the Create a notebook dialog box, type MyElectives-xx. Substitute your first and last initials for *xx*.

4   Click the Create notebook button.

OneNote creates the new notebook and makes the notebook active.

5   Click the Section button to add a section in the new notebook.

6   Type Child Lit and then press Enter.

7   Click above the dimmed line in the page title area in the Notebook content pane, type Children's Literature, and then press Enter.

8 Insert the PowerPoint presentation **ChildLitPres** on the page using the File button on the Insert tab and type The Butter Battle Book by Dr. Seuss as note text below the file icon.

9 Add a second section named *Film* with the page title *Film Genres*. Insert the Word document **ApNowReflectionPaper** as a file and type Paper on Apocalypse Now movie as note text below the file icon.

You decide to share the notebook with a classmate taking the same electives as you, so you can each add notes to the notebook.

10 Click the Share button near the upper right corner of the window below the Title bar.

The Share pane opens at the right side of the OneNote window.

11 Click in the *Type email addresses* text box and then type the email address for the classmate with whom you have been partnered for this topic. If necessary, use the email address for a friend or relative.

12 Click the Share button.

The *This notebook shared with* section of the Share pane is updated with the name(s) of people with whom the notebook was successfully shared.

13 Close OneNote.

Optional

14 Open a browser window, navigate to https://outlook.live.com, and sign in if you are not automatically signed in.

15 View the message with subject text similar to *MyElectives-xx has been shared with you*, and click the View in OneDrive button to open the notebook in OneNote Online. Dismiss any messages that appear about new features.

16 Add a note of your choosing to one of the pages and then close the browser window.

quick steps

Create a New Notebook
1. Click Show Notebook List button.
2. Click Notebook button.
3. Type name for new notebook.
4. Click Create notebook button.

Share a Notebook
1. Click Share button.
2. Type email address.
3. Click Share button.

Tutorial

Sharing a Notebook

app tip

By default, each person with whom you share a notebook can make changes to the notebook. To share a notebook and only allow the other person to view the content, click the permissions option box arrow (displays *Can edit*) and then click *Can view*.

Topics Review

Topic	Key Concepts
4.1 Adding Sections and Pages in a Notebook	**OneNote** is a note-taking application referred to as a *digital notebook*.
	A **OneNote notebook** is organized into sections (like dividers in a binder), with each section holding one or more pages.
	When you start the OneNote app for Windows 10, the default notebook for the signed in user opens. All OneNote notebooks are stored on OneDrive.
	To create a new section, click the **Section button**, type the section name, type a page title, and then press Enter.
	To add a new page to a section, make it active if necessary, click the **Page button**, type the page title, and then press Enter.
4.2 Adding Notes to Pages and Inserting Web Content	Click on a page where you want a note to appear and then type the note text. Each note on a page is stored within a **note container**, which is a box that surrounds the note text.
	Drag the gray bar along the top of the note container to move a note.
	Select text in a note container using the selection handle at the left of the note container.
	Use the **Highlight button** on the Home tab to add color to notes, similar to using a highlighter to emphasize text in a textbook.
	A web address is automatically converted to a hyperlink in a note container.
	A portion of a web page can be copied and pasted into a notebook.
4.3 Inserting Files into a Notebook	A OneNote notebook can be used as a repository to collect all the files related to a course, subject, or other topic.
	Buttons on the Insert tab are used to insert an image, a file as an icon linked to the source document, or a file embedded on a page with the **Insert Printout from PDF** option.
4.4 Tagging Notes	A **tag** is a category assigned to a note. Tags are useful to identify notes that you want to flag for later review or follow-up. OneNote includes the **Tag This Note button** on the Home tab with a list of predefined tags, such as *Important* or *Question*.
	Click to place an insertion point at the beginning of note text and then add the desired tag from the Home tab.
4.5 Searching Notes and Tags	OneNote searches all pages in all open notebooks for a keyword or phrase typed in the search text box, or for a tag selected in the Tags section of the search list. Click the Search icon (magnifying glass) to begin a search.
	OneNote highlights matches to the search keyword or phrase on the active page and displays pages with matches on the Pages tab in the search results list in the Search pane.
	Narrow the scope of a search by changing the *All Notebooks* option to *Current Notebook*, *Current Section*, or *Current Page*.
4.6 Creating a New Notebook and Sharing a Notebook	Display the Notebooks list by clicking the **Show Notebook List button**.
	Click the **Notebook button**, type a name for a notebook, and then click the Create notebook button to create a new notebook for organizing notes.
	Click the **Share button** to open the Share pane in which you type the email address for each person that you want to share the notebook with.

Communicating and Scheduling Using Outlook

Chapter 5

Outlook is often referred to as a **personal information management (PIM)** application. A PIM application lets you organize items such as email messages, appointments or meetings, events, contacts, to-do lists, and notes. Reminders and flags help you remember and follow up on activities.

In the workplace, Outlook is often used with an Exchange server, which allows employees within the organization to easily share calendars, schedule meetings, and assign tasks with one another. You can use Outlook on your home PC or mobile device to connect to the mail server operated by your ISP and manage your messages. Outlook also lets you organize your time, activities, address book, and to-do list.

In this chapter, you will learn how to use Outlook for creating and sending email messages; scheduling appointments, events, and meetings; creating contacts; and maintaining a to-do list.

If you do not have access to the Outlook application on your desktop or laptop PC, you can use the free, web-based version by signing in with your Microsoft account at Outlook.com. You can use the same features on Outlook.com to practice the skills taught in this chapter; however, the screens shown will not match what you see in the browser, and the step-by-step instructions will vary because the web application uses a different interface. Where possible, instructions or marginal notes direct you to the method used at Outlook.com. In some cases, a feature is not available in the web-based edition, meaning you will have to skip some instructions.

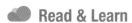 **Read & Learn**

Learning Objectives

5.1 Create, send, read, reply to, and forward email messages

5.2 Attach a file to a message, delete a message, and empty the Deleted Items folder

5.3 Preview, open, and save a file attachment

5.4 Schedule an appointment and an event

5.5 Schedule an appointment that repeats at fixed intervals, and edit an appointment

5.6 Schedule and accept a meeting request

5.7 Add and edit contact information

5.8 Add, update, and delete a task

5.9 Search Outlook messages, appointments, contacts, and tasks

Content Online

The online course includes additional training and assessment resources.

5.1 Using Outlook to Send Email

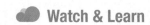 **Watch & Learn**

● ─ ─ ─ ─ ─ ─ ─ Skills

Create and send an
email message

Reply to a message

Forward a message

Electronic mail (email) is communication between individuals by means of sending and receiving messages electronically. Email is the business standard for communication in the workplace. Individuals also use email to communicate with relatives and friends around the world. While text messaging is popular for brief messages between individuals, email is still used to send longer messages.

Setting Up Outlook

The screen that you see when you start **Outlook** for the first time depends on whether a prior version of Outlook existed on the computer you are using. Outlook can transfer information from an older version of the application to a new data file. If no prior data file exists, Outlook will present a dialog box to set up a new email account. By default, Outlook inserts the Microsoft account email address you used to sign in on the device you are using. If you see the message shown in Figure 5.1a, type your email address if the email address shown is not the correct address. Click the Connect button to instruct Outlook to set up a new email profile. Type your password if a Windows Security dialog box appears and then click OK. When the message displays that the account was successfully added (Figure 5.1b), click Done.

Note: The instructions in this chapter assume Outlook has already been set up and that you are connected to the internet with an always-on connection at school or at home. If necessary, connect to the internet and sign in to your email account before starting the topic activities. Check with your instructor for assistance if you are not sure how to proceed.

Click *Advanced options* if you want to set up your email account manually by entering the incoming and outgoing mail server addresses provided by your ISP for a non-Microsoft email account.

Type another email address here and click Next if you want to set up Outlook to show messages from more than one email account. Click Done when finished.

a   b

Figure 5.1

(a) The startup dialog box is shown when Outlook cannot locate an email profile from a prior version of Outlook on the device. (b) The dialog box after an account is successfully added is shown.

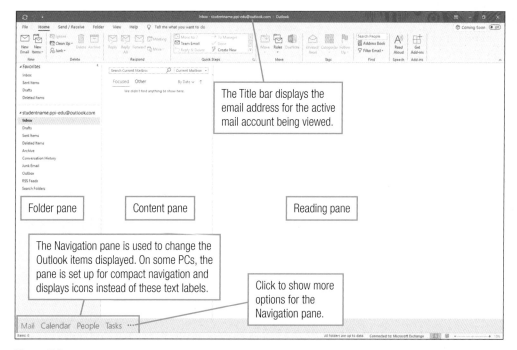

The Title bar displays the email address for the active mail account being viewed.

Folder pane

Content pane

Reading pane

The Navigation pane is used to change the Outlook items displayed. On some PCs, the pane is set up for compact navigation and displays icons instead of these text labels.

Click to show more options for the Navigation pane.

Figure 5.2

The Outlook window starts with the Inbox folder in Mail shown. Outlook checks for new messages automatically when the program is started.

Once Outlook has been set up with an email account, the Outlook window appears (Figure 5.2). By default, **Mail** is the active component. The mail folder shown when Outlook starts is **Inbox**. Messages in the Content pane are shown with the newest message received at the top of the message list. The **Focused Inbox** is turned on by default. In this view, Inbox messages are separated into two tabs: Focused and Other. The Focused tab displays the most important emails. All other messages are accessible on the Other tab. Messages such as newsletters or machine-generated emails are automatically placed on the Other tab. You can tailor the placement of messages from one tab to the other to meet your needs. For example, if a message appears in the Other list that you want in Focused, right-click the message header and then click *Move to Focused* so that future messages from the same sender will appear in the Focused list.

The left pane, called the *Folder pane*, is used to switch the display to another mail folder. At the bottom of the Folder pane is the Navigation pane, used to navigate to another Outlook component, such as Calendar. The right pane, called the *Reading pane*, displays the contents of the selected message.

Creating and Sending a Message

Click the **New Email button** in the New group on the Home tab to start a new email message. Type the recipient email address in the *To* text box, type a brief description in the *Subject* text box, and then type your message text in the white message text box. Click the Send button when finished.

Note: Check with your instructor for instructions on whom you should exchange messages and meeting requests with for this chapter. Your instructor may designate an email partner for each person or allow you to choose your email partner. If necessary, send messages to yourself.

●------- app tip

Click the View tab, click the Folder Pane button in the Layout group, and choose *Normal, Minimized,* or *Off* to change the Folder pane. The Reading Pane button in the same group is used to display the Reading pane at the right or bottom of the screen or to turn off the Reading pane.

 Tutorial

Creating and Sending a Message

1 Click in the search text box on the taskbar, type Outlook, and then press Enter to start Outlook. If you are using Outlook.com, open a browser window, navigate to https://outlook .live.com, and sign in to your Microsoft account if you are not automatically signed in.

Step 3

2 Dismiss any messages that may pop up with information about new features in Outlook.

3 Click the New Email button in the New group on the Home tab. In Outlook.com, click <u>New message</u> in the browser window.

4 Type the email address for the recipient in the *To* text box.

For a message to be sent to multiple recipients, type a comma (,) or a semicolon (;) between email addresses in the *To* text box.

5 Press the Tab key twice or click in the *Subject* text box.

6 Type Social Media Project and then press Enter.

7 With the insertion point positioned at the top of the message text box, type the following text:

Hi [Recipient's Name], [press Enter twice]

I think we should do our project on Pinterest.com. Pinterest is a virtual pinboard where people pin pictures of things they have seen on the internet that they want to share with others. [press Enter twice]

What do you think?

8 Press Enter twice at the end of the message text and then type your name as the sender.

9 Click the Send button.

Step 9

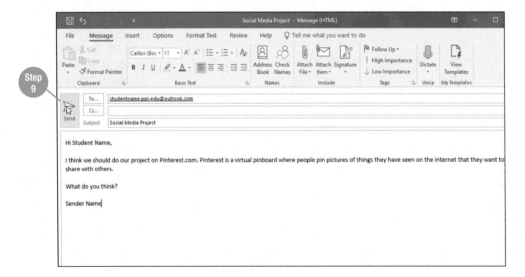

---------- **Oops!**

Type your email password after starting Outlook, if Outlook is not set up with the password saved on the device.

----- **in the know**

As a courtesy to the recipient, always include a *Subject* line that accurately describes the purpose of the message. People who receive many email messages in a day use the subjects to prioritize messages.

Replying to a Message

New messages appear at the top of the message list in the Content pane with message headers that show the sender, subject, time, and first line of message. Click to select a message header and reply directly from the Reading pane using the **Reply button**. Replying from the Reading pane is called an **inline reply**. You can also double-click the message header in the Content pane to open the message in a Message window.

 Tutorial

Replying to a Message

10 Click the Send/Receive All Folders button on the Quick Access toolbar to update the Content pane. Skip this step if you can already see the message sent to you by a classmate or yourself from Step 9.

Step 10

Send/Receive All Folders (F9)
Send and receive items such as mail messages, calendar appointments and tasks in all folders.

11 Click to select the message header for the message received from Step 9, if the message is not already selected, and then read the message text in the Reading pane.

12 Click the Reply button in the Reading pane.

Step 11

Step 12

13 Type the reply message text shown in the image below and then click the Send button.

Pop Out ✕ Discard

To... Student Name <studentname.ppi-edu@outlook.com>

Cc...

Subject RE: Social Media Project

Outlook inserts *RE:* in front of the *Subject* text when you reply to a message.

Student Name,

I agree. I have a few images we can use if you want to set up a sample account at Pinterest.com.

Sender Name

Step 13

Forwarding a Message

Forward a message if you want someone else to receive a copy of a message you have received. Click the **Forward button**, type the email address for the person to whom you want to forward the message, type a brief explanation, and then click Send. Think carefully before forwarding a message to be certain that the original sender would not object to another person reading the message without his or her permission. If in doubt, do not forward a message.

14 With the message header for the message selected in Step 11 still active, click the Forward button in the Reading pane.

Reply Reply All Forward
Student Name <studentna
Social Media Project

Step 14

15 Type the email address for another classmate in the *To* text box.

16 Click in the message text box above the original message text, type the text shown in the image below, and then click the Send button.

Step 15

Pop Out ✕ Discard

ⓘ You are not responding to the latest message in this conversation. Click here to open it.

To... studentname@ppi-edu.net

Cc...

Subject FW: Social Media Project

Outlook inserts *FW:* in front of the *Subject* text when you forward a message.

Hi Student Name,

Do you want to join our group for the social media project? See message below discussing Pinterest.com.

Sender Name

Step 16

---- **quick steps**

Create and Send an Email Message
1. Click New Email button.
2. Type address in *To* text box.
3. Type brief description in *Subject* text box.
4. Type message text in message text box.
5. Click Send.

Reply to a Message
1. Click Reply button in Reading pane.
2. Type reply message.
3. Click Send.

Forward a Message
1. Click Forward button in Reading pane.
2. Type address in *To* text box.
3. Type message.
4. Click Send.

------ **app tip**

Use Reply All to send a reply to messages that include more than one person. Use good judgment with Reply All and be sure that all the other recipients really need to see your response.

🌩 **Tutorial**

Forwarding a Message

5.2 Attaching a File to a Message and Deleting a Message

Files are often exchanged between individuals via email. To attach a file to an email message, use the **Attach File button** in the Include group on the Message tab. The recipient of an email message with a file attachment can choose to open the file from the mail server or save it to a storage medium to open later.

Messages that are no longer needed should be deleted to keep your mail folders a manageable size. You can delete a message in the Inbox folder if you replied to the message because you can view the original text with your reply in the Sent Items folder. Set aside a time each day or week to clean up your Inbox by deleting messages.

1. With Outlook open and Inbox the active folder, click the New Email button.

2. Type the email address for the recipient in the *To* text box.

As you begin typing an email address, Outlook suggests email addresses that match what you type based on people you have messaged recently in the *Recent People* list or at some other time in the *Other Suggestions* list. This feature is referred to as **AutoComplete**. Rather than type the entire email address, you can click the correct recipient in the list. People in the workplace who use Outlook connected to a mail server called an *Exchange server* can send a message to someone within the organization by typing the name of the recipient instead of the full email address.

3. Press the Tab key twice or click in the *Subject* text box.

4. Type Picture for Pinterest and then press Enter.

5. With the insertion point positioned in the message text box, type the following text:

   Hi [Recipient's Name], [press Enter twice]

   Attached is a picture we can put on Pinterest.

6. Press Enter twice at the end of the message text and then type your name as the sender.

7. Click the Attach File button in the Include group on the Message tab in the message window.

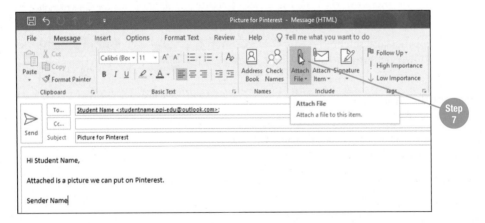

8. Click *Browse This PC*.

The *Recent Items* list from the Attach File button displays file names for files you have worked on recently that you can attach to a message with one click.

9. In the Insert File dialog box, navigate to the StudentDataFiles folder on your storage medium and then double-click *Ch5*.

 Watch & Learn

------- Skills

Attach a file to a message

Delete a message

Empty Deleted Items folder

Tutorial

Attaching a File to a Message

10 Double-click the image file *MurresOnIce.jpg*.

Outlook adds the file to an *Attached* area below the *Subject* text box.

11 Click the Send button.

Over time, your mail folders (Inbox and Sent Items) become filled with messages that are no longer needed. To delete a message, select the message header in the Content pane and then click the Delete button in the Delete group on the Home tab. Deleted messages are moved to the **Deleted Items** folder where the message can be restored if needed. Periodically empty the Deleted Items folder to permanently delete the messages.

file attached in Step 10

12 Click the Send/Receive All Folders button on the Quick Access Toolbar to update the Inbox. Skip this step if you can already see the message sent to you by a classmate or yourself in Step 11.

13 Click *Sent Items* in the Folder pane.

14 If necessary, click to select the message header for the message with the picture attached that you sent to a classmate or yourself in this topic.

15 Click the Delete button in the Delete group on the Home tab.

16 Click *Deleted Items* in the Folder pane.

Notice the message you deleted appears in the Content pane.

17 Right-click *Deleted Items* in the Folder pane and then click *Empty Folder*.

18 Click Yes in the Microsoft Outlook message box asking whether you want to continue to permanently delete everything in the Deleted Items folder.

19 Click *Inbox* in the Folder pane.

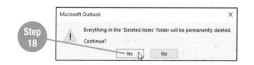

5.3 Previewing File Attachments and Using File Attachment Tools

 Watch & Learn

When you receive an email message with a file attached, you can preview, open, print, save, remove, or copy the file attachment from the Reading pane or from a message window. Click the down-pointing arrow next to the file name to select an action in the option list, or click the file name in the Reading pane to preview the attachment. During preview, the message text disappears, replaced with the contents of the attached file, and the Attachment Tools Attachments tab becomes active. Some files cannot be viewed within the Reading pane. In those instances, double-click the file name to open the file attached to the message.

------- skills

Preview a file attachment
Open a file attachment
Save a file attachment

1. With Outlook open and Inbox the active folder, click the message header for the message with the subject *Picture for Pinterest*.

2. Click the file ***MurresOnIce.jpg*** in the Reading pane. Do *not* click the down-pointing arrow at the right of the file name.

Outlook removes the message text and displays in the Reading pane the picture attached to the message. Notice also that the Attachment Tools Attachments tab is active on the ribbon.

------- app tip

If you are using Outlook .com, clicking the file name in the message pane previews the file in a separate pane. Click the Close button (displays as ×) in the preview pane when finished viewing the image. An Attachment Tools ribbon tab is not available in Outlook.com. Instead, you have two options: Download and Save to OneDrive.

3. Click *Back to message* at the top of the Reading pane to restore the message text.

4. Click the New Email button and then type the email address for the recipient in the *To* text box.

5. Click in the *Subject* text box and then type Presentation for Business Class.

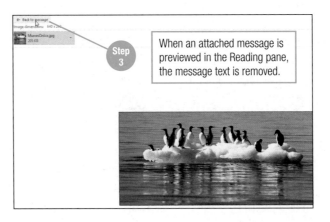

When an attached message is previewed in the Reading pane, the message text is removed.

6. Type the following text in the message text box:

Hi [Recipient's Name], [press Enter twice]

Attached is the PowerPoint presentation for our group project. [press Enter twice]

[Sender Name]

7. Click the Attach File button in the Include group on the Message tab and then click *Browse This PC*.

8. In the Insert File dialog box, with the Ch5 folder in StudentDataFiles the active folder, double-click the file ***SpeechTechniques.pptx***.

9. Click the Send button.

10 Click the Send/Receive All Folders button on the Quick Access Toolbar to update the Inbox folder if the message sent to you in Step 9 is not in your Inbox.

11 Click the message header for the message with the subject *Presentation for Business Class*.

12 Click the down-pointing arrow at the right of the file **SpeechTechniques.pptx** in the Reading pane and then click *Preview*.

13 Scroll down the Reading pane to the last slide in the presentation.

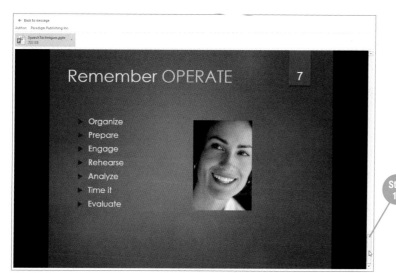

14 Click the Open button in the Actions group on the Attachment Tools Attachments tab.

  PowerPoint starts with the attached file open. The presentation opens in **Protected View**, which allows you to read the file content in the source application; however, editing is not permitted until you click the Enable Editing button on the Message bar.

15 Close PowerPoint to return to Outlook.

16 Click the Save As button in the Actions group on the Attachment Tools Attachments tab.

17 In the Save Attachment dialog box, navigate to the CompletedTopics folder on your storage medium and then create a new folder named *Ch5*.

18 Double-click the *Ch5* folder and then click the Save button.

19 Click the Show Message button in the Message group on the Attachment Tools Attachments tab to close the presentation preview in the Reading pane.

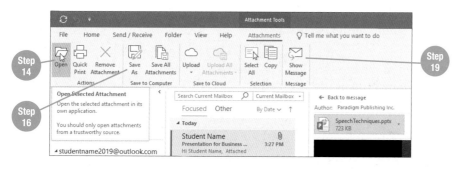

5.4 Scheduling Appointments and Events in Calendar

The **Calendar** component in Outlook is used to schedule appointments and events, such as meetings or conferences. An **appointment** is any activity where you want to track the day or time that the activity begins and ends in your schedule or when you want to be reminded to be somewhere. An appointment in Calendar can be a class, a meeting, a medical test, or a lunch date.

Note: In this topic and the next two topics, you will schedule appointments, an event, and a meeting in October 2021. Check with your instructor for alternate instructions.

1 With Outlook open and Inbox the active folder, click *Calendar* on the Navigation pane.

Mail Calendar People Tasks •••
Items: 4   Unread: 2

Your Navigation pane may display icons instead of these text labels.

Step 1

Outlook displays the current date, week, or month in the Content pane in Day, Week, or Month view. A **Date Navigator** displays at the top of the Folder pane with the current month and next month, along with directional arrows to browse forward or back to upcoming or previous months. Open the **Go To Date** dialog box to display a date further out.

2 Click the Day button in the Arrange group on the Home tab if Day is not the current view, and then click the Go to Date dialog box launcher at the lower right of the Go To group.

Step 2

3 In the Go To Date dialog box, type 10/11/2021, and then press Enter or click OK.

Step 3

In Outlook.com, the Go To Date dialog box is not available. Click the down-pointing arrow next to the date displayed at the top of the Appointment area to jump to a specific date. Click the up or down arrow to change the year, click the month button, and then click the day within the month.

4 Click next to 9:00 a.m. in the Appointment area, type Meet with program adviser, and then press Enter or click in another time slot outside the appointment box.

Step 4

Step 5

By default, Outlook schedules an appointment for a half hour.

5 Drag the bottom boundary of the appointment box to 10:00 a.m.

6 Click next to 11:00 a.m. in the Appointment area.

7 Click the New Appointment button in the New group on the Home tab.

Step 7

In Outlook.com click *New Event* in the browser window. Use the **New Appointment button** to open an Appointment window, where you can provide details about the appointment or select options to apply to the appointment.

(8) Type Intern Interview in the *Subject* text box.

(9) Press Tab or click in the *Location* text box and then type Room 3001.

(10) Click the *End time* option box arrow and then click *12:00 PM (1 hour)*.

(11) Click the Save & Close button in the Actions group on the Appointment tab.

An **event** differs from an appointment in that it is an activity that lasts an entire day or longer. Examples of events include conferences, trade shows, or vacations. An event does not occupy a time slot in the Calendar.

(12) Click the New Items button in the New group on the Home tab and then click *All Day Event* to open an Event window.

In Outlook.com, click the *All day* option to change an appointment to an all day event.

(13) Type Career Fair in the *Subject* text box.

(14) Press Tab or click in the *Location* text box and then type Student Center.

quick steps

Schedule an Appointment
1. Display the Calendar.
2. Display date for appointment.
3. Click next to appointment time, type description, and press Enter.

OR

1. Display the Calendar.
2. Display date for appointment.
3. Click next to appointment time.
4. Click New Appointment button.
5. Enter appointment details in Appointment window.
6. Click Save & Close.

Schedule an Event
1. Display the Calendar.
2. Display event date.
3. Click New Items button, then *All Day Event.*
4. Type event description.
5. Click in *Location* text box and type event location.
6. Click Save & Close.

Tutorials

Scheduling an Appointment

Scheduling Events in Calendar

(15) Click the Save & Close button in the Actions group on the Event tab.

Notice the event appears at the top of the Appointment area (Figure 5.3).

Figure 5.3

Event information appears in a banner along the top of the day in the Appointment area.

5.5 Scheduling a Recurring Appointment and Editing an Appointment

An appointment that occurs on a regular basis at fixed intervals need only be entered once and set up as a recurring appointment. To do this, open the Appointment Recurrence dialog box by clicking the **Recurrence button** in the Options group on the Appointment tab or the Calendar Tools Appointment tab. Enter the recurrence pattern for a repeating appointment, click OK, and then save and close the appointment.

① With Outlook open and Calendar active for October 11, 2021, click the Forward button to display October 12, 2021, in the Appointment area.

② Click next to 3:00 p.m. in the Appointment area, type Math Extra Help Sessions, and then press Enter.

③ With the Math Extra Help Sessions appointment box selected in the Appointment area, click the Recurrence button in the Options group on the Calendar Tools Appointment tab.

By default, Outlook sets the *Recurrence pattern* details for the appointment to recur *Weekly* at the same day and time as the appointment.

④ In the Appointment Recurrence dialog box, select *25* in the *End after* text box in the *Range of recurrence* section and then type 6.

⑤ Click OK.

A recurring icon displays at the right end of the appointment box in the Appointment area for any appointment that repeats.

⑥ Click *19* in the October 2021 calendar in the Date Navigator to display the appointments for the next Tuesday and view the recurring appointment.

Watch & Learn

------ Skills

Schedule a recurring appointment

Edit an appointment

Tutorials

Scheduling a Recurring Appointment

------ Oops!

Using Outlook.com? Set the recurrence option by changing the *Repeat* option to *Every week* and changing the end date to November 16, 2021.

------ app tip

Consider entering your class schedule in the Outlook calendar for the current semester as recurring appointments.

7. Click *26* in the October 2021 calendar in the Date Navigator to view the Math Extra Help Sessions appointment in the Appointment area.

8. Click the Go to Date dialog box launcher in the Go To group, type 11/23/2021 in the Go To Date dialog box, and then press Enter or click OK. Notice the Math Extra Help Sessions appointment does not appear in the Appointment area because the range of recurrence has ended.

Assign options or tags to an existing appointment by selecting the appointment and using the buttons on the Calendar Tools Appointment tab. Change the subject, location, day, or time of an appointment by double-clicking an appointment to open the Appointment window.

9. Display October 11, 2021, in the Calendar.

10. Click to select the appointment scheduled at 11:00 a.m.

A selected appointment box displays with a black outline. A pop-out opens at the left with the appointment details when you point at an appointment.

11. Click the High Importance button in the Tags group on the Calendar Tools Appointment tab.

    Skip Step 11 if you are using Outlook.com. The High Importance tag is not available.

12. Click the Open button in the Actions group.

    If you are using Outlook.com, click the *Edit* option.

13. Click the calendar icon at the right end of the *Start time* text box.

14. Click *12* in the calendar.

15. Click Save & Close in the Actions group on the Appointment tab.

16. Display October 12, 2021, in the Appointment area.

    Notice the revised Intern Interview appointment appears next to 11:00 a.m. You can also move an

appointment using a drag-and-drop technique. In Day view, drag an appointment box to another time slot on the same day. Display the Calendar in Week view and drag an appointment box from one day to another day in the same week, and change the start time if needed. In Month view, drag an appointment box from one day to another. The appointment is moved with the same start time.

5.6 Scheduling a Meeting

Schedule a meeting by displaying the day in the Appointment area, selecting the time, and then clicking the **New Meeting button** in the New group on the Home tab. In the Meeting window *To* text box, enter the email addresses for the individuals in your invite list. Enter the meeting subject, location, and other details as needed and then click the Send button. Meeting attendees receive a **meeting request** email message. Responses to the meeting request are sent back to the meeting organizer via buttons in the email message window or Reading pane.

●------- Skills

Schedule a meeting

Respond to a meeting request

1. With Outlook open and Calendar active with October 12, 2021, displayed in the Appointment area, click next to 1:00 p.m.

2. Click the New Meeting button in the New group on the Home tab.

3. Type the email address for the classmate with whom you have been exchanging email messages in the *To* text box.

Note: If you have been sending email messages to yourself in this chapter, send the meeting request message to a friend or relative, or use an email address for yourself that is not your Microsoft account address. You cannot send a meeting request to the same email sending the request. You will not be able to complete Step 8 to Step 16 if you do not receive a meeting request message from someone else.

●------- Oops!

Using Outlook.com? Type the email address for the meeting request in the *Invite attendees* text box.

4. Press Tab or click in the *Subject* text box and then type Fundraising Planning Meeting.

5. Press Tab or click in the *Location* text box and then type Room 1010.

6. Click the *End time* option box arrow and then click *2:30 PM (1.5 hours)*.

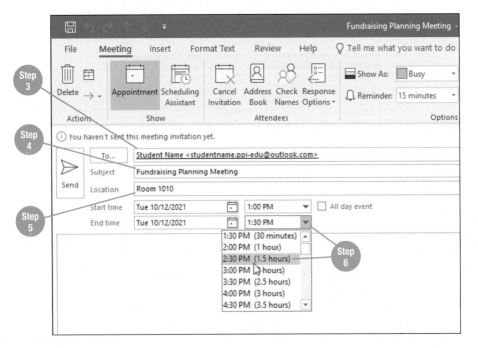

●------- app tip

Consider using the space in the message text box below *End time* to type a meeting agenda or other explanatory text to inform attendees about the purpose of the meeting.

7. Click the Send button.

⑧ Click *Mail* on the Navigation pane.

⑨ Click the Send/Receive All Folders button on the Quick Access Toolbar to update your Inbox, if the meeting request message sent to you by a classmate at Step 7 has not been received.

⑩ Click the message header for the meeting request to view the message details in the Reading pane.

Buttons along the top of the Reading pane or in the Respond group on the Meeting tab in a message text box for a meeting request are used to respond to the meeting organizer. Click the **Accept button** to send a reply that you will attend the meeting. Use the Tentative, Decline, or Propose New Time buttons if you are not required or unable to attend a scheduled meeting. Outlook also provides a Calendar button at the top of the Reading pane, which is used to view your appointments for the meeting day and time to see if you are available before you send a response to the meeting organizer.

⑪ Double-click the message header to open the meeting request message with the Meeting tab active.

Note that you will see two entries for the meeting in the message window. One entry is the meeting that you created in Step 1 to Step 7. You are referred to as the *meeting organizer* for this meeting. The other entry is a result of the meeting request sent to you by someone else for which you are a *meeting invitee*.

⑫ Click the Accept button in the Respond group on the Meeting tab.

⑬ Click *Send the Response Now*.

A meeting request email message is deleted from the Inbox after you respond to the meeting invitation.

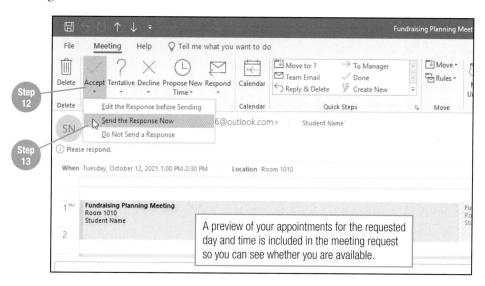

A preview of your appointments for the requested day and time is included in the meeting request so you can see whether you are available.

⑭ Click *Sent Items* in the Folder pane.

⑮ Click the message header for the message sent to the meeting organizer with your Accepted reply and then read the message in the Reading pane.

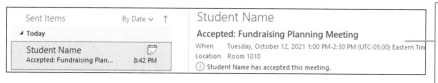

This is the default reply sent to a meeting organizer when a meeting invitation is accepted. Use the *Edit the Response before Sending* option to type your own message.

⑯ Click *Inbox* in the Folder pane.

quick steps

Schedule a Meeting
1. Display Calendar.
2. Navigate to meeting date.
3. Click next to meeting time.
4. Click New Meeting button.
5. Enter meeting details.
6. Click Send.

Accept a Meeting Request
1. Display Inbox.
2. Select meeting request message header OR open Meeting window.
3. Click Accept button.
4. Click *Send the Response Now*.

Tutorial
Scheduling a Meeting

5.7 Adding and Editing Contacts in People

The **People** component in Outlook is used to store and organize contact information, such as email addresses, mailing addresses, telephone numbers, and other information about the people with whom you communicate. Think of People as an electronic address book. To add information about a person, click the **New Contact button** in the New group on the Home tab. Contacts display alphabetically in the *People* list in the Content pane. Click a contact name to display the information about the person in the Reading pane.

Add a Contact
Edit a Contact

1. With Outlook open and Inbox the active folder, click *People* on the Navigation pane.

2. Click the New Contact button in the New group.

3. Type Tory Nguyen in the *Full Name* text box in the Contact window.

4. Press Tab or click in the *Company* text box.

Notice the *File as* text box automatically updates when you move past the *Full Name* entry, with the last name of the person followed by the first name. The *File as* entry is used to organize the *People* list alphabetically by last names.

5. Type NuWave Personnel in the *Company* text box.

6. Press Tab or click in the *Job title* text box and then type Recruitment Specialist.

7. Click in the *Email* text box and then type tory@ppi-edu.net.

8. Click in the *Business* text box in the *Phone numbers* section and then type 8885559840.

9. Click in the *Mobile* text box in the *Phone numbers* section, type 8885553256, and then press Tab.

Notice that the phone numbers automatically format to show brackets around the area code, a space, and a hyphen in the number when you move past the field. In Outlook.com, the formatting of telephone numbers does not occur. Type the brackets and hyphens if desired.

10. Click the Add Contact Picture control that displays as a silhouette in a box between the name and business card sections in the Contact window.

Oops!

Using Outlook.com? Click *New contact* to enter the information in the browser window. Outlook.com uses a different order and input grouping. For example, type the first name and last name in separate areas. Use the *Add more* option at the bottom of the window to find additional entry options not shown. For example, click *Add More* and point to the *Work* option to find the *Job title* entry.

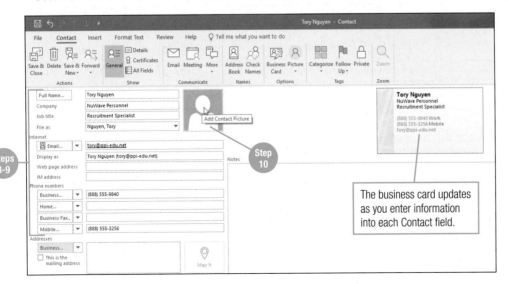

The business card updates as you enter information into each Contact field.

11 In the Add Contact Picture dialog box, navigate to the Ch5 folder in StudentDataFiles and then double-click the image file ***ToryNguyen.jpg***.

12 Click the Save & Close button in the Actions group on the Contact tab.

Contact information for the selected person displays in the Reading pane with options for communicating with the person, such as sending an email message.

13 Double-click *Tory Nguyen* in the *People* list. In Outlook.com, click the *Edit contact* option in the Reading pane to reopen the Contact window.

quick steps

Add a Contact
1. Display People.
2. Click New Contact button.
3. Enter contact information as required.
4. Click Save & Close.

Edit a Contact
1. Double-click name in *People* list.
2. Edit information as required.
3. Click Save & Close.

Tutorial
Adding People

14 Click at the end of the telephone number *(888) 555-9840* in the *Business* text box, press the spacebar, and then type extension 3115.

15 Click in the *Notes* text box and then type the following text:

NuWave Personnel was recommended by Dana. Tory is also the regional director.

16 Click the Save & Close button. The updated information displays in the Reading pane.

17 Double-click in any white space below the last entry in the *People* list to open a new Contact window.

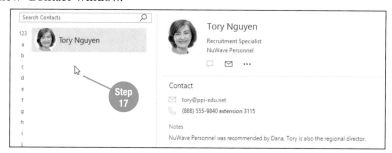

18 Enter the name of your instructor in the *Full Name* text box, the name of your school in the *Company* text box, and the email address for your instructor in the *Email* text box, and then click the Save & Close button.

5.8 Adding and Editing Tasks

Watch & Learn

------- skills

Add a task

Edit a task

Delete a task

Mark a task complete

Tutorial

Adding Tasks

The **Tasks** component in Outlook maintains a to-do list. You can track information about each task, such as how much of the task is completed, how much time has been spent on the task, and the priority of the task. In **To-Do List** view, uncompleted tasks are shown grouped in descending order by the due date.

1. With Outlook open and People active, click *Tasks* on the Navigation pane.

2. Click *To-Do List* in the Current View group on the Home tab if To-Do List is not the active view.

3. Click in the text box at the top of the To-Do List that displays the dimmed text *Type a new task*, type Do research on Pinterest, and then press Enter.

4. Type Gather images to create Pinterest pinboard and then press Enter.

5. Type Create resume for Career Fair and then press Enter.

Adding a task using the *Type a new task* text box adds the entry in the To-Do List with a Today follow-up flag by default. In the next steps, you will open a Task window using the **New Task button** to add a task with more details and options.

6. Click the New Task button in the New group on the Home tab.

7. Type Prepare study notes for exams in the *Subject* text box.

8. Click the *Priority* option box arrow and then click *High*.

9. Click the calendar icon at the right end of the *Due date* text box, navigate to the last month of the current semester, and then click the Monday one week before the last week of your semester.

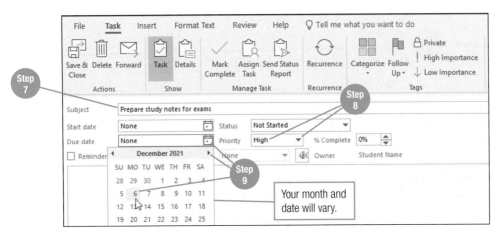

10. Click the Save & Close button in the Actions group on the Task tab.

Editing or updating a task can include activities such as assigning or changing a due date, assigning a priority, entering the percentage of completion, or changing the status of a task. When a task is completed, use the **Remove from List button** in the Manage Task group on the Home tab to remove the follow-up flag on the task, or the **Mark Complete button** to remove the task from the To-Do List.

11 Click *Do research on Pinterest* to select the task. Notice the task details in the Reading pane.

12 Click the Remove from List button in the Manage Task group on the Home tab.

Notice the task is removed from the To-Do List. You can also use the Delete button in the Delete group on the Home tab to remove a task you have completed.

quick steps

Add a Task
1. Display Tasks.
2. Click in *Type a new task* text box, type task description, and press Enter.

OR
1. Display Tasks.
2. Click New Task button.
3. Enter task details.
4. Click Save & Close.

Tutorial

Editing Tasks

13 Double-click the task *Create resume for Career Fair* to open the Task window.

14 Click the Mark Complete button in the Manage Task group on the Task tab.

The Task window closes, and the entry is removed from the To-Do List.

15 Double-click the task entry *Gather images to create Pinterest pinboard*.

16 Click the *Status* option box arrow and then click *Waiting on someone else*.

17 Click in the text box with white space below the *Reminder* options and then type Waiting for Leslie to send me images from her renovation clients.

18 Click the Save & Close button. Notice the updated task details appear in the Reading pane.

19 Display the Inbox folder in Mail.

5.9 Searching Outlook Items

The search feature in Outlook, referred to as **Instant Search**, is used to locate a message, appointment, contact, or task. A search text box located between the ribbon and content is used to find items. Outlook begins a search as soon as you begin typing an entry in the search text box. Matched items are highlighted in the search results. Once located, you can open an item to view or edit the information by double-clicking the entry in the filtered search results list.

1. With Outlook open and Inbox the active folder in Mail, click in the search text box at the top of the Content pane (contains the dimmed text *Search Current Mailbox*).

2. Type pinterest.

Outlook immediately begins matching items as you type characters. Matched words are highlighted in both the Content pane and Reading pane in the filtered search results list. Notice also the Search Tools Search tab is active.

3. Click the Current Folder button in the Scope group on the Search Tools Search tab.

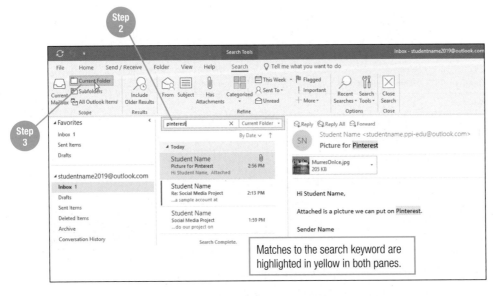

Matches to the search keyword are highlighted in yellow in both panes.

4. Click each message in the search results list to view the message in the Reading pane.

Notice that for each message, *Pinterest* is highlighted in the Reading pane. Use buttons in the Scope and Refine groups on the Search Tools Search tab to further eliminate messages that do not meet the criterion for content you are trying to find. You can search for a message by typing a sender name, a subject, or any keyword or phrase that exists in the message.

5. Click *Close Search* in the search text box to close the search results list and return the Inbox to the full message list.

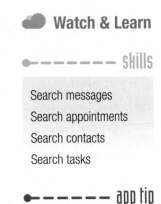

Watch & Learn

skills

Search messages
Search appointments
Search contacts
Search tasks

app tip

The keyboard shortcut Ctrl + E opens the search text box.

6 Display the Calendar.

7 Click in the search text box at the upper right of the Appointment area (contains the dimmed text *Search Calendar*) and then type career fair.

Outlook displays the appointment found with the search keywords in a filtered list. The search keywords are highlighted in yellow within the entry.

8 Double-click the entry in the filtered list to view the details in the Event window and then close the window.

●---- **quick steps**

Search for an Outlook Item
1. Display Mail, Calendar, People, or Tasks.
2. Click in search text box.
3. Type search keyword.

☁ **Tutorial**

Searching for People and Appointments

9 Click *Close Search* to restore the Calendar to the appointments for the current day.

10 Display People.

11 Click in the search text box at the top of the *People* list (contains the dimmed text *Search Contacts*), type nuwave, and then press Enter.

Outlook displays the contact for Tory Nguyen, who works at NuWave Personnel. You can use the search feature to find any Outlook item by any entry in the message, appointment, contact, or task. For example, you could find a contact by name, job title, company name, or telephone number.

12 Click *Close Search* to restore the *People* list.

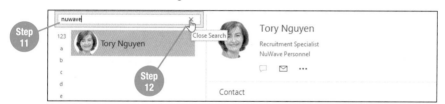

13 Display Tasks.

14 Click in the search text box at the top of the task list (contains the dimmed text *Search To-Do List* or *Search Tasks*, depending on the active selection in the Folder pane) and then type leslie.

15 Click to select the task entry *Gather images to create Pinterest pinboard* and then view the task details with *Leslie* highlighted in yellow in the Reading pane.

Outlook can locate a task by searching text in any task option.

16 Click *Close Search* to restore the To-Do List.

17 Display Mail with the Inbox folder.

18 Close Outlook.

Topic	Key Concepts
5.1 Using Outlook to Send Email	**Outlook** is an application for organizing messages, appointments, contacts, and tasks referred to as a **personal information management (PIM)** application.
	Electronic mail (email) is the exchange of messages between individuals electronically.
	When Outlook is started, **Mail** is the active component within Outlook, with the Inbox folder shown by default.
	The **Inbox** displays messages with the newest message received on the **Focused Inbox** tab at the top of the Content pane. The Focused tab shows your important messages—those that are not newsletters or machine-generated emails, which appear on the Other tab.
	Create and send a new email message using the **New Email button** in the New group on the Home tab.
	Click the message header for a new message received to read the message contents in the Reading pane.
	Reply directly to a message by clicking the **Reply button** in the Reading pane (referred to as an **inline reply**).
	Send a copy of a message you have received to someone else using the **Forward button**.
5.2 Attaching a File to a Message and Deleting a Message	Attach a file to a message using the **Attach File button** in the Include group on the Message tab.
	As you type an email address in the *To* text box, the **AutoComplete** feature shows email addresses in a *Recent People* list and an *Other Suggestions* list that match what you are typing. As you type, click an entry in the list if the correct recipient appears before you finish typing.
	Delete messages from mail folders that are no longer needed to keep folders a manageable size.
	Deleted messages are moved to the **Deleted Items** folder.
	Empty the Deleted Items folder to permanently delete messages.
5.3 Previewing File Attachments and Using File Attachment Tools	Preview a file attached to a message by clicking the file name in the Reading pane.
	While a file is being previewed, message text is temporarily removed from the Reading pane.
	Some files cannot be viewed in the Reading pane and must be viewed by double-clicking the file name to open the file in the source application.
	Open or save a file using buttons in the Actions group on the Attachment Tools Attachments tab or with the options accessed by clicking the down-pointing arrow at the right of the file name in the Reading pane.
	A file opened from a message is opened in **Protected View** in the source application, which allows you to read the contents. You cannot edit the file until you click the Enable Editing button on the Message bar.

continued…

Topic	Key Concepts
5.4 Scheduling Appointments and Events in Calendar	The **Calendar** component is used to schedule appointments and events. An **appointment** is any activity for which you want to record the occurrence by day and time. A **Date Navigator** at the top of the Folder pane displays the current month and next month with directional arrows to browse to the previous or next month. Use the **Go To Date** dialog box to navigate directly to a specific date you want to display in the Appointment area. Click next to the time in the Appointment area and then type a description to enter a new appointment. Click the **New Appointment button** in the New group on the Home tab to enter details for a new appointment in an Appointment window. An **event** is an appointment that lasts an entire day or longer. Click the New Items button in the New group on the Home tab and then click *All day event* to create an event in an Event window.
5.5 Scheduling a Recurring Appointment and Editing an Appointment	An appointment that occurs at fixed intervals on a regular basis can be entered once, and Outlook schedules the remaining appointments automatically. Click the **Recurrence button** in the Options group on the Appointment tab to set the recurrence pattern and range of recurrence details for a recurring appointment. Click to select an appointment in the Appointment area to assign options or tags to the appointment using buttons on the Calendar Tools Appointment tab. Open the Appointment window to make changes to the subject, location, day, or time of a scheduled appointment. You can also move an appointment by dragging the appointment box to another day or time in Day view or Week view. In Month view, drag an appointment box to another day at the same appointment start time.
5.6 Scheduling a Meeting	A meeting is an appointment to which you invite people. Click the **New Meeting button** in the New group on the Home tab to create a new meeting by entering the email addresses for meeting attendees, as well as and the meeting particulars. Information about a meeting is sent to people via a **meeting request**, which is an email message sent to meeting participants. A meeting attendee responds to a meeting request from the Reading pane or the message window by clicking a response button, such as the **Accept button**.
5.7 Adding and Editing Contacts in People	Use the **People** component to store and organize contact information for people with whom you communicate. Click the **New Contact button** or double-click in a blank area in the *People* list to open a Contact window and add contact information. Click the Add Contact Picture control in the Contact window to select an image file for a contact in the Add Contact Picture dialog box and display the image next to the name in the *People* list. Double-click a name in the *People* list to edit contact information in the Contact window.

continued…

Topic	Key Concepts
5.8 Adding and Editing Tasks	Use **Tasks** in Outlook to maintain a to-do list.
	Click in the *Type a new task* text box to add a task to the **To-Do List**, or click the **New Task button** to enter a new task in a Task window.
	Open a Task window to add a due date or to add other task information, such as a priority or status.
	Select a task and click the **Remove from List button** to remove the follow-up flag on the task, which also removes the task from the To-Do List.
	Select a task or open a task in the Task window and use the **Mark Complete button** to indicate a task is completed. Completed tasks are removed from the To-Do List view.
5.9 Searching Outlook Items	The **Instant Search** feature is a search text box at the top of Mail, Calendar, People, and Tasks in which you search for an Outlook item by typing a keyword or phrase.
	Matched items start to appear in a filtered list as soon as you type characters in the search text box. Continue typing the search keyword or phrase to continue filtering the list.
	Matches to the search keyword or phrase are highlighted in the filtered lists and in content in the Reading pane for a selected item.
	Use buttons on the Search Tools Search tab to further refine a search.
	Click *Close Search* in the search text box to remove the filtered list and redisplay all items.

 Topics Review

Creating, Editing, and Formatting Word Documents

Microsoft Word (referred to as Word) is a **word processing application** used to create documents that are mostly text. Word documents can also include images, charts, tables, or other visual objects to make the document more interesting and the content easier to understand. Letters, essays, reports, invitations, recipes, agendas, contracts, and resumes are examples of documents that can be created using Word.

Word automatically corrects some errors as you type and indicates other potential spelling and grammar errors for you to consider. Other features provide tools to format and enhance a document. In this chapter, you will learn how to create, edit, and format documents. You will create new documents starting from a blank page and other documents by selecting from the Template gallery in Word.

If necessary, review the Office essentials you learned in Chapter 3 before starting to do the work in this chapter. It is assumed that you have the skills to start an application; save, open, and print a document; and perform commands using the Quick Access Toolbar, ribbon, dialog boxes, and task panes.

Learning Objectives

6.1 Create a new document and insert, delete, and edit text

6.2 Insert symbols and check spelling and grammar

6.3 Find and replace text

6.4 Move text and create bulleted and numbered lists

6.5 Format text using font options, and change paragraph alignment

6.6 Indent paragraphs, change line spacing, and change spacing before and after paragraphs

6.7 Apply a style to text and change the style set

6.8 Create a new document from a template

Read & Learn

Content Online
The online course includes additional training and assessment resources.

6.1 Creating and Editing a New Document

The Word Start screen appears when Word is initially opened. You can choose to open an existing document, create a new blank document, or search for and select a template to create a new document. Creating a new document includes typing the document text, editing the text, and correcting errors. As you type, features in Word help you fix common typing errors and apply formatting to characters or paragraphs.

1 Start Word.

2 On the Word Start screen, click *Blank document* in the Templates gallery and compare your screen with the one shown in Figure 6.1.

Table 6.1 on the next page describes the elements shown in Figure 6.1.

3 Type Social Bookmarking and press Enter.

Notice that extra space is automatically added below the text before the next line.

4 Type the text on the next page, allowing the lines to end automatically; press Enter only where indicated.

Word moves text to a new line automatically when you reach the end of the current line. This feature is called **wordwrap**. Word displays a red wavy line below a word not recognized by the software. These red wavy lines indicate possible spelling errors. If a red wavy line appears below a word spelled correctly, you can ignore it. If the red wavy line appears for a typing error, correct the typing mistake by pressing the Backspace key to delete the character(s) and then type the correct character(s). You will learn other editing methods later in this topic.

Watch & Learn

Hands On Activity

------- Skills

Enter text

Describe AutoCorrect actions

Describe AutoFormat actions

Edit, insert, and delete text

Tutorials

Exploring the Word Start Screen

Entering Text

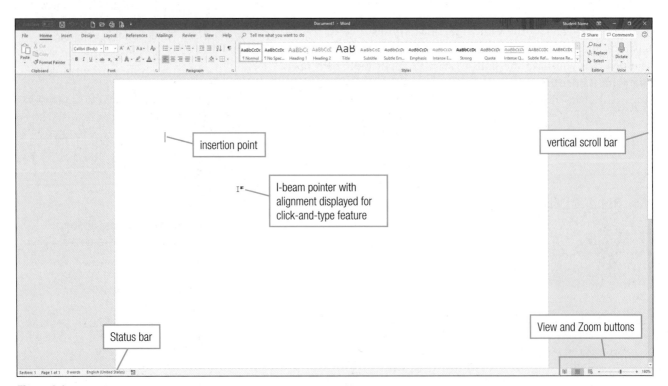

Figure 6.1

A new blank document screen is shown. The default settings in Word display a new document in Print Layout view. Your display may vary if settings have been changed on the computer you are using. See Table 6.1 on the next page for a description of screen elements.

Table 6.1 Word Features

Feature	Description
Insertion point	A blinking vertical bar indicates where the next character typed will appear.
I-beam pointer	This pointer appears for text entry or selection when you move the pointer using a mouse or trackpad. The I-beam pointer displays with a paragraph alignment option (left, center, or right) depending on the location of the I-beam within the current line. You can double-click and type text anywhere on a page, and the alignment option will be left-aligned, center-aligned, or right-aligned. This feature is called **click and type**.
Status bar	The status bar displays page numbers with total number of pages and number of words in the current document. The right end of the Status bar has view and zoom options. The default view is Print Layout view, which displays how a page will look when printed with the current print options.
Vertical scroll bar	Use the scroll bar to view parts of a document not displayed in the current window.
View and Zoom buttons	By default, Word opens in Print Layout view. Other view buttons include Read Mode and Web Layout. Read Mode view maximizes reading space and removes editing tools, providing a more natural environment for reading. In Web Layout view, the document displays the page width, text, and formatting options as the document would look in a browser. Zoom buttons, as you learned in Chapter 3, are used to enlarge or shrink the display.

Social bookmarking websites are used to organize, save, and share web content. Links are called bookmarks and include tags, which are keywords you assign to the content when you create the bookmark. [press Enter]

Many websites now include icons for popular social bookmarking sites that capture the page references for bookmarking. Another way to bookmark a page is to add the bookmarklet for the social bookmarking site you use to your browser's toolbar. Bookmarklets add a bookmark instantly when clicked. [press Enter]

5 Type teh and press the spacebar. Notice that Word changes the text to *The*.

A feature called **AutoCorrect** changes commonly misspelled words as soon as you press the spacebar and capitalizes the first character in a new sentence if the first character is typed lowercase.

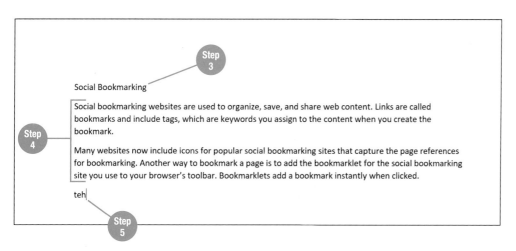

●－－－－－－ app tip

AutoCorrect also fixes common capitalization errors, such as two initial capitals and no capital in the name of a day. AutoCorrect also turns off the Caps Lock key and corrects text when a new sentence is started with the key left on. Use Undo if AutoCorrect changes text that you don't want changed.

 Tutorial

Undoing an AutoCorrect Correction

6. Type popular social bookmarking site Pinterest.com is used to pin pictures found on the Web to virtual pinboards. and press Enter.

7. Type a study by a marketing company found that 1/2 of frequent web surfers use a social bookmarking site, with Pinterest the 1st choice for most females. and press Enter.

Notice that Word automatically corrects the capitalization of the first word in the sentence, *1/2* is changed to a fraction character (½), and *1st* is automatically formatted as an ordinal, with the *st* displayed as superscript text (superscript characters are smaller text placed at the top of the line). The **AutoFormat** feature automatically changes some fractions, ordinals, quotes, hyphens, and hyperlinks as you type. AutoFormat also converts straight apostrophes (') or quotation marks (") to smart quotes ('smart quotes'), also called *curly quotes* ("curly quotes").

● – – – – – – app tip

AutoFormat does not recognize all fractions. For example, typing *1/3* will not format to the one-third fraction character. You will learn about inserting symbols for these characters in the next topic.

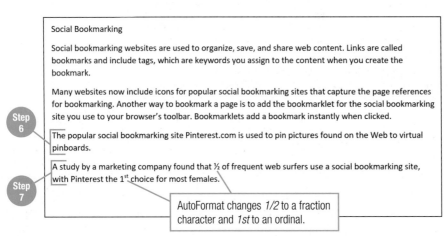

Social Bookmarking

Social bookmarking websites are used to organize, save, and share web content. Links are called bookmarks and include tags, which are keywords you assign to the content when you create the bookmark.

Many websites now include icons for popular social bookmarking sites that capture the page references for bookmarking. Another way to bookmark a page is to add the bookmarklet for the social bookmarking site you use to your browser's toolbar. Bookmarklets add a bookmark instantly when clicked.

Step 6 The popular social bookmarking site Pinterest.com is used to pin pictures found on the Web to virtual pinboards.

Step 7 A study by a marketing company found that ½ of frequent web surfers use a social bookmarking site, with Pinterest the 1st choice for most females.

AutoFormat changes *1/2* to a fraction character and *1st* to an ordinal.

8. Click the Save button on the Quick Access Toolbar.

The Save As backstage area appears because this is the first time the document has been saved.

9. Click *This PC* and then click *Browse*, or click the option in the Save As backstage area for your storage medium if you are not saving to a USB flash drive.

10. Navigate in the Save As dialog box to the CompletedTopics folder on your storage medium and then create a new folder, *Ch6*.

11. Double-click the new folder *Ch6*.

12. Select the current text in the *File name* text box, type SocialMediaProject-YourName, and then press Enter or click the Save button.

☁ **Tutorials**

Saving with the Same Name

Saving with a New Name

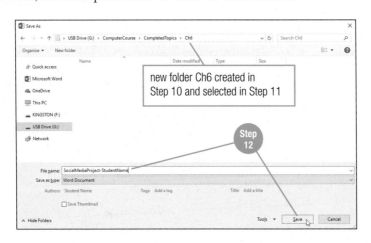

new folder Ch6 created in Step 10 and selected in Step 11

Step 12

When creating a new document, changes often need to be made to the text after the text has been typed. You may need to correct typing errors, change a word or phrase to some other text, add new text, or remove text. Making changes to a document after the document has been typed is called **editing**. The first step to edit text is to move the insertion point to the location of a change.

13 Click to position the insertion point at the beginning of the last paragraph that begins with the text *A study by a marketing company* (insertion point will be blinking just left of *A*), type Experian Hitwise, and then press the spacebar.

Word automatically inserts the new text and moves existing text to the right.

> Experian Hitwise A study by a marketing company found that ½ of frequent web surfers use a social bookmarking site, with Pinterest the 1st choice for most females.

14 With the insertion point still positioned at the left of *A* in *A study*, press the Delete key until you have removed *A study by*, type (, click to position the insertion point just after the *y* in *company*, and then type) conducted a survey of frequent web surfers and.

15 Position the insertion point just left of *½*, press the Delete key until you have removed *½ of frequent web surfers*, and then type one-half.

16 Position the insertion point at the left of *1st*, delete *1st*, and then type first.

17 Position the insertion point below the last paragraph and then type your first and last name.

18 Check your text with the document shown in Figure 6.2. If necessary, make further corrections by moving the insertion point and inserting and deleting characters as needed.

Social Bookmarking

Social bookmarking websites are used to organize, save, and share web content. Links are called bookmarks and include tags, which are keywords you assign to the content when you create the bookmark.

Many websites now include icons for popular social bookmarking sites that capture the page references for bookmarking. Another way to bookmark a page is to add the bookmarklet for the social bookmarking site you use to your browser's toolbar. Bookmarklets add a bookmark instantly when clicked.

The popular social bookmarking site Pinterest.com is used to pin pictures found on the Web to virtual pinboards.

Experian Hitwise (a marketing company) conducted a survey of frequent web surfers and found that one-half use a social bookmarking site, with Pinterest the first choice for most females.

Student Name

Figure 6.2
The document text for **SocialMediaProject-StudentName** is displayed.

19 Click the Save button on the Quick Access Toolbar. Leave the document open for the next topic.

Because the document has already been assigned a file name in Step 12, the Save button saves the document changes using the same name.

quick steps

Create a New Document
1. Start Word.
2. Click *Blank document*.
3. Type text.

Save a New Document
1. Click Save button on the Quick Access Toolbar.
2. Navigate to drive and folder.
3. Enter file name.
4. Click Save.

Save a Document Using the Existing Name
Click Save button on the Quick Access Toolbar.

Edit a Document
1. Position insertion point at location of change.
2. Type new text or delete text as needed.
3. Save changes.

Tutorial

Moving the Insertion Point and Inserting and Deleting Text

Oops!

Insertion point will not go below last paragraph? Click to place the insertion point at the end of the last sentence and then press Enter to move down to a blank line.

app tip

You can move the insertion point by pressing the Up, Down, Left, or Right Arrow keys to move within a document. Hold down an arrow key to rapidly move the insertion point.

6.2 Inserting Symbols and Completing a Spelling and Grammar Check

In some documents, you need to insert a symbol or special character, such as a copyright symbol (©), registered trademark (™), or a fraction character for a fraction that AutoCorrect does not recognize, such as one-third (⅓). Symbols and special characters are inserted using the **Symbol gallery** or the Symbol dialog box.

The **Check Document button** on the Review tab opens the Editor task pane. The Result(s) button near the top of the pane displays the number of errors detected with the *Corrections* list showing the number of errors categorized as *Spelling* or *Grammar*. The Spelling feature matches words in the document with words in a dictionary and flags a word not found as a possible error. When you click the Result(s) button to review potential errors, the Editor task pane changes to display suggestions for a word not found and give options to ignore, to change, or to add the word to the dictionary. The feature also checks for duplicate words, with an option to remove the repeated word. The Check Document feature helps you correct many errors; however, you still need to proofread each document. For example, the errors in the following sentence escaped detection: The plain fair was expensive!

1. With the **SocialMediaProject-YourName** document open, position the insertion point after *n* in *Experian* in the last paragraph.

2. Click the Insert tab.

3. Click the Symbol button in the Symbols group.

4. Click *Trade Mark Sign*. Note that the symbol may appear in a different position than shown in the image at the right.

Step 3

Step 4

5. Position the insertion point after the period at the end of the paragraph that begins *Experian* and press the spacebar to insert a space.

6. Type The survey sample size of 1,000 interviews provides a standard error at 95% confidence of and then press the spacebar.

7. Click the Symbol button and then click *More Symbols*.

Step 7

8. In the Symbol dialog box, with *Font* set to *(normal text)* and *Subset* set to *Letterlike Symbols*, scroll up the symbol list until the *Subset* changes to *Latin-1 Supplement*, click ±, and then click the Insert button.

Watch & Learn

Hands On Activity

●────────── Skills

Insert a symbol and special character

Check spelling and grammar

Tutorials
Inserting Symbols

Inserting Special Characters

●────────── Oops!

Different font and/or subset? Use the *Font* or *Subset* option box arrow to change the option to *(normal text)* and *Letterlike Symbols* if the Symbol dialog box has different settings.

Scroll up almost to the top of the dialog box in Step 8 until the *Subset* changes to *Latin-1 Supplement* and you can see the plus-minus symbol.

Step 8

9 Click the Close button to return to the document and then type 3%.

You may have noticed the Plus-Minus Sign symbol in the Symbol gallery. In Steps 7 to 9, you practiced using the Symbol dialog box so that you will know how to find a symbol that is not displayed in the Symbol gallery.

Experian™ Hitwise (a marketing company) conducted a survey of frequent web surfers and found that one-half use a social bookmarking site, with Pinterest the first choice for most females. The survey sample size of 1,000 interviews provides a standard error at 95% confidence of ±3%.

Student Name

Step 9

10 Click the Review tab and then click the Check Document button in the Proofing group.

11 Click the 1 Result button near the top of the Editor task pane to check the error detected by Word.

12 When the word *Hitwise* is selected, click *Ignore All* in the Editor task pane.

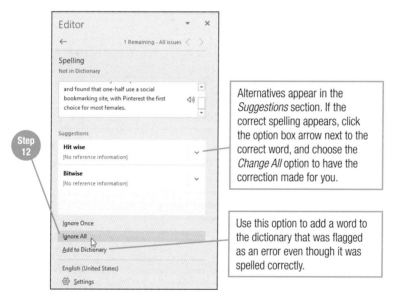

Alternatives appear in the *Suggestions* section. If the correct spelling appears, click the option box arrow next to the correct word, and choose the *Change All* option to have the correction made for you.

Use this option to add a word to the dictionary that was flagged as an error even though it was spelled correctly.

13 If the spelling feature stops at other typing errors in your document, click the option box arrow next to the correct spelling entry in the *Suggestions* section, and then click *Change All*. If the correct spelling is not offered, click in the document at the end of the typing mistake, press the Backspace key to delete the characters, type the correct text, and then click the Resume button in the Proofing task pane.

14 Click OK at the message that the spelling and grammar check is complete and then close the Editor task pane.

15 Save the document using the same name. Leave the document open for the next topic.

6.3 Finding and Replacing Text

The **Find** command moves the insertion point to each occurrence of a word or phrase. Find is helpful if you think you have overused a particular term and want to review how many times it appears in a document, or if you want to move the insertion point to a specific location in the document very quickly and a unique word or phrase exists near the location. **Replace** looks for each occurrence of a word or phrase and automatically changes the text to another word or phrase that you specify. Use Replace to make a global change throughout the document, such as changing a person's name in a will or legal contract.

1 With the **SocialMediaProject-YourName** document open, click at the top left of the document to position the insertion point at the beginning of the title text.

2 Click the Home tab.

3 Click the Find button in the Editing group. Do *not* click the down-pointing arrow on the button.

This opens the Navigation pane at the left side of the Word document window.

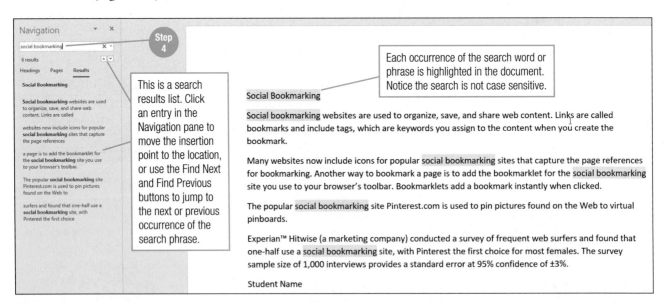

4 Type social bookmarking in the search text box.

When you finish typing, Word highlights in the document all the occurrences of the search word or phrase and displays the search results below the search text box. The total number of occurrences appears at the top of the *Results* list. Each entry in the search results list is a link that moves to the search word location in the document when clicked (Figure 6.3).

Figure 6.3
Search results for *social bookmarking* are highlighted in the **SocialMediaProject-YourName** document.

5 Click each entry one at a time in the *Results* list in the Navigation pane.

Notice that each occurrence of the search word is selected as you move to the phrase location.

Watch & Learn

Hands On Activity

● ─ ─ ─ ─ ─ ─ ─ SKILLS

Use Find Command

Use Replace Command

Tutorials

Finding Text

Navigating Using the Navigation Pane

● ─ ─ ─ ─ ─ app tip

You can find text using a partial word search. For example, enter *exp* to find *Experian*, *expert*, and *experience*.

⑥ Click the Close button at the top right of the Navigation pane to close the pane.

⑦ Press Ctrl + Home to position the insertion point at the beginning of the document.

Find and Replace searches begin from the location of the insertion point in the document. Move the insertion point when necessary before a Replace command.

⑧ Click the Replace button in the Editing group on the Home tab.

⑨ In the Find and Replace dialog box, with *social bookmarking* selected in the *Find what* text box, type bookmarklet.

⑩ Press Tab or click in the *Replace with* text box and then type bookmark button.

⑪ Click the Replace All button.

Use the Find Next button to have Word stop at each occurrence instead of globally replacing with Replace All. When Word stops, click the Replace button or Find Next button to move to the next occurrence.

⑫ Click OK at the message that 2 replacements were made.

⑬ Click the Close button to close the Find and Replace dialog box.

Notice that Word matches the correct case of a word when the word is replaced at the beginning of a sentence, as seen in the last sentence of the paragraph that begins with *Many websites now include*.

⑭ Save the document using the same name. Leave the document open for the next topic.

◗- - - - quick steps

Find Text
1. Position insertion point at beginning of document.
2. Click Find button.
3. Type search text.
4. Review *Results* list.

Replace Text
1. Position insertion point at beginning of document.
2. Click Replace button.
3. Type *Find what* text.
4. Press Tab or click in *Replace with* text box.
5. Type replacement text.
6. Click Replace All.
7. Click OK.
8. Click Close button.

◯ Tutorial

Finding and
Replacing Text

◗- - - - - - - Oops!

No replacements made at Step 12? Click OK and check your spelling in the *Find what* text box. Correct the text and try Replace All again. Still have 0 replacements? Cancel the Replace command and check the spelling of *bookmarklet* within your document. Correct the text in the document and repeat Steps 8 to 12.

6.4 Moving Text and Inserting Bullets and Numbering

Watch & Learn

Hands On Activity

The Cut button in the Clipboard group on the Home tab is used to move a selection of text from one location in the document to another location. Bulleted and numbered lists set apart information that is structured in short phrases or sentences. A bulleted list is text set apart from a paragraph with a list of items that are in no particular sequence. The **Bullets button** in the Paragraph group is used to create this type of list. A numbered list is used for a sequential list of tasks, items, or other text and is created using the **Numbering button** in the Paragraph group.

- - - - - - - - Skills

Move text
Create a bulleted list
Create a numbered list

1. With the **SocialMediaProject–YourName** document open, position the insertion point at the beginning of the paragraph that begins with *The popular social bookmarking site.*

2. Click the Show/Hide button in the Paragraph group on the Home tab.

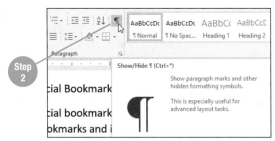

Show/Hide turns on the display of hidden formatting symbols. For example, each time you press Enter, a paragraph symbol (¶) is inserted in the document. Each time you press the spacebar, a dot is inserted (·). Revealing these symbols is helpful when you are preparing to move or copy text because you often want to make sure you move or copy the paragraph symbol with the paragraph.

3. Select the paragraph *The popular social bookmarking site Pinterest.com is used to pin pictures found on the Web to virtual pinboards.* Make sure to include the paragraph formatting symbol at the end of the text in the selection as shown in the image below.

● - - - - - - - Oops!

Forgot how to select text? Refer to Topic 3.4 in Chapter 3 for help with selecting text and objects.

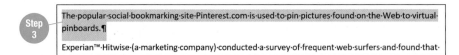

4. Click the Cut button in the Clipboard group on the Home tab.

The text is removed from the current location and placed in the Clipboard.

5. Position the insertion point at the beginning of the paragraph that begins with *Many websites now include.*

6. Click the top of the Paste button in the Clipboard group. Do *not* click the down-pointing arrow on the button.

text pasted in Step 6

Whenever you paste text with buttons in a gallery, a Paste Options button appears that can change how the text is pasted. The button disappears when you start a new task or press the Esc key.

7 Click the Show/Hide button to turn off the display of hidden formatting symbols.

8 Position the insertion point after the period that ends the sentence *The popular social networking site Pinterest.com is used to pin pictures found on the Web to virtual pinboards*, press the spacebar, type Other social bookmarking sites include:, and then press Enter.

9 Click the left part of the Bullets button in the Paragraph group. Do *not* click the down-pointing arrow on the button.

Step 9

This action indents and then inserts the default bullet character, which is a solid round bullet. To choose a different bullet symbol, click the Bullets button arrow to choose another bullet character in the Bullet Library.

10 Type Mix.com and press Enter.

11 Type Pinboard.in and press Enter.

12 Type Digg.com and press Enter.

13 Type Folkd.com.

The popular social bookmarking site Pinterest.com is used to pin pictures found on the Web to virtual pinboards. Other social bookmarking sites include:

Steps 10-13

- Mix.com
- Pinboard.in
- Digg.com
- Folkd.com

14 Position the insertion point after the period that ends the sentence *Bookmark buttons add a bookmark instantly when clicked*, press the spacebar, type To add a bookmark button:, and then press Enter.

15 Click the left part of the Numbering button in the Paragraph group. Do *not* click the down-pointing arrow on the button.

Step 15

This indents and inserts *1.* followed by a tab. To choose another number style, such as *1)* or *A.*, click the Numbering button arrow to choose another number option in the Numbering Library.

16 Type Display the browser's Favorites toolbar or Bookmarks bar. and then press Enter.

17 Type Right-click the bookmark button and then choose the Add to favorites option. and then press Enter.

18 Type Choose the Add button at the dialog box that appears.

Many websites now include icons for popular social bookmarking sites that capture the page references for bookmarking. Another way to bookmark a page is to add the bookmark button for the social bookmarking site you use to your browser's toolbar. Bookmark buttons add a bookmark instantly when clicked.

Steps 16-18

1. Display the browser's Favorites toolbar or Bookmarks bar.
2. Right-click the bookmark button and then choose the Add to favorites option.
3. Choose the Add button at the dialog box that appears.

19 Save the document using the same name. Leave the document open for the next topic.

quick steps

Move Text
1. Select text.
2. Click Cut button.
3. Position insertion point.
4. Click Paste button.

Create a Bulleted List
1. Click Bullets button.
2. Type first list item.
3. Press Enter.
4. Type second list item.
5. Press Enter.
6. Continue typing until finished.

Create a Numbered List
1. Click Numbering button.
2. Type first numbered item.
3. Press Enter.
4. Type second numbered item.
5. Press Enter.
6. Continue typing until finished.

Tutorials

Creating Bulleted Lists

Creating Numbered Lists

6.5 Formatting Text with Font and Paragraph Alignment Options

Changing the appearance of text is called **formatting**. Changing the appearance of characters is called **character formatting**. Changing the appearance of a paragraph is called **paragraph formatting**. Some people format text as they type the document by changing the character or paragraph format option before typing the text. Depending on the format option in use, you may have to turn off the option after typing text, or change to another format option. For example, if you want to apply bold to text as you type, turn on the bold feature, type the text, and then turn off the bold feature. Other people type the document text first and then apply formatting options. For many formatting options, the first step in formatting text that has already been typed is to select the characters or paragraphs to be changed.

Applying Character Formatting

The Font group on the Home tab contains buttons to change character formatting. A **font** includes the design and shape of the letters, numbers, and special characters of a particular typeface. A large collection of fonts is available, from simple to artistic character design. The font size is set in points, with one point equal to approximately 1/72 of an inch in height. The default font in a new document is 11-point Calibri.

The Font group includes buttons to increase or decrease the font size; change the case; change the font style (bold, italic, or underline) or font color; highlight text; add the effects strikethrough, subscript, or superscript; or add an artistic look using the Text Effects and Typography button (outline, shadow, glow, and reflection accents).

1. With the **SocialMediaProject-YourName** document open, select the title text, *Social Bookmarking*.

2. Click the *Font* option box arrow on the Mini toolbar.

3. Scroll down and then click *Century Gothic*.

4. With the title text still selected, click twice the Increase Font Size button on the Mini toolbar or in the Font group on the Home tab.

The first time you increase the font size, the size changes to 12 points. The second time, the size changes to 14 points and continues to increase 2 point sizes each time until you reach 28. After 28 points, the size changes to 36, 48, and then 72.

5. With the title text still selected, click the Bold button on the Mini toolbar or in the Font group on the Home tab.

6. With the title text still selected, click the Font Color button (*not* the Font Color button arrow) on the Mini toolbar or in the Font group.

The default Font Color is Red.

Watch & Learn

Hands On Activity

— — — — — — — **Skills**

Change font and font options

Change paragraph alignment

●— — — — — — **app tip**

Click the Font group dialog box launcher to open the Font dialog box for text effects options not available on the ribbon, such as double strikethrough and small caps.

●— — — — — — **Oops!**

Mini toolbar disappeared? This happens when you move the mouse pointer away from the toolbar after selecting text. Use the buttons on the ribbon to format the text.

Tutorial

Applying Font Formatting Using the Font Group

7 Click in the document away from the selected title to deselect the text.

Applying Paragraph Formatting

The Paragraph group on the Home tab contains the buttons used to change paragraph formatting. The bottom row of buttons in the group contains the buttons for changing the alignment of paragraphs from the default **Align Left** to **Center**, **Align Right**, or **Justify**. Justified text adds space within a line so that the text is distributed evenly between the left and right margins. You will explore other buttons in the Paragraph group in the next topic.

8 Click to place the insertion point anywhere within the title text *Social Bookmarking*.

To format a single paragraph, you do not need to select the paragraph text, because paragraph formatting applies to all text within the paragraph to the point where the Enter key was pressed.

9 Click the Center button in the Paragraph group.

10 Click to place the insertion point anywhere within the first paragraph of text and then click the Justify button in the Paragraph group.

Justified text spreads the lines out so that the text ends evenly at the right margin.

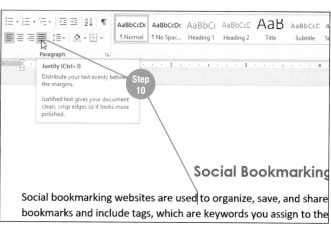

11 With the insertion point still positioned in the first paragraph, click the Align Left button in the Paragraph group.

To change the paragraph alignment for more than one paragraph in a continuous sequence, select the paragraphs first and then click the desired alignment option on the ribbon.

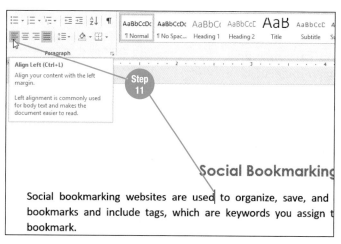

12 Save the document using the same name. Leave the document open for the next topic.

quick steps

Change Font
1. Select text.
2. Click *Font* option box arrow.
3. Scroll down to desired font.
4. Click font option.

Increase Font Size
1. Select text.
2. Click Increase Font Size button.

Change Font Color to Red
1. Select text.
2. Click Font Color button.

Change Paragraph Alignment
1. Click in paragraph.
2. Click Align Left, Center, Align Right, or Justify button.

Tutorial

Changing Paragraph Alignment

6.6 Indenting Text and Changing Line and Paragraph Spacing

Paragraphs are indented to set the paragraph apart from the rest of the document. In reports, essays, or research papers, long quotes are indented. A paragraph can be indented for the first line only or for all lines in the paragraph. Paragraphs can also be indented from the right margin. A paragraph where the first line remains at the left margin but subsequent lines are indented is called a **hanging indent**. Hanging indents are used in bulleted lists, numbered lists, bibliographies, and lists of cited works.

Use the **Line and Paragraph Spacing button** in the Paragraph group on the Home tab to change the spacing between lines of text within a paragraph and to change the spacing before and after paragraphs.

1 With the **SocialMediaProject-YourName** document open, position the insertion point at the left margin of the first paragraph (begins with the text *Social bookmarking websites*).

2 Press the Tab key.

Pressing the Tab key indents the first line of a paragraph 0.5 inch and is referred to as a *first line indent*. The AutoCorrect Options button also appears. Use the button when it appears to change the first line indent back to a Tab, to stop setting indents when you press Tab, or to change other AutoFormat options.

3 Position the insertion point anywhere within the second paragraph (begins with the text *The popular*).

4 Click the Increase Indent button in the Paragraph group on the Home tab.

The **Increase Indent button** indents all lines of a paragraph 0.5 inch. Click the button more than once if you want to move the paragraph farther away from the margin. Each time the button is clicked, the paragraph is indented another 0.5 inch.

5 With the insertion point still positioned in the second paragraph, click the Decrease Indent button in the Paragraph group.

Decrease Indent button moves the paragraph back toward the left margin. When a paragraph has been indented more than one position, clicking the Decrease Indent button moves the paragraph back towards the left margin 0.5 inch each time the button is clicked.

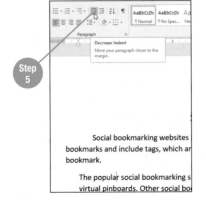

6 Position the insertion point anywhere within the third paragraph (begins with the text *Many websites now include*).

7 Click the Line and Paragraph Spacing button in the Paragraph group and then click *Line Spacing Options*.

8 Select the current entry in the *Left* text box and then type 0.5.

9 Select the current entry in the *Right* text box and then type 0.5.

10 Click OK.

The paragraph is indented from both margins by 0.5 inch.

11 With the insertion point still positioned in the paragraph that begins with the text *Many websites*, click the Line and Paragraph Spacing button and then click *Line Spacing Options*.

12 Change the entry in the *Left* and the *Right* text boxes to *0*.

13 Click the *Special* option box arrow and then click *First line*.

14 Click OK.

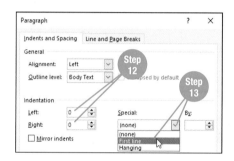

15 Format the second paragraph, which begins with the text *The popular*, and the last paragraph, which begins with the text *Experian*, with a first line indent by opening the Paragraph dialog box and then changing the *Special* option to *First line*.

16 Click the Select button in the Editing group on the Home tab and then click *Select All*.

Another way to select all the text in a document is to use the keyboard shortcut Ctrl + A.

17 Click the Line and Paragraph Spacing button and then click *1.5*.

The line spacing is changed to 1.5 lines for the entire document. Notice the other line spacing options are *1.0*, *1.15*, *2.0*, *2.5*, and *3.0*.

18 With the entire document still selected, click the Line and Paragraph Spacing button and then click *Remove Space After Paragraph*.

19 Click in any text in the document to deselect the text.

20 Save the document using the same name. Leave the document open for the next topic.

quick steps

Indent a Paragraph from Both Margins
1. Position insertion point in paragraph.
2. Click Line and Paragraph Spacing button.
3. Click *Line Spacing Options*.
4. Change *Left* value.
5. Change *Right* value.
6. Click OK.

Add Space Before Paragraph or Remove Space After Paragraph
1. Position insertion point or select paragraphs.
2. Click Line and Paragraph Spacing button.
3. Click *Add Space Before Paragraph* or *Remove Space After Paragraph*.

app tip

Open the Paragraph dialog box to specify the amount of space to insert before and after a paragraph, measured in points, in the *Before* and *After* text boxes in the *Spacing* section.

Tutorials

Changing Line Spacing

Changing Spacing Before and After Paragraphs

6.7 Formatting Using Styles

 Watch & Learn

 Hands On Activity

━━━━━━ SKills

Apply styles
Change style set

A **style** is a set of predefined formatting options that can be applied to selected text or paragraphs with one step. The Styles gallery on the Home tab displays style options. You can also create your own style. Use the More button at the bottom of the scroll bar in the Styles gallery to access the options *Create a Style, Clear Formatting*, and *Apply Styles*.

Once styles have been applied to text in the document, buttons in the Document Formatting group on the Design tab change the **style set**. A style set changes the look of a document by applying a group of formatting options to the active style. Each style set has different formatting options associated with it.

1. With the **SocialMediaProject-YourName** document open, click the File tab and then click *Save As*.

2. Click the <u>More options</u> hyperlink in the current file name section in the right panel of the backstage area.

3. Click in the *File name* text box in the Save As dialog box to deselect the file name, and then click a second time to place the insertion point at the end of the word *Project* and before *-YourName*.

4. Type WithStyles.

   The file name is now **SocialMediaProjectWithStyles-YourName**.

5. Click the Save button.

6. Position the insertion point anywhere within the title text *Social Bookmarking*.

7. Click the *Title* style in the Styles gallery on the Home tab.

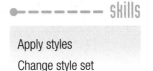 **Tutorial**

Applying Styles and Style Sets

8. Position the insertion point anywhere within the first paragraph of text below the title.

9. Click the *Quote* style option in the Styles gallery. If the *Quote* style option is not visible, click the More button () at the bottom of the scroll bar at the right of the Styles gallery and then click the *Quote* style option.

Format Using Styles
1. Select text or position insertion point.
2. Click desired style option.

Change Style Set
1. Click Design tab.
2. Click desired style set.

Step 9

Social Bookmarking

Social bookmarking websites are used to organize, save, and share web content. Links are called bookmarks and include tags, which are keywords you assign to the content when you create the bookmark.

first paragraph with *Quote* style preview

10 Select *Pinterest.com* in the second paragraph and then click the *Intense Reference* style.

11 Deselect *Pinterest.com*.

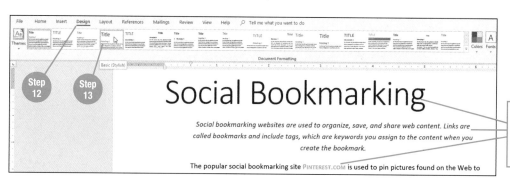

Step 10

Once styles have been applied to text, you can experiment with various style sets in the Document Formatting group on the Design tab. Changing the style set changes font and paragraph formatting options.

12 Click the Design tab.

13 Click the *Basic (Stylish)* style set in the Document Formatting gallery (fourth option from left).

Step 12   Step 13

Social Bookmarking

Social bookmarking websites are used to organize, save, and share web content. Links are called bookmarks and include tags, which are keywords you assign to the content when you create the bookmark.

The popular social bookmarking site PINTEREST.COM is used to pin pictures found on the Web to

The *Basic (Stylish)* style set causes the look of the document to change.

14 Position the insertion point anywhere within the title text *Social Bookmarking*, click the Home tab, and then click the *Heading 1* style.

The title text formats with the options for the Heading 1 style in the new style set. The formatting applied by a style is determined by the **theme**. Each theme has a color scheme and a font scheme that affect style options. You can change the theme by choosing another theme option in the Themes gallery in the Document Formatting group on the Design tab.

☁ **Tutorial**

Applying and Modifying a Theme

Step 14

Social Bookmarking

Social bookmarking websites are used to organize, save, and share web content. Links are

15 Save the document using the same name (**SocialMediaProjectWithStyles -YourName**).

16 Click the File tab and then click *Close* to close the document, leaving Word open for the next topic.

6.8 Creating a New Document from a Template

A **template** is a document that has been created with formatting options applied. Several professional-quality templates for various types of documents are available that you can use rather than creating a new document from scratch. At the Word Start screen, browse and preview available templates by category, or type a keyword for the type of document you are looking for in the search text box (contains the text *Search for online templates*) and browse the templates in the search results. The New backstage area is used to browse for a template.

1. Click the File tab and then click *New*.

2. In the New backstage area, click *Business* in the *Suggested searches* section.

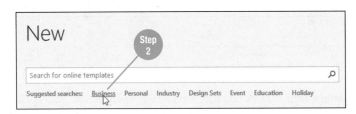

3. Scroll down and review the various types of business templates available, then click the Back button (left arrow) at the top of the New backstage area.

4. Click in the search text box, type time sheet, and then press Enter or click the Start searching icon (magnifying glass at the end of the search text box).

5. Click the *Time sheet* template in the Templates gallery that looks like the one in the image shown below.

   A preview of the template opens with a description that provides information on the template design.

6. Click the Create button.

Watch & Learn

Hands On Activity

●━━━━━━━━ skills

Create a new document from a template

Tutorial
Creating a Document Using a Template

●━━━━━━━ Oops!

Your *Time sheet* template looks different? Available templates are changed often. Look for the template closest to the one displayed. If necessary, adjust the remaining instructions to suit the available template.

7 Click *[Company Name]* and then type A+ Tutoring Advantage.

8 Click *[Street Address]* and then type 1015 Montreal Way.

9 Click *[City, ST ZIP Code]* and then type St. Paul, MN 55102.

10 Click *[phone]* and then type 888-555-3125.

11 Click *[fax]* and type 888-555-3445.

12 Click next to *Employee Name* and then type your name.

13 Complete the remainder of the time sheet document using the text shown in Figure 6.4.

quick steps

Create New Document from a Template
1. Click File tab.
2. Click *New*.
3. Browse or search for template design.
4. Click desired template.
5. Click Create button.
6. Complete document as required.

A+Tutoring Advantage
1015 Montreal Way
St. Paul, MN 55102
Phone 888-555-3125   Fax 888-555-3445

Steps 7-11

TIME SHEET

Step 12

Employee Name:	Student Name	Title:	Computer Tutor
Employee Number:	101	Status:	Part-time
Department:	Computers	Supervisor:	Dayna Summerton

Date	Start Time	End Time	Regular Hrs.	Overtime Hrs.	Total Hrs.
Oct 12	9:00 am	12:00 pm	3.0		3.0
Oct 13	1:00 pm	4:30 pm	3.5		3.5
Oct 14	7:00 pm	9:30 pm	2.5		2.5
Oct 15	10:00 am	1:00 pm	3.0		3.0
		Weekly Totals	12.0		12.0

Employee signature: _____   Date: _____

Supervisor signature: _____   Date: _____

Figure 6.4
Shown is a completed **Oct12to15TimeSheet-YourName** document.

app tip

[Company Name] is referred to as a *text placeholder.* Look for these placeholders in a template to indicate where to personalize the document. Other templates include descriptive text within the template that describes how to use the template.

14 Save the completed time sheet in the Ch6 folder in the CompletedTopics folder on your storage medium as **Oct12to15TimeSheet-YourName**. Click OK when a message displays that the document will be upgraded to the newest file format.

Microsoft Word   ?   X

Your document will be upgraded to the newest file format.

While you'll get to use all the new features in Word, some minor layout changes are possible. If you prefer not to upgrade, press cancel and check the maintain compatibility checkbox.

☐ Do not ask me again

Tell Me More...   OK   Cancel

Step 14

15 Close the document.

Topics Review

Topic	Key Concepts
6.1 Creating and Editing a New Document	A **word processing application** is software used to create documents that are composed mostly of text.
	Start a new blank document from the Word Start screen.
	Creating a new document includes typing text, editing text, and correcting errors.
	The term **wordwrap** describes Word moving text to the next line automatically when you reach the right margin.
	Double-clicking on the page in blank space and typing is referred to as **click and type**. Text is automatically aligned left, center, or right depending on the location in the line at which click and type occurs.
	As you type new text, **AutoCorrect** fixes common misspellings, and **AutoFormat** automatically converts some text to fractions, ordinals, quotes, hyphens, and hyperlinks.
	A change made to text that has already been typed is referred to as **editing** and involves inserting, deleting, and replacing characters.
	The first step in editing is to position the insertion point at the location of the change.
6.2 Inserting Symbols and Completing a Spelling and Grammar Check	Symbols or special characters, such as a copyright symbol or registered trademark, are entered using the **Symbol gallery** or Symbol dialog box.
	The **Check Document** button is used to match words in the document with words in the dictionary; words not found are flagged as potential errors. Click the Result(s) button near the top of the Editor task pane to review potential errors found.
	A word not found in the dictionary is highlighted, and suggestions for replacement appear in the Editor task pane.
	Ignore Once, Ignore All, and *Add to Dictionary* are options in the Editor task pane to respond to each potential error. Alternative words appear in the *Suggestions* section. A suggested word can be substituted for the error using the option box arrow next to the correctly spelled alternative.
6.3 Finding and Replacing Text	The **Find** command highlights all occurrences of a keyword or phrase and provides in the Navigation pane a link to each location in the document.
	Use the **Replace** command if you want Word to automatically change each occurrence of a keyword or phrase with another word or phrase.
	Word matches the case of the word when the word is replaced at the beginning of a sentence.
6.4 Moving Text and Inserting Bullets and Numbering	A bulleted list is set apart from the paragraph and is entered in no particular sequence. The **Bullets button** in the Paragraph group on the Home tab is used to type a bulleted list.
	A numbered list is a sequential series of tasks or other items that are each preceded by a number created using the **Numbering button** in the Paragraph group.
	Displaying hidden formatting symbols is helpful when moving text to make sure the paragraph symbol is selected before cutting the text. Turn on the display of hidden formatting symbols using the Show/Hide button in the Paragraph group.
	Selected text is moved by clicking the Cut button in the Clipboard group, moving the insertion point to the desired location, and then clicking the Paste button in the Clipboard group.

continued...

Topic	Key Concepts
6.5 Formatting Text with Font and Paragraph Alignment Options	Changing the appearance of text is called **formatting**. **Character formatting** involves applying changes to the appearance of characters, whereas **paragraph formatting** changes the appearance of an entire paragraph.
	A **font** is also called a *typeface* and refers to the design and shape of letters, numbers, and special characters. Change a font, font size, case, font style, and font color; highlight text; and add font effects to change character formats.
	Change a paragraph's alignment from the default **Align Left** to **Center**, **Align Right**, or **Justify** using the buttons in the Paragraph group on the Home tab.
	Justified text has extra space within a line so that the left and right margins are even.
6.6 Indenting Text and Changing Line and Paragraph Spacing	A paragraph in which all lines are indented except the first line is called a **hanging indent**.
	Change line spacing and the amount of space before and after a paragraph using options from the **Line and Paragraph Spacing button** in the Paragraph group or in the Paragraph dialog box.
	Press Tab at the beginning of a paragraph to indent only the first line or change *Special* to *First line* in the Paragraph dialog box.
	Indent all lines of a paragraph using the **Increase Indent button** or change the *Left* text box entry in the Paragraph dialog box.
	A paragraph indents 0.5 inch each time the Increase Indent button is clicked.
	Use the **Decrease Indent button** to move a paragraph closer to the left margin; the paragraph moves left 0.5 inch each time the button is clicked.
	Indent a paragraph from both margins using the *Left* and *Right* text boxes in the Paragraph dialog box.
6.7 Formatting Using Styles	Format text by applying a **style**, which is a set of predefined formatting options.
	Change the **style set** using buttons in the Document Formatting group on the Design tab. Each style set applies a different set of formatting options for the styles on the Home tab, meaning you can change the appearance of a document by changing the style set.
	A **theme** is a set of colors, fonts, and font effects that alter the appearance of a document.
6.8 Creating a New Document from a Template	A **template** is a document that is already set up with text and/or formatting options.
	Browse available templates in the Template gallery on the Word Start screen or in the New backstage area.
	Find a template by browsing the gallery by a category or by typing a keyword in the search text box.
	Click a template design to preview the template and create a new document based upon the template.
	Within a template, text placeholders or instructional text is included to help you personalize the document.

 Topics Review

Enhancing a Word Document with Special Features

Several features in Word allow you to add visual appeal, organize information, or format a document for a special purpose, such as a research paper. Word provides different views to work in, making navigating a document easy. Word integrates collaborative tools, such as comments, to help you effortlessly work on a document with multiple people. Word also provides several templates to help you build professional documents without spending a lot of time on design. For example, Word offers résumé and cover letter templates to help you build job search documents.

In this chapter, you will enhance documents already typed by inserting images, adding borders and shading to text, and inserting a text box. You will add text to an existing document in a column-and-row format by inserting a table. To finalize an academic research paper, you will learn to format an essay according to the MLA style guide, insert citations, and create a Works Cited page. Lastly, you will create a résumé and cover letter using templates.

Throughout the step-by-step instructions, you will notice prompts to save the document you're working on. These prompts are simply reminders. You are encouraged to save more frequently to avoid losing your work.

Learning Objectives

7.1 Insert, edit, and label images in a document

7.2 Add borders and shading to text and insert a text box in a document

7.3 Insert a table in a document

7.4 Format and modify a table

7.5 Change layout options

7.6 Add text and page numbers in a header for a research paper

7.7 Insert and edit citations in a research paper

7.8 Create a Works Cited page for a research paper and display a document in different views

7.9 Insert and reply to comments in a document

7.10 Create a résumé and cover letter from templates

Read & Learn

Content Online

The online course includes additional training and assessment resources.

7.1 Inserting, Editing, and Labeling Images in a Document

Watch & Learn

Hands On Activity

Adding a graphic element, such as an image, not only adds visual appeal to a document but can also help a reader understand content. You can insert an image from a web resource using the **Online Pictures button** in the Illustrations group on the Insert tab. Once an image has been inserted, you can change the way text wraps around the sides of the image using the **Layout Options button** that appears. Resize the image with the selection handles or drag the image to move it to another location in the document. Use buttons on the contextual Picture Tools Format tab to edit the image.

━━━━━━━ skills

Insert an image from a web resource

Insert an image from a file on your computer

Edit an image

Insert a caption

Inserting an Image from an Online Source

You can search for and insert an image from the web using the search text box in the Online Pictures dialog box. By default, Bing search results apply a copyright filter displaying images tagged with a Creative Commons license. This means that to use the image in a document, you need to provide attribution (credit to the image author). Word provides a hyperlink to the source website of an image inserted from the Online Pictures dialog box.

1   Start Word and open **InsulaSummary** from the Ch7 folder in StudentDataFiles. If necessary, click the Enable Editing button to close Protected view.

2   Click the File tab and then click *Save As*. Navigate to the CompletedTopics folder on your storage medium and create a new folder, *Ch7*. Double-click *Ch7*, click twice in the *File name* text box after the *y* in *InsulaSummary* and before the period, type - followed by your name, and then click the Save button. The file name is now **InsulaSummary-YourName.docx**.

3   Click to place the insertion point at the beginning of the first paragraph.

4   Click the Insert tab and then click the Online Pictures button in the Illustrations group.

5   With the insertion point positioned in the search text box, type brain and then press Enter.

━━━━━━ app tip

The Online Video button in the Media group on the Insert tab is used to add videos to a Word document.

Step 4

Step 5

Images are updated often. Your screen may display different imagery.

Images you have stored on OneDrive can be seen by clicking the OneDrive button.

6   If necessary, scroll down the search results list to the checked image shown in the Step 6 illustration, click to select the image, and then click the Insert button. If you cannot locate the image shown, close the Online Pictures dialog box and then insert the image using the Pictures button in the Illustrations group (see Steps 13 to 14). Use the image **Brain.jpg** in the Ch7 folder in StudentDataFiles.

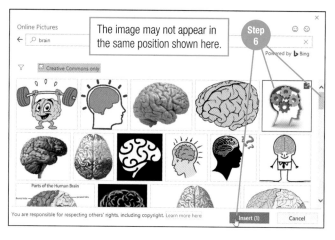

7   Click the Layout Options button located at the upper right of the inserted image.

8   Click *Square*, the first option in the *With Text Wrapping* section in the Layout Options gallery, and then click the Close button.

The Layout Options gallery allows you to control how text wraps around the image and to control whether the image should remain fixed at its current position or move with the text. Notice also that the Picture Tools Format tab becomes active when an image is selected. You will work with buttons on this tab later in this topic.

9   If necessary, scroll down to see the selection handles along the bottom of the image. Drag the bottom right corner selection handle on the image up and left until the image is resized to the approximate size shown in the Step 9 illustration. (You do not need to match the size exactly.)

10   Move the mouse pointer anywhere over the image and then drag the image right until the right edge of the image is aligned at the right margin. Use the green alignment guides to help you position the image as shown in the Step 10 illustration.

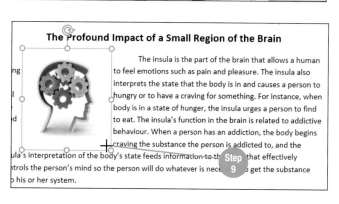

When the mouse pointer is positioned over an image, the pointer displays with a four-headed arrow attached. The four-headed arrow indicates a move command will occur when you drag the mouse.

Use the green alignment guides to help you place the image.

11   Save the revised document using the same name (**InsulaSummary-Your Name**).

Inserting an Image from a File

Images you have scanned or imported from a digital camera to a storage device, or other images you have saved on any storage medium, can be inserted into a document using the **Pictures button** in the Illustrations group. The Layout Options button also appears for an image inserted from a file.

12. Click to place the insertion point at the beginning of the second paragraph.

13. Click the Insert tab and then click the Pictures button in the Illustrations group.

14. Navigate to the Ch7 folder in the StudentDataFiles folder on your storage medium and then double-click *CampusBldg.jpg*.

15. Click the Layout Options button, click *Square*, and then close the Layout Options gallery.

16. Resize the image to the approximate size shown in the Step 16 illustration below and align the photo at the left margin.

Tutorial

Inserting, Sizing, and Positioning an Image

app tip

Create your own images by drawing Shapes, creating SmartArt or WordArt, or adding a chart or screenshot. Explore these features if you want to add a graphic but do not have an image available.

Editing a Picture

Buttons on the Picture Tools Format tab are used to edit an image. Use buttons in the Adjust group to modify the appearance of an image, such as the sharpness, contrast, or color tone, or to apply an artistic effect. Add a border or image effect with options in the Picture Styles group. Change the image position, text wrapping option, order, alignment, or rotation with buttons in the Arrange group. Crop or specify exact measurements for the image height and width with buttons in the Size group.

17. Click to select the image at the right margin in the first paragraph.

18. Click *Drop Shadow Rectangle* (fourth option) in the Picture Styles group on the Picture Tools Format tab.

app tip

The Alt Text button in the Accessibility group on the Picture Tools Format tab opens the Alt Text pane. In this pane, you can type a description of the image for a visually impaired person who is using a screen reader to read the document.

Tutorial

Formatting an Image

19. Click to select the image at the left margin in the second paragraph.

20. Click the Corrections button in the Adjust group and then click *Sharpen: 50%* (last option) in the *Sharpen/Soften* section.

Notice details in the image are more pronounced. The Corrections gallery contains two options to show more softness and two options to show more sharpness in the image. Use the thumbnails in the *Brightness/Contrast* section to show more or less brightness or contrast.

Inserting a Caption with an Image

Adding a caption below an image helps a reader understand the context of the image, or captions can serve as figure numbers to chronologically order images; e.g. in a formal report. With the **Insert Caption** feature, Word automatically numbers images, inserting the number after the label *Figure*.

21. With the image in the second paragraph still selected, click the References tab.

22. Click the Insert Caption button in the Captions group.

23. With the insertion point positioned in the *Caption* text box, press the spacebar and then type Insula research is done at many universities.

24. Press Enter or click OK.

25. Click in the document away from the caption box to deselect the caption.

Use the Caption feature in a formal report, such as a research paper with several illustrations, to automatically generate a Table of Figures from the caption text added to graphical objects. You can learn how to generate a Table of Figures using the Tell Me feature or Help task pane (see Chapter 3, Topic 3.6).

26. Save the revised document using the same name (**InsulaSummary -YourName**). Leave the document open for the next topic.

quick steps

Insert Online Image
1. Position insertion point.
2. Click Insert tab.
3. Click Online Pictures button.
4. Type search word or phrase.
5. Click desired image.
6. Click Insert.

Insert Image from a File
1. Position insertion point.
2. Click Insert tab.
3. Click Pictures button.
4. Navigate to drive and folder.
5. Double-click desired image.

Edit an Image
1. Select image.
2. Change layout options, resize, move, or otherwise edit image using buttons on the Picture Tools Format tab.

Insert a Caption
1. Select image.
2. Click References tab.
3. Click Insert Caption button.
4. Type caption text.
5. Click OK.

 Tutorial

Creating and Customizing Captions

7.3 Inserting a Table

A table organizes and presents data in columns and rows. Text is typed within a **table cell**, which is a rectangular box that is the intersection of a column with a row. When you create a table, you specify the number of columns and rows the table will hold, and Word creates a blank grid into which you type the table text. Text that you want to place side by side in columns, or in rows, is ideal for a table. For example, a price list or a catalog with items, descriptions, and prices is best typed in a three-column table.

You can also create a table using the Quick Tables feature. A **Quick Table** is a predefined and formatted table with sample data that you can replace with your own text.

1. Open the document **RezMealPlans** from the Ch7 folder in StudentDataFiles. If necessary, click the Enable Editing button to close Protected view.

2. Save the document as **RezMealPlans-YourName** in the Ch7 folder in CompletedTopics.

3. Click to place the insertion point at the left margin in the blank line below the subheading *Meal Plans with Descriptions.*

4. Click the Insert tab and then click the Table button in the Tables group.

5. Click the square in the grid that is three columns to the right and two rows down (*3x2 Table* displays above grid).

6. With the insertion point positioned in the first table cell, type Meal Plan Name and then press Tab or click in the next table cell.

7. Type Cost and then press Tab or click in the next table cell.

8. Type Description and then press Tab or click in the first table cell in the second row.

9. Type the second row of data as specified below. When you finish typing the text in the last column, press Tab to add a new row to the table automatically.

    Minimum $2,000   Suitable for students with small appetites who plan to be away from residence most weekends.

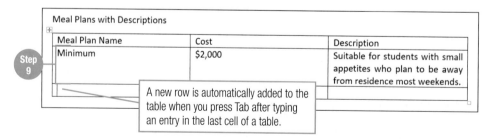

A new row is automatically added to the table when you press Tab after typing an entry in the last cell of a table.

10. Type the remainder of the table (starting with column 1, "Light") as shown in Figure 7.1 on the next page by completing steps similar to those in Steps 6 to 9, except do not press Tab after typing the last table cell entry.

Watch & Learn

Hands On Activity

Skills

Insert a table

Type text in a new table grid

Tutorial

Creating a Table

---

app tip

The advantage to using a table versus typing information in tabbed columns is that information can wrap within a table cell.

Meal Plans with Descriptions

Meal Plan Name	Cost	Description
Minimum	$2,000	Suitable for students with small appetites who plan to be away from residence most weekends.
Light	$2,200	Best plan for students with a lighter appetite who spend occasional weekends on campus.
Full	$2,400	Full is the most popular plan. This plan is for students with an average appetite who will stay on campus most weekends.
Plus	$2,600	Students with a hearty appetite who will stay on campus most weekends choose the Plus plan.

Figure 7.1

Text for the first table in the **RezMealPlans-YourName** document is shown.

⑪ Click to place the insertion point at the left margin in the blank line below the subheading *Meal Plan Fund Allocations*.

⑫ Click the Insert tab, click the Table button, and then click *Insert Table*.

You can also insert a new table using a dialog box in which you specify the number of columns and rows.

⑬ With the value in the *Number of columns* text box already set to *5*, press Tab or select the value in the *Number of rows* text box, type 5, and then press Enter or click OK.

⑭ Type the text in the new table as shown in Figure 7.2. Click in the paragraph below the table after typing the text in the last table cell.

⑮ Save the document using the same name (**RezMealPlans-YourName**). Leave the document open for the next topic.

Step 12

Step 13

quick steps

Insert a Table
1. Click Insert tab.
2. Click Table button.
3. Click square in drop-down grid that represents the desired number of columns and rows.
4. Type table text.
OR
1. Click Insert tab.
2. Click Table button.
3. Click *Insert Table*.
4. Type number of columns.
5. Type number of rows.
6. Click OK.
7. Type table text.

Click outside the table grid after typing the last table cell entry to avoid adding a new row to the table.

Meal Plan Fund Allocations

Meal Plan Name	Total Cost	Operating Fund	Basic Fund	Flex Fund
Minimum	$2,000	$200	$1,575	$225
Light	$2,200	$200	$1,725	$275
Full	$2,400	$200	$1,775	$425
Plus	$2,600	$200	$1,850	$550

Note that the Basic fund is tax exempt and is designed for use at all on-campus restaurants. Flex fund purchases are taxable.

Figure 7.2

Text for the second table in the **RezMealPlans-YourName** document is shown.

7.4 Formatting and Modifying a Table

Once a table has been created, use buttons on the Table Tools Design and Table Tools Layout tabs to format the table and to add or delete rows and columns. Choose from a predesigned collection of formatting options to add borders, shading, and color to a table from the **Table Styles** gallery.

1. With the **RezMealPlans-YourName** document open, click to place the insertion point in any table cell within the first table.

2. Click the Table Tools Design tab.

3. Click the More button located at the bottom of the scroll bar in the Table Styles gallery.

4. Click *Grid Table 4 – Accent 2* (tenth option in second row of *Grid Tables* section; the option's location may vary depending on your screen size and resolution setting).

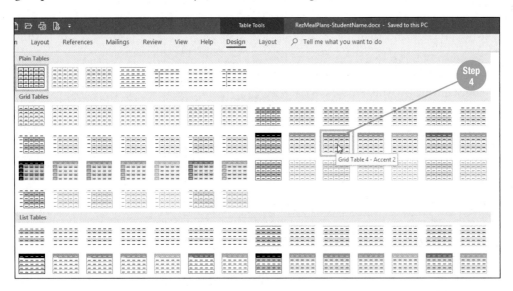

Notice the formatting applied to the column headings and text in the first column. A row with shading and other formatting applied uniformly to every other row to make the data easier to read is referred to as a **banded row**. The border around each cell is now colored orange. The check boxes in the Table Style Options group, the Shading button in the Table Styles group, and the buttons in the Borders group are used to further modify the table formatting.

5. Click the *First Column* check box in the Table Style Options group to clear the check mark.

Notice the bold formatting is removed from the text in the first column.

☁ **Watch & Learn**

☁ **Hands On Activity**

●━━━━━━ **skills**

Apply and customize a table style

Insert and delete rows and columns

Change column width

Change cell alignment

Merge cells

●━━━━ **quick steps**

Format a Table
1. Position insertion point within table cell.
2. If necessary, click Table Tools Design tab.
3. Click desired Table Style option.
4. Customize Table Style Options, Shading, or Borders as desired.

Insert Columns or Rows
1. Position insertion point in desired table cell.
2. If necessary, click Table Tools Layout tab.
3. Click Insert Above, Insert Below, Insert Left, or Insert Right button.

Delete Columns or Rows
1. Position insertion point in desired table cell.
2. If necessary, click Table Tools Layout tab.
3. Click Delete button.
4. Click *Delete Cells, Delete Columns, Delete Rows,* or *Delete Table.*

☁ **Tutorial**

Changing the Table Design

⑥ Select the column headings in the first row of the table, click the Shading button arrow on the Mini toolbar or in the Table Styles group, and then click *Orange, Accent 2, Darker 50%* (sixth option in last row of *Theme Colors* section).

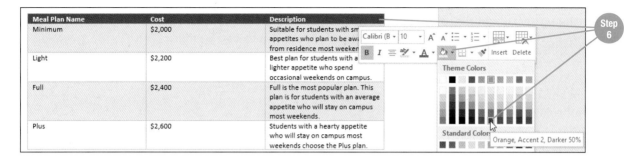

Inserting and Deleting Columns and Rows

Buttons in the Rows & Columns group on the Table Tools Layout tab are used to insert or delete columns or rows. Position the insertion point within a table row and click the Insert Above or Insert Below button to add a new row to the table. The Insert Left and Insert Right buttons are used to add a new column to the table.

Position the insertion point within a table cell, select multiple rows or columns or select the entire table, and then click the Delete button to delete cells, a column, a row, or the entire table.

⑦ Click to place the insertion point within any table cell in the third row of the first table (begins with *Light*).

⑧ Click the Table Tools Layout tab.

⑨ Click the Delete button in the Rows & Columns group.

⑩ Click *Delete Rows*.

⑪ Click to place the insertion point within any table cell in the third row of the second table (begins with *Light*), click the Delete button, and then click *Delete Rows*.

⑫ Click to place the insertion point within any table cell in the last column of the first table.

⑬ Click the Insert Left button in the Rows & Columns group.

A new column is created between the *Cost* and *Description* columns. Notice that Word adjusts each column width. New rows are inserted by following a similar process.

⑭ Click to place the insertion point within the table cell in the first row of the new column (between *Cost* and *Description*) and then type Daily Spending.

⑮ Type the values below the column heading in rows 2, 3, and 4 as follows:

$18.35

$22.00

$23.85

Modifying Column Width and Alignment and Merging Cells

Adjust the width of a column by dragging the border line between columns left or right. You can also enter precise width measurements in the *Width* text box in the Cell Size group on the Table Tools Layout tab. Use the buttons in the Alignment group to align text within cells horizontally and/or vertically. Combine two or more cells into one cell using the Merge Cells button, or divide a cell into two or more cells using the Split Cells button in the Merge group.

● **Tutorial**

Changing the Table Layout

16 Click to place the insertion point within any table cell in the second column of the first table (column heading is *Cost*).

17 Click the *Table Column Width* option box down arrow in the Cell Size group until the value is *1"*.

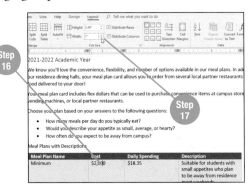

18 Click to place the insertion point within any table cell in the last column of the first table (column heading is *Description*) and then click the *Table Column Width* option box up arrow until the value is *2.3"*.

19 With the insertion point still positioned within the last column of the first table, click the Select button in the Table group and then click *Select Column*.

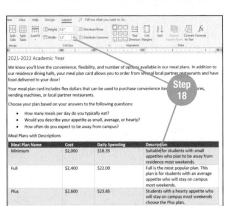

20 Click the Align Top Center button in the Alignment group (second button).

21 Select the first column in the first table (column heading is *Meal Plan Name*) and then click the Align Center button in the Alignment group (second button in second row).

22 Repeat Step 21 to Align Center the second and third columns in the first table.

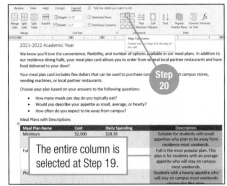

The entire column is selected at Step 19.

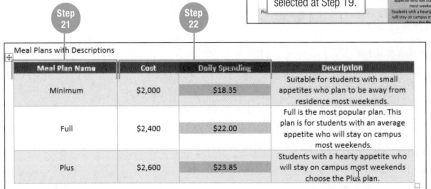

23 Click to place the insertion point within any table cell in the first row of the second table and then click the Insert Above button in the Rows & Columns group.

24 With the new row already selected, click the Merge Cells button in the Merge group.

25 With the new row still selected, type Breakdown of Meal Plan Cost by Fund and then click the Align Top Center button in the Alignment group.

quick steps

Modify Column Width
1. Position insertion point within table cell in desired column.
2. If necessary, click Table Tools Layout tab.
3. Change *Width* measurement value to desired width.

Modify Cell Alignment
1. Select column, row, or table cells.
2. If necessary, click Table Tools Layout tab.
3. Click desired button in Alignment group.

Merge or Split Cells
1. Select column, row, or table cells.
2. If necessary, click Table Tools Layout tab.
3. Click Merge Cells or Split Cells button.

Meal Plan Fund Allocations

Breakdown of Meal Plan Cost by Fund				
Meal Plan Name	Total Cost	Operating Fund	Basic Fund	Flex Fund

Step 25

26 Point in the second table at the beginning of the text *Total Cost* (second column, second row) until the pointer displays as a black diagonal arrow (➚), then drag the mouse right and down to select the column headings and all the values in columns 2, 3, 4, and 5. Click the Align Center button.

You cannot use the Select Column option from the Select button to select the columns, because this option includes the first merged row.

27 Click to place the insertion point within any table cell in the second table, click the Select button and then click *Select Table*.

You can also select a table by clicking the Table selection handle at the upper left of the table.

28 Click the Table Tools Design tab.

29 Click the Borders button arrow in the Borders group and then click *No Border*.

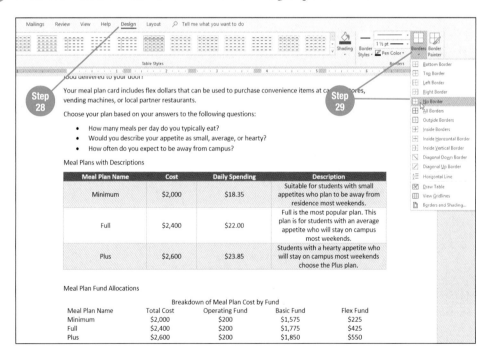

app tip

Create a table for any type of columnar text instead of setting tabs. Tables are simpler to create and have several formatting options.

30 Click in the paragraph below the table to deselect the table.

31 Apply the Heading 2 style to the headings *Meal Plans with Descriptions* and *Meal Plan Fund Allocations* above the first and second tables.

32 Save the document using the same name (**RezMealPlans-YourName**) and then close the document.

 Tutorial

Customizing Cells in a Table

7.5 Changing Layout Options

By default, new documents in Word are set up for a letter-size page (8.5 × 11 inches) in portrait orientation with 1-inch margins at the left, right, top, and bottom. When the page is vertical (taller than it is wide) it is in **portrait** orientation. In portrait orientation, a page has a standard 6.5-inch line length (8.5 inches minus 2 inches for the left and right margins). This is the orientation commonly used for documents and books. You can change to **landscape** orientation (the page is rotated to make it wider than it is tall). In landscape orientation, the text has a 9-inch line length (11 inches minus 2 inches for the left and right margins).

The Page Setup group on the Layout tab contains buttons to change the margins and page orientation. A Size button allows you to change to a legal size page (8.5 × 14 inches), another predefined page size, or set a custom page width and height. The Columns button formats a document into two or more newspaper-style columns.

1. Open the document **ChildLitBookRpt** from the Ch7 folder in StudentDataFiles. If necessary, click the Enable Editing button to close Protected view.

2. Save the document as **ChildLitBookRpt-YourName** in the Ch7 folder in CompletedTopics.

3. Click the Layout tab.

4. Click the Orientation button in the Page Setup group and then click *Landscape*.

Notice the width of the page is extended, and the page is now wider than it is tall.

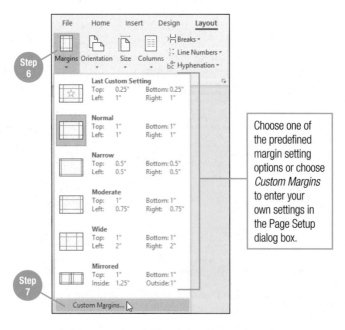

5. Scroll down to view the document in landscape orientation.

6. With the insertion point positioned at the top of the document, click the Margins button in the Page Setup group.

7. Click *Custom Margins*.

Watch & Learn

Hands On Activity

-------- skills

Change page orientation
Change margins
Insert a page break

Tutorials

Changing Page Orientation

Changing Margins

8 With the insertion point positioned in the *Top* text box in the *Margins* section in the Page Setup dialog box, press Tab twice or select the current value in the *Left* text box, and then type 1.2.

9 Press Tab or select the current value in the *Right* text box, type 1.2, and then press Enter or click OK.

10 Scroll down to view the document with the new left and right margin settings.

Sometimes you want to end a page before the point at which Word automatically ends a page and starts a new page (referred to as a **soft page break**). Soft page breaks occur when the maximum number of lines that can fit within the current page size and margins has been reached. A page break that you insert at a different location is called a **hard page break**. Insert hard page breaks as your last step in preparing a document, because hard page breaks do not adjust if you add or delete text.

11 Click to place the insertion point at the left margin next to the subtitle *The Allegories* near the bottom of page 1.

12 Click the Insert tab.

13 Click the Page Break button in the Pages group.

Notice that all the text from the insertion point onward is moved to page 2.

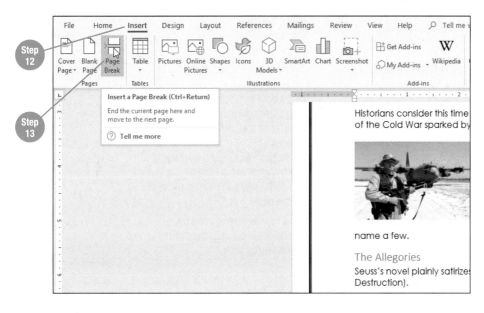

14 Scroll up and down to view the book report with the new page break.

15 Save the document using the same name (**ChildLitBookRpt-YourName**).

16 Close the document.

quick steps

Change to Landscape Orientation
1. Click Layout tab.
2. Click Orientation button.
3. Click *Landscape*.

Change Margins
1. Click Layout tab.
2. Click Margins button.
3. Click predefined margin option.
OR
1. Click Layout tab.
2. Click Margins button.
3. Click *Custom Margins*.
4. Enter custom measurements.
5. Click OK.

Insert a Hard Page Break
1. Position insertion point.
2. Click Insert tab.
3. Click Page Break button.

app tip

To delete a page break, position the insertion point after the last character on the page where the break occurs and then press the Delete key.

Tutorial
Inserting and Removing a Page Break

7.6 Adding Text and Page Numbers in a Header for a Research Paper

During the course of your education, chances are you will have to submit a research paper or essay that is formatted for a specific **style guide** (a set of rules for paper formatting and referencing). Style guides are used in academic and professional writing; MLA (Modern Language Association) and APA (American Psychological Association) are two organizations that publish widely used guides. See Table 7.1 for general MLA and APA guidelines. Always check an instructor's assignment instructions for additional requirements that may be unique to the guidelines set forth in Table 7.1.

Table 7.1 Formatting and Page Layout Guidelines for MLA and APA

Layout Item	MLA	APA
Paper size and margins	8.5 × 11" with 1-inch margins	8.5 × 11" with 1-inch margins
Font size	12-point; typeface is not specified but should be easily readable	12-point, with Times New Roman the preferred typeface
Line and paragraph spacing	2.0 with no spacing between paragraphs	2.0 with no spacing between paragraphs
Paragraph indent	Indent first line 0.5 inch	Indent first line 0.5 inch
Page numbering	Top right of each page with one space after your last name	Top right of each page with the title of the paper all uppercase at the left margin on the same line

Title page	No (unless specifically requested by your instructor)	Yes
		Running head: title of the paper at the left margin all uppercase with page number at the right margin 1 inch from the top; in the upper half of the page centered horizontally include:
		    Title of the paper
		    Your name
		    School name

First page	Top left corner (double-spaced):
	Your name
	Instructor's name
	Course title
	Date
	A double space after date
	Title (title case), centered
	Begin the paper (left-aligned)
		Center the word *Abstract* at the top of the page.
		    Type a brief summary of the paper in a single paragraph in block format (no indents). Limit yourself to approximately 150 words.
		    Start a new page after the abstract page, center the paper title (title case) at the top of the new page, and then begin typing the paper.

Bibliography	Create a separate Works Cited page at the end of the document organized alphabetically by author.	Create a separate References page at the end of the document organized alphabetically by author.

A **header** is text that appears at the top of each page, and a **footer** is text that appears at the bottom of each page. Word provides several predefined headers and footers or you can create your own. Page numbering is added within a header or footer using the **Page Number button** in the Header & Footer group on the Header & Footer Tools Design tab.

 Watch & Learn

 Hands On Activity

● ━ ━ ━ ━ ━ ━ ━ **skills**

Add text in a header

Insert page numbers in a header in MLA style

 Tutorials

Formatting a Report in APA Style

Formatting a Report in MLA Style

● ━ ━ ━ ━ ━ **go online**

https://CA3.Paradigm Education.com/MLA Guide

Go here for a comprehensive MLA guide.

1 Open the document **China&TibetEssay** from the Ch7 folder in StudentDataFiles. If necessary, click the Enable Editing button to close Protected view.

2 Save the document as **China&TibetEssay-YourName** in the Ch7 folder in CompletedTopics.

3 Scroll down and review the formatting in the essay. Notice the paper size, font, margins, line and paragraph spacing, and first line indents are already formatted.

4 Position the insertion point at the beginning of the document and replace the text *Michael Seguin* with your first and last name.

The first four lines of this report are set up in MLA format for a first page; however, you need to add the page numbering for an MLA report.

5 Click the Insert tab and then click the Header button in the Header & Footer group.

quick steps

Insert a Header or Footer
1. Click Insert tab.
2. Click Header or Footer button.
3. Click built-in option or choose *Edit Header* or *Edit Footer*.
4. Type text and/or add options as needed.
5. Click Close Header and Footer button.

Insert Page Numbering
1. Click within Header or Footer pane at desired location.
2. Click Page Number button.
3. Point to *Current Position*.
4. Click desired page number option.
5. Click Close Header and Footer button.

Step 5

6 Click *Edit Header*.

The document text is dimmed and a Header pane appears above a dashed line. In the Header pane, you type the text that you want to appear at the top of each page and/or insert page numbering. A Header or Footer pane is divided into three sections: left, center, and right.

7 Press Tab twice to move the insertion point to the right section, type your last name, and then press the spacebar.

8 Click the Page Number button in the Header & Footer group on the Header & Footer Tools Design tab.

9 Point to *Current Position* and then click *Plain Number*.

Step 8

Step 9

10 Select your last name and the page number in the Header pane.

11 Click the *Font* option box arrow on the Mini toolbar, scroll down the font list, and then click *Times New Roman*.

12 Click the *Font Size* option box arrow on the Mini toolbar and then click *12*.

13 Click within the Header pane to deselect the text.

14 Click the Close Header and Footer button in the Close group on the Header & Footer Tools Design tab.

Tutorials

Editing a Header and Footer

Inserting and Removing Page Numbers

Creating a Different First Page Header and Footer

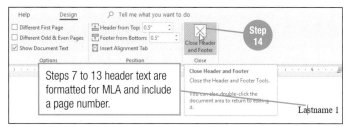

Step 14

Steps 7 to 13 header text are formatted for MLA and include a page number.

Lastname 1

15 Scroll down through the document to view the page number on each page.

16 Save the document using the same name (**China&TibetEssay-YourName**). Leave the document open for the next topic.

7.7 Inserting and Editing Citations

In an academic paper, direct quotations copied from sources or content you have paraphrased from another source need to be referenced in a **citation**. A citation tells the reader the source for the information you are quoting or paraphrasing. The first time you insert a citation for a source, add the information about the source. The next time you need to cite the same source, insert the citation by choosing the source entry in the *Insert Citation* list. To add a page number in a citation, click in the citation text and click the Citation Options arrow to open the Edit Citation dialog box.

① With the **China&TibetEssay-YourName** document open, click the References tab.

② Look at the *Style* option in the Citations & Bibliography group. If the *Style* is not *MLA*, click the *Style* option box arrow and then click *MLA*.

③ Scroll down the first page, click to place the insertion point left of the period at the end of the quotation in the first sentence in the second paragraph that begins *China currently claims . . .* and then press the spacebar.

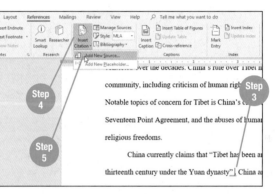

④ Click the Insert Citation button in the Citations & Bibliography group.

⑤ Click *Add New Source*.

⑥ Click the *Type of Source* option box arrow, scroll down the list box, and then click *Web site* in the Create Source dialog box.

⑦ Click in the *Author* text box and then type Bajoria, Jayshree.

⑧ Click in the *Name of Web Page* text box and then type The Question of Tibet.

⑨ Press Tab or click in the *Year* text box and then type 2008.

⑩ Continue to press Tab or click in the designated text boxes and type the information as follows:

Month	December	*Month Accessed*	November
Day	5	*Day Accessed*	15
Year Accessed	2021	*Medium*	Web

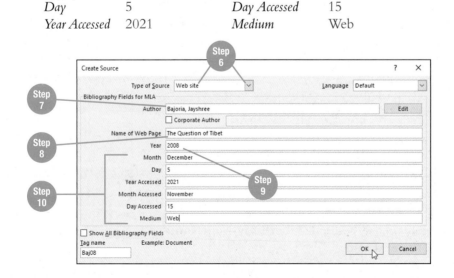

—————— **SKills**

Insert a citation

Edit a citation

●———— **in the know**

In the seventh edition of the MLA handbook, URLs are no longer required. MLA advises writers to include URLs only if a reader is unlikely to find the source without the web address.

11 Click OK. The citation is inserted using the correct formatting as per MLA style.

12 Scroll down if necessary, click to place the insertion point left of the period at the end of the quoted text in the fifth sentence in the second paragraph that begins *Not until the 18th century . . .*, press the spacebar, click the Insert Citation button, and then click *Add New Source.*

13 Click the *Type of Source* option box arrow, scroll up, and then click *Book*.

14 Enter the information in the designated text boxes in the Create Source dialog box as follows and click OK when finished.

Author	Praag, Michael C.
Title	The Historical Status of Tibet: History, Rights, and Prospects in International Law
Year	1987
City	Boulder
Publisher	Westview Press
Medium	Print

quick steps

Insert a Citation with a New Source
1. Position insertion point.
2. Click References tab.
3. Click Insert Citation button.
4. Click *Add New Source.*
5. If necessary, change *Type of Source.*
6. Enter required information.
7. Click OK.

Insert a Citation with an Existing Source
1. Position insertion point.
2. Click References tab.
3. Click Insert Citation button.
4. Click required source.

Edit a Citation
1. Position insertion point in citation text.
2. Click Citation Options arrow.
3. Click *Edit Citation.*
4. Type page or other reference.
5. Click OK.

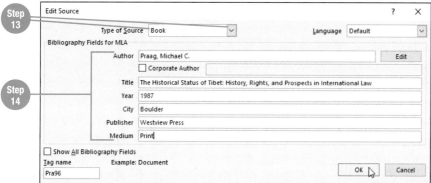

15 Click to place the insertion point in the *(Praag)* citation and then click the Citation Options arrow that appears.

16 Click *Edit Citation.*

17 Type 3 in the *Pages* text box in the Edit Citation dialog box and then press Enter or click OK.

For citations that refer to a print-based source, open the Edit Citation dialog box using the Citation Options arrow to enter the page number quoted or paraphrased.

Tutorials

Inserting Sources and Citations

Editing a Citation and Source

18 Click to place the insertion point left of the period at the end of the fourth sentence in the third paragraph on page 2, which begins *While independence was . . .* and then press the spacebar.

19 Click the Insert Citation button and then click *Bajoria, Jayshree.*

20 Save the document using the same name (**China&TibetEssay-YourName**). Leave the document open for the next topic.

7.8 Creating a Works Cited Page and Using Word Views

The **Bibliography button** in the Citations & Bibliography group on the References tab is used to generate a **Works Cited** page for MLA papers or a References page for APA papers. The MLA style guide requires a Works Cited page to be on a separate page at the end of the document and organized alphabetically by author's name, or by title when an author's name is absent.

Word provides various ways to view a document, including Read Mode view, which provides maximum screen space for reading longer documents.

1. With the **China&TibetEssay-YourName** document open, press Ctrl + End to move the insertion point to the end of the document.

2. Click the Insert tab and then click the Page Break button in the Pages group to start a new page.

3. Click the References tab.

4. Click the Bibliography button in the Citations & Bibliography group.

5. Click *Works Cited*.

Word automatically generates the Works Cited page. In the next steps, you will format the text to match the font, size, and spacing of the rest of the document.

6. If necessary, scroll up to view the Works Cited page.

7. Select all the text on the Works Cited page.

Word surrounds the text on the page with a border and displays a Bibliographies button and an Update Citations and Bibliography button at the top of the placeholder.

8. Click the Home tab and then make the following changes to the selected text:
   a. Change the font to 12-point Times New Roman.
   b. Change the line spacing to 2.0.
   c. Open the Paragraph dialog box and change *Before* and *After* in the *Spacing* section to *0 pt.*

9. Select the title text *Works Cited*, change the font color to Automatic (black), and center the title.

Watch & Learn

Hands On Activity

● — — — — — — Skills

Create a Works Cited page

Browse a document in different views

Tutorial

Inserting a Works Cited Page

● — — — — — app tip

Do not change formatting until you are sure your Works Cited page is complete, because the page will revert to predefined formats if you make changes to sources and then update the Works Cited page.

Use the Bibliographies button to change to a different bibliography style or to convert the Works Cited page to static text that can be edited.

Regenerate the Works Cited page using this button if you make a change to any of the source information.

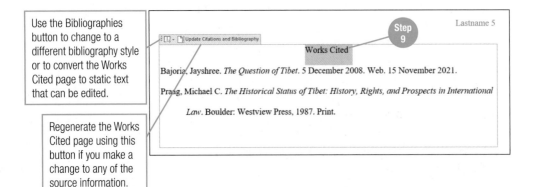

The default view for new documents is **Print Layout view**, which displays the document as it will appear when printed. **Read Mode view** displays a document full screen in columns, allowing you to read longer documents more easily without screen elements such as the Quick Access Toolbar and ribbon. **Draft view** hides print elements, such as headers and footers. **Web Layout view** displays a document as it would appear in a browser, and **Outline view** displays content as bulleted points.

10 Press Ctrl + Home to move the insertion point to the beginning of the document.

11 Click the View tab and then click the Read Mode button in the Views group.

Use Read Mode to view a document without editing.

• — — — — quick steps

Generate a Works Cited Page
1. Position insertion point at end of document.
2. Insert page break.
3. Click References tab.
4. Click Bibliography button.
5. Click *Works Cited*.
6. Format as required.

Change Document View
1. Click View tab.
2. Click desired view button.

Tutorial

Changing Document Views

12 Click the View tab, point to *Layout*, and then click *Paper Layout* to display the document as single pages. Skip this step if your screen is already displaying the document as single pages.

13 Scroll down to the end of the document to view the document in Read Mode, click the View tab, point to *Layout*, and then click *Column Layout*.

14 Click the Previous Screen button (left-pointing arrow inside circle at the middle left of the screen) to move back to the previous screen until you have returned to the beginning of the document.

15 Click the View tab and then click *Edit Document* to return to Print Layout view.

16 Click the Draft button in the Views group on the View tab and then scroll through the document to view the document without the header or margins.

17 Click the Print Layout button near the right end of the Status bar.

Read Mode and Print Layout buttons are also at the right end of the Status bar.

• — — — — — — app tip

In Print Layout view, turn on the Navigation pane (View tab, *Navigation Pane* check box in the App tip on page 167) and click *Pages* at the top of the pane to move through a document by clicking miniature page thumbnails.

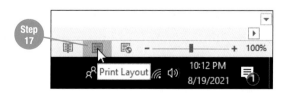

18 Save the document using the same name (**China&TibetEssay-YourName**). Leave the document open for the next topic.

7.9 Inserting and Replying to Comments

A **comment** is a short note associated with text that provides explanatory information to a reader. Comments are useful for individuals when working on a document with another person or team to give explanations, feedback, or to pose a question to other reviewers of the document. You can reply to a comment made by someone else and mark a comment resolved when a question is answered.

A comment and all replies added to a document are tagged with the user name of the comment writer and the date and the time the comment text was inserted.

1 With the **China&TibetEssay-YourName** document open, click to place the insertion point at the beginning of the first paragraph in the document.

2 Select the words *Sakya Lama* in the second sentence in the first paragraph.

3 Click the Review tab.

4 Click the New Comment button in the Comments group.

Word opens a new comment box (referred to as a *comment balloon*) in the Markup Area. The **Markup Area** is at the right side of the screen, where comments and other document changes, such as insertions and deletions, are displayed when the Track Changes feature is turned on.

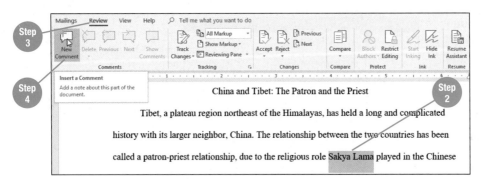

5 Type Consider adding more explanation about Sakya Lama and the Yuan dynasty and then click in the document outside the comment box.

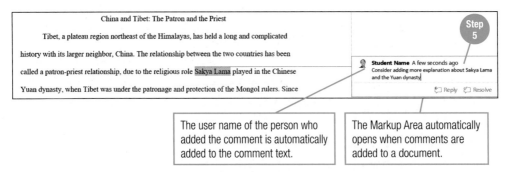

The user name of the person who added the comment is automatically added to the comment text.

The Markup Area automatically opens when comments are added to a document.

6 Select *modern historians* in the third sentence in the second paragraph.

7 Click the New Comment button.

8 Type Provide a few names of modern historians? and then click in the document.

 Watch & Learn

 Hands On Activity

------- Skills

Insert comments
Change the markup view
Reply to a comment
Resolve a comment

 Tutorial
Inserting Comments

 ------ app tip

When a document has been shared with others, the Real Time Presence feature lets you see who else is editing the document you have open and the changes each person is making in real time.

⑨ Position the insertion point at the beginning of the document.

⑩ Click the Display for Review option box arrow in the Tracking group (currently displays *All Markup* or *Simple Markup*) and then click *No Markup*.

Notice the two comments on page 1 are removed from the document display.

⑪ Click the Display for Review option box arrow and then click *Simple Markup*.

Simple Markup view displays a red line from the document text to the associated comment when you click inside a comment in the Markup Area. Other edited text displays a vertical red bar in the margin area next to insertions or deletions to highlight areas in the document where changes have been made.

⑫ Click in the first comment balloon on page 1.

Notice Word displays a red line pointing to the text for which the comment is associated. The comment box also displays a Reply option and Resolve option.

⑬ Click *Reply* in the first comment box.

⑭ Type Asked Dr. Smith and he said this is not necessary and then click in the document.

Notice the reply comment text is indented below the original comment in a conversation-style dialogue.

⑮ Scroll down if necessary, point to the second comment balloon on page 1, and then click *Reply*.

⑯ Type I'll check with Jose to see if he wants to include a few names.

⑰ Scroll up if necessary and then click *Resolve* in the first comment balloon.

⑱ Click in the document outside the comment box.

Notice the comment text is dimmed for the resolved comment. You can also delete a comment instead of marking the comment resolved.

⑲ Save the document using the same name (**China&TibetEssay-YourName**).

⑳ Close the document.

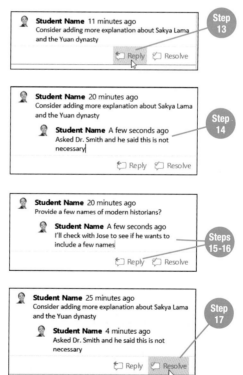

● ━ ━ ━ **quick steps**

Insert a Comment
1. Select text.
2. Click Review tab.
3. Click New Comment button.
4. Type comment text.
5. Click in document.

Reply to a Comment
1. Point to comment balloon.
2. Click *Reply*.
3. Type reply text.
4. Click in document.

Resolve a Comment
1. Point to comment balloon.
2. Click *Resolve*.

☁ **Tutorial**

Managing Comments

7.10 Creating a Résumé and Cover Letter from Templates

Word provides several professionally designed and formatted résumé and cover letter templates that take the work out of designing and formatting these two crucial documents, letting you focus your efforts on writing documents that will win you a job interview!

1. Click the File tab and then click *New*.

2. In the New backstage area, click in the search text box, type entry level resume, and then press Enter or click the Start searching icon.

3. Click the thumbnail for *Entry-level resume* in the Templates gallery.

4. Click the Create button in the preview window.

5. Double-click *YOUR NAME* in the First Page Header pane and then type Dana Jelic. Note that the text will appear all uppercase.

6. Select *Sreet Address, City, ST ZIP Code* and press Delete.

7. Select *Phone* and then type 800-555-4577.

8. Select *Email* and then type jelic@ppi-edu.net.

9. Select *Website*, press Delete, and then click the Close Header and Footer button in the Close group on the Header & Footer Tools Design tab.

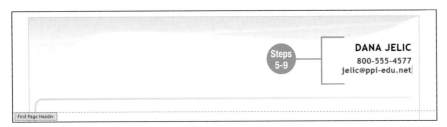

10. Type the remainder of the document by selecting text below a heading and typing text, by deleting template text, and by formatting text to match Figure 7.3.

11. Save the document as **JelicResume-YourName** in the Ch7 folder in CompletedTopics.

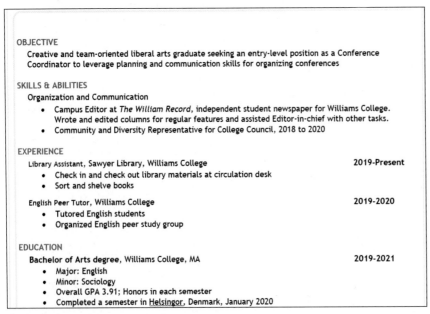

Figure 7.3

Shown is the résumé text for Topic 7.10.

Watch & Learn

Hands On Activity

------- Skills

Create a résumé

Create a cover letter

Tutorial

Changing Vertical Alignment

12 Close the résumé document and then display the New backstage area.

13 Type entry level cover letter in the search text box and then press Enter or click the Start searching icon.

14 Select and create a document using the template *Cover letter for entry-level resume.*

15 Create the letter as shown in Figure 7.4 by completing steps similar to those in Steps 5 through 10. (Note that the letter closing in the template is not shown in Figure 7.4. Use the default text in this section.)

quick steps

Create a Résumé
1. Click File tab.
2. Click *New*.
3. Type resume or other phrase in search text box and press Enter.
4. Click desired template.
5. Click Create button.
6. Edit as required.

Create a Cover Letter
1. Click File tab.
2. Click *New*.
3. Type cover letter or other search phrase in search text box and press Enter.
4. Click desired template.
5. Click Create button.
6. Edit as required.

Dana Jelic
100 Main Street
Anywhere Town, MA 01267

May 12, 2021

Ms. Patel
Conference Manager
Anywhere Town College
50 Hall Drive
Anywhere Town, MA 01267

Dear Ms. Patel:

I am writing in response to your advertisement in The Williams Record for a Conference Coordinator. After reading your job description, I am confident that my planning and organizational skills and my passion for representing Williams College are a perfect match for this position. As a graduate of Williams College, I am very familiar with the college venues and local area attractions.

I would bring to Williams College a broad range of skills, including:

• Excellent time management skills
• Ability to organize complex tasks
• Experienced communicator

I would welcome the opportunity to further discuss this position with you. If you have questions or would like to schedule an interview, please contact me by phone at 800-555-4577 or by email at jelic@ppi-edu.net. I have enclosed my resume for your review, and I look forward to hearing from you.

Figure 7.4
Use this cover letter text for Topic 7.10.

16 Click the Layout tab and then click the Page Setup dialog box launcher.

17 Click the Layout tab in the Page Setup dialog box.

18 Click the *Vertical alignment* option box arrow, click *Center*, and then click OK.

19 Save the document as **JelicCoverLetter-YourName** in the Ch7 folder in CompletedTopics and then close the document.

app tip

Vertically center a letter to make sure the letter has a professional appearance. For short letters, add extra space between letter elements to balance the content on the page.

Topics Review

Topic	Key Concepts
7.1 Inserting, Editing, and Labeling Images in a Document	Graphic elements assist with comprehension and/or add visual appeal to documents.
	Insert an image from a web resource or OneDrive using the **Online Pictures button** in the Illustrations group on the Insert tab.
	Click the **Layout Options button** to control how text wraps around the image and to change the position of the image on the page.
	Use the **Pictures button** to insert an image from a file stored on your computer or other storage medium.
	Edit the appearance of an image and/or add special effects using buttons on the Picture Tools Format tab.
	A caption is explanatory text above or below an image that is added using the **Insert Caption** feature on the References tab.
	Word automatically numbers images as Figures and can generate a Table of Figures automatically.
7.2 Adding Borders and Shading, and Inserting a Text Box	Add a border or **shading** to paragraphs to make text stand out on a page. Shading is color applied to the page behind the text.
	A page border surrounds the entire page and is added using the **Page Borders button** on the Design tab.
	Apply a border to selected text using the **Borders gallery** from the Borders button arrow in the Paragraph group on the Home tab.
	Shading is added using the Shading button arrow in the Paragraph group.
	A **pull quote** is a quote typed inside a text box.
	Insert text inside a box using the **Text Box button** in the Text group on the Insert tab.
7.3 Inserting a Table	A table is a grid of columns and rows in which you type text and is used when you want to arrange text side by side or in rows.
	A **table cell** is a rectangular-shaped box in the table grid that is the intersection of a column and a row. Text in the table is typed inside table cells.
	A **Quick Table** is a predesigned table with sample data, such as a calendar or a tabular list.
	Create a table by clicking a square in the table grid accessed from the Insert tab that represents the number of columns and rows or by entering the number of columns and rows in the Insert Table dialog box.
	Pressing Tab in the last table cell automatically adds a new row to the table.

continued…

Topic	Key Concepts
7.4 Formatting and Modifying a Table	Apply a predesigned collection of borders, shading, and color to a table using an option from the **Table Styles** gallery.
	Shading or other formatting applied to every other row to make the table data easier to read is called a **banded row**.
	Check boxes in the Table Style Options group on the Table Tools Design tab are used to customize the formatting applied from a Table Style.
	Apply shading or borders using buttons in the Table Styles group and Borders group on the Table Tools Design tab.
	New rows and columns are inserted above, below, left, or right of the active table cell using buttons in the Rows & Columns group on the Table Tools Layout tab.
	Remove selected table cells, rows, or columns or the entire table using options from the Delete button in the Rows & Columns group.
	Adjust the width of a column by changing the *Width* text box value in the Cell Size group on the Table Tools Layout tab or by dragging the column border.
	Buttons to change alignment options for selected table cells are found in the Alignment group on the Table Tools Layout tab.
	Cells in a table can be merged or split using buttons in the Merge group on the Table Tools Layout tab.
7.5 Changing Layout Options	**Portrait** orientation means the text on the page is oriented to the taller side (8.5-inch width), while **landscape** orientation rotates the text to the wider side of the page (11-inch measurement becomes the page width).
	Change the margins by choosing one of the predefined margin options or by entering measurements for the top, bottom, left, and right margins at the Page Setup dialog box.
	A **soft page break** is a page break that Word inserts automatically when the maximum number of lines that can fit on a page has been reached.
	A **hard page break** is a page break inserted by you in a different location than where the soft page break occurred.
7.6 Adding Text and Page Numbers in a Header for a Research Paper	A **style guide** is a set of rules for formatting and referencing academic papers.
	A **header** is text that appears at the top of each page, while a **footer** is text that appears at the bottom of each page.
	Page numbers are added to a document at the top or bottom of a page within a Header or Footer pane using the **Page Number button** on the Header & Footer Tools Design tab.
	Click the Insert tab and choose the Header or Footer button to create a header or footer in the Header or Footer pane.

continued...

Topic	Key Concepts
7.7 Inserting and Editing Citations	A **citation** provides a reader with the reference for information quoted or paraphrased within an academic paper.
	Check the *Style* option in the Citations & Bibliography group on the References tab for the correct style guide and change the option, if necessary, before inserting a citation or creating sources.
	Position the insertion point where a citation is needed and use the Insert Citation button on the References tab to create a reference.
	Click *Add New Source* in the *Insert Citation* list to enter information for a new reference for a citation in the Create Source dialog box.
	Click in citation text, click the Citation Options arrow that appears, and then click *Edit Citation* to add a page number to the reference.
	Add a citation for a source that has already been defined by positioning the insertion point, clicking the Insert Citation button, and then clicking the source entry in the list.
7.8 Creating a Works Cited Page and Using Word Views	A Works Cited page is a separate page at the end of the document with the references used for the paper.
	Use the **Bibliography button** in the Citations & Bibliography group on the References tab to generate a **Works Cited** page formatted for the MLA style guide.
	Print Layout view displays the document as it will appear when printed.
	Read Mode view displays a document full screen in columns or pages without editing tools.
	Draft view hides print elements, such as headers, footers, and page numbering.
	Web Layout view displays the document as a web page.
	Outline view displays content as bullet points.
7.9 Inserting and Replying to Comments	A **comment** is a short note associated with text that provides explanatory information or poses a question to a reader.
	Select text that you want to associate with a comment and type the comment text inside a comment balloon by clicking the New Comment button on the Review tab.
	Comment balloons display in the **Markup Area**, which is a pane that opens at the right side of the document when comments are added.
	A document with comments can be displayed with *No Markup*, *Simple Markup*, or *All Markup* view, which refers to the way comment boxes and other editing changes are displayed.
	Point at a comment balloon and use the *Reply* option to enter reply text that responds to a comment.
	Mark a comment as complete to retain the comment text but display the comment dimmed in the Markup Area by pointing at the comment balloon and clicking the *Resolve* option.
7.10 Creating a Résumé and Cover Letter from Templates	In the New backstage area, search for a résumé template and a cover letter template in various styles, themes, and purposes.
	Personalize a résumé and cover letter template by selecting existing text and typing new text or by selecting and deleting text not needed.

 Topics Review

Creating, Editing, and Formatting Excel Worksheets

Chapter **8**

Microsoft Excel (referred to as Excel) is a **spreadsheet application** used to create, process, and present information that is organized in a grid of columns and rows. In Excel, data can be calculated, analyzed, and graphed in a chart. The ability to do "what-if" analysis is a popular feature of the application. In this type of analysis, one or more values are changed to view the effect on other values. Excel is used for budget, income, expense, investment, loan, schedule, grading, attendance, inventory, and research data. Any information that can be set up in a grid-like structure is suited to Excel.

A file that you save in Excel is called a **workbook**. A workbook contains a collection of worksheets. A **worksheet** is the structure into which you enter, edit, and manipulate data. Think of a workbook as a binder and a worksheet as a page within the binder. Initially, a workbook has only one worksheet (page), but you can add more as needed.

Many of the features that you learned about in Word operate the same or similarly in Excel, which will make learning Excel faster and easier. You will begin by creating new worksheets in a blank workbook and then open other worksheets to practice navigating, editing, sorting, and formatting tasks.

Learning Objectives

8.1 Create and edit a new worksheet

8.2 Format cells with font, number, border, and merge and center options

8.3 Adjust column width and row height, and change cell alignment

8.4 Use the Fill feature to enter and copy data, and use AutoSum to add a column or row of values

8.5 Insert and delete rows and columns

8.6 Sort data and apply cell styles

8.7 Change page orientation, scale a worksheet, and display formulas in cells

8.8 Insert and rename a worksheet, copy cells, and indent data within a cell

8.9 Use Go To to move to a cell, freeze panes, apply shading options, and wrap text and rotate cell entries

Read & Learn

Content Online

The online course includes additional training and assessment resources.

8.1 Creating and Editing a New Worksheet

When you create a new blank workbook, you begin with a blank worksheet, which is divided into columns and rows. The intersection of a column and a row is called a **cell**, and in each cell you can type text, a value, or a formula. The cell with the green border is called the **active cell**. The active cell is the location in which the next entry you type is stored. The active cell is also the cell affected by the next command (action) you perform. Each cell is identified with the letter of the column and the number of the row that intersect to form the cell. For example, A1 refers to the cell in column A, row 1. A new workbook starts with one worksheet labeled *Sheet1* that has columns labeled A to Z, AA to AZ, BA to BZ, and so on to the last column, which is labeled XFD. Rows are numbered 1, 2, 3, up to 1,048,576.

Creating a New Worksheet

Begin a new worksheet by entering titles, column headings, and row headings to give the worksheet an organizational layout and provide context for the reader. Next, enter values in the columns and rows. Complete the worksheet by inserting formulas that perform calculations or otherwise summarize data.

1. Start Excel.
2. At the Excel Start screen, click *Blank workbook* in the Templates gallery. Compare your screen with the one shown in Figure 8.1 and read the descriptions of screen elements in Table 8.1 on the next page.

Watch & Learn

Hands On Activity

------- skills

Start a new workbook
Enter text and values
Create formulas
Edit cells

Tutorial
Opening a Blank Workbook

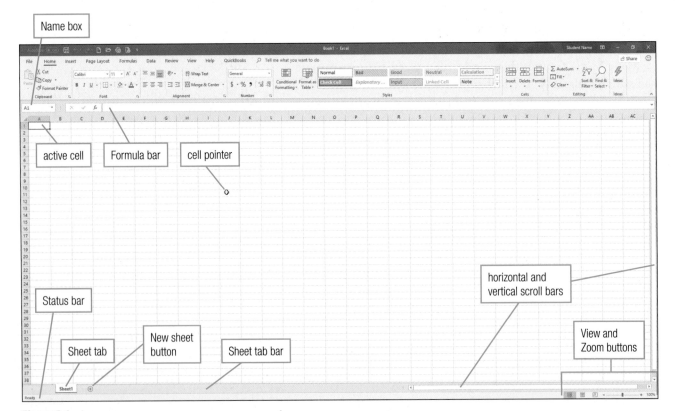

Figure 8.1

A new blank Excel worksheet is shown here. The worksheet area below the ribbon is divided into columns and rows, creating cells into which data and formulas are typed and stored.

Table 8.1 Excel Features

Feature	Description
Active cell	This location is where the next typed data will be stored and that will be affected by the next command. Make a cell active by clicking it or by moving to it using the arrow keys.
Cell pointer	This icon (⊕) displays when you are able to select cells with the mouse by clicking or dragging. On a touch device with no mouse attached, tap a cell to display selection handles (round circles) at the upper left and bottom right corners.
Formula bar	Bar that displays contents stored in the active cell and is also used to create formulas
Horizontal and vertical scroll bars	Tools used to view parts of a worksheet not displayed in the current viewing area
Name box	Box that displays the address or name of the active cell
New sheet button	Button on the Sheet tab bar used to insert a new worksheet
Sheet tab	This tab displays the name of the active worksheet. By default, new sheets are named *Sheet#* where *#* is the number of the sheet in the workbook.
Sheet tab bar	Bar that displays sheet tabs and is used to navigate between worksheets
Status bar	Bar that displays messages indicating the current mode of operation; e.g., *Ready* indicates the worksheet is ready to accept new data
View and Zoom buttons	These buttons are used to change the appearance of the worksheet. Excel opens in Normal view. Other view buttons include Page Layout and Page Break Preview. Zoom buttons are used to enlarge or shrink the display.

Entering Text and Values

When you start a new worksheet, the active cell is A1 at the upper left corner of the worksheet. Entries are created by activating a cell and typing text, a value, or a formula.

3 With A1 the active cell, type Car Purchase Cost and then press Enter or click cell A2 to make A2 the active cell.

4 Type Preowned Ford Focus Sedan and then press Enter twice or click cell A4.

5 Type Total Purchase Price and then click cell A6.

6 Type Loan Details: and then click cell B7.

7 Type the remaining row headings by moving the active cell and typing the text shown in the image at the right.

8 Click cell F4, type 16700.00, and then click cell E7.

By default, text entries align at the left edge of a cell. Numeric entries align at the right edge of a cell, and zeros to the right of a decimal are not stored or displayed. You will learn how to format a cell to display the decimal place values in Topic 8.2.

● — — — — — **app tip**

You can use arrow keys to move up, down, left, or right from cell to cell.

☁ **Tutorial**

Entering Data

9 Type the remaining values by activating the cell and typing the numbers shown in the image below.

	A	B	C	D	E	F
1	Car Purchase Cost					
2	Preowned Ford Focus Sedan					
3						
4	Total Purchase Price				16700	
5						
6	Loan Details:					
7		Amount of payment			470.05	
8		Term			36	
9		Total loan payments				
10						
11	Down payment made at purchase				1700	

Step 9

Creating Formulas to Perform Calculations

A **formula** is used to perform mathematical operations on values. A formula entry begins with the equals sign (=) to indicate to Excel the entry that follows is a calculation. Following the equals sign, type the first cell address that contains a value you want to use, type a mathematical operator, and then type the second cell address. Continue typing mathematical operators and cell addresses until finished. The mathematical operators are + (addition), − (subtraction), * (multiplication), / (division), and ^ (exponentiation).

10 Click cell E9 to make it the active cell and then type =e7*e8.

11 Click the Enter button on the Formula bar.

Excel calculates the result and displays the value in E9. Notice that the cell in the worksheet area displays the formula result, while the Formula bar displays the formula used to calculate the result. Notice also that Excel capitalizes column letters in cell addresses within formulas.

Another way to enter a formula is to use the pointing method. In this method, you click the desired cells instead of typing their cell addresses.

12 Make F13 the active cell and then type =.

13 Click cell E9.

A moving dashed border surrounds E9, the cell is color coded, and the address E9 is inserted in both cell F13 and the Formula bar.

14 Type +.

15 Click cell E11 and then click the Enter button on the Formula bar or press Enter.

16 Make F15 the active cell, type the formula =f13-f4 or enter the formula using the pointing method, and then click the Enter button on the Formula bar or press Enter.

The result, 1921.8, displays in the cell.

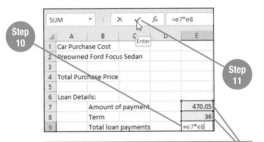

Step 10

Step 11

Color references display as you click cells to build a formula. These colors make it easy to check the values that are part of the formula or to help find errors.

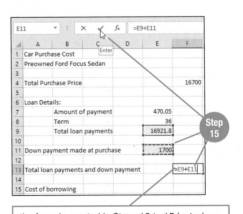

Step 15

the formula created in Steps 12 to 15 by typing the equals sign (Step 12), clicking cells (Steps 13 and 15), and typing the operator (Step 14)

Tutorials

Entering Formulas Using the Keyboard

Entering Formulas Using the Mouse

— — — — — — — Oops!

Clicked the wrong cell? Just click the correct cell—the cell reference can be changed until you type an operator. You can also press the Esc key to start over.

Tutorial

Determining the Order of Operations

Editing Cells

An entire cell entry can be changed by making the cell active and typing a new entry to replace the existing contents. Double-click a cell to open it for editing in the worksheet area; this will allow you to change the entry rather than replace it. You can also edit the content in a cell by making the cell active and then inserting or deleting characters or spaces in the Formula bar.

To delete the contents of an active cell, click the cell and then press the Delete key or click the **Clear button** in the Editing group on the Home tab and then click *Clear All*.

17 Make E7 the active cell, type 480.95, and then press Enter.

Notice that the new payment amount causes the values in E9, F13, and F15 to update.

These values are updated automatically when the new loan payment is entered in E7.

18 Double-click cell F4, position the insertion point between *6* and *7*, press Backspace to remove *6*, type *5*, and then click any other cell.

19 Make E11 the active cell, click in the Formula bar, position the insertion point between *1* and *7*, press Backspace to remove *1*, and then click any other cell.

20 Save the new workbook as **CarCost-YourName** in a new folder *Ch8* in the CompletedTopics folder on your storage medium. Leave the workbook open for the next topic.

8.2 Formatting Cells

Much like the Home tab in Word, the Home tab in Excel contains the formatting options for changing the appearance of text, values, or formula results. The Font group contains buttons to change the font, font size, and font color and to apply bold, italic, underline, borders, and shading. The Alignment group contains buttons to align text or values within the cell edges.

Selecting Cells and Applying Font Formatting

To select cells using a mouse: Select adjacent cells with a mouse by positioning the cell pointer (⬧) in the starting cell and dragging in the required direction until all the desired cells have been included in a shaded selection rectangle. Select nonadjacent cells by holding down the Ctrl key while you click the mouse in each desired cell. The Quick Analysis button displays when a group of cells has been selected. You will learn about the options available from this button in Chapter 9.

   To select cells using touch: Selecting cells on a touch device in Excel is similar to selecting text in Word, with the exception that two selection handles display in the active cell, as shown in Figure 8.2. Tap inside the selection area to display the Mini toolbar.

1. Tap starting cell to display selection handles.

2. Slide finger over selection handle in the direction required until remaining cells are selected.

Quick Analysis button

Figure 8.2
Selecting cells on a touch device is not much different from selecting cells using a mouse.

① With the **CarCost-YourName** workbook open, starting at cell A1, select all the cells down and right to F15.

   A rectangular-shaped group of cells is referred to as a **range**. A range is referenced with the address of the cell at the upper left corner, a colon (:), and the address of the cell at the lower right corner. For example, the reference for the range selected in Step 1 is A1:F15.

② Click the *Font* option box arrow in the Font group on the Home tab, scroll down, and then click *Century Gothic*.

③ Click any cell to deselect the range.

④ Select A1:A2 and then click the Bold button in the Font group.

Notice the entire text in A1 and A2 is bold, including the characters that spill over the edge of column A into columns B, C, and D. This is because the entire text entry is stored in the cell that was active when the text was typed. Overflow text that displays in adjacent columns is not problematic when the adjacent columns are empty. You will learn how to widen a column to fit overflow text in the next topic.

☁ **Tutorial**

Applying Font Formatting

⑤ Click cell F15 and then click the Bold button.

Formatting Numbers

Cells in a new worksheet are in the General format, which has no specific appearance options. Buttons in the Number group on the Home tab are used to format the appearance of values in a worksheet. Add a dollar symbol, insert commas to indicate thousands, and/or adjust the number of decimal places to improve the appearance of values. Use the Percent Style format to convert decimal values to percentages and include the percent symbol. The *Number Format* option box (displays *General*) offers other formats for dates, times, fractions, or scientific values and is used to open the Format Cells dialog box from the *More Number Formats* option (Figure 8.3).

⑥ Select E4:F15.

⑦ Click the Comma Style button in the Number group.

Comma Style formats values with a comma in thousands and two decimal places.

⑧ Click cell F4 and then click the Accounting Number Format button in the Number group.

Accounting Number Format adds a currency symbol ($ for the United States and Canada), commas in numbers above 1,000, and two decimal places. Use the *Accounting Number Format* option box arrow to choose a different currency symbol (such as €, which stands for Euro).

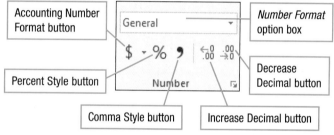

Figure 8.3

Shown are the buttons in the Number group on the Home tab. Click the *Number Format* option box arrow for more options.

● ─ ─ ─ ─ ─ ─ app tip

Excel automatically widens columns as needed when you apply a format that adds more characters to a column, such as Comma Style.

⑨ Click cell E7 and then click the Accounting Number Format button.

⑩ Select F13:F15 and then click the Accounting Number Format button.

    The Accounting Number format aligns the currency symbol at the left edge of the cell. The *Currency* option (an option in the *Number Format* drop-down list), places the currency symbol immediately left of the value in the cell. Formatting values using the *Currency* option means that the currency symbols do not align at the same position in the cell if the length of the values varies. Use the Accounting Number Format option if you want all dollar symbols to align at the same position.

⑪ Click cell E8 and then click the Decrease Decimal button in the Number group twice.

    One decimal place is removed from the active cell or range each time you click the **Decrease Decimal button**. Click the **Increase Decimal button** to add one decimal place.

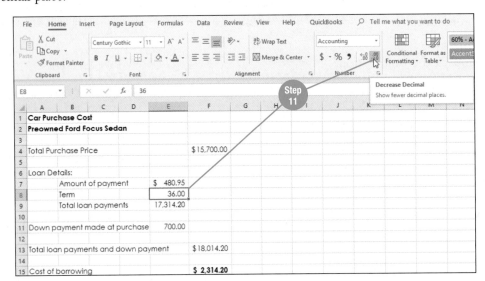

☁ **Tutorials**

Applying Formatting Using the Format Cells Dialog Box

Applying Number Formatting

Adding Borders

Borders in various styles and colors can be added to the top, left, bottom, or right edge of a cell. Borders are used to underscore column headings or totals or to otherwise emphasize cells.

⑫ Click cell F13.

⑬ Click the *Bottom Border* button arrow in the Font group.

⑭ Click *Top and Bottom Border*.

⑮ Click cell F15.

⑯ Click the *Top and Bottom Border* button arrow and then click *Bottom Double Border*.

☁ **Tutorial**

Adding Borders to Cells

17 Click any other cell to view the border style applied to F15.

Top and Bottom Border option applied to cell F13 in Steps 12 to 14.

Bottom Double Border option applied to cell F15 in Steps 15 to 16.

Merging and Centering Cells

A worksheet title is often centered across the columns used in the worksheet. The **Merge & Center button** in the Alignment group on the Home tab is used to combine a group of cells into one large cell and center its contents. The Merge & Center button arrow on the Merge & Center button lets the user alter the Merge & Center option (to merge without centering, or to unmerge a merged cell).

18 Select A1:F1.

19 Click the Merge & Center button in the Alignment group.

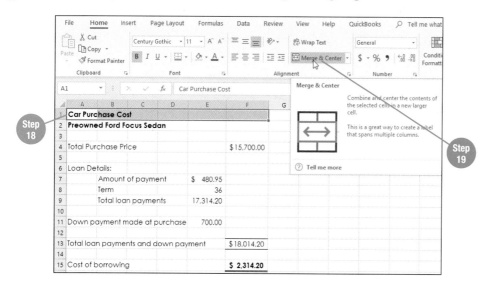

20 Select A2:F2 and then click the Merge & Center button.

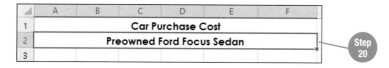

Step 20

21 Save the workbook using the same name (**CarCost-YourName**). Leave the workbook open for the next topic.

quick steps

Change a Font
1. Select cell(s).
2. Click *Font* option box arrow.
3. Click desired font.

Change Number Format
1. Select cell(s).
2. Click Accounting Number Format button, Percent Style button, or Comma Style button.

OR

1. Select cell(s).
2. Click *Number Format* option box arrow.
3. Click desired format option.

Adjust Decimal Places
1. Select cell(s).
2. Click Increase Decimal or Decrease Decimal button.

Add Borders
1. Select cell(s).
2. Click Borders button arrow.
3. Click border style.

Merge Cells
1. Select cells.
2. Click Merge & Center button.

Tutorial

Merging and Centering Cells

8.3 Adjusting Column Width and Row Height and Changing Cell Alignment

In a new worksheet, each column width is 8.43 and each row height is 15. The column width value is the number of characters at the default font that can be displayed in the column. The row height value is a points measurement, with 1 point being approximately 1/72 of an inch. Make cells larger by widening the width of a column or by increasing the height of a row. In many instances, Excel automatically makes columns wider and rows taller to accommodate the cell entry, formula result, or format that you apply. Manually changing the column width or the row height is a technique used to add more space between cells to improve readability or emphasize a section of the worksheet.

1. With the **CarCost-YourName** workbook open, make active any cell in column E.

2. Click the Format button in the Cells group on the Home tab and then click *Column Width*.

3. Type 15 in the *Column width* text box in the Column Width dialog box and then press Enter or click OK.

4. Make active any cell in column F, click the Format button, and then click *Column Width*.

5. Type 10 in the Column Width dialog box and then press Enter or click OK.

Notice the cells with values in column F have been replaced with a series of pound symbols (#####). This occurs when the column width is too narrow to display all the characters.

6. Make F4 the active cell.

7. Click the Format button and then click *AutoFit Column Width*.

AutoFit changes the width of the column to fit the contents of the active cell. F4 was made active in Step 6 because this cell has one of the longest numbers in the column. Notice the pound symbols have disappeared, and the values are redisplayed now that the column is wide enough.

Excel displays a series of pound symbols (#####) in any cell that is too narrow to display the full entry. This occurs when you have changed a column width, making the width too narrow as you did in Step 5.

Watch & Learn

Hands On Activity

●————————— Skills

Adjust column width

Adjust row height

Change cell alignment

Tutorials

Adjusting Column Width and Row Height

Applying Alignment Formatting

●—————— app tip

You can also change the column width or row height using the mouse by dragging the column boundary at the right of the column letter or the row boundary below the row number. Drag the boundary line right or left to increase or decrease the column width or down or up to increase or decrease the row height. Double-click the boundary line to AutoFit the width or height.

8 Select A1:A2.

To change the height or width of more than one row or column at the same time, you first select cells in the rows or columns to be changed.

9 Click the Format button and then click *Row Height*.

10 Type 26 in the *Row height* text box in the Row Height dialog box, and then press Enter or click OK.

The Alignment group on the Home tab contains buttons to align the entry of a cell horizontally and/or vertically. You can align cell content at the left, center, or right horizontally or at the top, middle, or bottom vertically within the cell boundaries. The **Middle Align button** centers text vertically between the top and bottom edges within a cell.

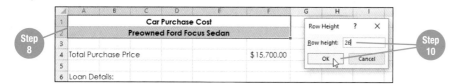

11 With A1:A2 still selected, click the Middle Align button in the Alignment group.

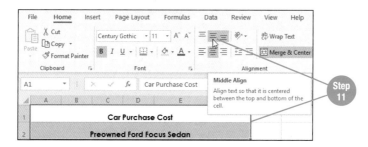

12 Make active any cell in row 15.

13 Click the Format button, click *Row Height*, type 26, and then press Enter or click OK.

14 Select A15:F15 and then click the Middle Align button.

15 Click any cell to deselect the range and then compare your worksheet to the one shown in the image above.

16 Save the workbook using the same name (**CarCost-YourName**).

17 Click the File tab and then click *Close* to close the workbook.

quick steps

Change Column Width
1. Activate any cell in column.
2. Click Format button.
3. Click *Column Width*.
4. Type width.
5. Click OK.

Change Row Height
1. Activate any cell in row.
2. Click Format button.
3. Click *Row Height*.
4. Type height.
5. Click OK.

AutoFit Column Width or Row Height
1. Activate cell with longest column or tallest row contents.
2. Click Format button.
3. Click *AutoFit Row Height* or *AutoFit Column Width*.

8.4 Entering or Copying Data with the Fill Command and Using AutoSum

 Watch & Learn

 Hands On Activity

●------- Skills

Use Auto Fill to enter a series

Use Fill Right to copy a value

Use the fill handle to enter data

Add values in a column with AutoSum

The **Auto Fill** feature is used to enter data automatically based on a pattern or series that exists in an adjacent cell or range. For example, if *Monday* is entered in cell A1, Auto Fill can enter *Tuesday*, *Wednesday*, and so on automatically in the cells immediately to the right of or below A1. Excel fills many common text or number series, and also detects patterns for other data when you select the first few entries in a list. When no pattern or series applies, the **Fill** feature is used to copy an entry or formula across or down to other cells.

The **Flash Fill** feature automatically fills data as soon as a pattern is recognized. When Flash Fill presents a suggested list in dimmed text, press Enter to accept the suggestions, or ignore the suggestions and continue typing. A Flash Fill Options button with options to undo Flash Fill, accept the suggestions, or select changed cells appears when a list is presented.

Using Auto Fill and Fill Right

1. Click the File tab, click *New*, and then click *Blank workbook*.

2. Type the text entries in A2:A13 as shown in the image at the right.

3. Change the width of column A to 18.

4. Make B1 the active cell, type Sep, and then click the Enter button on the Formula bar.

5. Select B1:I1.

6. Click the Fill button in the Editing group, and then click *Series*.

7. Click *AutoFill* in the *Type* section in the Series dialog box and then click OK.

Auto Fill enters the column headings *Oct* through *Apr* in the selected range.

8. Make B3 the active cell, type 875, and then click the Enter button.

9. Select B3:I3, click the Fill button, and then click *Right*.

Fill Right copies the entry in the first cell to the other cells within the selected range.

 Tutorial
Populating Data
Using Flash Fill

10 Enter the remaining values as shown in the Step 10 illustration at the right. In rows 5, 6, and 7, use Fill Right to enter the data.

	A	B	C	D	E	F	G	H	I
1		Sep	Oct	Nov	Dec	Jan	Feb	Mar	Apr
2	Expenses								
3	Housing	875	875	875	875	875	875	875	875
4	Food	260	340	310	295	320	280	300	345
5	Transportation	88	88	88	88	88	88	88	88
6	Smartphone	48	48	48	48	48	48	48	48
7	Internet	42	42	42	42	42	42	42	42
8	Entertainment	150	110	95	175	100	85	95	120
9	Total Expenses								

Step 10

Using the Fill Handle to Copy Cells

The **fill handle** is a small, green square at the lower right corner of the active cell or range. The fill handle is used to copy data from a cell or range to adjacent cells.

To use the fill handle with a mouse: When you point at the fill handle with a mouse, the cell pointer changes appearance from the large white cross to a thin, black crosshairs (**+**). Drag right or down when you see the thin, black crosshairs to copy data or a formula to the cells right or below the active cell or to extend a series, such as September or Monday, from the active cell to adjacent cells.

To use the fill handle on a touch device: Tapping a cell on a touch device displays the active cell with two selection handles instead of the fill handle. See Figure 8.4 for instructions on how to use the fill handle on a touch device.

Figure 8.4

The steps to using the fill handle on a touch device are shown here. First, (a) tap inside the cell and tap the AutoFill button, resulting in (b) the selection handles disappearing and the fill handle and fill icon displaying. Next, (c) slide right or down to highlight the cells you want filled, resulting in (d) Excel copying the entry to the selected cells.

11 Make B11 the active cell, type *1750*, and then click the Enter button.

12 Point to the fill handle in B11 and then drag the fill handle right to I11 when you see the pointer change to a thin, black crosshairs.

The value *1750* is copied to the cells in the selected range when you release the mouse.

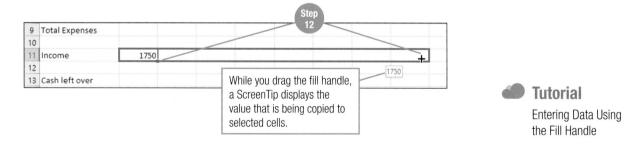

Step 12

While you drag the fill handle, a ScreenTip displays the value that is being copied to selected cells.

🫧 **Tutorial**

Entering Data Using the Fill Handle

Using the SUM function and AutoSum

To add the expenses in B9, you could type the formula *=B3+B4+B5+B6+B7+B8*; however, Excel includes a built-in preprogrammed function called SUM that can be used to add a column or row of numbers. The SUM function is faster and easier to use. To add the expenses in B9 using SUM, you would type the formula *=SUM(B3:B8)*. Notice after *=SUM* you need to provide only the range of cells to add enclosed in parentheses, rather than all the individual cell references and addition symbols. Because the SUM function is used frequently, an **AutoSum button** is included in the Editing group on the Home tab and the AutoSum feature automatically detects the range to be added.

13 Make B9 the active cell.

14 Click the AutoSum button in the Editing group on the Home tab.

Excel inserts the formula *=SUM(B3:B8)* in B9 with the suggested range B3:B8 selected. In most cases, the suggested range is correct; however, always check the entry before completing the formula because sometimes AutoSum assumes you want to add values above the active cell when you intend to add values to the left. If necessary, you can drag the mouse to select a different range before completing the formula.

Step 14

Tutorial

Entering Formulas Using the AutoSum Button

	A	B	C	D	E	F	G	H	I
1		Sep	Oct	Nov	Dec	Jan	Feb	Mar	Apr
2	Expenses								
3	Housing	875	875	875				875	875
4	Food	260	340	310				300	345
5	Transportation	88	88	88				88	88
6	Smartphone	48	48	48				48	48
7	Internet	42	42	42				42	42
8	Entertainment	150	110	95				95	120
9	Total Expenses	=SUM(B3:B8)							
10		SUM(**number1**, [number2], ...)							

SUM fx =SUM(B3:B8)

With the active cell B9 when the AutoSum button was clicked, Excel suggests the values above the active cell as the range to be added.

15 Press Ctrl + Enter.

Ctrl + Enter is the keyboard shortcut to complete the entry and keep the current cell active—the equivalent of clicking the Enter button on the Formula bar.

16 With B9 the active cell, point to the fill handle and then drag the fill handle right to I9 when you see the pointer change to a thin, black crosshairs.

In this instance, using the fill handle copies the formula in B9 to the selected cells. The **Auto Fill Options button** appears when you release the mouse after dragging the fill handle to copy a cell. Use the button to fill the cells with the formatting options only from the copied cell (no data is copied) or to copy the data with no formatting options (only data is copied). The button disappears when you start typing data in a new cell.

Tutorial

Copying Formulas

8	Entertainment	150	110	95	175	100	85	95	120
9	Total Expenses	1463	1503	1458	1523	1473	1418	1448	1518
10									
11	Income	1750	1750	1750	1750	1750	1750	1750	1750

Step 16

Auto Fill Options button

17 Make B13 the active cell, type =b11-b9, and then click the Enter button or press Ctrl + Enter.

18 With B13 the active cell, drag the fill handle right to I13.

11	Income	1750	1750	1750	1750	1750	1750	1750	1750
12									
13	Cash left over	287	247	292	227	277	332	302	232
14									

Step 18

19 Make J1 the active cell, type Total, and then press Enter.

20 Make J3 the active cell and then click the AutoSum button.

In this instance, Excel suggests the range B3:I3 in the SUM function. Excel looks for values immediately above or to the left of the active cell. Because no value exists above J3, Excel correctly suggests adding the values to the left in the same row.

21 Click the Enter button to accept the formula.

Step 20

22 With J3 the active cell, drag the fill handle down to J13.

23 Make J10 the active cell, and then press the Delete key.

24 Make J12 the active cell and then press the Delete key.

	A	B	C	D	E	F	G	H	I	J
1		Sep	Oct	Nov	Dec	Jan	Feb	Mar	Apr	Total
2	Expenses									
3	Housing	875	875	875	875	875	875	875	875	7000
4	Food	260	340	310	295	320	280	300	345	2450
5	Transportation	88	88	88	88	88	88	88	88	704
6	Smartphone	48	48	48	48	48	48	48	48	384
7	Internet	42	42	42	42	42	42	42	42	336
8	Entertainment	150	110	95	175	100	85	95	120	930
9	Total Expenses	1463	1503	1458	1523	1473	1418	1448	1518	11804
10										
11	Income	1750	1750	1750	1750	1750	1750	1750	1750	14000
12										
13	Cash left over	287	247	292	227	277	332	302	232	2196

Step 24

25 Save the new workbook as **SchoolBudget-YourName** in the Ch8 folder in CompletedTopics on your storage medium. Leave the workbook open for the next topic.

8.5 Inserting and Deleting Rows and Columns

New rows or columns are inserted or deleted using the Insert or Delete buttons in the Cells group on the Home tab. New rows are inserted above the row in which the active cell is positioned, and new columns are inserted to the left. Cell references within formulas and formula results are automatically updated when new rows or columns with data are added to or removed from a worksheet.

To insert a new row, activate any cell in the row below where a new row is required and click *Insert Sheet Rows* from the **Insert button** option list.

● ———————— Skills

Insert a new row

Insert a new column

Delete a row

1 With the **SchoolBudget-YourName** workbook open, make any cell in row 4 active.

	A	B	C	D	E	F	G	H	I
1		Sep	Oct	Nov	Dec	Jan	Feb	Mar	Apr
2	Expenses								
3	Housing	875	875	875	875	875	875	875	87
4	Food	260	340	310	295	320	280	300	34
5	Transportation	88	88	88	88	88	88	88	8

Step 1

2 Click the Insert button arrow in the Cells group on the Home tab.

3 Click *Insert Sheet Rows*.

A new blank row is inserted between *Housing* and *Food*.

4 Type the following entries in the cells indicated:

A4	Utilities	F4	128
B4	110	G4	106
C4	115	H4	118
D4	132	I4	112
E4	147		

● ——————— Oops!

Only one cell is inserted instead of an entire row? Clicking the top part of the Insert button inserts a cell instead of an entire new row. Use Undo and then try again, making sure to click the arrow on the bottom part of the Insert button to access the option list.

5 Make J3 the active cell and then drag the fill handle down to J4 to copy the SUM formula to the new row.

	A	B	C	D	E	F	G	H	I	J
1		Sep	Oct	Nov	Dec	Jan	Feb	Mar	Apr	Total
2	Expenses									
3	Housing	875	875	875	875	875	875	875	875	7000
4	Utilities	110	115	132	147	128	106	118	112	968
5	Food	260	340	310	295	320	280	300	345	2450

Step 4   Step 5

6 Select A1:A2, click the Insert button arrow, and then click *Insert Sheet Rows*.

Two rows are inserted above A1. You can also insert multiple rows by selecting the row numbers along the left edge of the worksheet area and displaying the contextual shortcut menu. To do this, point to the first row number until the pointer displays as a right-pointing black arrow (➡), hold down the left mouse button, drag down to the last row number and release the mouse. Multiple rows will be highlighted in the worksheet area. Right-click within the selection area and then click *Insert*.

	A	B	C	D	E	F	G	H	I	J
1										
2										
3		Sep	Oct	Nov	Dec	Jan	Feb	Mar	Apr	Total
4	Expenses									
5	Housing	875	875	875	875	875	875	875	875	7000

Step 6

⑦ Make the new cell A1 the active cell and then type Proposed School Budget.

⑧ Make the new cell A2 the active cell and then type First Year of Program.

⑨ Select A1:J1 and then click the Merge & Center button in the Alignment group.

⑩ Select A2:J2 and then click the Merge & Center button.

	A	B	C	D	E	F	G	H	I	J
1					Proposed School Budget					
2					First Year of Program					
3		Sep	Oct	Nov	Dec	Jan	Feb	Mar	Apr	Total
4	Expenses									
5	Housing	875	875	875	875	875	875	875	875	7000
6	Utilities	110	115	132	147	128	106	118	112	968

⑪ Make any cell in column J active.

⑫ Click the Insert button arrow and then click *Insert Sheet Columns*.

A new column is inserted between *Apr* and *Total*. Notice also an **Insert Options button** (◉) appears below and right of the active cell. Options from this button are used to format the new column with the same formatting options as the column at its left or right, or to clear formatting in the new column.

To delete a single row or column, position the active cell within that row or column, and then click *Delete Sheet Rows* or *Delete Sheet Columns* in the **Delete button** option list. To remove multiple rows or columns from the worksheet, begin by selecting the range of rows or columns to be deleted before clicking the Delete button arrow.

⑬ Make any cell in row 10 active.

⑭ Click the Delete button arrow and then click *Delete Sheet Rows*.

Row 10 is removed from the worksheet, and existing rows below are shifted up to fill in the space. Delete a column by performing actions similar to those in Steps 13 to 14 except click *Delete Sheet Columns* in the Delete option list.

⑮ Save the workbook using the same name (**SchoolBudget-YourName**). Leave the workbook open for the next topic.

3		Sep	Oct	Nov
4	Expenses			
5	Housing	875	875	875
6	Utilities	110	115	132
7	Food	260	340	310
8	Transportation	88	88	88
9	Smartphone	48	48	48
10	Internet	42	42	42
11	Entertainment	150	110	95

☁ **Tutorial**
Deleting Columns and Rows

8.6 Sorting Data and Applying Cell Styles

Data in cells within a range in Excel can be reordered by sorting in either ascending or descending order on one or more columns. For example, you can sort a list of names and cities first by the city and then by the last name. To sort the entire worksheet by one column, make active any cell in the column by which to order the data, click the **Sort & Filter button** in the Editing group on the Home tab and then click *Sort A to Z* or *Sort Z to A*. To sort a portion of the cells within a worksheet or to sort by more than one column, select the range and open the Sort dialog box from the Sort & Filter button option list.

Watch & Learn

Hands On Activity

------- *Skills*

Sort rows of data

Apply cell styles

Tutorial

Sorting Data

1 With the **SchoolBudget–YourName** workbook open, select A5:K10.

To sort the list of expenses alphabetically in ascending order, notice you do not include the heading (in A4) or the totals (in A11:K11) in the sort range.

Step 1

4	Expenses									
5	Housing	875	875	875	875	875	875	875	875	7000
6	Utilities	110	115	132	147	128	106	118	112	968
7	Food	260	340	310	295	320	280	300	345	2450
8	Transportation	88	88	88	88	88	88	88	88	704
9	Smartphone	48	48	48	48	48	48	48	48	384
10	Entertainment	150	110	95	175	100	85	95	120	930
11	Total Expenses	1531	1576	1548	1628	1559	1482	1524	1588	12436
12										

2 Click the Sort & Filter button in the Editing group on the Home tab.

3 Click *Sort A to Z*.

4 Click any cell to deselect the range, and review the new order of the expenses.

5 Select A5:K10.

6 Click the Sort & Filter button and then click *Custom Sort*.

7 Click the *Sort by* option box arrow in the *Column* section (currently displays *Column A*) in the Sort dialog box, and then click *Column K*.

8 Click the *Order* option box arrow (currently displays *Smallest to Largest*), and then click *Largest to Smallest*.

9 Click OK.

The data within the range A5:K10 is rearranged in descending order from highest expense total to lowest.

10 Click any cell to deselect the range, and review the new order of expenses.

Similar to the Styles feature in Word, **Cell Styles** in Excel offers a set of predefined formatting options that can be applied to a single cell or a range. Using Cell Styles to format a worksheet is fast and promotes consistency. The Cell Styles gallery groups styles by the sections *Good, Bad and Neutral*; *Data and Model*; *Titles and Headings*; *Themed Cell Styles*; and *Number Format*.

11 Click cell A1 and then the More button in the Styles group on the Home tab.

Step 11

More
A colorful style is a great way to make important data stand out on the sheet.

quick steps

Sort a Range by the First Column
1. Select range.
2. Click Sort & Filter button.
3. Click *Sort A to Z* or *Sort Z to A*.

Custom Sort
1. Select range.
2. Click Sort & Filter button.
3. Click *Custom Sort*.
4. Change options and/or add levels as needed.
5. Click OK.

Apply Cell Styles
1. Select cell or range.
2. Click desired cell style in Cell Styles gallery.

12 Click *Heading 1* in the *Titles and Headings* section of the Cell Styles gallery.

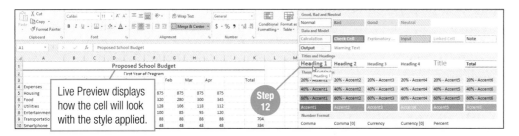

Live Preview displays how the cell will look with the style applied.

Step 12

13 Click cell A2, click the More button in the Cell Styles gallery, and then click *Heading 4* in the *Titles and Headings* section.

14 Click cell A4, hold down the Ctrl key, click cell A13, click cell A15, and then release the Ctrl key. With the three cells selected, apply the Heading 4 cell style.

15 Select B3:K3, apply the Accent1 style (first option in last row) in the *Themed Cell Styles* section of the Cell Styles gallery, and then center the content of those cells.

16 Select B5:K15 and apply the Comma [0] style in the *Number Format* section of the Cell Styles gallery.

17 Select B15:K15 and apply the Total style in the *Titles and Headings* section of the Cell Styles gallery.

18 Click any cell to deselect the range and compare your worksheet with the one shown in Figure 8.5.

Oops!

No Cell Styles gallery? On smaller displays, the gallery is accessed by clicking the Cell Styles button in the Styles group on the Home tab.

	A	B	C	D	E	F	G	H	I	J	K
1	Proposed School Budget										
2	First Year of Program										
3		Sep	Oct	Nov	Dec	Jan	Feb	Mar	Apr		Total
4	Expenses										
5	Housing	875	875	875	875	875	875	875	875		7,000
6	Food	260	340	310	295	320	280	300	345		2,450
7	Utilities	110	115	132	147	128	106	118	112		968
8	Entertainment	150	110	95	175	100	85	95	120		930
9	Transportation	88	88	88	88	88	88	88	88		704
10	Smartphone	48	48	48	48	48	48	48	48		384
11	Total Expenses	1,531	1,576	1,548	1,628	1,559	1,482	1,524	1,588		12,436
12											
13	Income	1,750	1,750	1,750	1,750	1,750	1,750	1,750	1,750		14,000
14											
15	Cash left over	219	174	202	122	191	268	226	162		1,564

Figure 8.5
The **SchoolBudget-YourName** worksheet will display in sorted order and with cell styles applied from this topic.

 Tutorials

Applying Cell Styles

Applying and Modifying Themes

19 Save the workbook using the same name (**SchoolBudget-YourName**). Leave the workbook open for the next topic.

8.7 Changing Orientation and Scaling, Displaying Cell Formulas, and Exporting a Worksheet

By default, new Excel workbooks have print options set to print the active worksheet on a letter-size page (8.5 × 11 inches), in portrait orientation, with 0.75-inch top and bottom margins, and 0.7-inch left and right margins. Preview a new worksheet before printing to determine whether these print options are appropriate.

Workbooks are often circulated electronically by email or by other means of electronic file transfer. In that case, a workbook is often distributed as a PDF file, which is essentially an electronic view of a printed worksheet. When a workbook is exported in PDF format, the PDF is created using the print options in effect. Preview a worksheet and change print options as needed before exporting in PDF file format.

1. With the **SchoolBudget-YourName** workbook open, click the File tab, click *Print*, and then compare your screen with the one shown in Figure 8.6.

2. Click the Next Page button at the bottom of the preview panel to view the second page of the worksheet.

3. Click the *Orientation* button arrow (currently displays *Portrait Orientation*) in the *Settings* section and then click *Landscape Orientation*.

Notice the worksheet now fits on one page. Landscape is a common layout used for wide worksheets. Print options are saved with the workbook content.

Watch & Learn

Hands On Activity

------- Skills

Preview a worksheet

Change orientation

Display cell formulas

Change scaling

Export worksheet as PDF

Tutorials

Displaying Formulas

Printing a Worksheet

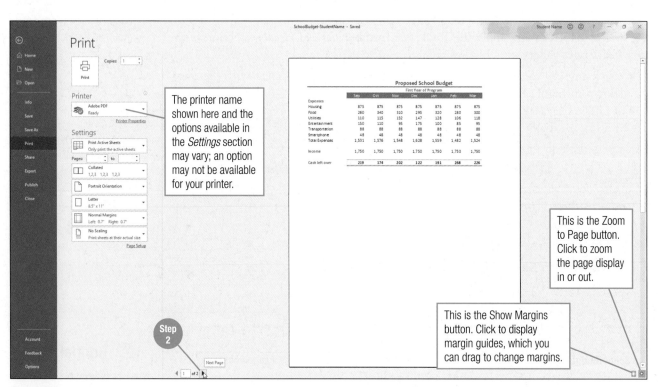

The printer name shown here and the options available in the *Settings* section may vary; an option may not be available for your printer.

This is the Zoom to Page button. Click to zoom the page display in or out.

This is the Show Margins button. Click to display margin guides, which you can drag to change margins.

Figure 8.6

The Print backstage area is shown with the first page displayed for the **SchoolBudget-StudentName** worksheet.

④ Click Back to return to the worksheet and then save the revised workbook using the same name (**SchoolBudget–YourName**).

On a printed copy of the worksheet, only the formula result is printed. You may want to print a second copy of the worksheet with the formulas displayed in the cell as a backup or documentation strategy for a complex or otherwise important worksheet.

⑤ Click the Formulas tab.

⑥ Click the Show Formulas button in the Formula Auditing group.

The **Show Formulas button** is a toggle button that switches the display between showing the formula in each cell and showing the result in each cell. Ctrl + ` (grave accent, usually positioned on the keyboard above the Tab key), is the keyboard command to turn on or turn off the display of formulas.

●‑ ‑ ‑ ‑ **quick steps**

Change the Orientation
1. Display Print backstage area.
2. Click *Orientation* button arrow.
3. Click *Landscape Orientation*.

Display Cell Formulas
1. Click Formulas tab.
2. Click Show Formulas button.

Scale a Worksheet
1. Display Print backstage area.
2. Click *Scaling* option box arrow.
3. Click required scaling option.

Export a Worksheet
1. Click File tab.
2. Click *Export*.
3. Click Create PDF/XPS button.
4. Click Publish button.

⑦ Scroll right if necessary to review the worksheet with formulas displayed.

⑧ Display the Print backstage area.

⑨ Click the *Scaling* option box arrow (currently displays *No Scaling*) in the *Settings* section and then click *Fit Sheet on One Page*.

Fit Sheet on One Page shrinks the size of text on the printout to fit all columns and rows on one page.

⑩ Click Back to return to the worksheet.

⑪ Use Save As to save a copy of the worksheet with the formulas displayed, named **SchoolBudgetFormulas–YourName** in the Ch8 folder in CompletedTopics.

⑫ Click the File tab and then click *Export*.

⑬ Click the Create PDF/XPS button on the right panel of the Export backstage area.

⑭ Click the Publish button in the Publish as PDF or XPS dialog box, accepting the default file name and storage location options.

⑮ If the PDF document opens in a new window, close the window to return to Excel.

⑯ Close the workbook.

●‑ ‑ ‑ ‑ ‑ ‑ **app tip**

Other methods used to print wide worksheets using less paper are to decrease the margins, and change the scaling percentage. Options to change the page layout for printing purposes are also found on the Page Layout tab of the ribbon.

8.8 Inserting and Renaming a Worksheet, Copying Cells, and Indenting Cell Contents

A workbook can contain more than one worksheet. Use multiple worksheets as a method to organize or group data into manageable units. For example, a homeowner might have one household finance workbook and keep track of bills and loans in one worksheet, savings and investments in a second worksheet, and a household budget in a third worksheet. Insert, rename, and navigate between worksheets using the sheet tabs on the **Sheet tab bar**. Use the **New sheet button** on the Sheet tab bar to add a new worksheet to the workbook.

1. Open the **SchoolBudget-YourName** workbook.

2. Click the New sheet button on the Sheet tab bar.

   A new worksheet with the name Sheet2 is added to the workbook to the right of the Sheet1 worksheet and made the active worksheet.

3. Click the Sheet1 tab to make Sheet1 the active worksheet.

4. Right-click the Sheet1 tab and then click *Rename*.

5. Type First Year and then press Enter.

6. Right-click the Sheet2 tab, click *Rename*, type Second Year, and then press Enter.

7. Click the First Year tab to make First Year the active worksheet.

8. Select A4:A15 and then click the Copy button in the Clipboard group on the Home tab.

9. Click the Second Year tab, click cell A4, and then click the Paste button. Do *not* click the down-pointing arrow.

10. Click the Paste Options button and then click *Keep Source Column Widths* (second option in second row in *Paste* section).

11. Click the First Year tab, select A1:K3, and then click the Copy button.

12. Click the Second Year tab, click cell A1, and then click the Paste button.

13. Edit the content in cell A2 in the Second Year worksheet to change *First* to *Second* so that the title now reads *Second Year of Program*.

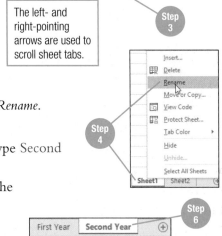

The left- and right-pointing arrows are used to scroll sheet tabs.

Step 2
Step 3
Step 4
Step 6
Step 10

Step 13

—————— Skills

Insert a new worksheet

Rename worksheets

Copy cells

Indent cells

————— app tip

Other options on the sheet tab shortcut menu are used to delete, move, copy, hide, or protect entire sheets and to change the color of the background in the sheet tab.

————— Oops!

Pasted to the wrong starting cell? Drag the border of the selected range to the correct starting point, or use Cut and Paste to move cells.

Tutorials

Inserting and Renaming Worksheets

Copying and Pasting Cells between Worksheets

14 Enter the data in the Second Year worksheet as shown in Figure 8.7. Complete the worksheet by entering and copying formulas for the cells in row 11, row 15, and column K. Refer to the entries in the First Year worksheet if you need help with the formulas. Apply the Comma [0] cell style to all the values and the Total cell style to the cells in row 15.

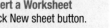

quick steps

Insert a Worksheet
Click New sheet button.
Rename a Worksheet
1. Right-click sheet tab.
2. Click *Rename*.
3. Type new name.
4. Press Enter.
Indent Cells
1. Activate cell or select range.
2. Click Increase Indent button.

	A	B	C	D	E	F	G	H	I	J	K
1					Proposed School Budget						
2					Second Year of Program						
3		Sep	Oct	Nov	Dec	Jan	Feb	Mar	Apr		Total
4	Expenses										
5	Housing	910	910	910	910	910	910	910	910		
6	Food	245	330	298	285	308	275	295	355		
7	Utilities	112	118	140	151	131	118	122	124		
8	Entertainment	160	95	100	185	110	95	90	125		
9	Transportation	90	90	90	90	90	90	90	90		
10	Smartphone	50	50	50	50	50	50	50	50		
11	Total Expenses										
12											
13	Income	1,800	1,800	1,800	1,800	1,800	1,800	1,800	1,800		
14											
15	Cash left over										

Figure 8.7
The completed Second Year worksheet is shown here.

The **Increase Indent button** in the Alignment group on the Home tab moves an entry approximately one character width inward from the left edge of a cell each time the button is clicked. Use this feature to indent entries in a list below a subheading. The **Decrease Indent button** moves an entry approximately one character width closer to the left edge of the cell each time the button is clicked.

15 With Second Year still the active worksheet, select A5:A10 and then click the Increase Indent button in the Alignment group.

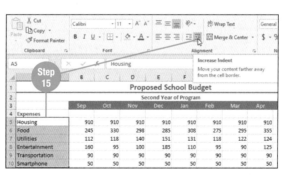

16 Click cell A11 and then click the Increase Indent button twice.

17 Click the Page Layout tab.

18 Click the Orientation button in the Page Setup group and then click *Landscape*.

19 Make First Year the active worksheet. If necessary, press the Esc key to remove the moving marquee from the copied cells in A1:A2.

20 Select A5:A10, click the Home tab, and then click the Increase Indent button.

21 Click cell A11 and then click the Increase Indent button twice.

22 Save the workbook using the same name (**SchoolBudget-Your Name**) and then close the workbook.

Tutorial
Moving Cells

app tip

Each worksheet has its own page layout and print options.

8.9 Using Go To; Freezing Panes; and Shading, Wrapping, and Rotating Cell Entries

In large worksheets where you cannot see all cells at once, the **Go To** and **Go To Special** commands accessed from the **Find & Select button** in the Editing group on the Home tab are used to move the active cell to a specific location in a worksheet. Column or row headings not visible when you scroll right or down beyond the viewing area can be fixed in place using the **Freeze Panes** buton. The position of the active cell when the *Freeze Panes* option is used determines which rows and columns remain fixed in place—all columns left and all rows above the active cell are frozen.

1. Open the **NSCSuppliesInventory** workbook from the Ch8 folder in StudentDataFiles. If necessary, click the Enable Editing button to close Protected view.

2. Save the workbook as **NSCSuppliesInv-YourName** in the Ch8 folder in CompletedTopics.

3. Scroll down the worksheet area until the titles and column headings are no longer visible.

4. Click the Find & Select button in the Editing group on the Home tab and then click *Go To*.

5. Type a4 in the *Reference* text box in the Go To dialog box and then press Enter or click OK.

6. Click the Find & Select button and then click *Go To Special*.

7. Click *Last cell* in the Go To Special dialog box and then click OK.

Use the *Last cell* option in the Go To Special dialog box in a large worksheet to quickly move the active cell to the bottom right of the worksheet.

8. Use the Go To command to move the active cell back to A4.

9. Scroll up until you can see the first three rows, containing titles and column headings.

10. With A4 still the active cell, click the View tab and then click the Freeze Panes button in the Window group.

11. Click *Freeze Panes*.

 Watch & Learn

 Hands On Activity

------------ Skills

Use Go To

Freeze panes

Add fill color

Wrap text

Rotate text

●------------ app tip

Ctrl + G is the keyboard command for Go To.

 Tutorials

Navigating and Scrolling

Freezing and Unfreezing Panes

●------------ app tip

Once cells have been frozen, the *Freeze Panes* option from the Freeze Panes button changes to *Unfreeze Panes*.

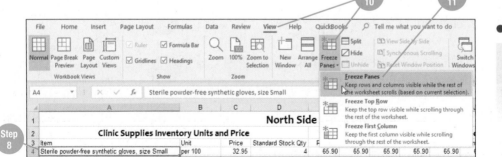

12 Scroll down several rows past all data. Notice that rows 1 to 3 do not scroll out of the viewing area.

●--- quick steps

Column headings can be formatted to stand out from the rest of the worksheet by shading the background of the cell using the **Fill Color button** in the Font group on the Home tab or by rotating the cell entries. Cells with long entries can be housed in narrower columns by formatting the text to automatically wrap within the width of the cell using the **Wrap Text button** in the Alignment group. In Steps 13 to 20, you will format worksheet headings to match the headings shown in Figure 8.8.

Freeze Panes
1. Activate cell below and right of cells to freeze.
2. Click View tab.
3. Click Freeze Panes button.
4. Click *Freeze Panes*.
Shade Cell Background
1. Select cell or range.
2. Click Fill Color button arrow.
3. Click desired color.
Rotate Cells
1. Select cell or range.
2. Click Orientation option in Alignment group.
3. Click desired rotate option.

13 Scroll to the top of the worksheet and then click cell A1.

14 Click the Home tab, click the Fill Color button arrow in the Font group, and then click *Orange, Accent 6* (last color in first row of *Theme Colors* section).

15 Select A2:M2, click the Fill Color button arrow and then click *Orange, Accent 6, Lighter 60%* (last option in third row of *Theme Colors* section).

16 Select A3:M3, click the Fill Color button arrow, and then click *Orange, Accent 6, Lighter 80%* (last option in second row of *Theme Colors* section).

17 Make M3 the active cell, change the row height to 30, and change the column width to 10.

18 With M3 still the active cell, click the Wrap Text button in the Alignment group.

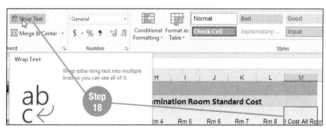

The column heading is visible again, with the text wrapping within the cell.

19 Make D3 the active cell, change the column width to 9, and then click the Wrap Text button.

20 Select E3:L3, click the Orientation button in the Alignment group, and then click *Angle Counterclockwise*.

Angle Counterclockwise rotates the text within the cell boundaries 45 degrees.

21 Click any cell to deselect the range and then display the Print backstage area.

22 Change settings to *Landscape Orientation* and *Fit All Columns on One Page* and then go back to the worksheet display.

23 Save the workbook using the same name (**NSCSuppliesInv-YourName**) and then close the workbook.

 Tutorials

Adding Fill Color to Cells

Using Format Painter and the Repeat Command

	A	B	C	D	E	F	G	H	I	J	K	L	M
1	North Side Medical Clinic												
2	Clinic Supplies Inventory Units and Price					Patient Examination Room Standard Cost							
3	Item		Unit	Price	Standard Stock Qty	Rm 1	Rm 2	Rm 3	Rm 4	Rm 5	Rm 6	Rm 7	Rm 8	Total Cost All Rooms

Figure 8.8

The **NSCSuppliesInv-StudentName** worksheet with the formatted headings is shown.

Topics Review

Topic	Key Concepts
8.1 Creating and Editing a New Worksheet	A **spreadsheet application** is software in which data is created, analyzed, and presented in a grid-like structure of columns and rows.
	A **workbook** is an Excel file that consists of a collection of individual **worksheets**.
	A new workbook opens with a blank worksheet into which you add text, insert values, and create formulas.
	The intersection of a column and a row is called a **cell**.
	The **active cell** is indicated with a green border and is the place where the next data typed will be stored or the next command will be acted upon.
	Create a worksheet by making a cell active and typing text, a value, or a formula.
	A **formula** is used to perform mathematical operations on values.
	Formula entries begin with an equals sign and are followed by cell references with operators between the references.
	Edit a cell by typing new data to overwrite existing data, by double-clicking to open the cell for editing, or by inserting or deleting characters in the Formula bar.
	Press the Delete key or use the **Clear button** in the Editing group on the Home tab to delete the contents in the active cell.
8.2 Formatting Cells	The Font group on the Home tab contains buttons to change the font, font size, font color, and font style of selected cells.
	Select cells with the mouse by positioning the cell pointer over the starting cell and dragging in the required direction.
	Select cells using touch by tapping the starting cell and then sliding your finger over a selection handle until the remaining cells are inside the selection rectangle.
	A rectangular-shaped group of cells is called a **range** and is referenced with the starting cell address, a colon, and the ending cell address (e.g., A1:F15).
	By default, cells in a new worksheet have the General format, which has no specific formatting options.
	The **Comma Style** format option adds a comma in thousands and two decimal places to numbers.
	The **Accounting Number Format** option adds a dollar symbol, a comma in the thousands place, and displays two digits after the decimal point for numbers.
	The **Decrease Decimal button** and **Increase Decimal button** in the Number group on the Home tab remove or add one decimal place each time the button is clicked.
	Borders in various styles and colors can be added to the edges of a cell using the Bottom Border button arrow in the Font group on the Home tab.
	The **Merge & Center button** in the Alignment group on the Home tab is often used to center a worksheet title over multiple columns.

continued…

Topic	Key Concepts
8.3 Adjusting Column Width and Row Height, and Changing Cell Alignment	A technique to add more space between cells to improve readability or emphasize a section is to widen a column or increase the height of a row.
	Open the Column Width dialog box from the Format button in the Cells group on the Home tab to enter a new value for the width of the column in which the active cell is positioned.
	Excel displays a series of pound symbols when a column width is too narrow to display all the cell contents.
	AutoFit changes the width of a column to fit the contents of the active cell.
	Open the Row Height dialog box from the Format button in the Cells group on the Home tab to enter a new value for the height of the row in which the active cell is positioned.
	Align the content in a cell within the cell boundaries at the left, center, or right horizontally, or top, middle, or bottom vertically using buttons in the Alignment group.
	The **Middle Align button** in the Alignment group on the Home tab centers cell contents vertically.
8.4 Entering or Copying Data with the Fill Command and Using AutoSum	**Auto Fill** can be used to automatically enter data in a series or pattern based upon an entry in an adjacent cell. When no pattern is detected, the **Fill** feature copies an entry or formula to other cells.
	The **Flash Fill** feature automatically suggests entries when a pattern is detected.
	Select a range and use the Fill button to open the Series dialog box or choose the *Down, Right, Up,* or *Left* option to copy an entry. For example, **Fill Right** copies the entry in the first cell to the cells that are right of the starting cell within the selected range.
	The small, green square at the lower right of an active cell is the **fill handle** and can be used to copy data and formulas or to enter a series by dragging the fill handle to adjacent cells.
	The **AutoSum button** in the Editing group on the Home tab enters a SUM function to add a column or row of numbers in the active cell.
	The **Auto Fill Options button** appears after dragging the fill handle with options for copying the data.
8.5 Inserting and Deleting Rows and Columns	A new row is inserted above the active cell or selected range.
	A new column is inserted left of the active cell or selected range.
	Use the **Insert button** in the Cells group on the Home tab to insert new rows or columns.
	Options for formatting new rows or columns are available from the **Insert Options button** that appears when rows or columns are inserted.
	Delete rows or columns using options from the **Delete button** in the Cells group on the Home tab.
8.6 Sorting Data and Applying Cell Styles	Select a range and choose the sort order option from the **Sort & Filter button** in the Editing group on the Home tab to arrange the rows by the entries in the first column.
	Open the Sort dialog box to sort by more than one column or to choose a different column in the range by which to sort.
	Cell Styles are a set of predefined formatting options applied to selected cells using options in the Cell Styles gallery in the Styles group on the Home tab.
	Use Cell Styles to format cells with a group of options faster and/or to promote consistency among worksheets.

continued...

Topic	Key Concepts
8.7 Changing Orientation and Scaling, Displaying Cell Formulas, and Exporting a Worksheet	New workbooks print on a letter-size page, in portrait orientation, with top and bottom margins of 0.75 inches, and left and right margins of 0.7 inches.
	Change print options even if you are only exporting the workbook as a PDF because PDFs are generated using the print settings.
	Change to landscape orientation using the Orientation option box in the Print backstage area.
	Landscape is a common layout used for wide worksheets.
	Turn on or turn off the display of formulas in cells by clicking the Formulas tab and then clicking the **Show Formulas button** in the Formula Auditing group.
	The **Fit Sheet on One Page** scaling option scales text on a printout so that all columns and rows print on one page.
	Export a worksheet as a PDF document by clicking the File tab, *Export*, and then the Create PDF/XPS button in the right panel of the Export backstage area.
8.8 Inserting and Renaming a Worksheet, Copying Cells, and Indenting Cell Contents	The **Sheet tab bar** near the bottom left of the window is used to insert, rename, and navigate among sheets in a workbook.
	Click the **New sheet button** on the Sheet tab bar to insert a new worksheet.
	Right-click a sheet tab and click *Rename* to type a new name for a worksheet.
	Copy and paste cells between worksheets using the Copy and Paste buttons in the Clipboard group.
	Keep Source Column Widths from the Paste Options button lets you paste new cells with the same column width as the source cell.
	The **Increase Indent button** moves an entry approximately one character width inward from the left edge of the cell each time the button is clicked.
	The **Decrease Indent button** moves an entry approximately one character width closer to the left edge of the cell each time the button is clicked.
8.9 Using Go To; Freezing Panes; and Shading, Wrapping, and Rotating Cell Entries	The **Go To** dialog box and **Go To Special** dialog box from the **Find & Select button** in the Editing group on the Home tab are used to move to a specific cell in a large worksheet.
	Freeze Panes fixes rows and/or columns in place for scrolling in large worksheets so that column and row headings do not scroll out of the viewing area.
	All rows above and all columns left of the active cell are frozen when Freeze Panes is turned on.
	Cells are shaded with color using the **Fill Color button** in the Font group on the Home tab.
	Long text entries in cells can be displayed in narrow columns by wrapping text within the cell column width using the **Wrap Text button** in the Alignment group on the Home tab.
	Angle Counterclockwise is an option from the Orientation button in the Alignment group on the Home tab that rotates text within a cell 45 degrees.

 Topics Review

Inserting Functions and Enhancing an Excel Worksheet

Several hundred preprogrammed formulas grouped by category in the function library are used to perform data analysis, decision making, and data modeling. With each application update, the function library is updated and expanded. To enter references for some formulas correctly, you need to understand the difference between an absolute and a relative cell address. Creating a range name to reference a cell or a block of cells makes creating and understanding a formula easier.

There are all sorts of creative ways to enhance the look of an Excel worksheet. Charts present data in a visual snapshot. Data organized in a list can be defined as a table. Excel offers various design styles with formatting options, and the ability to sort or filter lists of data. As you design your data into a more visually appealing presentation, Page Layout view is useful for previewing page layout and print options and for adding headers or footers to worksheets that will be printed. You can then use comments to collaborate with multiple people that are editing or reviewing a worksheet.

In this chapter, you continue working with formulas by learning the types of references used in formulas and how to use functions to perform statistical, date, financial, and logical analysis. Next, you explore strategies for presenting data using charts, comments, and tables as well as formatting a worksheet using page layout options and print options.

Learning Objectives

9.1 Create formulas with absolute addresses and range names

9.2 Create formulas with AVERAGE, MAX, and MIN statistical functions

9.3 Enter and format dates and use the TODAY function

9.4 Perform decision making using the logical IF function

9.5 Use the PMT function to calculate a loan payment

9.6 Create and edit a pie chart

9.7 Create and edit a column chart

9.8 Create and edit a line chart

9.9 Use Page Layout view, insert a header, change margins, and center a worksheet

9.10 Create and edit sparklines and insert comments into a worksheet

9.11 Sort and filter a range defined as a table

Read & Learn

Content Online
The online course includes additional training and assessment resources.

9.1 Using Absolute Addresses and Range Names in Formulas

The formulas created in the previous chapter used a type of cell reference called a **relative address**, where each column letter and row number changes to the destination column or row when the formula is copied. For example, the formula *=SUM(A4:A10)* becomes *=SUM(B4:B10)* when copied from a cell in column A to a cell in column B. Relative addressing is the most common addressing method.

Sometimes you need a formula in which one or more addresses should not change when the formula is copied. In these formulas, use a cell reference that is an **absolute address**. A dollar symbol precedes a column letter and/or row number in an absolute address, for example, *=$A$10*. Some formulas have both a relative and an absolute reference; referred to as a **mixed address**. See Table 9.1 for formula addressing examples. A range name is a text label to describe the value stored in a cell.

Table 9.1 Cell Addressing and Copying Examples

Formula	Type of Reference	Action if Formula Is Copied
=B4*B2	relative	Both addresses will update.
=$B$4*$B$2	absolute	Neither address will update.
=B4*$B$2	mixed	The address B4 will update; the address $B$2 will not update.
=B4*$B2	mixed	The address B4 will update; the row number in the second address will update, but the column letter will not.
=B4*B$2	mixed	The address B4 will update; the column letter in the second address will update, but the row number will not.

① Start Excel and open the workbook **FinancialPlanner** from the Ch9 folder in StudentDataFiles on your storage medium. If necessary, click the Enable Editing button to close Protected view.

② Use Save As to save a copy of the workbook as **FinancialPlanner-YourName** in a new folder, Ch9, in the CompletedTopics folder on your storage medium.

③ Review the worksheet, noticing the three rates in row 2; these rates will be used to calculate gross pay, payroll deductions, and savings.

④ Click cell C4, type =b4*b2, and then click the Enter button on the Formula bar or press Ctrl + Enter.

⑤ Use the fill handle in C4 to copy the formula to C5:C30.

Notice the entry #VALUE! in cell C5, which is an **error value**. An error value appears when Excel cannot calculate a formula.

⑥ Click cell C5 and read the formula in the Formula bar.

The #VALUE! error occurred because the content stored in B3 is a label (Estimated Hours) and has no mathematical value. Although you see results in

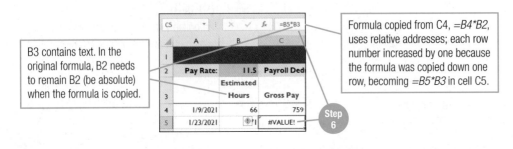

B3 contains text. In the original formula, B2 needs to remain B2 (be absolute) when the formula is copied.

Formula copied from C4, =B4*B2, uses relative addresses; each row number increased by one because the formula was copied down one row, becoming =B5*B3 in cell C5.

the cells C6:C30, the calculated values are not the correct gross pay amounts. For example, the formula in C6 is =*B6*B4*, which is multiplying 58 × 66, returning the result *3828*. The correct calculation should be 58 × 11.5, returning the result 667.

7 Select C5:C30 and press the Delete key, or click the Clear button in the Editing group on the Home tab and then click *Clear All*.

8 Click cell C4, click at the end of the formula in the Formula bar, press Backspace twice to delete B2 content, and then type $B$2 so that the formula now reads =*B4*$B$2*.

9 Click the Enter button on the Formula bar or press Ctrl + Enter, and then use the fill handle in C4 to copy the formula to C5:C30.

10 Click cell D4, type the formula =c4*e2, and then press Ctrl + Enter.

You can also press function key F4 to make the cell address absolute. F4 cycles through variations of addressing for the address in which the insertion point is positioned each time the key is pressed. The first variation is an absolute reference.

11 Click cell E4, type the formula =c4-d4, and then press Ctrl + Enter.

12 Select D4:E4 and then use the fill handle to copy the formulas to D5:E30.

A cell or a range in a formula can be referenced by a descriptive label, making the formula easier to understand. For example, the formula =*Hours*PayRate* is readily understood. Names are also used when a formula needs an absolute reference, because the cell referenced in a range name is automatically an absolute address. Assign a range name using the **Name box** (left of the Formula bar).

13 Click cell G2, click in the Name box, type SaveRate, and then press Enter.

A range name can use letters, numbers, and some symbols. Spaces are not valid in a range name, and the first character in a name must be a letter, an underscore, or a backslash (\).

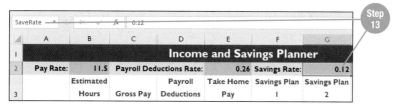

14 Click cell F4, type =e4*SaveRate, and then press Ctrl + Enter.

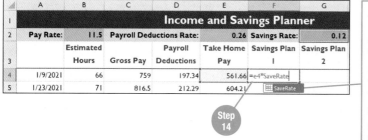

15 Use the fill handle in F4 to copy the formula to F5:F30.

16 Save the revised workbook using the same name (**FinancialPlanner-YourName**). Leave the workbook open for the next topic.

9.2 Entering Formulas Using Statistical Functions

A preprogrammed formula in Excel is called a **function**. In the previous chapter, you learned how to use the AutoSum function, which is the formula to add a series of values. The function library in Excel contains more than 400 preprogrammed formulas grouped into 13 categories. All formulas based on functions begin with the name of the function followed by the function parameters in parentheses. The parameters for a function (referred to as an **argument**) vary depending on the formula chosen and can include a value, a cell reference, a range, multiple ranges, or a combination of values with cell references.

1 With the **FinancialPlanner-YourName** workbook open, click cell I4.

2 Click the AutoSum button arrow in the Editing group on the Home tab and then click *Average*.

Excel inserts *=AVERAGE(B4:H4)* in the cell with the range B4:H4 selected. In this instance, Excel suggests the wrong range.

3 With the range B4:H4 highlighted in the formula cell, select B4:B30, and then press Enter or click the Enter button on the Formula bar.

Excel displays the result *68.96296296* in the formula cell, which is the arithmetic mean of the hours in column B. If empty cells or cells containing text are included in the formula argument, they are ignored.

Excel provides the format for the function argument in a ScreenTip.

4 Click cell I5, click the AutoSum button arrow, and then click *Max*.

5 Type *=b4:b30* and then press Enter or click the Enter button.

Excel returns the value *80* in the formula cell. MAX returns the largest value found in the range included in the argument.

6 Click cell I6 if I6 is not the active cell, type *=min(b4:b30)*, and then press Enter or click the Enter button.

The result *48* is displayed in I6. MIN returns the smallest value within the range included in the argument.

Excel's Insert Function dialog box assists with finding and entering functions and their arguments into a formula cell. A variety of methods can be used to open the Insert Function dialog box, including clicking the Insert Function button on the Formula bar, or clicking the Formulas tab and then clicking the Insert Function button in the Function Library group.

7 Click cell I8 and then click the Insert Function button on the Formula bar (button at the right of the Enter button).

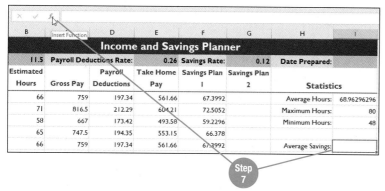

quick steps

AVERAGE, MAX, or MIN Functions
1. Activate formula cell.
2. Click AutoSum button arrow.
3. Click required function.
4. Type or select argument range.
5. Press Enter.

8 Click the *Or select a category* option box arrow and then click *Statistical*.

9 Click *AVERAGE* in the *Select a function* list box and then click OK.

10 Type f4:f30 in the *Number1* text box in the Function Arguments dialog box and then press Enter or click OK.

11 Click cell I9, click the AutoSum button arrow, and then click *More Functions*.

12 With the current text already selected in the *Search for a function* text box, type max and then click the Go button.

13 With MAX selected in the *Select a function* list box, click OK.

14 Type f4:f30 in the *Number1* text box in the Function Arguments dialog box, and then press Enter or click OK.

15 Click cell I10, click the AutoSum button arrow, and then click *Min*.

16 Type f4:f30 and then press Enter.

17 Save the revised workbook using the same name (**FinancialPlanner-YourName**). Leave the workbook open for the next topic.

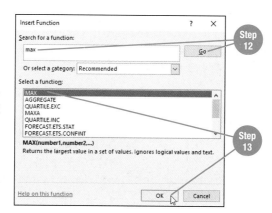

Tutorial

Using Statistical Functions

app tip

The *Count Numbers* option in the AutoSum drop-down list returns the number of cells within a range that have values. Use this function to return a count of values in a list.

9.3 Entering, Formatting, and Calculating Dates

 Watch & Learn

Hands On
Activity

A date typed into a cell in normal date format, such as *May 1, 2021* or *5/1/2021*, is stored as a value. For example, entering May 1, 2021 in cell A1 displays *1-May-21* in the worksheet area and *5/1/2001* in the Formula bar. Excel assigns a value to a cell containing a date. For a date of May 1, 2021, the value assigned to cell A1 would be 44317. The value assigned to a date represents the number of days that have passed since January 1, 1900. (January 1, 1900, is assigned the value 1.)

A time entered into a cell is stored as a decimal value representing a fraction of a day. For example, entering 12:00 pm into cell A1 displays *12:00 PM* in the worksheet area, *12:00:00 PM* in the Formula bar, and Excel assigns the value 0.5 to the cell (one-half of the day has passed).

A formula can reference a cell that contains a date or a time, since the entry is considered a value by Excel. A variety of date and time formats can be applied to cells containing dates. Examples of worksheets that use dates or times in formulas include worksheets to calculate elapsed time such as scheduling, hours worked, memberships, vacation durations, seniority, or employee service.

● - - - - - - - SKills

Enter a valid date

Enter the current date using a function

Create a formula using a date

Format dates

1   With the **FinancialPlanner-YourName** workbook open, click cell I2.

2   Type 12/20/2021 and then press Ctrl + Enter.

3   Notice that *Date* appears in the *Number Format* option box in the Number group on the Home tab. Table 9.2 gives examples of cell entries that Excel recognizes as valid dates.

● - - - - - - Oops!

General instead of *Date* appears? Excel did not recognize your entry as a valid date. Generally, this is because of a typing error. Try Step 2 again. Still *General*? You may need to check the Region in the Control Panel.

Table 9.2 Entries Excel Recognizes as Valid Dates or Times

Dates	Times
12/20/21; 12-20-21	4:45 (stored as 4:45:00 AM)
Dec 20, 2021	4:45 PM (stored as 4:45:00 PM)
20-Dec-21 or 20 Dec 21 or 20/Dec/21	16:45 (stored as 4:45:00 PM)

Note: The year can be entered as two digits or four digits and the month as three characters or spelled in full. Times are generally entered as hh:mm, but in situations that require a higher level of accuracy, they are entered as hh:mm:ss.

4   With I2 still the active cell, press the Delete key to clear the contents, type =today(), and then press Ctrl + Enter.

Excel enters the current date into the cell. No argument is required for this function. The TODAY function updates the cell entry to the current date whenever the worksheet is opened or printed. Do not use =*TODAY()* if you want the date to stay the same. Another DATE function that returns the current date is the NOW function. Entering =*NOW()* into a cell enters the current date along with the current time.

5   Click cell B3, click the Insert button arrow in the Cells group on the Home tab, and then click *Insert Sheet Columns*.

⑥ With B3 still the active cell, type Pay Date and then click A3.

⑦ Type End Date in A3 and then press Ctrl + Enter.

⑧ Select A3:B3 and then click the Center button in the Alignment group.

⑨ Click cell B4, type =a4+7, and then press Ctrl + Enter.

Excel returns *1/16/2021* in B4, which is seven days from January 9, 2021.

⑩ Use the fill handle in B4 to copy the formula to the range B5:B30.

⑪ Select A4:B30.

⑫ Click the *Number Format* option box arrow (the arrow next to *Date*) and then click *More Number Formats*.

⑬ With *Date* selected in the *Category* list box in the Format Cells dialog box, scroll down the *Type* list box and then click *14-Mar-12* (the Sample preview box will display *9-Jan-21*).

⑭ Click OK.

⑮ Click any cell to deselect the range.

⑯ Scroll down and review the dates in column A and column B.

You can also enter a date into a cell using a DATE function. A DATE function uses the argument *(Year,Month,Day)*. For example, the entry *=DATE(2021,12,20)* enters the date December 20, 2021 in a cell.

⑰ Save the revised workbook using the same name (**FinancialPlanner-YourName**). Leave the workbook open for the next topic.

9.4 Using the IF Function

Logical functions are used when you need a formula to perform a calculation based on a condition or comparison of a cell with a value or the contents of another cell. For example, in column G of the Income and Savings Planner worksheet, you calculated a savings value based on the take-home pay amounts in column F. Suppose you decide that you cannot afford to contribute to your savings plan unless your take-home pay is more than $500. The formula in column G does not accommodate this restriction; however, an IF formula can compare each take-home pay value with a set value and calculate the savings for those payroll earnings over the minimum.

1. With the **FinancialPlanner-YourName** workbook open, click cell H4.

2. Click the Formulas tab.

Functions are grouped on the Formulas tab in the Function Library group by category buttons. Click a button to view a list of functions in a drop-down list.

3. Click the Logical button in the Function Library group and then click *IF*.

Excel opens the Function Arguments dialog box for the IF statement. An IF statement has three arguments: *Logical_test*, *Value_if_true*, and *Value_if_false*.

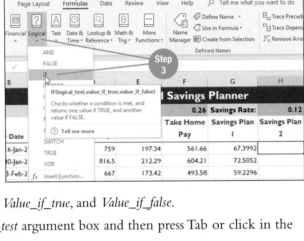

4. Type f4>500 in the *Logical_test* argument box and then press Tab or click in the *Value_if_true* argument box.

A logical test is a statement to evaluate a comparison and perform one of two actions. The statement *f4>500* tells Excel to determine whether the value in F4 is greater than 500. Either the value is greater than 500 *(true)* or the value is not greater than 500 *(false)*. See Table 9.3 on the next page for more examples of logical tests.

5. Type f4*SaveRate and then press Tab or click in the *Value_if_false* argument box.

Enter in the *Value_if_true* argument box the formula to calculate when the logical test proves true. In this instance, if the value in F4 is greater than 500, Excel will multiply the value in F4 times the value in the cell named *SaveRate (.12)*.

6. Type 0 and then click OK.

 — — — — **app tip**

Formulas, values, or text are all valid entries for the *Value_if_true* and *Value_if_false* argument boxes.

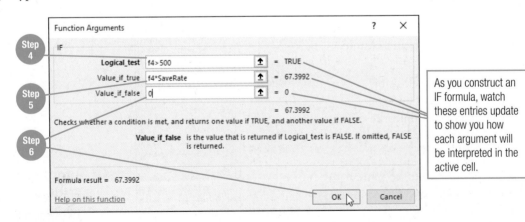

As you construct an IF formula, watch these entries update to show you how each argument will be interpreted in the active cell.

In the *Value_if_false* argument box, enter the formula to calculate when the logical test proves false. In this formula, if the value in F4 is 500 or less, zero is entered in the cell because you have decided that you cannot afford to contribute to your savings plan for earnings below the set value.

7 Look in the Formula bar at the IF statement entered into cell H4: *=IF(F4>500,F4*SaveRate,0)*.

Using the Function Arguments dialog box to build an IF statement is a good idea because the commas and parentheses are inserted automatically in the correct positions within the formula.

8 Use the fill handle in H4 to copy the formula to the range H5:H30.

9 Click any cell to deselect the range and then scroll down to view the results in H5:H30. Notice the cells with 0 occur in a row where the take-home pay value in column F is 500 or less.

10 Select C4:H30 and then click the Quick Analysis button that appears below the selection.

11 Click the Totals tab and then click the Sum button in the Totals gallery (first button).

Excel creates SUM functions in row 31 for each column in the selected range. Using the Quick Analysis button saves time when you need to add totals to multiple columns.

12 Select D4:H31, click the Home tab, and then click the Comma Style button in the Number group.

13 Apply the Comma Style format to C2 and then J4:J10.

14 Apply the Percent Style format to F2 and H2.

15 Select C31:H31 and then add a Top and Double Bottom Border.

16 Save the revised workbook using the same name (**FinancialPlanner-YourName**). Leave the workbook open for the next topic.

quick steps

IF Function
1. Activate formula cell.
2. Click Formulas tab.
3. Click Logical button.
4. Click *IF*.
5. Type *Logical_test* statement and press Tab.
6. Type value or formula in *Value_if_true* argument box and press Tab.
7. Type value or formula in *Value_if_false* argument box.
8. Click OK.

app tip

The Percent Style number format multiplies the value in the cell by 100 and adds a percent symbol (%) to the cell.

	A	B	C	D	E	F	G	H	I	J
1					Income and Savings Planner					
2	Pay Rate:		11.50	Payroll Deductions Rate:		26%	Savings Rate:	12%	Date Prepared:	9/7/2018
3	End Date	Pay Date	Estimated Hours	Gross Pay	Payroll Deductions	Take Home Pay	Savings Plan 1	Savings Plan 2	Statistics	
4	9-Jan-21	16-Jan-21	66	759.00	197.34	561.66	67.40	67.40	Average Hours:	68.96
5	23-Jan-21	30-Jan-21	71	816.50	212.29	604.21	72.51	72.51	Maximum Hours:	80.00
6	6-Feb-21	13-Feb-21	58	667.00	173.42	493.58	59.23	-	Minimum Hours:	48.00
7	20-Feb-21	27-Feb-21	65	747.50	194.35	553.15	66.38	66.38		
8	6-Mar-21	13-Mar-21	66	759.00	197.34	561.66	67.40	67.40	Average Savings:	70.42
9	20-Mar-21	27-Mar-21	60	690.00	179.40	510.60	61.27	61.27	Maximum Savings:	81.70
10	3-Apr-21	10-Apr-21	63	724.50	188.37	536.13	64.34	64.34	Minimum Savings:	49.02

First 10 rows of worksheet with formatting applied in Steps 12 to 14

Table 9.3 IF Statement Logical Test Examples

Logical Test	Condition Evaluated	IF Statement Example
F4>=500	Is the value in F4 greater than or equal to 500?	=IF(F4>=500,F4*SaveRate,0)
F4<500	Is the value in F4 less than 500?	=IF(F4<500,0,F4*SaveRate)
F4<=500	Is the value in F4 less than or equal to 500?	=IF(F4<=500,0,F4*SaveRate)
F4=$K$2	Is the value in F4 equal to the value in K2? Assume value in K2 is the take-home pay value for which you will set aside savings.	=IF(F4=$K$2,F4*SaveRate,0)
Hours<>0	Is the value in the cell named *Hours* not equal to 0?	=IF(Hours<>0,Hours*PayRate,0) Calculates Gross Pay when hours have been logged

Tutorial

Using Logical IF Functions

9.5 Using the PMT Function

Financial functions in Excel can be used for a variety of tasks that involve saving or borrowing money, such as calculating the future value of an investment, calculating the present value of an investment, or calculating borrowing criteria, such as interest rates, terms, or payments. If you are considering a loan or mortgage, use the Excel PMT function to determine an estimated loan payment. The PMT function uses a specified interest rate, number of payments, and loan amount to calculate a regular payment. Once a payment is displayed, you can change the interest rate, term, or loan amount to find a payment with which you are comfortable.

1. With the **FinancialPlanner-YourName** workbook open, click the LoanPlanner sheet tab.

2. Click cell B7.

3. Click the Formulas tab, click the Financial button in the Function Library group, scroll down the list, and then click *PMT*.

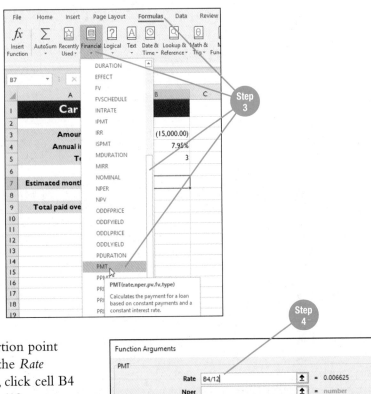

4. With the insertion point positioned in the *Rate* argument box, click cell B4 and then type /12.

●————— Oops!

Can't see B4? Drag the Function Arguments Title bar right until the dialog box is no longer obscuring your view of columns A and B.

Cell references can be entered in the Function Arguments dialog box by clicking a cell in the worksheet area or by typing the cell reference. The interest rate in cell B4 is expressed as the interest rate per year. Typing */12* after B4 causes Excel to divide the interest rate in B4 by 12 to calculate the monthly interest rate. To use the PMT function correctly, you need to ensure that the time periods are all the same. To find a monthly payment, you need to make sure the rate and terms are also in monthly units. Most lending institutions express interest with the annual rate (not monthly) but compound the interest monthly.

5 Click in the *Nper* argument box, click cell B5, and then type *12.

The value in B5 is the number of years you will take to pay back the loan. Multiplying the value times 12 will convert the value to the number of months to repay the loan. Most lending institutions express the repayment term in years (not months).

6 Click in the *Pv* argument box and then click B3.

Pv stands for *present value* and represents the amount you want to borrow (referred to as the *principal*). Notice the amount borrowed is entered as a negative value in this worksheet. By default, Excel considers payments as negative values because money is subtracted from your bank balance when you make a loan payment. By entering a negative number for the amount borrowed, the PMT formula will return a positive value for the calculated loan payment. Whether you prefer to display a negative value for the amount borrowed or for the estimated monthly loan payment is a matter of personal preference; both options are acceptable.

7 Click OK.

Excel returns the payment *$469.70* in B7. The PMT formula assumes a constant payment and a constant interest rate. Do not use the PMT function to estimate a loan payment where the payment or the interest rate is variable.

quick steps

PMT Function
1. Activate formula cell.
2. Click Formulas tab.
3. Click Financial button.
4. Scroll down list.
5. Click *PMT*.
6. Enter *Rate* particulars.
7. Enter *Nper* particulars.
8. Enter *Pv* value or reference.
9. Click OK.

8 Look in the Formula bar at the PMT statement entered into the active cell =*PMT(B4/12,B5*12,B3)*.

9 Click cell B9, type =b7*b5*12, and then press Ctrl + Enter.

Excel calculates the total cost for the loan to be $16,909.18.

app tip

Type a negative symbol in front of PMT if the amount borrowed is a positive value in the worksheet and you want the calculated payment value to also be a positive value. For example, =-PMT(B4/12,B5*12,B3).

	A	B
1	**Car Loan Planner**	
2		
3	Amount borrowed:	$ (15,000.00)
4	Annual interest rate:	7.95%
5	Term in years:	3
6		
7	Estimated monthly payment:	$469.70
8		
9	Total paid over life of loan:	=b7*b5*12

Step 9

10 Change the value in B5 from *3* to *4*.

Notice that increasing the term one more year reduces your monthly payment to 365.84; however, the total cost of the loan increases to $17,560.41 because you are making 12 more payments and are being charged interest for an additional year.

11 Save the revised workbook using the same name (**FinancialPlanner-YourName**) and then close the workbook.

Tutorial

Using Financial Functions

9.6 Creating and Modifying a Pie Chart

Watch & Learn

Hands On
Activity

Charts provide a visual snapshot of data. Charts illustrate trends, proportions, and comparisons more distinctly than numbers alone. Excel provides 15 categories of charts with multiple styles in each category. The Quick Analysis button recommends charts based on the type of data you are analyzing and allows you to preview the chart style with selected data. A **pie chart** is a circular graph with each data point (pie slice) sized to show its proportion to the total of all points within the selected range. A frequent use of pie charts is by governments to illustrate how tax dollars are allocated across programs and services.

- - - - - - - skills

Create a pie chart

Add data labels

Modify the legend position

Edit the chart title

1. Open the workbook **SocialMediaStats**. If necessary, click the Enable Editing button to close Protected view.

2. Use Save As to save a copy of the workbook as **SocialMediaStats-YourName** in the Ch9 folder in CompletedTopics on your storage medium.

3. Select A5:B9 in the SocialMediaWebsites worksheet.

Before you can insert a chart, you first need to select the data that you want Excel to represent in a chart.

4. Click the Quick Analysis button that appears below the selection area and then click the Charts tab.

5. Click *Pie*.

Excel graphs the data in a pie chart and places the chart overlapping the cells within a chart object window. Notice also that the chart object is selected with selection handles, three chart editing buttons, and the Chart Tools Design and Chart Tools Format tabs in the ribbon.

- - - - - - app tip

Roll the mouse over the chart options offered from the Quick Analysis button to see a live preview of the data graphed in the chart above the gallery.

6. Position the mouse pointer over any white unused area inside the chart borders and then drag the chart to the approximate location shown below.

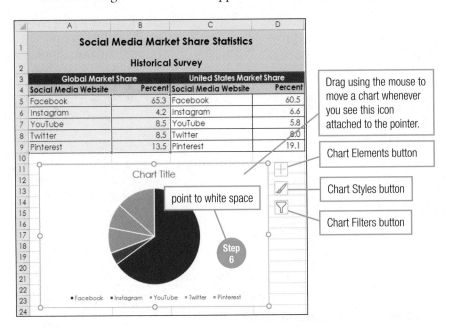

Drag using the mouse to move a chart whenever you see this icon attached to the pointer.

Chart Elements button

Chart Styles button

Chart Filters button

7　Click the Chart Elements button (displays as a plus symbol next to the chart).

8　Click the *Data Labels* check box to insert a check mark, click the right-pointing arrow that appears at the right end of the *Data Labels* option, and then click *Outside End*.

Although pie charts show proportions well, adding data labels allows a reader to include context with the size of each pie slice.

quick steps

Create a Pie Chart
1. Select range.
2. Click Quick Analysis button.
3. Click Charts tab.
4. Click *Pie*.
5. Move and/or modify chart elements as required.

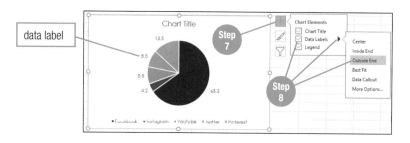

9　With Chart Elements still displayed, point to the *Legend* option, click the right-pointing arrow that appears, and then click *Right*.

10　Click to select the *Chart Title* object inside the chart window, select the text *Chart Title*, type Global Market Share, and then click in any white, unused area within the chart to deselect the title.

Global Market Share

11　Select C5:D9 and insert a second pie chart, as shown in Figure 9.1, by completing steps similar to those in Steps 4 to 10. In Step 10, type United States Market Share as the chart title.

12　Save the revised workbook using the same name (**SocialMediaStats-YourName**). Leave the workbook open for the next topic.

Tutorials

Creating Charts

Formatting with Chart Buttons

app tip

A popular technique to emphasize a pie slice is to move the slice away from the rest of the pie (called a *point explosion*). To do this, click to select the pie slices, then click to isolate the individual slice and drag the slice away from the pie.

Figure 9.1

The completed side-by-side pie charts are shown for the **SocialMediaStats-YourName** workbook.

9.7 Creating and Modifying a Column Chart

🌥 **Watch & Learn**

🌥 **Hands On Activity**

● – – – – – – – 𝖲𝗄𝗂𝗅𝗅𝗌

Create a column chart

Change the chart style

Change the chart color scheme

Add axis titles

🌥 **Tutorial**

Changing Chart Design

In a **column chart**, each data point is a colored bar that extends up from the **category axis** (horizontal axis, also called *x-axis*) with the bar height representing the value of the data point on the **value axis** (vertical axis, also called *y-* or *z-axis*). Use a column chart to compare one or more series of data side by side. Column charts are often used to identify trends or illustrate comparisons over time or by categories.

1. With the **SocialMediaStats-YourName** workbook open, click the Facebook sheet tab.

2. Select A7:B14.

3. Click the Quick Analysis button, click the Charts tab, and then click Clustered Column (first button).

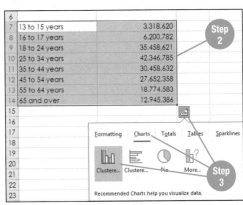

4. Position the mouse pointer over any white unused area inside the chart borders and then drag the chart to position the top left corner in row 1 under column letter C.

5. Point to the bottom right–corner selection handle. When the mouse pointer changes to a diagonal two-headed white arrow, drag the pointer down and right to resize the chart, releasing the mouse when the bottom right corner is at the lower right border of J16.

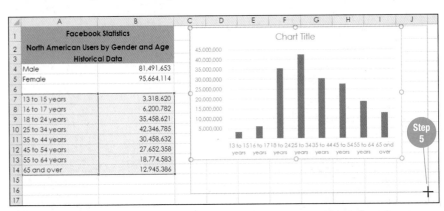

6. Click the Chart Styles button (displays as a paintbrush next to the chart).

7. Scroll down to the bottom of the Style list and then click the last option in the gallery (*Style 16*).

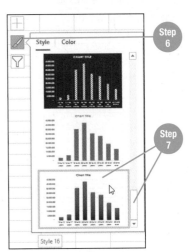

8   With the Chart Styles gallery still open, click the Color tab and then click the third row in the *Colorful* section (*Colorful Palette 3*).

9   Click the Chart Elements button.

More Chart Elements options appear for a column chart than a pie chart because data points are graphed on two axes. For example, you can add titles to the horizontal and vertical axes on the chart to describe the values and add context for each bar. You can also add a data table, add error bars, show or hide gridlines, or add a trendline on the chart. The chart title, data labels, and legend options for a column chart are the same chart elements used for a pie chart that you learned about in the previous topic.

10   Click the *Axis Titles* check box to insert a check mark.

Excel adds an Axis Title object to the vertical axis and to the horizontal axis.

11   Right-click inside the Axis Title object along the vertical axis (displays *Axis Title* rotated 90 degrees), and then click *Edit Text*.

12   Press Delete until the text *Axis Title* is removed, and then type North American Users.

13   Click to select the *Axis Title* object along the horizontal axis and then press Delete to remove the object.

14   Click to select the *Chart Title* object, select the text *Chart Title*, type Facebook Audience by Age Group, and then click in the worksheet area outside the chart to deselect the chart.

15   Compare your chart to the one shown in Figure 9.2. If necessary, redo an action in Steps 4 to 14.

16   Save the revised workbook using the same name (**SocialMediaStats-YourName**). Leave the workbook open for the next topic.

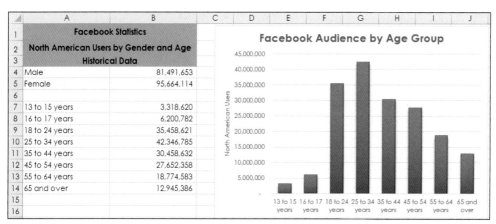

Figure 9.2

Shown is the completed column chart for the Facebook worksheet in the **SocialMediaStats-YourName** workbook.

9.8 Creating and Modifying a Line Chart

Line charts are best suited for data where you want to illustrate trends and changes in values over a period of time. With a **line chart**, a reader can easily spot a trend or identify growth spurts, dips, or unusual points in the series. Line charts are also often used to help predict future values based on the direction of the line.

Watch & Learn

Hands On Activity

●━ ━ ━ ━ ━ ━ Skills

Create a line chart

Move a chart to a new sheet

Format an axis

Format data labels

1. With the **SocialMediaStats–YourName** workbook open, click the FacebookUserTimeline sheet tab.

2. Select A4:B18.

3. Click the Quick Analysis button, click the Charts tab, and then click *Line*.

4. Click the Move Chart button in the Location group on the Chart Tools Design tab.

5. Click the *New sheet* option, type FBTimelineChart, and then press Enter or click OK.

   Click the **Move Chart button** to move a chart to its own chart sheet. Excel automatically scales the chart to fit a letter-size page in landscape orientation.

6. Click the second option in the Chart Styles gallery (*Style 2*) on the Chart Tools Design tab.

7. Click the Change Colors button in the Chart Styles group and then click the third row in the *Colorful* section (*Colorful Palette 3*).

8. Click to select the *Chart Title* object, select the text *Chart Title*, and then type Facebook Active Users Historical Timeline.

Notice the dates in column A were incorrectly converted when the chart was created, changing *Dec* to *Jan*. You will correct the dates in Steps 9 to 12.

9. Click any date along the bottom of the chart to select the category axis. Make sure you see a border and selection handles around the axis labels.

10. Double-click inside the border of the selected axis labels to open the Format Axis task pane at the right side of the window.

11. Click *Text axis* in the *Axis Options* section.

   Notice the axis labels change to display the December dates as they appeared in the worksheet.

12. Close the Format Axis task pane.

●━ ━ ━ ━ ━ ━ Oops!

No border around dates? Click the axis labels a second time. Sometimes the chart is selected the first time you click.

13 Click any data value on a data point to select the entire series of data labels.

14 Right-click any selected data value and then click *Format Data Labels*.

The Format Data Labels task pane displays.

15 Click *Above* in *Label Position* in the *Label Options* section.

16 Click the Text Options tab and then click *Text Fill* to expand the options list.

17 Click the Color button and then click *Black, Text 1* (second color in first row).

18 Close the Format Data Labels task pane and then click in the window outside the chart borders to deselect the data labels.

19 Compare your chart with the chart shown in Figure 9.3 and make corrections if necessary.

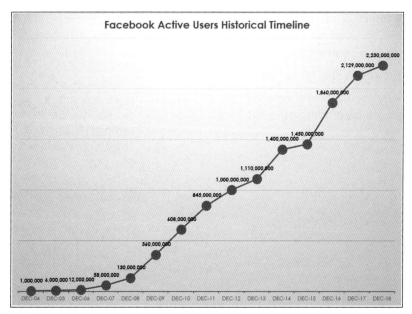

Figure 9.3

Shown is the line chart in a new chart sheet in the **SocialMediaStats-YourName** workbook.

20 Save the revised workbook using the same name (**SocialMediaStats-YourName**). Leave the workbook open for the next topic.

9.9 Using Page Layout View, Adding a Header, and Changing Margins

In **Page Layout view**, you can preview page layout options similarly to Print Preview; however, you also have the advantage of being able to edit the worksheet. The worksheet is divided into pages, with white space around the edges of each page displaying the size of the margins and a ruler along the top and left of the column letters and row numbers. Pages and cells outside the active worksheet are grayed out; however, you can click any page or cell to add new data.

1 With the **SocialMediaStats-YourName** workbook open, click the SocialMediaWebsites sheet tab.

2 Click the View tab and then click the Page Layout button in the Workbook Views group.

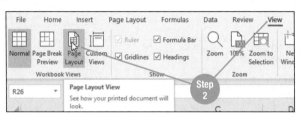

Notice in Page Layout view you can see the right pie chart is split over two pages.

3 Click the Page Layout tab, click the Orientation button in the Page Setup group, and then click *Landscape*.

Notice that changing the page orientation to print on the wider edge of the paper did not resolve fitting the entire worksheet on one page.

4 Click the *Width* option box arrow in the Scale to Fit group (displays *Automatic*) and then click *1 page*.

Inserting a Header or Footer

A header prints at the top of each page and a footer prints at the bottom of each page. Headers and footers are divided into three sections, with the left section left-aligned, the center section centered, and the right section right-aligned by default.

5 Click the dimmed *Add header* text near the top center of the page.

The Header pane opens with three text boxes in which you can type header text and add header and footer options, such as images, page numbering, the current date or time, and file or sheet names.

6 Type your first and last names.

7 Click in the right box in the Header pane.

8 Click the Sheet Name button in the Header & Footer Elements group on the Header & Footer Tools Design tab.

Step 8

Excel inserts the code &[Tab], which is replaced with the sheet tab name when you click outside the right text box.

9 Click the left box in the Header pane and then click the File Name button in the Header & Footer Elements group.

Excel inserts the code &[File], which is replaced with the file name when you click outside the left section text box.

Step 9

The &[Tab] code inserted in Step 8 is replaced with the sheet name when you click outside the Header box.

Header
&[File]   Student Name   SocialMediaWebsites

Social Media Market Share Statistics

10 Click any cell in the worksheet area.

Changing Margins

Worksheet margins are 0.75 inch at the top and bottom of the page and 0.7 inch at the left and right of the page, with the header or footer printing 0.3 inch from the top or bottom of the page. Adjust margins to add more space around the edges of a page, or between the header and footer text and the worksheet. Center a smaller worksheet horizontally and/or vertically to improve the page appearance.

11 Click the Page Layout tab, click the Margins button in the Page Setup group, and then click *Wide*.

The *Wide* preset margin option changes the top, bottom, left, and right margins to 1 inch and the header and footer margins to 0.5 inch.

12 Click the Margins button and then click *Custom Margins*.

13 Click the *Horizontally* and the *Vertically* check boxes in the *Center on page* section in the Page Setup dialog box to insert a check mark in each box and then click OK.

Step 11

Last Custom Setting
Top: 0.75"   Bottom: 0.75"
Left: 0.5"   Right: 0.5"
Header: 0.3"   Footer: 0.3"

Normal
Top: 0.75"   Bottom: 0.75"
Left: 0.7"   Right: 0.7"
Header: 0.3"   Footer: 0.3"

Wide
Top: 1"   Bottom: 1"
Left: 1"   Right: 1"
Header: 0.5"   Footer: 0.5"

Center on page
☑ Horizontally
☑ Vertically

Step 13

14 Click the Facebook sheet tab, change to Page Layout view, and modify print options by completing steps similar to those in Steps 3 to 13 to improve the appearance of the printed worksheet.

15 Save the revised workbook using the same name (**SocialMediaStats-YourName**) and then close the workbook.

quick steps

Add a Header
1. Display Page Layout view.
2. Click *Add header*.
3. Type header text in center text box, or click in left or right text boxes to type header text.
4. Click in worksheet area.

Change Margins
1. Click Page Layout tab.
2. Click Margins button.
3. Click preset option or click *Custom Margins* and change margins in Page Setup dialog box.

Center the Worksheet
1. Click Page Layout tab.
2. Click Margins button.
3. Click *Custom Margins*.
4. Click *Horizontally* and/ or *Vertically* check boxes.
5. Click OK.

app tip

Page Layout view is not available for chart sheets; however, you can add a header or change margins in Print Preview by using the Margins button or Page Setup hyperlink.

9.10 Creating and Modifying Sparklines and Inserting Comments

 Watch & Learn

 Hands On Activity

 Skills

Insert sparkline charts
Insert a comment
Edit a comment
Print comments

Tutorial

Summarizing Data with Sparklines

A **sparkline chart** is a miniature chart inserted into an individual cell within a worksheet. Sparkline charts are used to draw attention to trends or variations in data on a smaller scale than a column or line chart. Excel offers three types of sparkline charts: Line, Column, and Win/Loss.

A comment attached to a cell pops up when the reader points or clicks the cell. Comments are used to add explanatory information, pose questions, or provide other feedback to readers when a workbook is shared.

1. Open the workbook **SchoolBudget**. If necessary, click the Enable Editing button to close Protected view.

2. Use Save As to save a copy of the workbook as **SchoolBudget-YourName** in the Ch9 folder in CompletedTopics on your storage medium.

3. Click cell K3.

4. Click the Insert tab and then click the Column button in the Sparklines group.

5. Type b3:i3 in the *Data Range* text box in the Create Sparklines dialog box and then press Enter or click OK.

Excel embeds a column chart within the cell.

6. Use the fill handle in K3 to copy the sparklines column chart from K3 to K4:K11.

7. Click the *High Point* check box in the Show group on the Sparkline Tools Design tab to insert a check mark.

Excel highlights the bar in the column chart with the highest value by coloring it red. Other options on the tab are used to change the chart type or style, emphasize other points, display markers, or edit the data source.

app tip

Increase the row height and/or column width to enlarge sparkline charts.

8. Click cell K2, type Trend, and then click cell E9.

⑨ Click the Review tab and then click the New Comment button in the Comments group.

⑩ Type Assuming extra hours during Christmas break. and then click I3.

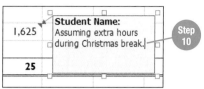

Excel inserts a red triangle in the upper right corner of a cell to indicate a comment exists for the cell.

⑪ Click the New Comment button, type May be able to use last month's rent., and then click any cell.

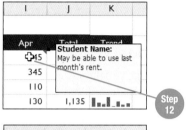

⑫ Point to I3 with the mouse to display the comment in a pop-up box.

⑬ Click I3 to activate the cell.

⑭ Click the Edit Comment button in the Comments group and edit the comment text to *May be able to use last month's rent*, which lowers this value to 55.

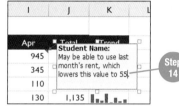

⑮ Click any cell to finish editing the Comment box.

⑯ Click the Show All Comments button in the Comments group to display both comment boxes in the worksheet.

⑰ Click the Show All Comments button to turn off the display of comment boxes.

By default, comments do not print with the worksheet. To print a version of the worksheet with comments shown, use the Show All Comments button to turn on the display of comments and print the worksheet. Alternatively, you can print comments on a separate page after the worksheet prints, which you will set up in Steps 18 to 20.

⑱ Click the File tab, click *Print*, and then click the <u>Page Setup</u> hyperlink at the bottom of the *Settings* section.

⑲ Click the Sheet tab in the Page Setup dialog box.

⑳ Click the *Comments* option box arrow, click *At end of sheet*, and then click OK.

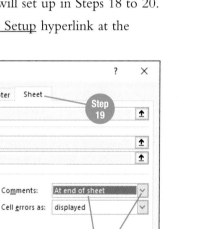

㉑ Click the Next Page arrow in the Print Preview panel to view the separate page with the comments and then click Back to return to the worksheet.

㉒ Save the revised workbook using the same name (**SchoolBudget-YourName**) and then close the workbook.

9.11 Working with Tables

A range of cells in a worksheet can for formatted as a table to analyze, sort, and filter data as an independent unit. A worksheet can have more than one table, which means you can isolate and analyze data in groups. A table also allows you to choose from a variety of preformatted table styles, which is faster than manually formatting a range. Use tables for any block of data organized in a list format.

A **filter** temporarily hides any data that does not meet a criterion. Use filters to look at subsets of data without deleting rows in the table.

① Open the workbook **CalorieActivityTable**. If necessary, click the Enable Editing button to turn off Protected view.

② Use Save As to save a copy of the workbook as **CalorieActivityTable-YourName** in the Ch9 folder in CompletedTopics on your storage medium.

③ Select A3:D23 and then click the Quick Analysis button.

④ Click the Tables tab and then click the Table button.

⑤ Select A1:A2, click the Fill Color button arrow, and then click *White, Background 1, Darker 5%* (first color in second row).

⑥ Click cell A4.

⑦ Click the Table Tools Design tab and then click the *White, Table Style Medium 1* option in the Table Styles gallery (option left of the active style).

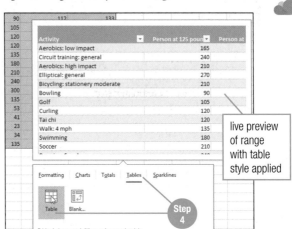

live preview of range with table style applied

⑧ Click the *Activity* column filter arrow (down-pointing arrow at the top of the *Activity* column).

⑨ Click *Sort A to Z*.

The table rows are sorted in ascending order by the activity descriptions.

🔟 Click the *Person at 155 pounds* column filter arrow.

A check box is included for each unique value within the column. You can filter a table by clearing check boxes for values or items you do not want to see in a filtered list, or use the *Filter by Color* and *Number Filters* options to specify a filter condition.

⓫ Point to *Number Filters* and then click *Greater Than*.

⓬ Type 200 with the insertion point already positioned in the text box next to *is greater than* in the Custom AutoFilter dialog box and then click OK.

Excel filters the table and displays only those activities in which the calories burned are more than 200 for 30 minutes of the activity by a person at 155 pounds.

⓭ Point to the *Person at 155 pounds* filter arrow. Notice the funnel icon displayed on the button and the ScreenTip that pops up telling you how the current worksheet data has been filtered.

Other indicators that the worksheet data is filtered are the blue row numbers (row numbers for hidden rows do not display) and the message on the Status bar that reads *9 of 20 records found* (next to *Ready*).

⓮ Click the *Person at 155 pounds* filter arrow and then click *Clear Filter From "Person at 155 pounds"*.

Clearing a filter redisplays the entire table.

⓯ Change the orientation to landscape and center the worksheet horizontally.

⓰ Save the revised workbook using the same name (**CalorieActivityTable –YourName**) and then close the workbook.

quick steps

Format a Table
1. Select range.
2. Click Quick Analysis button.
3. Click Tables tab.
4. Click *Table*.

Sort a Table
1. Click filter arrow at top of column to sort.
2. Click *Sort A to Z* or *Sort Z to A*.

Filter a Table
1. Click filter arrow at top of column to filter.
2. Clear check boxes for items you want to hide, or point to *Text Filters* or *Number Filters* and specify criterion.

app tip

You can filter a table by one column and then filter again by another column to further drill down to the data you want to analyze.

Tutorials
Sorting a Table
Filtering a Table

Topics Review

Topic	Key Concepts
9.1 Using Absolute Addresses and Range Names in Formulas	By default, a cell address in a formula is a **relative address**, which means the column letter or row number will update as the formula is copied relative to the destination column and row.
	A dollar symbol in front of a column letter or row number makes the cell reference an **absolute address**, and means the reference will not update when the formula is copied.
	A formula that has both relative and absolute addresses is referred to as a **mixed address**.
	Excel displays an **error value** in a cell when the formula cannot produce a calculated result.
	A descriptive label can be assigned to a cell or range and is created by typing the label in the **Name box**. Each cell reference in a range name is automatically made an absolute address.
	A range name can be used in a formula in place of the cell address(es).
9.2 Entering Formulas Using Statistical Functions	A preprogrammed formula in Excel is called a **function**.
	A formula that uses a function begins with the function name followed by the parameters for the formula (called the **argument**) within parentheses.
	The AVERAGE function returns the arithmetic mean from the range used in the formula.
	The MAX function returns the largest value from the range.
	The MIN function returns the smallest value from the range.
	The Insert Function dialog box accessed from the Insert Function button provides tools to find and enter a function and argument.
9.3 Entering, Formatting, and Calculating Dates	A valid date or time entered into a cell is stored as a numerical value and can be used in formulas.
	The TODAY function enters the current date into the cell and updates the date whenever the worksheet is opened or printed.
	Date and time cells can be formatted to a variety of month, day, and year combinations in the Format Cells dialog box with the *Date* category selected.
9.4 Using the IF Function	The IF function compares the contents in a cell with a set value and and performs one of two calculations depending on whether the comparison proves true or false.
	Use the Insert Function dialog box to assist with entering an IF statement's arguments.
	The *logical_test* argument is the statement you want Excel to evaluate to determine which calculation to perform.
	The *value_if_true* argument is the value or formula to return if the logical test proves true.
	The *value_if_false* argument is the value or formula to return if the logical test proves false.
9.5 Using the PMT Function	Financial functions can be used for a variety of calculations that involve saving or borrowing money.
	The PMT function calculates a regular loan payment from a specified interest rate, term, and amount borrowed.
	Make sure the interest rate and terms are in the same units as the payment you want calculated. For example, divide the interest rate by 12 and/or multiply the term times 12 to calculate a monthly payment from an annual rate or terms.
	In the PMT argument, *Rate* means the interest rate, *Nper* means the term, and *Pv* means the amount borrowed.

continued...

Topic	Key Concepts
9.6 Creating and Modifying a Pie Chart	Charts are often used to portray a visual snapshot of data.
	A **pie chart** shows each data point as a pie slice.
	The size of each slice in the pie chart represents the value of the data point in proportion to the total of all the values.
	Use the Charts tab in the Quick Analysis gallery to create a pie chart from a selected range.
	The Chart Elements button is used to add or modify a chart title, data labels, or legend.
9.7 Creating and Modifying a Column Chart	A **column chart** shows one bar for each data point extending upward from a horizontal axis with the height of the bar representing its value.
	The horizontal axis in a column chart is the **category axis**, also called the *x-axis*, and shows the labels for each bar.
	The vertical axis in a column chart is called the **value axis**, also known as the *y-* or *z-axis*, and is scaled to the values of the bars graphed.
	A column chart is often used to illustrate trends or comparisons over time or by category.
	The Chart Styles button is used to choose a preformatted style for a column chart or to change the color scheme.
	The *Axis Titles* option from the Chart Elements button is used to add titles to each axis in a column chart.
9.8 Creating and Modifying a Line Chart	A **line chart** helps a reader identify trends, growth spurts, dips, or unusual points in a data series.
	Use the **Move Chart button** in the Location group on the Chart Tools Design tab to move a chart from the worksheet into a chart sheet.
	A chart in a chart sheet is automatically scaled to fill a letter-size page in landscape orientation.
	Change axis options in the Format Axis task pane, or data label options in the Format Data Labels task pane.
9.9 Using Page Layout View, Adding a Header, and Changing Margins	In **Page Layout view** the worksheet is divided into pages, with white space depicting the size of the margins and a ruler along the top and left edges.
	You can see page layout and print options in Page Layout view while viewing and editing the worksheet.
	Add a header in Page Layout view by clicking the dimmed text *Add header*.
	Use buttons on the Header & Footer Tools Design tab to add options to a header or footer, such as a picture, page numbering, date or time, or file or sheet names.
	Change to a preset set of margins from the Margins button on the Page Layout tab, or choose *Custom Margins* to enter your own margin settings in the Page Setup dialog box.
	Open the Page Setup dialog box with the Margins tab active to center a worksheet horizontally and/ or vertically.

continued...

Topic	Key Concepts
9.10 Creating and Modifying Sparklines and Inserting Comments	A miniature chart embedded into a cell is called a **sparkline chart**.
	Sparkline charts emphasize trends or variations in data on a smaller scale.
	Activate a cell and choose a Line, Column, or Win/Loss sparkline chart from the Sparklines group on the Insert tab.
	Once created, add or modify sparkline options using buttons on the Sparkline Tools Design tab.
	A comment appears in a pop-up box when you point to or click a cell with an attached comment.
	Excel displays a red triangle in a cell containing a comment.
	Use the New Comment button on the Review tab to add a comment in the active cell.
	To change the text in an existing comment, activate the cell containing the comment and use the Edit Comment button.
	By default, comments do not print with the worksheet. Use the Show All Comments button to print a copy of the worksheet with the comments displayed, or print the comments on a separate page after the worksheet data by opening the Page Setup dialog box and changing the *Comments* option on the Sheet tab to *At end of sheet*.
9.11 Working with Tables	A block of data set up in list format can be formatted as a table for formatting, analyzing, sorting, or filtering purposes.
	A **filter** temporarily hides data that does not meet a criterion.
	Use a filter to review subsets of data without deleting rows.
	Click the filter arrow at the top of a column to sort or filter a table.
	Click the filter arrow at the top of a filtered column and then use the *Clear Filter From (column title)* option to redisplay the hidden rows in the table.

 Topics Review

Creating, Editing, and Formatting a PowerPoint Presentation

Presentations occur in meetings, seminars, and classrooms for a variety of purposes. Some presentations are informational, while others are designed to persuade you to buy a product or service. Some people use presentations at weddings, anniversaries, or family reunions to entertain an audience. In some organizations, presentations are used to provide information at a kiosk where a slide show runs continuously for individuals to view as they walk by or enter a booth. For example, at a trade show, a company might provide a slide show with information about a product. At school, you may have used a presentation as a study guide to prepare for an exam.

A presentation is made up of a collection of slides (referred to as a **slide deck**) containing text and multimedia. PowerPoint is a **presentation application** used to create a slide deck for presentations. In this chapter, you will learn how to create, edit, and format a presentation. You will create a presentation with a variety of text-based slide layouts; edit content and placeholders; move, duplicate, and delete slides; format slides using a variety of techniques; add notes and comments; and preview the presentation as a slide show. Finally, you will preview options for audience and speaker handouts.

Learning Objectives

10.1 Create a new presentation based on a theme, insert slides, and add content to slides

10.2 Change the design theme and theme variant, and insert a table

10.3 Format text using font and paragraph options

10.4 Create a slide with the comparison layout and select, resize, align, and move slide placeholders

10.5 Use Slide Sorter view and duplicate, move, and delete slides

10.6 Modify the slide master

10.7 Add notes and comments to slides

10.8 Run a presentation in Slide Show view and Presenter view

10.9 Prepare slides for audience handouts or speaker notes

Read & Learn

Content Online
The online course includes additional training and assessment resources.

10.1 Creating a New Presentation and Inserting Slides

Begin creating a new presentation on the PowerPoint Start screen by choosing a template, theme, and variant on a theme, or by starting with a blank presentation. The first slide in a presentation is a **title slide** with a text **placeholder** for a title and a subtitle. A placeholder is a rectangular container on a slide that can hold text or other content. Each placeholder on a slide can be manipulated independently.

PowerPoint starts a new presentation with a title slide displayed in Normal view. In Normal view, the current slide displays in widescreen format in the **slide pane**. Numbered slide thumbnails display in the **slide thumbnails pane**. A notes pane at the bottom of the slide pane and a Comments pane at the right of the slide pane can be opened as needed.

1. Start PowerPoint and then click the <u>More themes</u> hyperlink near the top right of the PowerPoint Start screen.

2. Click the *Ion* theme in the New backstage area.

The New backstage area has a gallery of design themes. Click to preview a theme along with the theme variants. A **variant** is a different style and color scheme included in the theme family.

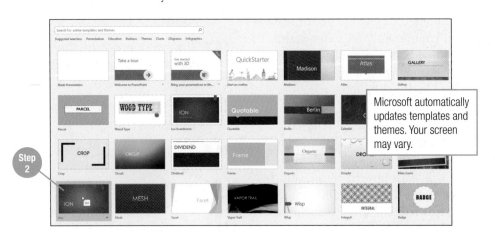

Step 2

Microsoft automatically updates templates and themes. Your screen may vary.

3. Click the last variant (orange color scheme), and then click the right-pointing arrow below the preview slide next to *More Images*.

Browse through the *More Images* slides to see a variety of content in the color scheme and view the theme or variant style and colors before making a selection.

Title Layout
SUBTITLE

Step 3

Click here if you want to close the preview to select another theme.

4. Click the second variant (blue color scheme), and then click the right-pointing arrow below the preview slide to view the blue color scheme with a Title and Content layout depicting a chart.

 Watch & Learn

 Hands On Activity

●——————— Skills

Create new presentation

Choose theme and theme variant

Insert slide

Edit text on slide

●—————— app tip

Double-click a theme to start a new presentation using the theme default style and color scheme.

 Tutorial

Opening a Presentation Based on a Template

5 Click the right-pointing arrow below the preview slide two more times to view other types of content with the blue color scheme.

6 With the Photo Layout preview displayed, click the Create button.

7 Compare your screen with the one shown in Figure 10.1.

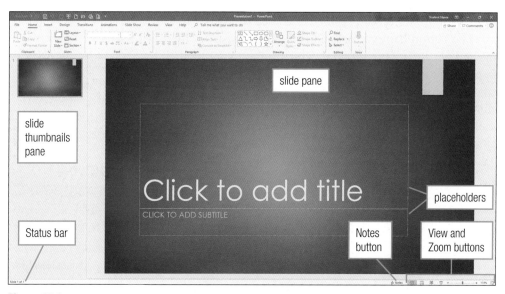

Figure 10.1

A new PowerPoint presentation with Ion theme and blue color variant in the default Normal view is shown above. See Table 10.1 for a description of screen elements.

Table 10.1 PowerPoint Features

Feature	Description
Notes button	Button to turn on or turn off the notes pane at the bottom of the slide pane
Placeholders	Containers in which you type or edit text, or insert other content such as an image or audio clip
Slide pane	Pane that displays the active slide; add or edit content on a slide in this area
Slide thumbnails pane	Pane that displays numbered thumbnails of the slides in the presentation; navigate to, insert, delete, or duplicate a slide in this pane
Status bar	Bar that displays active slide number with total number of slides in the presentation and displays a message about an action in progress
View and Zoom buttons	These buttons change the display of the PowerPoint window. View buttons in order are: Normal, Slide Sorter, Reading View, and Slide Show. Zoom buttons enlarge or shrink the display of the active slide.

quick steps

Start a New Presentation
1. Start PowerPoint.
2. Click More themes hyperlink.
3. Click theme.
4. Click variant.
5. Click Create button.

Insert a Slide
Click New Slide button in Slides group.
OR
1. Click New Slide button arrow.
2. Click required slide layout.

Edit Text
1. Activate slide.
2. Select text or click in placeholder and move insertion point as needed.
3. Type new text or change text as required.

Tutorial
Exploring the PowerPoint Screen

(8) Click anywhere in *Click to add title* on the title slide in the slide pane and then type Car Maintenance.

(9) Click anywhere in *CLICK TO ADD SUBTITLE* on the title slide in the slide pane and then type Tips for all seasons.

The subtitle text displays in all capital letters regardless of the case used when you type the text because the Ion theme uses the All Caps font effect for the subtitle text.

(10) Click in an unused area of the slide to deactivate the subtitle placeholder.

Inserting New Slides

The **New Slide button** in the Slides group on the Home tab is used to insert a new slide following the active slide. The button has two parts. Clicking the top part of the button adds a new slide with the Title and Content layout, which is the layout used most frequently. The content placeholder in this layout provides options to add text or a table, chart, SmartArt graphic, picture, or video to the slide. Click the New Slide button arrow to choose from a list of slide layouts and other new slide options. A **slide layout** is an arrangement of placeholders that determine the number, position, and type of content placeholders included on a slide.

(11) Click the top part of the New Slide button in the Slides group on the Home tab.

(12) Click anywhere in *Click to add title* in the title placeholder and then type Why maintain a car?.

(13) Click anywhere in *Click to add text* in the content placeholder, type Preserve vehicle value, and then press Enter.

Typing text in the content placeholder automatically creates a bulleted list. In the Ion theme, the bullet character is a green, right-pointing arrow.

(14) Type the remaining bulleted list items, pressing Enter after each item except the last one.

Prolong vehicle life

Improve driver safety

Spend less for repairs

Lower operating costs

Improve vehicle appearance

Reduce likelihood of breakdowns

Tutorial
Inserting and Deleting Text in Slides

app tip

Change the layout for a slide after a slide has been inserted using the Layout button in the Slides group on the Home tab.

Tutorials
Choosing a Slide Layout
Changing a Slide Layout
Inserting a New Slide

15 Click the top part of the New Slide button.

16 Type the text on the third slide as shown in the image below.

app tip

Press Ctrl + Enter to move to the next placeholder on a slide or to create a new slide when pressed in the last placeholder.

Editing Text on Slides

Activate the slide you want to edit by clicking the slide in the slide thumbnails pane. Select the text you want to change or click inside a placeholder to place an insertion point at the location where you want to edit text and then type new text, change text, or delete text as needed.

17 Click Slide 1 in the slide thumbnails pane.

18 Select *ALL SEASONS* in the subtitle text placeholder and then type car owners so that the subtitle text now reads *TIPS FOR CAR OWNERS*.

Tutorial

Checking Spelling

app tip

Always carefully spell check and proofread each slide in your pre-sentation. Start with the Spelling button in the Proofing group on the Review tab.

19 Click Slide 2 in the slide thumbnails pane.

20 Click at the beginning of the text in the third bulleted list item, delete *Improve*, and then type Sustain.

21 Click to place an insertion point within the title placeholder and edit the title text so that *m* in *maintain* and *c* in *car* are capital letters. The title should now read "Why Maintain a Car?"

22 Click in an unused area on the slide to deactivate the title placeholder.

23 Save the presentation as **CarMaintenance-YourName** in a new folder named *Ch10* in the CompletedTopics folder on your storage medium. Leave the presentation open for the next topic.

10.2 Changing the Theme and Inserting and Modifying a Table

The presentation theme and/or variant can be changed after a presentation has been created. To do this, click the Design tab and browse the themes and theme variants in the Themes and Variants galleries.

1. With the **CarMaintenance-YourName** presentation open, click Slide 1 in the slide thumbnails pane.

2. Click the Design tab.

3. Click the *Facet* theme in the Themes gallery (third option).

When deciding upon a theme, roll the mouse over the various theme options to view the active slide with a live preview of the theme. Changing the theme after slides have been created may cause some changes in capitalization in placeholders. For example, a theme that uses the All Caps font effect in a title or subtitle may mean that you have to do some corrections after the theme is changed if the new theme does not use All Caps.

4. Click the More button (⊽) at the bottom right of the Variants gallery.

5. Point to *Colors* and then click *Red Orange* in the Colors gallery.

From the Variant gallery More button are also options to customize the fonts, effects, or background styles used in the theme variant.

6. Click Slide 3 in the slide thumbnails pane.

Inserting a Table on a Slide

PowerPoint includes a Table feature for organizing text on a slide in columns and rows similar to the Table feature in Word. To insert a table on a slide, click the Insert Table button in the content placeholder.

7. Click the Home tab and then click the top part of the New Slide button to insert a new slide with the Title and Content layout.

8. Click anywhere in *Click to add title* in the title placeholder and then type Typical Annual Maintenance Costs.

9. Click the Insert Table button in the content placeholder.

☁ **Watch & Learn**

☁ **Hands On Activity**

●------- Skills

Change theme

Change variant

Insert a table on a slide

Modify table layout

☁ **Tutorials**

Applying a Design Theme

Changing and Modifying Design Themes

●------- Oops!

Design Ideas task pane opens? The Design Ideas task pane may appear when you are making changes to a presentation. The Designer feature works in the background to match content to professionally designed layouts. You can select a design by clicking an option in the task pane. Close the task pane if you don't want the pane taking up screen space.

☁ **Tutorial**

Creating a Table

10 Select *5* in the *Number of columns* text box in the Insert Table dialog box and then type 2.

11 Select *2* in the *Number of rows* text box, type 6, and then click OK.

PowerPoint inserts a table on the slide with the colors in the theme variant.

Insert Table	?	✕
Number of <u>c</u>olumns:	2	
Number of <u>r</u>ows:	6	
OK	Cancel	

Step 10
Step 11

12 With the insertion point positioned in the first cell in the table, type Type of Car and then press Tab or click in the second cell.

13 Type Cost.

14 Type the remaining entries in the table by pressing Tab to move to the next cell or by clicking in the next cell and then typing the text as follows:

Small size	$600
Medium size	$675
Large family sedan	$750
Minivan	$775
SUV	$825

Modifying a Table

The Table Tools Design and Table Tools Layout tabs provide options for modifying a table. These tools are the same table tools you learned in Word. Use the handles to enlarge or shrink the table size, or drag the border of a table to move it on the slide.

15 Drag the right-middle sizing handle to the left until the right border of the table ends approximately below the *c* in *Maintenance* in the title text, as shown in the image at right.

16 Click in any cell in the second column of the table.

17 Click the Table Tools Layout tab, click the Select button in the Table group, and then click *Select Column.*

18 Click the Center button in the Alignment group.

19 Click in any cell in the first column of the table, select the current entry in the *Width* text box in the Cell Size group, type 3.5, and then press Enter.

20 Drag the top border of the table to move it to the approximate location shown in the image at right.

21 Save the revised presentation using the same name (**CarMaintenance-YourName**). Leave the presentation open for the next topic.

Typical Annual Maintenance Costs

Type of Car	Cost
Small size	$600
Medium size	$675
Large family sedan	$750
Minivan	$775
SUV	$825

Step 15
Step 20

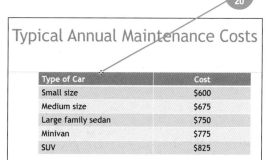

Typical Annual Maintenance Costs

Type of Car	Cost
Small size	$600
Medium size	$675
Large family sedan	$750
Minivan	$775
SUV	$825

quick steps

Change Theme
1. Click Design tab.
2. Click desired option in Themes gallery.
3. Click variant option.

Insert a Table on a Slide
1. Insert new slide.
2. Click Insert Table button in content placeholder.
3. Enter number of columns.
4. Enter number of rows.
5. Click OK.

Oops!

Pressed Tab after last entry and added a new row by mistake? Click the Undo button to remove the extra blank row.

Tutorial

Changing the Table Layout

Oops!

Table appears too small with first column wrapping text? You probably changed the width using the *Width* text box in the Table Size group instead of the Cell Size group. Use Undo and then try Step 19 again.

10.3 Formatting Text with Font and Paragraph Options

Font and paragraph formatting options in PowerPoint are the same as those in Word and Excel. Select text within a placeholder and apply a formatting option, or select a placeholder and apply a formatting option to all the text in the placeholder.

A multilevel bulleted list is created using the **Increase List Level button** and the **Decrease List Level button** in the Paragraph group on the Home tab. Each time you click the Increase List Level button, the insertion point or text is indented to the next tab and the bullet character changes to indicate the text is being demoted to the next list level. Use the Decrease List Level button to move the insertion point or text back to the previous tab and promote the text to the previous list level.

1. With the **CarMaintenance-YourName** presentation open, click Slide 3 in the slide thumbnails pane.

2. Insert a new slide with the Title and Content layout.

New slides are inserted after the active slide. The new slide should be positioned between the Fall and Winter Maintenance slide and the Typical Annual Maintenance Costs slide.

3. With the new Slide 4 the active slide, type Spring and Summer Maintenance as the slide title.

4. Type Thoroughly clean vehicle as the first bulleted list item in the content placeholder and then press Enter.

5. With the insertion point positioned at the beginning of the second bulleted list item, click the Increase List Level button in the Paragraph group on the Home tab.

6. Type Prevent rust by removing sand and salt accumulated from winter driving and then press Enter.

7. With the insertion point positioned at the beginning of the third bulleted list item, click the Decrease List Level button in the Paragraph group to move the bullet back to the previous level, type Check cooling system, and then press Enter.

8　Type the remaining text on the slide as shown in the image below, using the Increase List Level and Decrease List Level buttons as needed.

9　Select *12,000* in the content placeholder, click the Font Color button arrow on the Mini toolbar or in the Font group on the Home tab, and then click *Red, Accent 1* (fifth option in first row of *Theme Colors* section).

10　Click the Bold button in the Font group.

11　Click in the title text to activate the title placeholder.

12　Click the Center button in the Paragraph group.

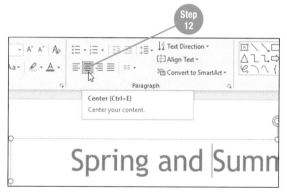

13　Click the Align Left button in the Paragraph group to return the title placeholder to the default paragraph alignment.

14　Save the revised presentation using the same name (**CarMaintenance -YourName**). Leave the presentation open for the next topic.

10.4 Selecting, Resizing, Aligning, and Moving Placeholders

Watch & Learn

Hands On Activity

The active placeholder displays with a border and selection handles, which are used to resize or move the placeholder. Paragraph or font options apply to the text in which the insertion point is positioned or to selected text. To apply a font or paragraph change to all the text in a placeholder, click the placeholder border to select the placeholder, which also removes the insertion point or deselects text.

Skills

Insert a slide with the comparison layout

Change a bulleted list to a numbered list

Resize a placeholder

Align a placeholder

Move a placeholder

1. With the **CarMaintenance-YourName** presentation open, click Slide 5 in the slide thumbnails pane.

2. Click the New Slide button arrow and then click *Comparison*.

3. With the new Slide 6 the active slide, type Top 5 Cars Rated by Maintenance Costs as the slide title.

4. Type the title and bulleted list text in the left and right content placeholders as shown in the image below.

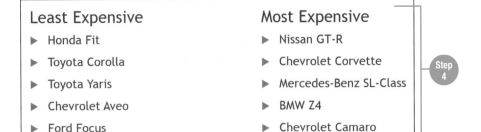

5. Click anywhere in the bulleted list below the heading *Least Expensive* to activate the placeholder.

6. Click anywhere along the border of the active placeholder to remove the insertion point, selecting the entire placeholder.

The placeholder border changes to a solid line from a dashed line when the entire placeholder is selected. The next action will affect all the text within the placeholder.

7. Click the Numbering button in the Paragraph group on the Home tab to change the bulleted list to a numbered list. Do *not* click the down-pointing arrow on the button.

Tutorial

Modifying Placeholders

Oops!

Only one bullet changed to a number? This occurs if you have an insertion point within the placeholder; only the item in the list at which the insertion point was positioned is changed. Go back to Step 6 and try again.

8 Click anywhere in the bulleted list below *Most Expensive*, click along the border of the active placeholder to select the entire placeholder, and then click the Numbering button.

9 Select the numbered list placeholder below the title *Least Expensive*.

10 Drag the right-middle sizing handle to the left until the right border of the placeholder is at the approximate location shown in the image below.

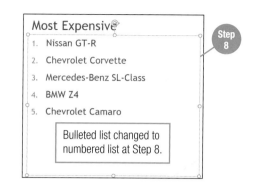

Most Expensive
1. Nissan GT-R
2. Chevrolet Corvette
3. Mercedes-Benz SL-Class
4. BMW Z4
5. Chevrolet Camaro

Step 8

Bulleted list changed to numbered list at Step 8.

11 Select the *Least Expensive* title placeholder and then drag the right-middle sizing handle to the left to resize the placeholder until the smart guide appears, indicating the title placeholder is the same width as the content placeholder below it.

Smart guides, also called *alignment guides*, appear automatically when moving or resizing objects. A **smart guide** is a colored horizontal or vertical guideline that helps you align, space, or size placeholders or objects evenly.

Least Expensive
1. Honda Fit
2. Toyota Corolla
3. Toyota Yaris
4. Chevrolet Aveo
5. Ford Focus

Step 10

Least Expensive
1. Honda Fit
2. Toyota Corolla
3. Toyota Yaris
4. Chevrolet Aveo
5. Ford Focus

Step 11

Smart guide helps resize close objects to the same width.

12 With the *Least Expensive* title placeholder still selected, drag the border of the placeholder right until the smart guides appear as shown in the image at right.

13 Select the numbered list placeholder below *Least Expensive* and drag right until left, right, top, and bottom smart guides appear, indicating the placeholder is aligned evenly with the placeholders above and right.

14 Save the revised presentation using the same name (**CarMaintenance-YourName**). Leave the presentation open for the next topic.

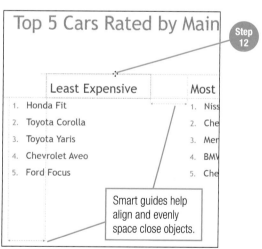

Top 5 Cars Rated by Main

Step 12

Least Expensive
1. Honda Fit
2. Toyota Corolla
3. Toyota Yaris
4. Chevrolet Aveo
5. Ford Focus

Most
1. Niss
2. Che
3. Mer
4. BMV
5. Che

Smart guides help align and evenly space close objects.

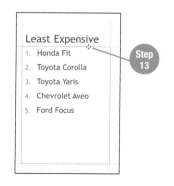

Least Expensive
1. Honda Fit
2. Toyota Corolla
3. Toyota Yaris
4. Chevrolet Aveo
5. Ford Focus

Step 13

10.5 Using Slide Sorter View and Moving, Duplicating, and Deleting Slides

Slide Sorter view displays all the slides in a presentation as slide thumbnails. Change to Slide Sorter view to perform slide management tasks. For example, you can easily rearrange the order of the slides by dragging a slide thumbnail to a new position within the slide deck. Select a slide in Slide Sorter view or Normal view to duplicate or delete the slide.

1 With the **CarMaintenance-YourName** presentation open, click the View tab and then click the Slide Sorter button in the Presentation Views group.

2 Click Slide 5 to select the slide.

3 Drag Slide 5 to place the slide to the right of Slide 2, and then release the mouse button.

As you drag to move a slide in Slide Sorter view, the existing slides rearrange around the slide and are automatically renumbered.

The pointer displays with a dimmed box attached when you drag to move a slide.

Duplicating a Slide

When you need to create a new slide with the same layout as an existing slide and with the placeholders sized, aligned, and positioned the same, make a duplicate copy of the existing slide. Once the slide is duplicated, all you have to do is change the text inside the placeholders. A duplicated slide is inserted in the presentation immediately after the slide selected to be duplicated.

④ Click to select Slide 6.

⑤ Right-click Slide 6 to display the shortcut menu.

⑥ Click *Duplicate Slide*.

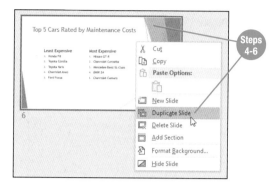

● – – – – **quick steps**

Slide Sorter View
Click Slide Sorter button on Status bar.
OR
1. Click View tab.
2. Click Slide Sorter button.

Move a Slide
Drag slide in Slide Sorter view to required location.

Duplicate a Slide
1. Select slide.
2. Display shortcut menu.
3. Click *Duplicate Slide*.

Delete a Slide
1. Select slide.
2. Display shortcut menu.
3. Click *Delete Slide*.

⑦ Double-click Slide 7 to return to Normal view.

Deleting a Slide

To delete slides in Slide Sorter view or Normal view, select the slide, display the shortcut menu, and then choose *Delete Slide* or press the Delete key. Multiple slides can be deleted all at once. To do this, hold down the Ctrl key while clicking each slide you want to remove. When all slides have been selected, right-click any selected slide and then choose *Delete Slide*.

Tutorial

Deleting Slides

⑧ Right-click Slide 7 in the slide thumbnails pane to display the shortcut menu.

⑨ Click *Delete Slide*.

⑩ Save the revised presentation using the same name (**CarMaintenance -YourName**). Leave the presentation open for the next topic.

10.6 Modifying the Slide Master

Each presentation that you create includes a slide master. A **slide master** determines the default formatting and paragraph options for placeholders when you insert new slides. If you want to make a change to a font or paragraph option for the entire presentation, making the change in the slide master will apply the change automatically to all slides in the presentation. For example, if you want a different font color for all the slide titles, change the color on the slide master.

1. With the **CarMaintenance-YourName** presentation open and the View tab active, click the Slide Master button in the Master Views group.

In **Slide Master view**, a slide master at the top of the hierarchy in the slide thumbnails pane controls the font, colors, paragraph options, and background for the entire presentation. Below the slide master is a variety of layouts for the presentation. Changes made to the slide master at the top of the hierarchy affect all the slide layouts below it except the title slide.

2. Scroll up the slide thumbnails pane to the first slide at the top of the hierarchy.

3. Click to select Slide 1.

4. Click the border of the slide master title placeholder on the slide master to select the placeholder.

5. Click the Home tab, click the Font Color button arrow, and then click *Dark Red, Accent 6* (last color in first row of *Theme Colors* section).

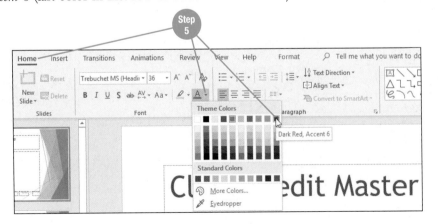

Watch & Learn

Hands On Activity

— — — — — Skills

Display slide master

Format placeholder on slide master

Tutorial

Formatting with a Slide Master

— — — — — app tip

Formatting changes made on individual slides override the slide master. Presentations should have a consistent look; therefore, limit individual slide formatting changes to only when necessary, such as to indicate a change in topic or speaker.

6 Click the border of the content placeholder to select the placeholder and then click the Bullets button arrow in the Paragraph group.

7 Click *Bullets and Numbering.*

8 Click the Color button in the Bullets and Numbering dialog box and then click *Dark Red, Accent 6* (last color in first row of *Theme Colors* section).

9 Click the *Hollow Square Bullets* option (first option in second row).

10 Click OK.

quick steps

Slide Master View
1. Click View tab.
2. Click Slide Master button.

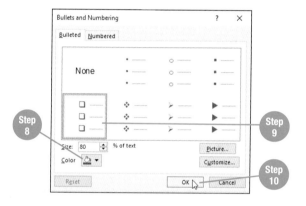

11 Click the Slide Master tab.

12 Click the Close Master View button in the Close group.

13 Click the Previous Slide or Next Slide buttons at the bottom of the vertical scroll bar or click each slide in the slide thumbnails pane to scroll through and view each slide in the presentation.

Notice that the font color for the title text and the bullet character are changed on each slide *after* the title slide. A title slide has its own slide master and is the first layout below Slide 1 in the slide master hierarchy.

14 Save the revised presentation using the same name (**CarMaintenance –YourName**). Leave the presentation open for the next topic.

app tip

Page Up and Page Down also display the previous or next slide in the presentation.

10.7 Adding Notes and Comments

Notes, generally referred to as *speaker notes*, are text typed in the **notes pane** below the slide pane in Normal view. Use notes to type reminders for the presenter or to add more details about the slide content for the person giving the presentation. In a presentation designed to be used as a self-study aid, text typed in the notes pane provides more detailed explanations to the learner.

Comments added to slides appear in the **Comments pane** at the right side of the slide pane. If you are creating a shared presentation, use comments to provide feedback or pose questions to others who will be editing the slide deck.

1 With the **CarMaintenance-YourName** presentation open, display Slide 1 in the slide pane.

2 Click the Notes button on the Status bar to turn on the display of the notes pane at the bottom of the slide pane. Skip this step if the notes pane is already visible.

3 Click anywhere in *Click to add notes* in the notes pane and then type Begin this slide with the statistic that approximately 5.2% of motor vehicle accidents are caused by vehicle neglect.

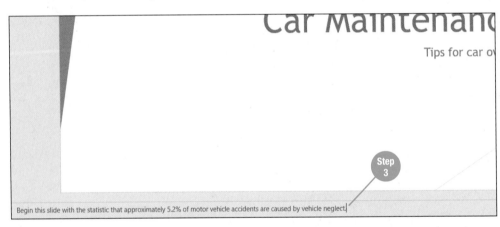

Begin this slide with the statistic that approximately 5.2% of motor vehicle accidents are caused by vehicle neglect.

4 Display Slide 3 in the slide pane.

5 Drag the top border of the notes pane upward to increase the height of the pane by approximately a half inch.

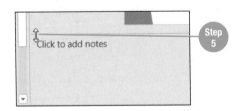

6 Click anywhere in *Click to add notes* in the notes pane and then type Mention that these costs are estimated for a driving distance of 12,000 miles (19,000 kilometers) per year.

7 Press Enter twice and then type Ask the audience if anyone wants to share the total amount paid each year to maintain his or her vehicle.

Mention that these costs are estimated for a driving distance of 12,000 miles (19,000 kilometers) per year.

Ask the audience if anyone wants to share the total amount paid each year to maintain his or her vehicle.

Watch & Learn

Hands On Activity

Skills

Display the notes and Comments panes

Add speaker notes

Add comments

Tutorial

Inserting and Deleting Comments

app tip

Text in the notes pane is visible to the presenter but not the audience during a slide show.

8 Click the Notes button to close the notes pane.

9 Click the Review tab and then click the top part of the Show Comments button in the Comments group to display the Comments pane at the right side of the slide pane.

You can also open the Comments pane by clicking the Comments button at the upper right corner of the ribbon. Either button displays or closes the Comments pane.

 quick steps

Add Notes
1. Activate required slide.
2. Click Notes button.
3. Type note text in notes pane.

Add Comments
1. Activate required slide.
2. Click the Review tab and then click the top part of the Show Comments button.
3. Click New button.
4. Type comment text.

10 Click the New button near the top of the Comments pane.

PowerPoint opens a comment box in the Comments pane with your account name associated with the comment.

11 Type Consider adding the source of these statistics to the slide.

12 Click Slide 4 in the slide thumbnails pane, click the New button in the Comments pane, and then type Add more information for any of these points?

13 Click on the slide to close the comment.

A *Reply* text box appears below the comment when the comment box is closed. Reviewers or other editors of the presentation can click in the *Reply* text box to provide feedback.

14 Click the Comments button at the upper right corner of the ribbon to close the Comments pane.

A comment balloon appears on the top left corner of a slide for which a comment has been added.

app tip

A prompt appears in the Status bar when you open a presentation that has comments, informing you of their existence in the file.

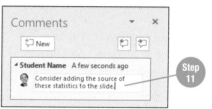

Use the Previous and Next buttons to navigate to all the comments in a presentation.

Click here to type a reply to a comment.

A comment balloon displays on slides with comments. Click the balloon to open the Comments pane and view the comments and replies.

Fall and Winter Maintenance

15 Save the revised presentation using the same name (**CarMaintenance -YourName**). Leave the presentation open for the next topic.

10.8 Displaying a Slide Show

Display the presentation in **Slide Show view** to preview the slides as they will appear to an audience. Each slide fills the screen with the ribbon and other PowerPoint elements removed; however, tools to navigate and annotate slides are available. Use the **From Beginning button** in the Start Slide Show group on the Slide Show tab to start the slide show at Slide 1.

In **Presenter view**, the slide show displays full screen on one monitor (the monitor the audience will see) and in Presenter view on a second monitor. Presenter view displays a preview of the next slide, notes from the notes pane, a timer, and a slide show toolbar along with other options.

1 With the **CarMaintenance-YourName** presentation open, click the Slide Show tab and then click the From Beginning button in the Start Slide Show group.

2 Click the right-pointing arrow that appears on the Slide Show toolbar near the lower left corner of the screen to move to Slide 2. Move the mouse toward the lower left corner of the screen to display the toolbar if the Slide Show toolbar is not visible.

You can also click anywhere on a slide or press the Page Down key to move to the next slide. The buttons on the Slide Show toolbar are shown in Figure 10.2 and described in Table 10.2 below.

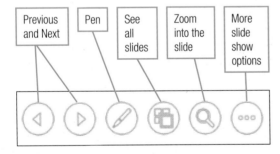

Figure 10.2
The Slide Show toolbar. See Table 10.2 for a description of each button.

Table 10.2 Slide Show Toolbar Buttons

Button	Description
Previous and Next	Displays the previous or next slide in the presentation
Pen	Displays a pop-up list of options for using the laser pointer, pen, or highlighter when running the presentation
See all slides	View all slides in the presentation similarly to Slide Sorter view. Use this option to jump to a slide out of sequence during a presentation
Zoom into the slide	Use this button to click on a portion of a slide that you want to enlarge to temporarily fill the screen for a closer look. Right-click or press the Esc key to restore the slide
More slide show options	Displays a pop-up list of options for customizing the presentation; use this button to end the show, access screen options (to show a black screen or a white screen) or display the taskbar

Watch & Learn

Hands On Activity

------ Skills

Display a presentation in Slide Show view

Display a presentation in Presenter view

------ app tip

Press F5 to start a slide show from Slide 1.

Tutorials

Running a Slide Show

Changing the Display when Running a Slide Show

③ Continue clicking the Next Slide arrow to navigate through the remaining slides in the presentation until the black screen appears.

After the last slide is viewed, a black screen is shown with the message *End of slide show, click to exit.* Many presenters leave the screen black when their presentation is ended until the audience has left because clicking to exit displays the presentation in Normal view on the screen.

④ Click anywhere on the black screen to return to Normal view.

⑤ Display Slide 1 in the slide pane and then click the Slide Show button on the Status bar.

The **Slide Show button** on the Status bar starts the slide show at the active slide.

⑥ Click the More slide show options button (button with three dots) on the Slide Show toolbar and then click *Show Presenter View.*

You can use Presenter view on a system with only one monitor to preview or rehearse a presentation. At a presentation venue, PowerPoint automatically detects the computer setup and chooses the correct monitor on which to show Presenter view.

⑦ Click the Next Slide button on the slide navigator near the bottom of Presenter view until you have navigated to Slide 3 (Figure 10.3).

⑧ Compare your screen with the one shown in Figure 10.3.

⑨ Continue clicking the Next Slide button until you reach Slide 6 and then click END SLIDE SHOW at the top of Presenter view.

⑩ Leave the presentation open for the next topic.

quick steps

Display a Slide Show
1. Click Slide Show tab.
2. Click From Beginning button.
OR
1. Display Slide 1.
2. Click Slide Show button on Status bar.

Display Presenter View
1. Display presentation as Slide Show.
2. Click More slide show options button.
3. Click *Show Presenter View.*

in the know

Many speakers include a closing slide as the last slide in a presentation that is left on the screen until the audience has left. The closing slide contains the speaker's contact information, a favorite or memorable quote related to the topic, or a thank-you message.

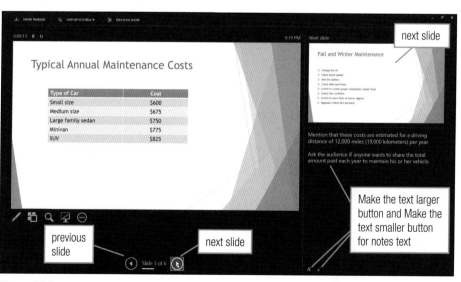

Figure 10.3
Shown above is Slide 3 of the **CarMaintenance-YourName** presentation in Presenter view.

app tip

You can also preview a slide show in Reading view where each slide fills the screen. A Title bar, Status bar, and Taskbar remain visible with buttons to navigate slides on the Status bar.

10.9 Preparing Audience Handouts and Speaker Notes

Some speakers provide audience members with a printout of the slide deck in a format that gives an individual room to handwrite notes during the presentation. PowerPoint provides several options for printing slides as handouts. Speakers who do not use Presenter view during a presentation may also print a copy of the slides with the notes included for reference during the presentation.

1. With the **CarMaintenance-YourName** presentation open, click the File tab and then click *Print*.

2. In the Print backstage area, click the *Full Page Slides* option box arrow in the *Settings* category.

3. Click *3 Slides* in the *Handouts* section.

    The option to print three slides per page provides horizontal lines next to each slide for writing notes, as shown in the Print Preview panel.

4. Click the *3 Slides* option box arrow and then click *6 Slides Horizontal*.

    Notice that the printout requires two print pages for the six slides in the presentation. By default, comments print with the presentation; the second page is for printing the comments.

5. Click the *6 Slides Horizontal* option box arrow and then click *Print Comments* to remove the check mark. The printout is now only one page.

6. Click the *6 Slides Horizontal* option box arrow and then click *Notes Pages* in the *Print Layout* section.

Notes Pages prints one slide per page with the slide at the top half of the page and notes or blank space in the bottom half.

7 Click the Next Page or Previous Page button until Slide 2 is displayed in the Print Preview panel.

8 Click the Next Page button to display Slide 3.

Notice the notes text is displayed below the slide.

9 Click the <u>Edit Header & Footer</u> hyperlink at the bottom of the *Settings* section.

The Header and Footer dialog box opens. In this dialog box, add text to print at the top or bottom of each handout. Many speakers put their professional affiliation, company name, or a copyright notice in a header or footer.

10 If necessary, click the Notes and Handouts tab.

11 Click the *Header* check box to insert a check mark, click in the *Header* text box, and then type your first and last names.

12 Click the *Footer* check box to insert a check mark, click in the *Footer* text box, and then type your school name.

13 Click the Apply to All button.

Click here to print the date at the top right of each page. By default, the date updates to the date the slides are printed; choose *Fixed* to enter a specific date.

14 Preview the header and footer text by scrolling through the remaining slides in the Print Preview panel.

15 Click the Back button to exit the Print backstage area.

16 Save the revised presentation using the same name (**CarMaintenance –YourName**) and then close the presentation.

Topics Review

Topic	Key Concepts
10.1 Creating a New Presentation and Inserting Slides	A **slide deck** is a collection of slides in a presentation.
	A **presentation application** is software used to create a slide deck. PowerPoint is the presentation application in the Office suite.
	A new presentation is created from the PowerPoint Start screen by choosing a template, a theme, or the blank presentation option.
	PowerPoint starts a new presentation with a title slide in widescreen format in Normal view.
	A **title slide** is the first slide in a presentation.
	A **placeholder** is a rectangular container in which you type text or insert other content.
	Normal view includes the **slide pane**, which displays the active slide on the right side of the screen, and the **slide thumbnails pane**, which displays numbered thumbnails of all the slides in a single column along the left side of the screen.
	A **variant** of a theme family is based upon the same theme but with different colors, styles, and effects.
	Add or edit text on a slide by clicking inside the placeholder and then typing or editing text.
	Use the **New Slide button** to add a slide to the presentation.
	A **slide layout** sets the number, placement, and type of placeholders on a slide.
10.2 Changing the Theme and Inserting and Modifying a Table	Change the theme and/or variant for a presentation after the presentation has been started using options on the Design tab.
	Insert a table on a slide using the Insert Table button within the content placeholder of a new slide.
	In the Insert Table dialog box, type the number of columns for the table, type the number of rows for the table, and then click OK.
	The Table Tools Design and Table Tools Layout tabs provide options to modify a table. These options are the same tools you learned for modifying a table in Word.
10.3 Formatting Text with Font and Paragraph Options	Select text within a placeholder or select the entire placeholder to apply formatting changes using options in the Font and Paragraph groups on the Home tab.
	Create a multilevel bulleted list using the **Increase List Level button** and the **Decrease List Level button** in the Paragraph group.
	Each time you click the Increase List Level button, the insertion point or text is indented to the next tab, and the level changes to the next level. Click the Decrease List Level button to move the insertion point or text back to the previous tab and level.
10.4 Selecting, Resizing, Aligning, and Moving Placeholders	The active placeholder displays with sizing handles and a border with which you can resize or move the placeholder.
	Click the border of a placeholder to remove the insertion point and select the entire placeholder to apply a formatting change.
	A **smart guide** is a colored line that appears on the slide as you resize or move a placeholder to assist in aligning the placeholder or evenly spacing the placeholder with other close objects.

continued…

Topic	Key Concepts
10.5 Using Slide Sorter View and Moving, Duplicating, and Deleting Slides	**Slide Sorter view** displays all slides as slide thumbnails and is used to rearrange the order of slides or otherwise manage slides in the presentation.
	Slide or drag a slide in Slide Sorter view to move the slide to a new position within the presentation. As you move a slide around in Slide Sorter view, existing slides adjust to make room and the slides are automatically renumbered.
	Duplicating a slide makes a copy of an existing slide with the placeholders sized, aligned, and positioned the same as the original slide. Use this method to create a new slide based on the same design as an existing slide that has had several placeholders customized.
	Delete a slide or group of slides by selecting the slide(s) to be removed and using the *Delete Slide* option from the shortcut menu or by pressing the Delete key.
10.6 Modifying the Slide Master	Each presentation has a **slide master** that determines the formatting and paragraph options for placeholders on slides.
	Display the slide master to make formatting changes that you want to apply to all slides in the presentation.
	Change to **Slide Master view** from the View tab to modify the slide master.
	In Slide Master view, the slide thumbnails pane displays the slide master at the top of the hierarchy.
	Below the slide master, individual slide layouts allow you to format a layout separately from the slide master.
10.7 Adding Notes and Comments	The **notes pane** appears along the bottom of the slide pane and is used to type speaker notes, reminders for the presenter, or more detailed information about the slide content for a reader.
	In a shared presentation, type questions or feedback about a slide for others who will be editing the slide deck in the **Comments pane**.
	Reveal or hide the notes pane with the Notes button on the Status bar.
	Reveal or hide the Comments pane by clicking the Comments button at the upper right corner of the ribbon or by clicking the Show Comments button in the Comments group on the Review tab.
	A comment is added to the active slide by clicking the New button in the Comments pane and then typing the comment text. Click on the slide when finished to close the comment.
	A *Reply* text box appears below a comment after the comment is completed for reviewers or editors to type a response to the comment author.

continued…

Topic	Key Concepts
10.8 Displaying a Slide Show	**Slide Show view** previews each slide as the audience will see it with a full screen.
	Display a slide show starting at Slide 1 by clicking the **From Beginning button** in the Start Slide Show group on the Slide Show tab.
	Presenter view works with two monitors, where one monitor displays the slide show to the audience, and the second monitor displays the slide show for the presenter with a preview of the next slide, timer controls, and the speaker notes in a larger display.
	The Slide Show toolbar provides buttons to navigate slides, annotate slides using the pen tool, see all slides, zoom into a slide, or access other slide show options during the presentation.
	After the last slide is shown, a black screen displays, indicating the end of the slide show.
	The **Slide Show button** on the Status bar starts the slide show from the active slide in the slide pane.
	Start a slide show and use the Show Presenter View option from the More slide show options button on the Slide Show toolbar to switch the view to Presenter view.
	PowerPoint automatically detects the correct monitor on which to display Presenter view.
10.9 Preparing Audience Handouts and Speaker Notes	Preview slides formatted as handouts in the Print backstage area using the *Full Page Slides* option box arrow in the *Settings* category.
	The *3 Slides* Handouts option provides lines next to each slide for writing notes.
	By default, comments print on a separate page after the slides; to prevent comments from printing, remove the check mark next to *Print Comments*.
	Choose the **Notes Pages** option to print one slide per page with the notes from the notes pane.
	Add header and/or footer text to a printout using the <u>Edit Header & Footer</u> hyperlink at the bottom of the *Settings* category in the Print backstage area to open the Header and Footer dialog box.

 Topics Review

Enhancing a Presentation with Multimedia and Animation Effects

Presentations are more engaging for audiences when multimedia is used to help speakers communicate their points. Incorporating images, sound, and video into slides in a slide deck can help an audience understand the content and remain focused on the presentation. Animation and transition effects focus attention and add interest when one slide is removed and the next slide appears on the screen or when new content appears on a slide. Several options are available in PowerPoint to add special effects to a presentation that will win over your audience.

Some presentations are not delivered in a venue where a speaker is controlling the slide advancement through the slide show. In these instances, a slide show is customized to run continuously based on a set time for each slide. A presentation delivered this way is called a *self-running presentation*.

In this chapter, you will learn how to add graphic images to slides using images, SmartArt, WordArt, charts, and drawn shapes. You will also learn to add text in a text box, add sound and video, and complete a slide show presentation by adding transitions and animation effects. Lastly, you will learn how to set up a slide show that advances through the slide deck automatically.

Learning Objectives

11.1 Insert and resize images on a slide

11.2 Insert and modify a SmartArt graphic on a slide

11.3 Convert existing text to a SmartArt graphic and insert and modify a WordArt object on a slide

11.4 Create and modify a chart on a slide

11.5 Draw and modify shapes and text boxes on a slide

11.6 Insert a video clip into a presentation

11.7 Insert a sound clip into a presentation

11.8 Add transition and animation effects into a slide show

11.9 Set up a self-running presentation

Read & Learn

Content Online

The online course includes additional training and assessment resources.

11.1 Inserting, Resizing, and Aligning Images

Adding an image, illustration, diagram, or chart on a slide emphasizes content, adds visual interest, and helps an audience understand and make connections with the information more easily than with text alone. As you did in Chapter 7, you can insert images from a file on your computer or from an online resource.

Inserting an Image from a File on Your Computer

To add an image to an existing slide, use the Pictures button in the Images group on the Insert tab to add the image stored in a file on your computer or a computer to which you are connected. Once inserted, move, resize, and/or modify the image using buttons on the Picture Tools Format tab. On a new slide, use the Pictures icon in the content placeholder to add an image to a slide.

1. Start PowerPoint and open the presentation **PaintedBunting** from the Ch11 folder in StudentDataFiles. If necessary, click the Enable Editing button to exit Protected view.

2. Use Save As to save a copy of the presentation as **PaintedBunting-YourName** in a new folder named *Ch11* in the CompletedTopics folder.

3. Browse through the presentation and read the slides.

4. Make Slide 2 the active slide in the slide pane.

5. Click the Insert tab and then click the Pictures button in the Images group.

6. Navigate to the Ch11 folder within StudentDataFiles on your storage medium in the Insert Picture dialog box and then double-click **PaintedBunting_NPS.jpg**.

7. Click anywhere on the image to select it. Using one of the four corner selection handles, resize the image to the approximate size shown in the image below.

8. With the mouse pointer positioned anywhere over the selected image, drag the image to the right side of the slide, aligning it with the horizontal and vertical smart guides that appear when the image is even with the top of the text and the right margin on the slide.

Align the image with horizontal and vertical smart guides.

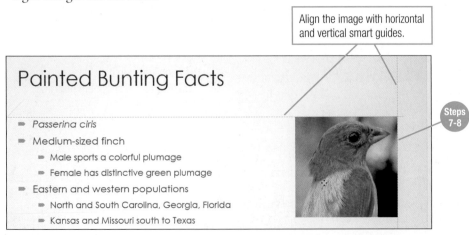

Watch & Learn

Hands On Activity

—————— Skills

Add an image from a file on your storage medium

Add an image from an online resource

Tutorial
Inserting, Sizing, and Positioning an Image

9 Insert the image **PaintedBunting_Female.jpg** near the bottom right of the slide (see image below), by completing steps similar to Steps 5 to 8.

Inserting an Image from a Web Resource

The Online Pictures button in the Images group on the Insert tab or in a content placeholder is used to find an image from a website. Use the search text box in the Online Pictures dialog box to type a word or phrase representing the image you need. As you learned in Chapter 7, search results displayed are from the Bing search engine and apply a copyright filter displaying images tagged with a Creative Commons license.

10 Make Slide 6 the active slide in the slide pane.

11 Click the Insert tab and then click the Online Pictures button.

12 With the insertion point positioned in the search text box, type team and then press Enter.

13 Double-click the image shown on the slide below. If you cannot locate the same image, close the Online Pictures dialog box and insert the image **Team.png** that is saved in the Ch11 folder in StudentDataFiles.

14 Resize and move the image to the left side of the bulleted list, aligning it with the horizontal and vertical smart guides that appear when the image is placed evenly with the top and left edge of the bulleted list, as shown on the slide below.

15 Save the revised presentation using the same name (**PaintedBunting -YourName**). Leave the presentation open for the next topic.

11.2 Inserting a SmartArt Graphic

SmartArt is a graphic object that visually communicates a relationship in a list, process, cycle, hierarchy, or other diagram. Begin creating a SmartArt graphic by choosing a predesigned layout and then adding text in the Text pane, or by typing text directly in the text placeholders within the shapes. You can add and delete shapes to the graphic as needed and choose from a variety of color schemes and styles. See Table 11.1 for a description of layout category diagrams created using SmartArt.

Table 11.1 SmartArt Graphic Layout Categories

Layout Category	Description
List	Show nonsequential tasks, processes, or other list items
Process	Illustrate a sequential series of steps to complete a process or task
Cycle	Show a sequence of steps or tasks in a circular or looped process
Hierarchy	Show an organizational chart or decision tree
Relationship	Show how parts or elements are related to one another
Matrix	Depict how individual parts or ideas relate to a whole or central idea
Pyramid	Show proportional or hierarchical relationships that build upward
Picture	Add pictures inside shapes with small amounts of text to display ideas, a process, or a relationship

1. With the **PaintedBunting-YourName** presentation open and Slide 6 the active slide in the slide pane, click the Insert tab.

2. Click the SmartArt button in the Illustrations group.

3. In the Choose a SmartArt Graphic dialog box, click *Process* in the Category pane (left pane), click *Basic Chevron Process* in the Layout pane (second option, fifth row in center pane), and then click OK.

PowerPoint places the SmartArt graphic in the center of the slide, overlapping existing content. Three shapes are automatically included in the *Basic Chevron Process* layout.

④ With the insertion point in the first bullet Text pane, type Band; click next to the second bullet or press the Down Arrow key and then type Observe; click next to the third bullet or press the Down Arrow key and then type Analyze.

The SmartArt graphic updates as each word is typed in the Text pane to display the text in the shape. You can also add text to the shapes by typing text directly within the text placeholders inside each shape.

⑤ Click the Close button to close the Text pane.

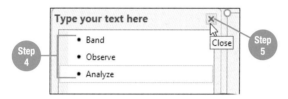

⑥ With the SmartArt Tools Design tab active, click the More button at the bottom of the SmartArt Styles gallery.

⑦ Click *Polished* (first option in *3-D* section).

⑧ Click the Change Colors button in the SmartArt Styles group and then click *Colorful – Accent Colors* (first option in the *Colorful* section).

⑨ Drag the border of the SmartArt graphic to reposition the graphic near the bottom center of the slide, and then click on a blank area on the slide to deselect the object (Figure 11.1).

⑩ Save the revised presentation using the same name (**PaintedBunting -YourName**). Leave the presentation open for the next topic.

Figure 11.1

The completed Slide 6 with SmartArt graphic is shown here.

● – – – – quick steps

Insert a SmartArt Graphic
1. Activate slide.
2. Click Insert tab.
3. Click SmartArt button.
4. Select category in left pane.
5. Select layout in center pane.
6. Click OK.
7. Add text in Text pane or in shapes.
8. Format and move graphic object as required.

● – – – – – – Oops!

Text pane is not open at Step 4? Click the arrow along the left border of the graphic to display the Text pane.

☁ Tutorial

Formatting SmartArt

11.3 Converting Text to SmartArt and Inserting WordArt

An existing bulleted list on a slide can be converted to a SmartArt graphic using the **Convert to SmartArt button** in the Paragraph group on the Home tab. **WordArt** is text that is created and formatted as a graphic object. With WordArt, you can create decorative text on a slide with a variety of WordArt Styles and text effects. A WordArt object can also have the text formed around a variety of shapes.

1. With the **PaintedBunting-YourName** presentation open, make Slide 5 the active slide in the slide pane.

2. Click in the bulleted list to activate the placeholder.

3. Click the Convert to SmartArt Graphic button in the Paragraph group on the Home tab.

4. Click *Hierarchy List* (second option in second row).

Step 3

Step 4

PowerPoint converts the text in the bulleted list into the selected SmartArt layout. Level 1 text from the bulleted list is placed inside shapes at the top level in the hierarchy diagram, with level 2 text in shapes below the corresponding level 1 box.

5. Close the Text pane if the Text pane is open.

6. Click in the second shape in the top level of the hierarchy, delete *Need to* and capitalize *m* (type M) so that the text inside the shape reads *Manage and preserve natural habitat.*

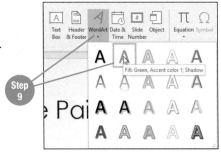

Step 6

7. Click anywhere along the border of the SmartArt object to select the entire SmartArt object and then change the SmartArt style and color scheme to the same style and color used in the SmartArt graphic on Slide 6.

8. Click on a blank area of the slide to deselect the SmartArt object and then click the Insert tab.

9. Click the WordArt button in the Text group and then click *Fill: Green, Accent color 1; Shadow* (second option in first row).

Step 9

10. With *Your text here* inside the WordArt object already selected, type Help Save the Painted Bunting!

11. Drag the border of the WordArt object to the bottom of the slide, as shown in the image below.

Step 11

Manage private and open public lands

Help Save the Painted Bunting!

☁ **Watch & Learn**

☁ **Hands On Activity**

●━━━━━━ Skills

Convert text to a SmartArt graphic

Insert and modify a WordArt object

☁ **Tutorials**

Converting Text and WordArt to a SmartArt Graphic

Inserting and Formatting WordArt

●━━━━━━ Oops!

Don't remember the style and color used on Slide 6? Refer to page 257, Steps 6 to 8 to see how the SmartArt graphic was formatted on Slide 6.

12 Click the Text Effects button in the WordArt Styles group on the Drawing Tools Format tab, point to *Glow*, and then click *Glow: 5 point; Lime, Accent color 3* (third option in first row of *Glow Variations* section).

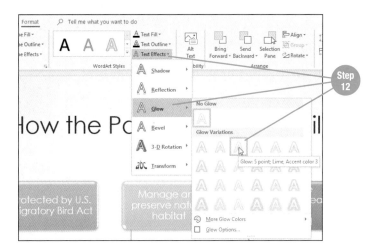

13 Click the Text Fill button and then click *Dark Teal, Accent 4* (eighth option in first row in *Theme Colors* section).

14 Click the Shape Effects button in the Shape Styles group, point to *Shadow*, and then click *Offset: Bottom Right* (first option in *Outer* section).

15 Click a blank area on the slide and compare your slide with the one shown in Figure 11.2. Redo any steps to make corrections as needed.

16 Save the revised presentation using the same name (**PaintedBunting-YourName**). Leave the presentation open for the next topic.

Figure 11.2

The completed Slide 5, with a WordArt object and a bulleted list converted to a SmartArt object, is shown.

11.4 Creating a Chart on a Slide

Charts similar to the ones you created with Excel in Chapter 9 can be added to a PowerPoint slide. Add a chart using the Insert Chart icon in a content placeholder or with the Chart button in the Illustrations group on the Insert tab. Charts are commonly used in presentations to display dollar figures, targets, budgets, comparisons, patterns, trends, or variations in numerical data.

1. With the **PaintedBunting-YourName** presentation open, make Slide 3 the active slide in the slide pane.

2. Click the Insert Chart icon in the content placeholder.

3. Click OK in the Insert Chart dialog box with *Column* selected in the All Charts category list and *Clustered Column* selected as the chart type.

Watch & Learn

Hands On Activity

━━━━━━━ Skills

Create a chart on a slide

Modify the chart style and color

Tutorials

Creating a Chart

Formatting with Chart Buttons

Changing the Chart Design

Step 2

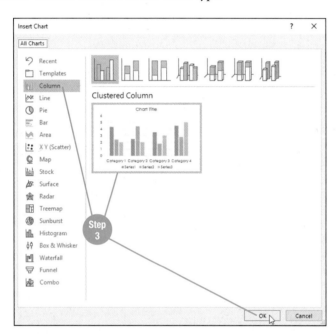

Step 3

PowerPoint displays a small worksheet with placeholder data and a chart on the slide, as shown in the image below. Data to be graphed is typed inside the worksheet, which updates the chart on the slide as you enter labels and values.

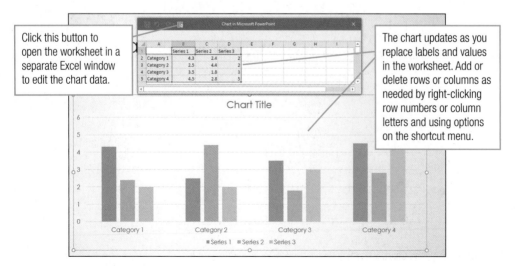

Click this button to open the worksheet in a separate Excel window to edit the chart data.

The chart updates as you replace labels and values in the worksheet. Add or delete rows or columns as needed by right-clicking row numbers or column letters and using options on the shortcut menu.

4 With B1 in the worksheet the active cell, type 2019.

5 Click C1 and then type 2020.

6 Type the remaining data in the cells in the worksheet as shown in the image below.

7 Close the worksheet.

quick steps

Insert a Chart
1. Activate slide.
2. Click Insert Chart icon in content placeholder.
3. Choose category and chart type.
4. Click OK.
5. Add data in chart data grid.
6. Close worksheet.
7. Format chart as required.

8 Click to select the chart title object, select the text *Chart Title*, and then type Monthly Sightings January to April.

9 Click the border of the chart to select the entire chart.

10 Click *Style 4* (fourth option) in the Chart Styles gallery on the Chart Tools Design tab.

app tip

A complex chart or a chart with a lot of data that updates regularly is best created in Excel and copied to a slide in PowerPoint. You will learn how to do this in Chapter 14.

11 Click the Change Colors button in the Chart Styles group and then click *Colorful Palette 2* (second row in *Colorful* section).

12 Click on the slide outside the chart to deselect the chart object and then compare your slide with the one shown in Figure 11.3.

13 Save the revised presentation using the same name (**PaintedBunting –YourName**). Leave the presentation open for the next topic.

Tutorial

Changing Chart Formatting

Oops!

Your chart data doesn't match Figure 11.3? Reopen the Excel worksheet to edit the entries you typed in Steps 4 to 6. To do this, select the chart object, click the Chart Tools Design tab, and then click the top part of the Edit Data button in the Data group.

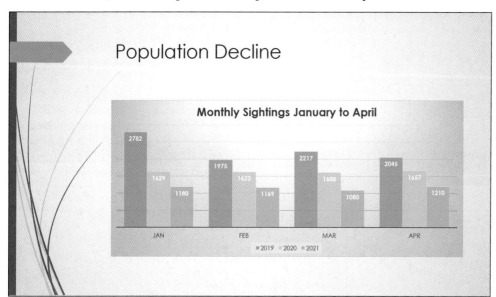

Figure 11.3

Shown is the completed Slide 3 with a Clustered Column Chart.

11.5 Drawing a Shape and Adding a Text Box

A graphic can be added to a slide by drawing a line, rectangle, circle, arrow, star, banner, or other shape. Once the shape is drawn, text can be added inside the shape, and the shape can be formatted by adding a visual effect or by changing the outline color or fill color. Draw a shape by clicking the **Shapes button** in the Illustrations group on the Insert tab and then selecting the desired shape in the list. To insert the shape at a preset size, click the slide where you want the shape to appear, or drag the crosshairs to create a shape the size that you want.

A text box is text inside a rectangular object that can be manipulated independently from other objects on a slide. To add a text box, click the Text Box button in the Text group on the Insert tab. When the mouse pointer displays as a down-pointing arrow, click on the slide at the position where the text box is to begin and then start typing—the text box width expands to accommodate the amount of text typed.

1. With the **PaintedBunting-YourName** presentation open and with Slide 3 the active slide in the slide pane, click the Insert tab.

2. Click the Shapes button in the Illustrations group.

3. Click the *Arrow: Striped Right* shape (fifth option in second row of the *Block Arrows* section).

A shape can be drawn one of two ways: move the crosshairs to the location where the shape is to appear and then click to insert the shape at the default shape size; or, at the desired position on the slide, drag the crosshairs until the shape is the desired height and width. In the next step, you will create a shape using the first method.

4. Click inside the chart above the JAN bar for 2020 (the bar with the value *1629*).

5. With the shape selected, type A 41% decline!

6. Drag the right-middle sizing handle to the right until the text fits on one line inside the arrow shape.

Watch & Learn

Hands On Activity

- - - - - - - Skills

Draw and modify a shape on a slide

Add text inside a shape

Format a shape

Create a text box on a slide

Tutorials

Inserting, Sizing, and Positioning Shapes

Formatting Shapes

Copying and Rotating Shapes

Inserting and Formatting Text Boxes

- - - - - - app tip

Use the yellow handles that appear for a selected shape to change the appearance of the shape. For example, the yellow handle at the top of the arrow can be used to change the length of the arrowhead.

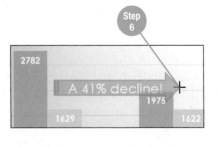

7. Drag the rotation handle (circled arrow above upper center sizing handle) in an upward diagonal direction toward the left until the shape is at the approximate angle shown in the image at the right.

8. Drag the border of the arrow shape down to the bottom left of the chart so that it points to the 2020 January bar, as shown in the image at right.

9. With the arrow shape still selected and the Drawing Tools Format tab active, click the More button at the bottom of the Shape Styles gallery and then click *Intense Effect – Turquoise, Accent 6* (last option in last row of *Theme Styles* section).

10. Click the Insert tab and then click the Text Box button in the Text group.

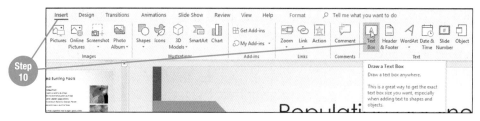

11. With the mouse pointer displayed as a down-pointing arrow, click anywhere below the chart at the left side to insert a text box with an insertion point.

12. Type Source: Painted Bunting Observer Team, University of North Carolina, Wilmington.

13. Click the border of the text box to remove the insertion point and select the entire placeholder, click the Bold button, and then click the Italic button in the Font group on the Home tab.

14. With the text box placeholder still selected, click the *Font Size* option box arrow and then click *14*.

15. Drag the border of the text box to align the text box at the center below the chart when the smart guides appear, as shown in the image below.

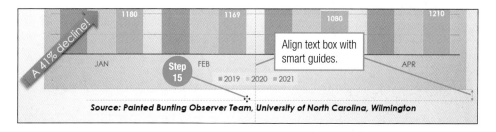

16. Save the revised presentation using the same name (**PaintedBunting -YourName**). Leave the presentation open for the next topic.

11.6 Adding Video to a Presentation

A high-quality video can demonstrate a process or task that is otherwise difficult to portray using descriptions or pictures. Video is effective for instructional purposes and when used appropriately provides a more enjoyable experience for the audience. Using PowerPoint, you can play a video from a file stored on your PC or link to a video on YouTube or another online source. Use the **Trim Video button** in the Editing group on the Video Tools Playback tab to crop a portion of the video at the beginning or end of the video clip.

1. With the **PaintedBunting–YourName** presentation open, make Slide 6 the active slide in the slide pane.

2. Insert a new slide with the Title and Content layout and then type A Beautiful Bird as the slide title.

3. Click the Insert Video icon in the content placeholder.

4. Click the Browse From a file hyperlink in the *From a file* section in the Insert Video dialog box.

5. Navigate to the Ch11 folder in StudentDataFiles and then double-click the file *PaintedBuntingVideo.mp4*.

6. Click the Play/Pause button below the video to preview the video clip. The video plays for approximately 52 seconds.

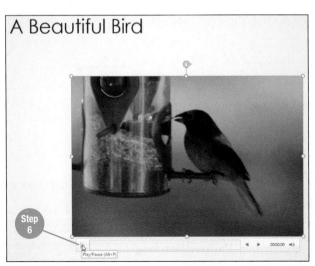

Watch & Learn

Hands On Activity

— — — — — — — Skills

Insert a video from a file

Trim the video

Set video playback options

Tutorial
Inserting and Modifying a Video File

● — — — — — — app tip

PowerPoint recognizes most video file formats, such as QuickTime movies, MP4 videos, MPEG movie files, Windows Media Video (.wmv) files, and Adobe Flash Media.

7 Click the Video Tools Playback tab.

8 Click the Trim Video button in the Editing group.

Step
8

quick steps

Add Video from a File on a PC
1. Click Insert Video icon in content placeholder.
2. Click Browse From a file.
3. Navigate to drive and/ or folder.
4. Double-click video file.
5. Edit and/or format video clip object as required.

Trimming a video allows you to display only a portion of a video file if the video is too long or if you want to cut parts at the beginning or end. Drag the green or red slider to start playing at a later starting point and/or end before the video is finished, or enter the start and end times in the Trim Video dialog box.

9 In the Trim Video dialog box, select the current entry in the *Start Time* text box and then type 00:10.

10 Select the current entry in the *End Time* text box and then type 00:30.

11 Click the Play button to preview the shorter video clip.

12 Click OK.

13 Click the *Start* option box arrow (displays *In Click Sequence*) in the Video Options group and then click *Automatically*.

The *Automatically* option means the video will begin playing as soon as the slide is displayed in the slide show.

14 Drag the video object left until the smart guide appears at the left, indicating the object is aligned with the slide title.

15 Click the Video Tools Format tab and then click the *Soft Edge Rectangle* option in the Video Styles group (third option).

16 Save the revised presentation using the same name (**PaintedBunting -YourName**). Leave the presentation open for the next topic.

11.7 Adding Sound to a Presentation

Adding music or other sound during a slide show is another way to interest and entertain your audience. For example, you might time introductory music to play while the title slide displays and your audience gathers, with the end of the music cueing the audience that the presentation is about to begin. Music can also be timed to play during a segment of a presentation to accompany a series of images. To add a sound clip or music to a presentation, activate the slide at which the sound should begin, click the **Audio button** in the Media group on the Insert tab, choose *Audio on My PC*, and then select the sound or music file in the Insert Audio dialog box.

1 With the **PaintedBunting-YourName** presentation open, make Slide 1 the active slide in the slide pane and then click the Insert tab.

2 Click the Audio button in the Media group and then click *Audio on My PC*.

3 Navigate to the Ch11 folder in StudentDataFiles and then double-click the file ***Allemande.mp3*** in the Insert Audio dialog box.

4 Drag the sound icon to position the icon and playback tools near the bottom right of the slide.

5 Click the Play/Pause button to listen to the recording. Click the Pause button after you have heard the beginning of the music clip for about 10 seconds.

The entire music clip plays for approximately two and a half minutes.

6 With the Audio Tools Playback tab active, click the *Hide During Show* check box in the Audio Options group to insert a check mark.

7 Click the *Start* option box arrow (displays *In Click Sequence*) and then click *Automatically*.

This option will start the music as soon as the slide is displayed in the slide show.

8 Click the *Loop until Stopped* check box to insert a check mark.

The *Loop until Stopped* option replays the music clip continuously until the slide is advanced during the slide show.

Watch & Learn

Hands On Activity

● ━ ━ ━ ━ ━ ━ ━ **Skills**

Insert sound from a file

Set audio playback options

Tutorial

Inserting and Modifying an Audio File

● ━ ━ ━ ━ ━ ━ **app tip**

PowerPoint recognizes most audio file formats, including MIDI files, MP3 and MP4 audio files, Windows audio files (.wav), and Windows Media Audio files (.wma).

⑨ Make Slide 7 the active slide in the slide pane and then insert the audio file **PaintedBunting_Song.mp3** on the slide by completing steps similar to those in Steps 2–8.

The audio recording of the painted bunting bird song is slightly less than two seconds in length.

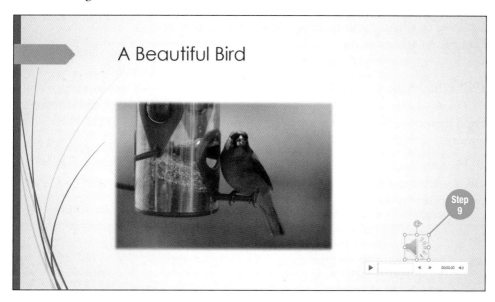

⑩ Insert a new slide after Slide 7 with the Title and Content layout and then type Photo, Video, and Audio Credits as the slide title.

⑪ Insert a table, type the information shown in Figure 11.4, and then adjust the layout using your best judgment for column widths and position on the slide.

Always credit the source of images, audio, and video used in a presentation if you did not create the multimedia yourself. In this instance, the music from Slide 1 is not credited because the recording is in the public domain and does not require attribution.

⑫ Save the revised presentation using the same name (**PaintedBunting –YourName**). Leave the presentation open for the next topic.

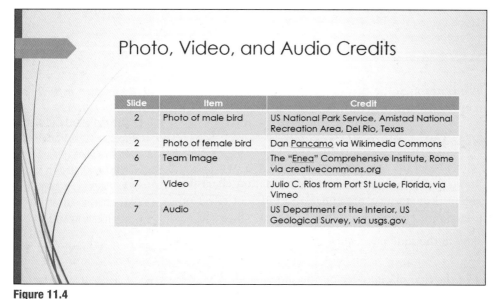

Slide	Item	Credit
2	Photo of male bird	US National Park Service, Amistad National Recreation Area, Del Rio, Texas
2	Photo of female bird	Dan Pancamo via Wikimedia Commons
6	Team Image	The "Enea" Comprehensive Institute, Rome via creativecommons.org
7	Video	Julio C. Rios from Port St Lucie, Florida, via Vimeo
7	Audio	US Department of the Interior, US Geological Survey, via usgs.gov

Figure 11.4
This table for Slide 8 shows multimedia credits.

11.8 Adding Transitions and Animation Effects to Slides for a Slide Show

Watch & Learn

Hands On Activity

A **transition** is a special effect that appears as one slide is removed from the screen and the next slide appears. **Animation** adds a special effect to an object on a slide that causes the object to move or change. Animation is a powerful way to enliven a presentation by focusing the viewer's attention on specific text or objects, but don't overuse transition and animation effects, as too much movement can become a distraction.

skills

1. With the **PaintedBunting-YourName** presentation open, make Slide 1 the active slide in the slide pane.

2. Click the Transitions tab and then click the More button at the bottom of the Transition to This Slide gallery.

3. Click the *Blinds* option in the *Exciting* section of the gallery.

Add a transition to all slides

Add an animation effect to an object on the slide master

Add an animation effect to an individual object

PowerPoint previews the effect with the current slide so that you can experiment with various transitions and effects before making your final selection.

4. Click the Apply To All button in the Timing group.

Add a sound effect that plays with the transition and/or speed up or lengthen the time of transition using the two options shown here.

Apply To All
Apply the current slide's transition, effects, and timing settings to the entire presentation.

Tutorials

Adding Slide Transitions

Adding Sound to Slide Transitions

5. Display the slide show, advance through the first three slides to view the transition effect, and then end the show to return to Normal view.

Applying Animation Effects Using the Slide Master

To apply the same animation effect to all the titles and/or bulleted lists in a presentation, apply the effect using the slide master. Generally, animation effects for similar objects should be consistent throughout a presentation; a different effect on each slide might become a distraction.

6. Make Slide 2 the active slide in the slide pane, click the View tab, and then click the Slide Master button.

7. Click to select the border of the title placeholder on the slide master.

app tip

Use the Effect Options button in the Transition to This Slide group to choose a variation for the selected transition (such as the direction the blinds move).

⑧ Click the Animations tab.

⑨ Click the *Split* option in the Animation gallery.

See Table 11.2 at the bottom of the page for a description of Animation categories.

 app tip

The Animation gallery provides the most popular effects. View more effects by category using the options at the bottom of the gallery. For example, *More Entrance Effects* displays all 40 options.

Tutorials

Applying and Removing Animations

Modifying Animations

⑩ Click to select the border of the content placeholder and then click the More button in the Animation gallery.

⑪ Click the Zoom animation in the *Entrance* section.

⑫ Click the *Start* option box arrow (displays *On Click*) in the Timing group and then click *After Previous*.

⑬ Select the current entry in the *Duration* text box, type 1.5, and then press Enter.

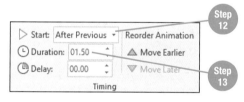

⑭ Click the Slide Master tab and then click the Close Master View button.

⑮ Make Slide 1 the active slide in the slide pane, run through the presentation in a slide show to view the transition and animation effects, and then return to Normal view.

Table 11.2 Animation Effects

Effect Section	Description
Entrance	Animates an object as it appears on the slide; most common animation effect
Emphasis	Animates text or object already in place by causing the object to move or to change in appearance; includes effects such as darkening, changing color, bolding, and underlining, to name a few
Exit	Animates the text or object after it has been revealed, such as by fading or flying off the slide
Motion Paths	Animates an object to move along a linear path, an arc, or some other shape

Applying Animation Effects to Individual Objects

As you previewed the slide show, you probably noticed that images and other objects, such as shapes or text boxes, appeared on the slide before the title. You may want these items to remain hidden until the title and text have been revealed. To apply animation to an individual object, display the slide, select the object to be animated, and then apply the desired animation option.

To copy an animation effect from one object to another, use the **Animation Painter button** in the Advanced Animation group on the Animations tab, which operates similarly to the Format Painter button that you learned to use in Chapter 3.

16 Make Slide 2 the active slide in the slide pane.

17 Click to select the male bird image at the upper right of the slide.

18 Click the Animations tab and then click the Wipe animation in the Animation gallery.

19 Click the *Start* option box arrow and then click *After Previous*.

20 Click to select the male bird image and then click the Animation Painter button in the Advanced Animation group.

21 With the mouse pointer displayed with the paint brush icon, click to select the female bird image at the lower right of the slide.

22 Make Slide 3 the active slide in the slide pane.

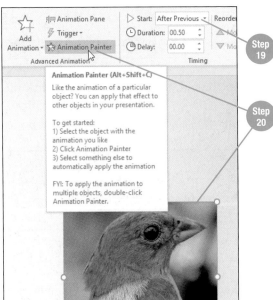

Animation Painter copies animation effects and animation options from one object to another.

●------- app tip

To adjust the order an object is animated, click the Animation Pane button in the Advanced Animation group, select the object you want to move in the Animation Pane, and then click the Move Earlier or Move Later button in the Reorder Animation group.

23 Click to select the text box object below the chart and then apply the Fly In animation option.

24 Click the *Start* option box arrow and then click *After Previous*.

25 Use the Animation Painter feature to copy the animation options from the text box object to the arrow object on Slide 3.

26 Make Slide 5 the active slide in the slide pane.

27 Click to select the WordArt object at the bottom of the slide, apply the Float In animation option, and then change the *Start* option to *After Previous*.

28 Make Slide 6 the active slide in the slide pane.

29 Click to select the image at the left side of the slide, apply the Shape animation, and then change the *Start* option to *After Previous*.

30 Click to select the SmartArt graphic placeholder at the bottom of the slide. Make sure the entire graphic is selected and not an individual shape within the graphic.

31 Apply the Fly In animation and then change the *Start* option to *After Previous*.

32 Click the Effect Options button and then click the *One by One* option in the *Sequence* section.

The *One by One* effect option causes each chevron in the graphic to animate on the slide one at a time, starting with the leftmost shape first.

33 Click to select the text box below the team image that contains copyright information, click the border of the text box to select the entire object, and then press the Delete key. Skip this step if you do not have a copyright text box below the team image.

34 Run through the presentation in a slide show from the beginning to view the revised animation effects. Return to Normal view when the slide show ends.

35 Save the revised presentation using the same name (**PaintedBunting -YourName**). Leave the presentation open for the next topic.

11.9 Setting Up a Self-Running Presentation

Some presentations are designed to be self-running, meaning that the slides are intended to be displayed continuously at a kiosk or on a PC by an individual instead of within a group setting where a speaker is leading the slide show. To create a presentation that advances through slides automatically, you need to set up a time for each slide to display and ensure that each slide animation is set to start automatically for each object. When the animation options and timing settings are complete, open the Set Up Show dialog box to change the show type to *Browsed at a kiosk* by clicking the **Set Up Slide Show button** in the Set Up group on the Slide Show tab.

1. With the **PaintedBunting-YourName** presentation open, use Save As to save a copy of the presentation in the current folder, naming it **PaintedBuntingSelfRunning-YourName**.

2. Make Slide 2 the active slide in the slide pane and then display the slide master.

3. Select the border of the title placeholder.

4. Click the Animations tab and then change the *Start* option in the Timing group to *After Previous*.

5. Close Slide Master view.

6. Make Slide 1 the active slide in the slide pane and then click to select the sound icon.

7. Click the Audio Tools Playback tab and then click the *Play Across Slides* check box in the Audio Options group to insert a check mark.

   This option will cause the music that starts at Slide 1 to continue playing through the remaining slides.

8. Click the Volume button and then click *Low*.

9. Make Slide 7 the active slide in the slide pane and then select and delete the sound icon to remove the audio.

10. Make Slide 8 the active slide in the slide pane and then select and delete the last row in the table. (Refer to Chapter 7, Topic 7.4, Steps 7–10 if you need assistance with this step.)

11. Click the Transitions tab.

12. Click the *After* check box in the *Timing* section to insert a check mark, select the current entry in the *After* text box, type 0:25, and then press Enter.

Watch & Learn

Hands On Activity

------------ Skills

Add timings to slides

Change the show type to kiosk

Tutorials

Setting Timings for a Slide Show

Looping a Slide Show Continuously

------- app tip

On the Slide Show tab, the Rehearse Timings feature lets you assign a time to each slide as you run through a slide show with a timer active and a Recording toolbar. Use the Next button on the Recording toolbar to advance each slide, and the time for the slide to remain on screen is automatically entered for the slide transition.

13 Click the Apply To All button.

All the slides will advance automatically after the same 25-second duration. To set individual transition times for slides, activate a slide and enter a different time in the *After* text box.

14 Make Slide 3 the active slide in the slide pane, select the entry in the *After* text box, type 0:10 and then press Enter.

15 Change the *After* time for Slide 5 and Slide 6 to 0:15 and for Slide 8 to 0:10.

16 Click the Slide Show tab and then click the Set Up Slide Show button in the Set Up group.

17 Click the *Browsed at a kiosk (full screen)* option in the *Show type* section in the Set Up Show dialog box.

18 Click OK.

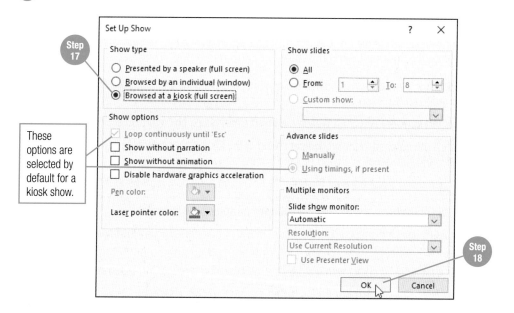

These options are selected by default for a kiosk show.

19 Start the slide show from the beginning and watch the presentation as it advances through all the slides automatically. End the show when the presentation starts at Slide 1 again by pressing the Esc key.

20 Save the revised presentation using the same name (**PaintedBuntingSelf Running-YourName**) and then close the presentation.

Topics Review

Topic	Key Concepts
11.1 Inserting, Resizing, and Aligning Images	An image in a file on your PC can be added to a slide using the Pictures button in the Images group on the Insert tab or with the Pictures icon in the content placeholder on a new slide.
	Resize, move, or edit an image by selecting the image and using the selection handles and/or buttons on the Picture Tools Format tab.
	Find an image from a website using the Online Pictures button in the Images group on the Insert tab.
11.2 Inserting a SmartArt Graphic	A **SmartArt** graphic is made up of shapes with text to illustrate information in lists, processes, cycles, hierarchies, or other diagrams.
	Add a SmartArt graphic on a slide using the SmartArt button in the Illustrations group on the Insert tab or the Insert a SmartArt Graphic icon in a content placeholder.
	Choose a SmartArt category and layout in the Choose a SmartArt Graphic dialog box and then click OK to enter the text for each item.
	Text can be added to shapes in the Text pane or by typing directly in a shape placeholder.
	Modify SmartArt styles or colors or edit the graphic using buttons on the SmartArt Tools Design tab.
11.3 Converting Text to SmartArt and Inserting WordArt	A bulleted list can be converted into a SmartArt graphic using the **Convert to SmartArt button** in the Paragraph group on the Home tab.
	WordArt is decorative text inside an independent graphic object on a slide.
	Create WordArt using the WordArt button in the Text group on the Insert tab.
	Type the WordArt text inside the text box and then add text effects, move, or otherwise edit the object using buttons on the Drawing Tools Format tab.
11.4 Creating a Chart on a Slide	Insert a chart using the Insert Chart icon in the content placeholder or the Chart button in the Illustrations group on the Insert tab.
	Choose the chart category and chart type in the Insert Chart dialog box and then click OK.
	Type the data to be graphed in the worksheet on top of the slide placeholders. As you replace the sample data in the worksheet, the chart on the slide updates.
	Modify the chart using the buttons on the Chart Tools Design and Chart Tools Format tabs.
11.5 Drawing a Shape and Adding a Text Box	Draw your own graphics on a slide using the **Shapes button** on the Insert tab.
	Type text inside a selected shape and then resize, move, or otherwise modify the shape using buttons on the Drawing Tools Format tab.
	A text box is a rectangular object with text that can be moved, resized, or formatted independently.
	Create a text box using the Text Box button in the Text group on the Insert tab.
11.6 Adding Video to a Presentation	Add a video clip to a slide with the Insert Video icon in a content placeholder or with the Video button in the Media group on the Insert tab.
	Select a video clip from a file on your PC or by finding a video clip at YouTube.
	The **Trim Video button** lets you change the starting and ending position of the video if you do not want to play the entire clip in a slide show.
	Change the *Start* option in the Video Options group on the Video Tools Playback tab to *Automatically* to begin playing a video as soon as the slide is displayed in a slide show.
	Options on the Video Tools Format tab are used to format the video object.

continued...

Topic	Key Concepts
11.7 Adding Sound to a Presentation	Add audio to a slide with the **Audio button** in the Media group on the Insert tab.
	Use buttons in the Audio Options group on the Audio Tools Playback tab to hide the sound icon during a slide show, start the audio automatically, play the sound in the background across all slides, or loop the audio continuously until the slide is advanced.
	Always credit the sources of all multimedia that you did not create yourself used in a presentation.
11.8 Adding Transitions and Animation Effects to Slides for a Slide Show	A **transition** is a special effect that appears as one slide is removed from the screen and another is revealed during a slide show.
	Animation causes an object to move or transform in some way.
	Select a transition in the Transition to This Slide gallery on the Transitions tab.
	The Apply To All button in the Timing group on the Transitions tab sets the same transition effect to all slides.
	Add an animation effect to a placeholder on the slide master to apply the effect to all slides in the presentation.
	Animation effects are selected in the Animation gallery on the Animations tab.
	Specify how the animation will start and the animation duration using options in the Timing group.
	Animation effects are grouped by: Entrance, Emphasis, Exit, and Motion Paths.
	Animate an individual object on a slide by selecting the object and then adding an animation effect from the Animation gallery.
	The **Animation Painter button** in the Advanced Animation group copies the animation effect and effect options from one object to another.
11.9 Setting Up a Self-Running Presentation	A self-running presentation is set up to run a slide show continuously.
	To create a self-running presentation, each slide needs to have a time entered in the *After* text box in the Timing group on the Transitions tab, and each animated object needs to be set to start automatically.
	Open the Set Up Show dialog box from the **Set Up Slide Show button** on the Slide Show tab, and then choose *Browsed at a kiosk (full screen)* to instruct PowerPoint to play the slide show continuously until stopped.

 Topics Review

Using and Querying an Access Database

Organizations and individuals rely on data to complete transactions, analyze reports, and make decisions. Data that is stored in an organized manner to provide information to meet a variety of needs is called a **database**. A database application is referred to as a **database management system (DBMS)**. Microsoft Access is a DBMS used to organize, store, and maintain data that is used mostly by small- to medium-size businesses.

You interact with a DBMS several times a day as you complete your daily activities. Examples of the types of transactions that involve a DBMS include withdrawing cash from your bank account, completing a purchase, looking up a price at a website, or programming your GPS to find a route to an address.

In this chapter, you will learn database terminology and how to navigate a DBMS, including how to open and close objects, add and maintain records using a datasheet and form, find and replace data, sort and filter data, and use queries to look up information and perform a calculation on a numeric field.

Learning Objectives

12.1 Identify a database table, query, report, and form; and define *field*, *field value*, and *record*

12.2 Add a record using a datasheet

12.3 Edit and delete records using a datasheet

12.4 Add, edit, and delete records using a form

12.5 Find and replace data, and adjust column widths in a datasheet

12.6 Sort and filter records in a datasheet and form

12.7 Create a query using a wizard

12.8 Create a query using Design view

12.9 Select records in a query using criteria

12.10 Select records in a query using AND and OR criteria, and sort query results

12.11 Modify a query, add a calculated field to a query, and preview a database object

Read & Learn

Content Online

The online course includes additional training and assessment resources.

12.1 Understanding Database Objects and Terminology

An Access database is structured and organized to keep track of a large amount of similar data. For example, a library database is organized so that information (such as the title, author, and publisher) is maintained for each book in the library catalog. Making sure that the data is entered and updated in the same manner for each item is important so that information is complete and accurate. For this reason, a database is created with a structure that defines the data that will be collected for each item. Working with objects and data in an existing database will help you understand the terms that are used and how data is organized before you create your own database.

Identifying Database Objects

An Access database is a collection of related objects in which data is recorded, edited, and viewed. Access opens with a Navigation pane along the left side of the window that is used to open an object. Objects are grouped in the Navigation pane by type. Tables, queries, forms, and reports are the four most common types of database objects and are described in Table 12.1.

Table 12.1 Four Most Common Access Objects

Object	Description
Table	Data is organized into tables, each of which opens in a datasheet that displays data in columns and rows. A table stores data about one topic or subject only. For example, in the LibraryFines database you will use in this chapter, one table contains data about each student, and another table contains data about each fine.
Query	A query is used to extract information from one or more tables in a single datasheet that displays all the data or a subset of data that meets a specific condition. For example, a query could display all library fines that have been issued, or only those fines that remain unpaid.
Form	A form provides a user-friendly interface to enter or update data where one record is viewed at a time. The layout of a form can be customized; for example, you can customize a layout to match closely an existing paper form used in a business.
Report	Reports are used for viewing or printing data from a table or query. Reports can include summary totals and a customized layout.

Watch & Learn

Hands On Activity

------- Skills

Open and close a database

Identify objects in a database

Open and close objects

Tutorials

Opening an Existing Database

Closing a Database and Closing Access

1. Start Access and open the database **LibraryFines** from the Ch12 folder in StudentDataFiles.
2. Click the Enable Content button in the security warning message bar that appears below the ribbon. Click Yes if you receive a prompt asking if you want to make the database a trusted document.

The security warning message bar appears each time you open a database unless the settings for Access on your PC have been changed. Microsoft disables some database content as a way to protect your PC from potentially harmful files that may be embedded in the database without your knowledge (such as a virus). The data files provided with this textbook are safe, so you can click the Enable Content button.

3. Compare your screen with the one shown in Figure 12.1 on the next page.

Figure 12.1

The **LibraryFines** database is shown opened in the Access window.

④ If necessary, drag the gray border along the right side of the Navigation pane to the right to expand the width of the pane until the title *All Access Objects* is entirely visible.

Opening and Closing Objects

Data in a database is organized by topic or subject about a person, place, event, item, or other category grouping in an object called a **table**. A database table is the first object that is created. The number of tables varies for each database depending on the information that needs to be stored. Tables are the building blocks for creating other objects, such as a query, form, or report. In other words, you cannot create a query, form, or report without first creating a table.

⑤ Double-click *Fines* in the Tables group in the Navigation pane.

The table opens in Datasheet view within a tab in the work area. A datasheet resembles a worksheet with data organized in columns and rows. The information about the subject or topic of a table (such as library fines) is divided into columns, each of which is called a **field**. A field should store only one unit of information about a person, place, event, or item. For example, a mailing address is split into at least four fields so the street address, city, state or province, and zip or postal code are separated. This allows the database to be sorted, filtered, or searched by any unit of information.

Each row in the datasheet displays all the fields for one person, place, event, or item and is called a **record**. The data that is stored in one field within a record is called a **field value**.

Tutorial

Opening and Closing an Object

app tip

Another way to open any database object is to right-click the object name in the Navigation pane and then click *Open*.

⑥ Double-click *Students* in the Tables group in the Navigation pane and then compare your screen with the one shown in Figure 12.2.

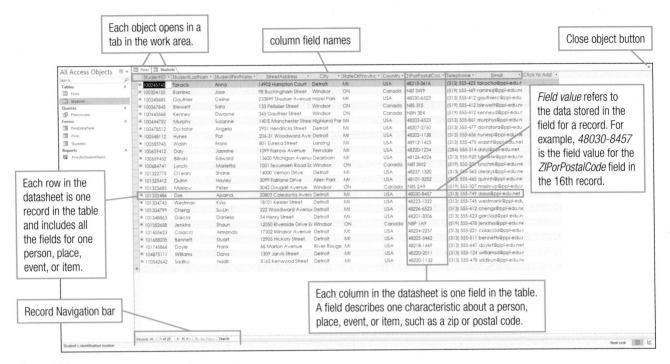

Each object opens in a tab in the work area.

column field names

Close object button

Field value refers to the data stored in the field for a record. For example, *48030-8457* is the field value for the *ZIPorPostalCode* field in the 16th record.

Each row in the datasheet is one record in the table and includes all the fields for one person, place, event, or item.

Record Navigation bar

Each column in the datasheet is one field in the table. A field describes one characteristic about a person, place, event, or item, such as a zip or postal code.

Figure 12.2
Shown is the Datasheet view for the Students table in the **LibraryFines** database.

⑦ Double-click *FinesByStudentName* in the Reports group in the Navigation pane and review the report content and layout in the work area.

A **report** is designed to view or print data from one or more tables or queries in a customized layout and with summary totals. In this report, library fines are arranged and grouped by student name.

⑧ Click the Close button at the upper right of the work area to close the report. Do *not* use the Close button at the upper right of the window, which exits Access.

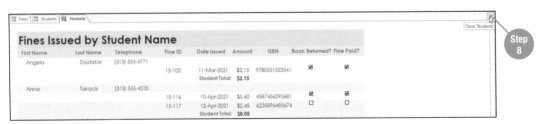

⑨ Double-click *FineEntryForm* in the Forms group in the Navigation pane.

A **form** is used to enter, update, or view one record at a time. Forms can be created that resemble paper-based forms used within an organization.

10 Click the Next record button (right-pointing arrow) on the Record Navigation bar located at the bottom of the form.

Buttons on the Record Navigation bar are used to move to the first record, previous record, next record, or last record. Use the search text box to navigate to a record by typing a field value.

11 Click the Previous record button (left-pointing arrow).

12 Click the Last record button (right-pointing arrow with vertical bar) to move to the last record in the form.

13 Click the First record button (vertical bar with left-pointing arrow) to move to the first record in the form.

14 Click the Close button at the upper right corner of the work area to close the form.

15 Double-click *FinesIssued* in the Queries group in the Navigation pane.

Open a Database Object
1. Open database file.
2. Double-click object name in Navigation pane.

previous record

new (blank) record

first record

last record

search text box

Step 10

A **query** opens in a datasheet and displays data from one or more tables. A query may display all the records or only a subset of records that meet a specific condition.

FineID	DateIssued	StudentFirstName	StudentLastName	Telephone	Amount	OverdueBookISBN	BookReturned	FinePaid
15-101	10-Mar-2021	Pat	Hynes	(313) 555-6569	$8.75	9780763843011	☑	☑
15-102	11-Mar-2021	Angela	Doxtator	(313) 555-4771	$2.15	9780531523541	☑	☑
15-103	12-Mar-2021	Pat	Hynes	(313) 555-6569	$1.25	9780412533145	☑	☐
15-104	12-Mar-2021	Marietta	Lynch	(519) 555-3214	$1.40	9784123524158	☑	☐
15-105	13-Mar-2021	Edward	Bilinski	(313) 555-9200	$4.25	9784125312517	☑	☑
15-106	13-Mar-2021	Stuart	Bennett	(313) 555-5112	$3.25	8745125412352	☑	☐
15-107	15-Mar-2021	Daniela	Garcia	(313) 555-6235	$6.50	6235841752358	☑	☑
15-108	15-Mar-2021	Dwayne	Kenney	(519) 555-4125	$12.50	6498536864758	☐	☐
15-109	15-Mar-2021	Daniela	Garcia	(313) 555-6235	$1.85	9774582368541	☑	☐
15-110	30-Mar-2021	Jasmine	Daly	(284) 555-3142	$2.40	9774586412352	☐	☐
15-111	30-Mar-2021	Pat	Hynes	(313) 555-6569	$3.25	9685412563258	☑	☑
15-112	04-Apr-2021	Peter	Maslov	(519) 555-3276	$7.85	3148578685035	☑	☐
15-113	06-Apr-2021	Dwayne	Kenney	(519) 555-4125	$4.60	1345685697566	☐	☐
15-114	08-Apr-2021	Sara	Blewett	(519) 555-4125	$3.50	8755745862538	☑	☑
15-115	10-Apr-2021	Su-Lin	Cheng	(313) 555-4125	$8.75	4574698541255	☑	☐
15-116	10-Apr-2021	Anna	Takacis	(313) 555-4235	$5.60	4587456595681	☑	☑
15-117	12-Apr-2021	Anna	Takacis	(313) 555-4235	$2.45	6235896485674	☐	☐

A query combines data from more than one table and displays the fields in a specified order.

16 Close the query and the two tables.

Close objects as soon as you are finished viewing or updating data. Some Access commands will not run if an object is open in the background.

17 Click the File tab and then click *Close*.

Always close a database file using the backstage area before exiting Access so that all temporary files used by Access while you are viewing and updating records are properly closed.

12.2 Adding Records to a Table Using a Datasheet

To add a new record to a table, open the table and click the **New (blank) record button** on the Record Navigation bar. Type the field values for the new record in each column, pressing Tab or Enter to move to the next column (field) in the datasheet. When you move past the last column in a new row in the datasheet, the record is automatically saved and another new blank record is open.

1 Open the database **LibraryFines**.

2 Click the File tab and then click *Save As* to open the Save As backstage area.

3 With *Save Database As* already selected in the *File Types* panel and *Access Database* already selected as the *Save Database As* option, click the Save As button.

4 In the Save As dialog box, navigate to the CompletedTopics folder on your storage medium, create a new folder *Ch12*, double-click the Ch12 folder, change the file name to **LibraryFines-YourName**, and then click the Save button.

5 Click the Enable Content button on the security warning message bar.

6 Double-click the Fines table to open the table.

7 Click the New (blank) record button on the Record Navigation bar.

8 Type 15-118 in the *FineID* field and then press Tab to move to the next field.

The field *StudentID* looks up names and ID numbers in the Students table using a drop-down list.

9 Click the down-pointing arrow in the *StudentID* field in the new record field just created, click *100478512 Angela Doxtator*, and then press Tab.

The student ID number becomes the field value, which is connected to Angela Doxtator's record in the Students table.

The Pencil icon indicates the record is being edited. The pencil disappears when Access saves the changes.

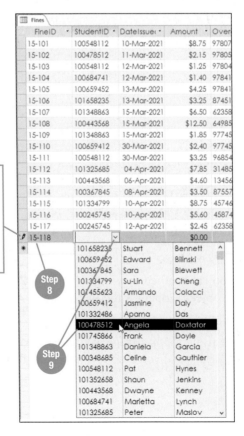

Watch & Learn

Hands On Activity

·------- Skills

Add a new record using a datasheet

Tutorial

Adding and Deleting Records in a Table

·------ app tip

New records can also be added by clicking the New button in the Records group on the Home tab, or by clicking in the first cell in the blank row at the bottom of the datasheet (next to the asterisk).

·------ app tip

You can also move to the next field by pressing the Enter key or by clicking in the next column.

⑩ Type 12apr2021 in the *DateIssued* field and then press Tab.

The date field has been set up to display underscores and dashes as soon as you begin typing to help you enter the date in the correct format, *dd-mmm-yyyy*. This configuration also ensures that all dates are entered consistently in the database. Access displays the date as *12-Apr-2021*, which is the format set up for date fields in the database.

⑪ Type 8.75 in the *Amount* field and then press Tab.

⑫ Type 4348973098226 in the *OverdueBookISBN* field and then press Tab.

15-116	100245745	10-Apr-2021	$5.60	4587456595681	☑	
15-117	100245745	12-Apr-2021	$2.45	6235896485674	☐	
15-118	100478512	12-Apr-2021	$8.75	4348973098226	☐	
*			$0.00		☐	

⑬ Press the spacebar to insert a check mark in the *BookReturned* field and then press Tab.

BookReturned is a field that has been set up to store only one of two possible field values: *Yes* or *No*. Inserting a check mark stores *Yes*, while an empty check box stores *No*.

⑭ Click the check box to insert a check mark in the *FinePaid* field and then press Tab.

⑮ Type 15apr2021 in the *DatePaid* field and then press Tab.

Moving to the next row in the datasheet automatically saves the record just typed and starts a new record.

15-117	100245745	12-Apr-2021	$2.45	6235896485674	☐	☐	
15-118	100478512	12-Apr-2021	$8.75	4348973098226	☑	☑	15-Apr-2021
*			$0.00		☐	☐	

⑯ Add the following field values in the new row in the fields indicated, pressing Tab after typing the data to move to the next field:

FineID	15-119	*OverdueBookISBN*	7349872345760
StudentID	101348863 Daniela Garcia	*BookReturned*	Yes
DateIssued	15apr2021	*FinePaid*	No (leave blank)
Amount	5.25	*DatePaid*	(leave blank)

15-118	100478512	12-Apr-2021	$8.75	4348973098226	☑	☑	15-Apr-2021	
15-119	101348863	15-Apr-2021	$5.25	7349872345760	☑	☐		
*			$0.00		☐	☐		

⑰ With the insertion point positioned in the *FineID* field in a new row, close the Fines table. Leave the database open for the next topic.

12.3 Editing and Deleting Records Using a Datasheet

Edit a field value in a table using a datasheet by opening the table, selecting the text to be changed, and then typing the new text, or by clicking in the table cell to place an insertion point and then inserting or deleting text as required. Select a record for deletion by clicking in the gray record selector bar along the left edge of the datasheet next to the record and then clicking the Delete button in the Records group on the Home tab. Access requires confirmation before deleting a record.

 Watch & Learn

 Hands On Activity

● ─ ─ ─ ─ ─ ─ ─ Skills

1 With the **LibraryFines-YourName** database open, double-click *Students* in the Tables group to open the table.

2 Select the text *Murphy* in the *StudentLastName* column in the sixth row in the datasheet and then type Hall as the new last name for Suzanne.

Edit a record using a datasheet

Delete a record using a datasheet

 Tutorial
Completing a Spelling Check

3 Press Tab eight times to move to the *Email* field.

4 Press F2 to open the field for editing, move the insertion point as needed, delete *murphy* at the beginning of the email address, and then type hall so that the email address becomes *halls@ppi-edu.net*.

5 Click at the end of *N8T 3W9* in the *ZIPorPostalCode* field in the second row in the datasheet to position the insertion point, press Backspace to remove *3W9*, and then type 2E6.

Changes made to field values in a record are automatically saved as soon as you place an insertion point in another record in the datasheet.

Country	ZIPorPostalCod	Telephone
USA	48215-3616	(313) 555-423
Canada	N8T 2E6	(519) 555-469
USA	48030-6523	(313) 555-412

Step 5

6 If necessary, scroll left until you can see the student names.

7 Click in the record selector bar (gray bar at left edge of datasheet) next to the record for the student *Das Aparna* when you see the mouse pointer change to a right-pointing black arrow (➡).

The gray bar at the left edge of the datasheet is used to select a record. The mouse pointer displays as a black right-pointing arrow when positioned next to a record in the record selector bar. The top of the record selector bar next to the first field name is called the **Select all button**. Clicking the Select all button selects all field values in all records in the table.

Edit a Record
1. Open table.
2. Click in table cell to place insertion point.
3. Insert or delete text as required.

Delete a Record
1. Open table.
2. Select record.
3. Click Delete button.
4. Click Yes.

Select all button

Record selector bar

Step 7

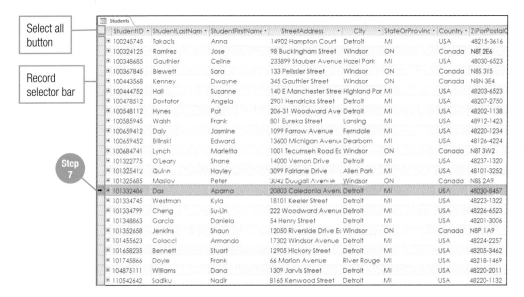

8 Click the Delete button in the Records group on the Home tab. Do *not* click the down-pointing arrow on the button.

Step 8

9 Click Yes at the Microsoft Access message box that appears asking whether you are sure you want to delete the record.

Step 9

Always exercise caution when you use the Delete command, because the Undo feature does not work to restore a record. Depending on the purpose of the database, deleting records is generally not done until the records to be deleted are first copied to an archive database (a copy of the database saved for historical record keeping). Alternatively, a database administrator may make an extra backup copy of the database for safekeeping before deleting records. In some workplaces, the delete option is made unavailable to all employees except a few authorized database administrators.

10 Close the Students table. Leave the database open for the next topic.

12.4 Adding, Editing, and Deleting Records Using a Form

A form is an Access object that provides a different view for the data stored in a table. Generally only one record at a time is displayed in a columnar layout instead of the spreadsheet-style layout presented in a datasheet. Forms are usually preferred over a datasheet for adding, editing, and deleting records because the user can focus on the data in one record at a time.

1. With the **LibraryFines-YourName** database open, double-click *FineEntryForm* in the Forms group to open the form.

2. Click the New (blank) record button on the Record Navigation bar.

3. Add the field values as shown in the image below, using Tab to move from one field to the next field. After typing the last entry, press Tab.

   A new blank form displays when you press Tab after the last field in a form.

4. Click the First record button on the Record Navigation bar to display the first record in the form.

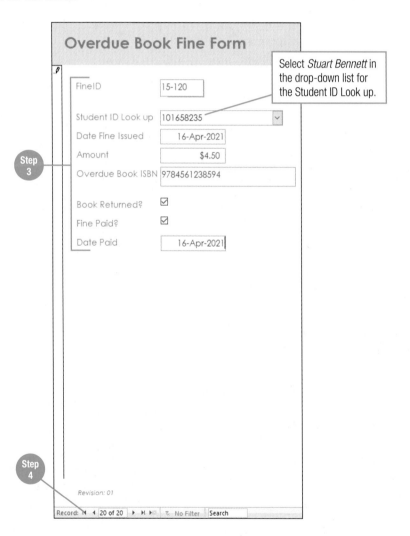

Select *Stuart Bennett* in the drop-down list for the Student ID Look up.

Overdue Book Fine Form

FineID: 15-120

Student ID Look up: 101658235

Date Fine Issued: 16-Apr-2021

Amount: $4.50

Overdue Book ISBN: 9784561238594

Book Returned? ☑

Fine Paid? ☑

Date Paid: 16-Apr-2021

Revision: 01

Record: 20 of 20   No Filter   Search

Step 3

Step 4

Watch & Learn

Hands On Activity

Skills

Add a record using a form

Edit a record using a form

Delete a record using a form

app tip

Print the current record displayed in a form by displaying the Print backstage area, clicking *Print*, and then clicking *Selected Record(s)* in the *Print Range* section of the Print dialog box.

Tutorials

Adding and Deleting Records in a Form

Navigating in Objects

⑤ Select $8.75 in the *Amount* field and then type 7.25.

quick steps

Delete a Record Using a Form
1. Open form.
2. Navigate to desired record.
3. Click Delete button arrow.
4. Click *Delete Record*.
5. Click Yes.

⑥ Click the Next record button two times to display record 3 in the form.

⑦ Click the Delete button arrow in the Records group on the Home tab and then click *Delete Record*.

Oops!

Only the current field value is deleted? This occurs when you do not use the arrow on the button to select the option to delete the entire record. Try Step 7 again, making sure to choose *Delete Record*.

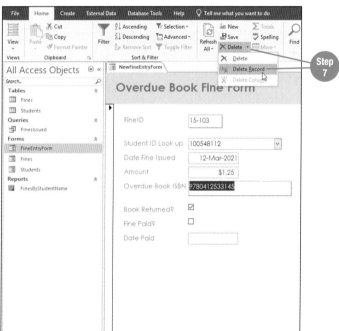

⑧ Click Yes at the message box that appears asking whether you are sure you want to delete the record.

⑨ Close the form. Leave the database open for the next topic.

12.5 Finding and Replacing Data and Adjusting Column Widths in a Datasheet

The Find feature locates a field value in a datasheet or form and moves the insertion point to each occurrence of the data. Find is helpful to locate a record that you need to edit when the datasheet contains hundreds of records. When a change needs to be made to all occurrences of a field value, use the Replace command to make the change automatically. The column width for a column in a datasheet can be made wider to fully display data for those fields that do not currently display all the field values.

1 With the **LibraryFines–YourName** database open, double-click *Fines* in the Tables group to open the table.

2 Click to place an insertion point within the *StudentID* field value in the first record.

3 Click the Find button in the Find group on the Home tab.

4 Type 101348863 in the *Find What* text box and then click the Find Next button.
The first record (record 6) that matches the field value is made active.

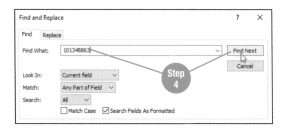

5 Continue clicking the Find Next button to review all occurrences of the matching field value.

6 Click OK at the message that Microsoft Access has finished searching records.

7 Click the Cancel button to close the Find and Replace dialog box.

8 Click to place an insertion point within the *FineID* field in the first record.

 Watch & Learn

 Hands On Activity

------ Skills

Find and replace data using a datasheet

Adjust column width in a datasheet

Tutorials

Finding Data

Finding and Replacing Data

Adjusting Field Column Width

------ Oops!

No records found? Click OK and then check that you typed the ID number without errors.

9 Click the Replace button in the Find group.

10 Type 15- in the *Find What* text box and then press Tab.

11 Type MCL- in the *Replace With* text box.

12 Click the *Match* option box arrow and then click *Any Part of Field*.

13 Click the Replace All button.

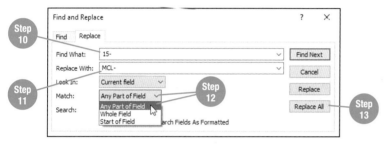

14 Click Yes at the message box asking whether you want to continue and informing you that the Replace operation cannot be undone.

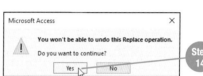

15 Click the Close button in the top right corner of the Find and Replace dialog box.

16 Click to place the insertion point in any field value within the *DateIssued* field.

17 Click the More button in the Records group on the Home tab and then click *Field Width*.

18 Click Best Fit in the Column Width dialog box.

Best Fit adjusts the width of the column to accommodate the length needed to display the longest field value.

19 Close the Fines table. Click Yes when prompted to save the changes to the layout of the table. Leave the database open for the next topic.

Saving changes to the layout of the table means that Access will retain the new column width for the *DateIssued* field when the table is reopened.

12.6 Sorting and Filtering Records

Records are initially arranged in the datasheet alphanumerically by the field in the table that has been defined as the primary key. A **primary key** is a field that contains the data that uniquely identifies each record in the table. Generally, the primary key is an identification number, such as *StudentID* in the Students table. To change the order of the records, click in the column to sort and then use the Ascending or Descending buttons in the Sort & Filter group on the Home tab.

① With the **LibraryFines-YourName** database open, double-click *Students* in the Tables group.

The primary key field in the Students table is the field named *StudentID*. Notice the records in the datasheet are arranged in order of the StudentID field values.

② Click to place an insertion point within any field value in the *StudentLastName* column.

③ Click the Ascending button in the Sort & Filter group on the Home tab.

Notice the records in the table are now arranged in order by the student last name field values.

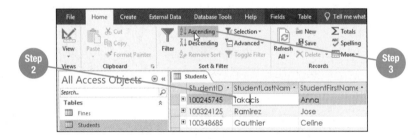

④ Close the Students table. Click Yes when prompted to save the changes to the design of the table.

Selecting Yes to save changes to the design of the table means that the table will remain sorted by the *StudentLastName* field when you reopen the datasheet. Each object based upon the Students table can have its own sort option saved.

⑤ Open the Students form.

⑥ Click the Next record button a few times to view the first few records. Notice the records are arranged by *StudentID*.

⑦ Click the First record button to return the display to the first record.

⑧ Click to place an insertion point in the *Student Last Name* field.

⑨ Click the Ascending button in the Sort & Filter group.

10 Scroll through the first 10 records in the form to view the sorted order and then close the form.

11 Open the Students table. Notice the up-pointing arrow next to *StudentLastName* in the field names row, indicating the records are arranged alphabetically in ascending order by the student last names.

StudentID ▾	StudentLastNam ▾	StudentFirstName ▾
⊞ 101658235	Bennett	Stuart
⊞ 100659452	Bilinski	Edward
⊞ 100367845	Blewett	Sara

Step 11

You can filter a datasheet in Access using the same techniques you learned for filtering a table in Excel in Chapter 9. Recall that a filter temporarily hides the rows that you do not want to view.

12 Click the filter arrow (down-pointing arrow) next to *Country*.

13 Click the check box next to *USA* to clear the check mark from the box and then click OK.

The datasheet is filtered to display records for students who reside in Canada only. The indicators that a datasheet is filtered include a funnel icon next to the filtered field name, the message *Filtered* (shaded with an orange background) on the Record Navigation bar, and also at the right end of the Status bar along the bottom of the window.

14 Click the Toggle Filter button in the Sort & Filter group to clear the filter, redisplaying all records in the datasheet.

Step 14

This is the filtered list of records after Step 13.

15 Close the Students table. Click No when prompted to save changes to the design of the table. Leave the database open for the next topic.

Note that a sort order can be saved with a datasheet, but a filter option is not saved when the table is closed.

 quick steps

Sort a Datasheet or Form
1. Open table or form.
2. Click in field by which to sort.
3. Click Ascending or Descending button.

Filter a Datasheet
1. Open table.
2. Click filter arrow next to field.
3. Clear check boxes as needed.
4. Click OK.

app tip

You can also click the funnel icon next to a field and then click the *Clear Filter* option to redisplay all records.

12.7 Creating a Query Using the Simple Query Wizard

Queries extract information from one or more tables in the database and display the results in a datasheet. Some queries display fields from more than one table in the same datasheet. For example, in the LibraryFines database, the student names are in one table and the fines are in another table; a query can combine the names and fines in one datasheet. Other queries are designed to answer a question about the data; for example, *Which library fines are unpaid?* The **Simple Query Wizard** assists a user with creating a query by prompting the user to make selections in a series of dialog boxes.

1. With the **LibraryFines–YourName** database open, click the Create tab.

2. Click the Query Wizard button in the Queries group.

3. Click OK in the New Query dialog box with *Simple Query Wizard* already selected.

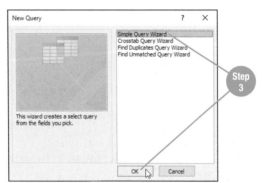

4. In the first Simple Query Wizard dialog box, click the *Tables/Queries* option box arrow and then click *Table: Students*. Skip this step if *Table: Students* is already displayed in the *Tables/Queries* option box.

   The first step in creating a query is to choose the tables or queries and the fields from each table or query that you want to display in a datasheet.

5. With *StudentID* already selected in the *Available Fields* list box, click the Add Field button (displays as a right-pointing arrow) to move *StudentID* to the *Selected Fields* list box.

Watch & Learn

Hands On Activity

●———————— Skills

Create a query using a wizard

Tutorial

Creating a Query Using the Simple Query Wizard

●———————— Oops!

Added the wrong field or the order of fields is wrong? Move a field back to the *Available Fields* list box by selecting the field and using the Remove Field button (left-pointing arrow).

6 Double-click *StudentFirstName* in the *Available Fields* list box to move the field to the *Selected Fields* list box.

Add fields to the *Selected Fields* list box in the order you want the fields displayed in the query results datasheet.

7 Double-click the following fields in the *Available Fields* list box to move each field to the *Selected Fields* list box.

> *StudentLastName*
> *Telephone*
> *Email*

8 Click the *Tables/Queries* option box arrow and then click *Table: Fines*.

9 Double-click the following fields in the *Available Fields* list box to move each field to the *Selected Fields* list box.

> *DateIssued*
> *Amount*
> *FinePaid*

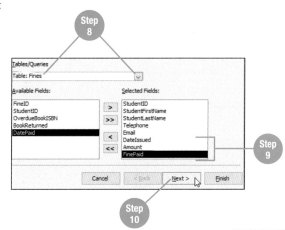

10 Click Next.

11 Click Next in the second Simple Query Wizard dialog box to accept *Detail (shows every field of every record)* for the query results.

12 Select the current text in the *What title do you want for your query?* text box in the third Simple Query Wizard dialog box, type StudentsWithFines, and then click Finish.

13 Review the query results datasheet. The first five rows are shown in the image below. Notice the fields are displayed in the order selected in the first Simple Query Wizard dialog box.

14 Close the StudentsWithFines query. Leave the database open for the next topic.

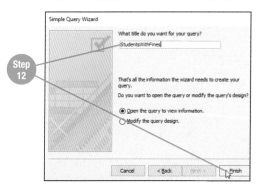

quick steps

Create a Query Using Simple Query Wizard
1. Click Create tab.
2. Click Query Wizard button.
3. Click OK.
4. Choose each table and/or query and fields in required order.
5. Click Next.
6. Click Next.
7. Type title for query.
8. Click Finish.

first five rows of query results datasheet

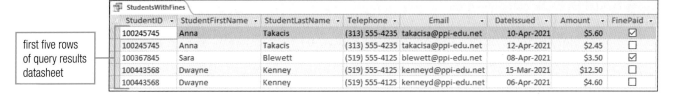

StudentsWithFines							
StudentID	StudentFirstName	StudentLastName	Telephone	Email	DateIssued	Amount	FinePaid
100245745	Anna	Takacis	(313) 555-4235	takacisa@ppi-edu.net	10-Apr-2021	$5.60	☑
100245745	Anna	Takacis	(313) 555-4235	takacisa@ppi-edu.net	12-Apr-2021	$2.45	☐
100367845	Sara	Blewett	(519) 555-4125	blewett@ppi-edu.net	08-Apr-2021	$3.50	☑
100443568	Dwayne	Kenney	(519) 555-4125	kenneyd@ppi-edu.net	15-Mar-2021	$12.50	☐
100443568	Dwayne	Kenney	(519) 555-4125	kenneyd@ppi-edu.net	06-Apr-2021	$4.60	☐

12.8 Creating a Query Using Design View

Every Access object has at least two views. In one view, you browse the data in the table, query, form, or report. This is the view that is active when you open the object from the Navigation pane. Another view, called **Design view**, is used to set up or define the structure and/or layout of a table, query, form, or report. A query can be created in Design view, which displays a blank grid into which you add the fields you want to display in the query results.

1. With the **LibraryFines -YourName** database open and with the Create tab active, click the Query Design button in the Queries group.

2. In the Show Table dialog box with the *Fines* table selected, click the Add button.

A field list box for the Fines table is added to the top of the *Query1* design grid in the work area.

3. Double-click *Students* in the Show Table dialog box.

A field list box for the Students table is added to the top of the design grid beside the Fines table field list box. A black join line connects the two tables. The black line displays 1 and an infinity symbol (∞), which indicates the type of relationship for the two tables. You will learn about relationships in the next chapter.

4. Click the Close button in the Show Table dialog box.

join line (shows tables are connected with a relationship)

5. Double-click *FineID* in the Fines table field list box.

FineID is added to the *Field* text box in the first column of the design grid. The blank columns in the bottom of the window represent the query results datasheet. Build a query by adding fields to the blank columns in the order you want them to appear in the datasheet. Double-clicking a field name in a table field list box in the top half of the window adds a field to the next available column, as you saw when you completed Step 5.

FineID is added here after you perform Step 5.

Watch & Learn

Hands On Activity

------ Skills

Create a query using Design view

Tutorials

Creating a Query in Design View

Creating a Query in Design View Using Multiple Tables

●------ Oops!

Closed the Show Table dialog box by mistake? Reopen the dialog box using the Show Table button in the Query Setup group on the Query Tools Design tab.

6 Double-click the following fields in the Fines table field list box to add each field to the next available column in the query design grid.

  DateIssued
  Amount
  BookReturned (scroll down the table field list box to the field)

7 Double-click the following fields in the Students table field list box to add each field to the next available column in the query design grid.

  StudentFirstName
  StudentLastName

8 Click the Run button in the Results group on the Query Tools Design tab to view the query results datasheet.

The **Run button** instructs Access to produce the query results datasheet by assembling the data from the tables according to the query instructions. A query is a set of instructions with table names and field names to display in a datasheet. The query results datasheet is not a duplicate copy of the data—each time a query is opened or run, the data is generated by extracting the field values from the tables. The first five rows in the query results datasheet are shown in the image below.

FineID	DateIssued	Amount	BookReturned	StudentFirstName	StudentLastName
MCL-116	10-Apr-2021	$5.60	☑	Anna	Takacis
MCL-117	12-Apr-2021	$2.45	☐	Anna	Takacis
MCL-114	08-Apr-2021	$3.50	☑	Sara	Blewett
MCL-108	15-Mar-2021	$12.50	☐	Dwayne	Kenney
MCL-113	06-Apr-2021	$4.60	☐	Dwayne	Kenney

first five rows of query results datasheet

9 Click the Save button on the Quick Access Toolbar.

10 Type FinesWithBookReturnList in the Save As dialog box and then press Enter or click OK.

11 Close the FinesWithBookReturnList query. Leave the database open for the next topic.

quick steps

Create a Query Using Design View
1. Click Create tab.
2. Click Query Design button.
3. Add tables to design grid.
4. Close Show Table dialog box.
5. Double-click field names in table field list boxes in desired order for query results datasheet.
6. Click Run button.
7. Click Save button.
8. Type query name.
9. Click OK.

12.9 Entering Criteria to Select Records in a Query

Watch & Learn

Hands On
Activity

╾ ─ ─ ─ ─ ─ ─ ─ skills

Select records in a query
using criteria

Tutorial
Adding a Criteria
Statement to a Query

Both query results datasheets for the queries you created using the Simple Query Wizard and using Design view displayed all records in the tables. Queries are often created to select records from tables that meet one or more conditions. For example, in this topic, you will add a criterion to display only those records in which the fines are unpaid. A query that extracts records based on criteria is called a **select query**.

1. With the **LibraryFines-YourName** database open, double-click the *StudentsWithFines* query.

2. Click the top part of the View button in the Views group on the Home tab.

The View button is used to switch between the query results datasheet and Design view.

3. Click in the *Criteria* box in the *FinePaid* column in the design grid, type No, press the spacebar, and then press Enter.

Access displays functions in a drop-down list as you type text that matches the letters in a function name. As you type *No*, the function wizard displays *Now* in a drop-down list. Typing a space after *No* causes the *Now* function to disappear. *FinePaid* is a field in which the field value is either *Yes* or *No*. By typing *No* in the *Criteria* box, you are instructing Access to select the records from the Fines table in which *No* is the field value for *FinePaid*.

Email	DateIssued	Amount	FinePaid
Students	Fines	Fines	Fines
☑	☑	☑	☑
			No

Step 3

●─ ─ ─ ─ ─ ─ ─ Oops!

Empty datasheet? Use the View button to return to Design view and check that *No* is in the *Criteria* box of the *FinePaid* column. A spelling mistake will cause an empty data-sheet.

4. Click the Run button.

Notice that 10 records are selected in the query results datasheet and that the check box in the *FinePaid* column for each record is empty.

StudentID	StudentFirstName	StudentLastName	Telephone	Email	DateIssued	Amount	FinePaid
100245745	Anna	Takacis	(313) 555-4235	takacisa@ppi-edu.net	12-Apr-2021	$2.45	☐
100443568	Dwayne	Kenney	(519) 555-4125	kenneyd@ppi-edu.net	15-Mar-2021	$12.50	☐
100443568	Dwayne	Kenney	(519) 555-4125	kenneyd@ppi-edu.net	06-Apr-2021	$4.60	☐
100659412	Jasmine	Daly	(284) 555-3142	dalyj@ppi-edu.net	30-Mar-2021	$2.40	☐
100684741	Marietta	Lynch	(519) 555-3214	lynchm@ppi-edu.net	12-Mar-2021	$1.40	☐
101325685	Peter	Maslov	(519) 555-3276	maslovp@ppi-edu.net	04-Apr-2021	$7.85	☐
101334799	Su-Lin	Cheng	(313) 555-4125	chengs@ppi-edu.net	10-Apr-2021	$8.75	☐
101348863	Daniela	Garcia	(313) 555-6235	garciad@ppi-edu.net	15-Mar-2021	$1.85	☐
101348863	Daniela	Garcia	(313) 555-6235	garciad@ppi-edu.net	15-Apr-2021	$5.25	☐
101658235	Stuart	Bennett	(313) 555-5112	bennetts@ppi-edu.net	13-Mar-2021	$3.25	☐
*							◼

This is the query results datasheet displaying unpaid fines only.

5. Click the File tab and then click *Save As*.

6. Click *Save Object As* in the *File Types* panel and then click the Save As button in the *Save the current database object* panel.

Step 6

7. Type UnpaidFines in the *Save 'StudentsWithFines' to* text box in the Save As dialog box and then press Enter or click OK.

Step 7

8. Close the UnpaidFines query.

9. Double-click the *StudentsWithFines* query.

10. Click the View button to switch to Design View.

11. Click in the *Criteria* box in the *DateIssued* column, type Between March 1, 2021 and March 31, 2021 and then press Enter.

12. Position the mouse pointer on the *DateIssued* right column boundary line in the gray bar above the columns and drag to the right when the mouse pointer displays with a black vertical bar and a left- and right-pointing arrow until the entire criteria statement is visible.

quick steps

Select Records in a Query
1. Open query.
2. Click View button.
3. Type criterion in *Criteria* box of field by which to select records.
4. Run query.
5. Save query or use Save As to save revised query using new name.

A criteria statement added to a date field is automatically converted to the date format *m/d/yyyy*, and a pound symbol (#) is added to the beginning and end of each date. Other ways to select records by date use the greater than (>) or less than (<) operator. For example, >*March 1, 2021* displays as >#3/1/2021# and selects all records in the table with a date *after* March 1, 2021. Table 12.2 provides more criteria statement examples.

Oops!

Syntax error message appears? A typing mistake in keywords *Between* or *And* or a typing error in the date is called a *syntax error*. Click OK to close the message and correct typing errors in the criteria statement.

Step 11   Step 12

13. Click the Run button. Notice only records with a fine issued in March 2021 are displayed.

14. Use *Save Object As* to save the revised query as *March2021Fines*.

15. Close the March2021Fines query. Leave the database open for the next topic.

Table 12.2 Criteria Examples

Field	Entry Typed in *Criteria* Box	Records Selected
Amount	<=5	Fines issued that were $5.00 or less
Amount	>5	Fines issued that were more than $5.00
DateIssued	March 15, 2021 (entry converts automatically to *#3/15/2021#*)	Fines issued on March 15, 2021
StudentLastName	Kenney (entry converts automatically to "Kenney")	Fines issued to student with the last name *Kenney*

12.10 Entering Multiple Criteria to Select Records and Sorting a Query

 Watch & Learn

 Hands On
Activity

●———————— Skills

Select records using
AND criteria

Select records using *OR*
criteria

Sort query results

Tutorials

Designing a Query
with an AND Criteria
Statement

Designing a Query
with an OR Criteria
Statement

Sorting Data and
Hiding Fields in
Query Results

More than one criterion can be entered in the query design grid to select records. For example, you may want a list of all unpaid fines that are more than $5.00. When more than one criterion is on the same row in the query design grid, it is referred to as an *AND* statement, meaning that each criterion must be met for a record to be selected. When more than one criterion is on different rows in the query design grid, it is referred to as an *OR* statement, meaning that any criterion can be met for a record to be selected.

1 With the **LibraryFines-YourName** database open, double-click the *UnpaidFines* query to open the query.

2 Click the top part of the View button in the Views group on the Home tab to switch to Design view.

3 Click in the *Criteria* box in the *Amount* column, type >5, and then press Enter.

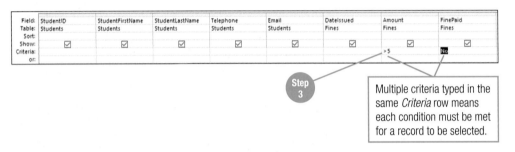

Step 3

Multiple criteria typed in the same *Criteria* row means each condition must be met for a record to be selected.

4 Click the Run button. Compare your results with the datasheet shown in the image below.

StudentID	StudentFirstName	StudentLastName	Telephone	Email	DateIssued	Amount	FinePaid
100443568	Dwayne	Kenney	(519) 555-4125	kenneyd@ppi-edu.net	15-Mar-2021	$12.50	☐
101325685	Peter	Maslov	(519) 555-3276	maslovp@ppi-edu.net	04-Apr-2021	$7.85	☐
101334799	Su-Lin	Cheng	(313) 555-4125	chengs@ppi-edu.net	10-Apr-2021	$8.75	☐
101348863	Daniela	Garcia	(313) 555-6235	garciad@ppi-edu.net	15-Apr-2021	$5.25	☐

This is the query results datasheet displaying unpaid fines over $5.00.

5 Use *Save Object As* to save the revised query as *UnpaidFinesOver$5*.

6 Close the UnpaidFinesOver$5 query.

7 Click the Create tab and then click the Query Design button.

8 Double-click *Students* in the Show Table dialog box and then click the Close button.

9 Double-click the following fields in the Students table field list box to add each field to the next available column in the query design grid.

>   *City*
>   *StudentID*
>   *StudentFirstName*
>   *StudentLastName*
>   *Telephone* (scroll down the table field list box to the field)

Field:	City	StudentID	StudentFirstName	StudentLastName	Telephone
Table:	Students	Students	Students	Students	Students
Sort:					
Show:	☑	☑	☑	☑	☑

Step 9

10 Click in the *Criteria* box in the *City* column, type Detroit, click in the row below *Detroit* (next to *or*), type Windsor, and then press Enter.

●---- quick steps

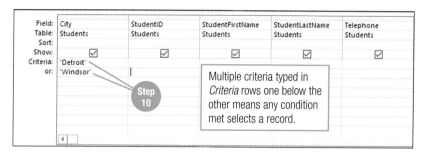

Select Records Using AND
1. Open query in Design view.
2. Type criterion in *Criteria* box of first field by which to select.
3. Type criterion in *Criteria* box of second field by which to select.
4. Run query.

Select Records Using OR
1. Open query in Design view.
2. Type criterion in *Criteria* box of first field by which to select.
3. Type criterion in *or* box of second field by which to select.
4. Run query.

Sort a Query
1. Open query in Design view.
2. Click in *Sort* box of column by which to sort.
3. Click *Sort* option box arrow.
4. Click *Ascending* or *Descending*.

Access inserts double quotation marks at the beginning and end of a criterion for a field that contains text, such as a city, name, or other field not used for calculating values.

11 Click the Run button.

Students who reside in Detroit *or* Windsor are displayed in the query results datasheet.

12 Click the View button to return to Design view.

A query is sorted by choosing *Ascending* or *Descending* in the *Sort* box of the column by which you want to sort. At Step 9, *City* was placed first in the design grid because Access sorts query results by column left to right. To arrange the records alphabetically by student last name grouped by cities, the *City* field needed to be positioned left of the *StudentLastName* field.

13 Click in the *Sort* box in the *City* column to place an insertion point and display the option box arrow, click the *Sort* option box arrow, and then click *Ascending*.

14 Click in the *Sort* box in the *StudentLastName* column, click the option box arrow that appears, and then click *Ascending*.

15 Click the Run button.

The query results datasheet is sorted alphabetically by city and then by the student last name within each city.

City	StudentID	StudentFirstName	StudentLastNam	Telephone
Detroit	101658235	Stuart	Bennett	(313) 555-511
Detroit	101334799	Su-Lin	Cheng	(313) 555-412
Detroit	101455623	Armando	Colacci	(313) 555-221
Detroit	100478512	Angela	Doxtator	(313) 555-477
Detroit	101348863	Daniela	Garcia	(313) 555-623
Detroit	100548112	Pat	Hynes	(313) 555-656
Detroit	101322775	Shane	O'Leary	(313) 555-365
Detroit	110542642	Nadir	Sadiku	(313) 555-478
Detroit	100245745	Anna	Takacis	(313) 555-423
Detroit	101334745	Kyla	Westman	(313) 555-745
Detroit	104875111	Dana	Williams	(313) 555-124
Windsor	100367845	Sara	Blewett	(519) 555-412
Windsor	101352658	Shaun	Jenkins	(519) 555-478
Windsor	100443568	Dwayne	Kenney	(519) 555-412
Windsor	100684741	Marietta	Lynch	(519) 555-321
Windsor	101325685	Peter	Maslov	(519) 555-327
Windsor	100324125	Jose	Ramirez	(519) 555-469

This query results datasheet displays students who reside in either Detroit or Windsor and is sorted first by *City* and then by *StudentLastName*.

16 Save the query and name it **DetroitAndWindsorStudents**.

17 Close the DetroitAndWindsorStudents query. Leave the database open for the next topic.

12.11 Modifying a Query, Calculating in a Query, and Previewing a Datasheet

Modify a query by adding and removing columns in the query design grid using buttons in the Query Setup group on the Query Tools Design tab. A calculated field can be created in a query that performs a mathematical operation on a numeric field. A database design best practice is to avoid including a field in a table for storing data that can be generated by performing a calculation on another field. For example, assume that in the LibraryFines database, each fine is assessed a $2.50 administrative fee. Because the fee is a constant value, adding a field in the table to store the fee is not necessary. In this topic, you will use a query to calculate the total fine, including the administrative fee.

1. With the **LibraryFines-YourName** database open, double-click the *FinesIssued* query to open the query.

2. Switch to Design view.

3. Click in any cell in the *Telephone* column in the query design grid.

4. Click the Delete Columns button in the Query Setup group on the Query Tools Design tab.

Buttons in the Query Setup group are used to modify a query by deleting columns or inserting new columns between existing fields.

5. Delete the *OverdueBookISBN* and *BookReturned* fields by completing steps similar to Steps 3 and 4.

6. With *FinePaid* the active field, click the Insert Columns button in the Query Setup group.

7. With an insertion point positioned in the *Field* box in the new column between *Amount* and *FinePaid*, type Fine with Admin Fee: [Amount]+2.50 and then press Enter.

8. Drag the right column boundary line in the gray bar above the calculated field until you can see the entire formula as shown in the image below. Note that Access drops the zero at the end of the formula.

Field:	FineID	DateIssued	StudentFirstName	StudentLastName	Amount	Fine with Admin Fee: [Amount]+2.5	FinePaid	
Table:	Fines	Fines	Students	Students	Fines		Fines	
Sort:								
Show:	☑	☑	☑	☑	☑	☑	☑	
Criteria:								
or:								

The text before the colon is the column heading for the new field *Fine with Admin Fee*. After the colon, the mathematical expression *[Amount]+2.5* is stored. A field name used in a formula is typed within square brackets.

9. Click the Run button.

Notice that the calculated field is not formatted the same as the *Amount* field, and that the column needs to be widened to display the entire column heading.

10. Click in any cell in the *Fine with Admin Fee* column, click the More button in the Records group, click *Field Width*, and then click the Best Fit button in the Column Width dialog box.

Watch & Learn

Hands On Activity

- - - - - - - - Skills

Delete and insert columns in a query

Create a calculated field

Format a field

Print Preview a datasheet

Tutorials

Performing Calculations in a Query

Previewing and Printing a Table

- - - - - - - - Oops!

Error message appears? Check your typing to make sure you typed a colon after *Fine with Admin Fee*, used square brackets, and that the entry has no other spelling errors.

app tip

Use the same mathematical operators in Access that you would use in a formula in Excel: + to add, - to subtract, * to multiply, and / to divide.

⑪ Switch to Design view.

⑫ Click to place an insertion point in the *Fine with Admin Fee* column heading in the query design grid and then click the Property Sheet button in the Show/Hide group on the Query Tools Design tab.

⑬ Click in the *Format* box in the Property Sheet task pane, click the option box arrow that appears, and then click *Currency*.

quick steps

Create a Calculated Field in a Query
1. Open query in Design view.
2. Insert column if necessary.
3. Click in *Field* box for calculated column.
4. Type formula.
5. Press Enter.
6. Run query.
7. Save query.

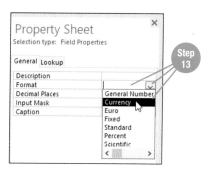

⑭ Close the Property Sheet task pane.

⑮ Click the Run button.

⑯ Use *Save Object As* to save the revised query as *FinesWithAdminFee*.

FineID	DateIssued	StudentFirstName	StudentLastName	Amount	Fine with Admin Fee	FinePaid
MCL-116	10-Apr-2021	Anna	Takacis	$5.60	$8.10	☑
MCL-117	12-Apr-2021	Anna	Takacis	$2.45	$4.95	☐
MCL-114	08-Apr-2021	Sara	Blewett	$3.50	$6.00	☑
MCL-108	15-Mar-2021	Dwayne	Kenney	$12.50	$15.00	☐
MCL-113	06-Apr-2021	Dwayne	Kenney	$4.60	$7.10	☐

These are the first five records in the FinesWithAdminFee query displaying the *Fine with Admin Fee* calculated column.

A table datasheet or query results datasheet should be viewed in Print Preview before printing to make adjustments as necessary to the orientation and margins.

⑰ Click the File tab, click *Print*, and then click *Print Preview* in the Print panel of the backstage area.

The entire datasheet does not fit on one page in the default portrait orientation.

⑱ Click the Landscape button in the Page Layout group on the Print Preview tab.

Notice that Access prints the query name and the current date at the top of the page and the page number at the bottom of the page.

⑲ Click the Close Print Preview button in the Close Preview group.

app tip

Access does not save page layout options for datasheets. For data that is printed frequently, a report object is created, which saves page layout and format options. You will learn how to create a report in Chapter 13.

⑳ Close the FinesWithAdminFee query.

㉑ Click the File tab and then click *Close* to close the LibraryFines database.

Topics Review

Topic	Key Concepts
12.1 Understanding Database Objects and Terminology	A **database** stores data in an organized manner to provide information for a variety of purposes.
	A **database management system (DBMS)** is application software to organize, store, and maintain a database.
	An Access database is a collection of objects used to enter, maintain, and view data.
	Access opens with a Navigation pane along the left side of the window used to select an object to open and view data.
	A **table** stores data about a single topic or subject such as people, places, events, or items.
	Each characteristic about the subject or topic of a table is called a **field**.
	The data stored in a field is called a **field value**.
	A set of fields for one person, place, event, item, or other subject of a table is called a **record**.
	A table opens in a datasheet where the columns are fields and the rows are records.
	A **report** is an object used to view or print data from tables in a customized layout and with summary totals.
	A **form** is another interface to view, enter, or edit data and displays only one record at a time in a customized layout.
	Use buttons on the Record Navigation bar to scroll records in a form.
	A **query** is used to combine fields from one or more tables in a single datasheet and may display all records or only some records that meet a condition.
12.2 Adding Records to a Table Using a Datasheet	New records are added to a table by opening the table datasheet and then clicking the **New (blank) record button** on the Record Navigation bar.
	Type field values in each column in the table datasheet, pressing Tab to move from one field to the next field.
	A field that displays with a down-pointing arrow means that you can enter the field value by selecting an entry from a drop-down list.
	Date fields can be set up to display underscores and hyphens to make sure dates are entered consistently in the correct format.
	A field that displays with a check box stores *Yes* if the box is checked and *No* if the box is left empty.
	Access automatically saves a new record as soon as you press Tab to move past the last field.
12.3 Editing and Deleting Records Using a Datasheet	Edit a field value in a datasheet by selecting text to be changed and typing new text, or by clicking to place an insertion point within a field (cell) and inserting or deleting text as required.
	Function key F2 opens a field for editing.
	The gray record selector bar along the left edge of a datasheet is used to select a record. At the top of the gray bar next to the first field name is the **Select all button**, which selects all field values in all records in the table.
	Click the Delete button in the Records group on the Home tab to delete the selected record from the table.
	Access requires that you confirm a deletion before the record is removed.
	Generally, records are not deleted until data has been copied to an archive database and/or a backup copy of the database has been made.

continued...

Topic	Key Concepts
12.4 Adding, Editing, and Deleting Records Using a Form	A form is the preferred object for adding, editing, and deleting records because one record at a time is displayed in a columnar layout in the work area.
	Add new records and edit field values in records using the same techniques that you used for adding and editing records using a datasheet.
	To delete a record using a form, display the record, click the Delete button arrow in the Records group on the Home tab, and then click *Delete Record*.
12.5 Finding and Replacing Data and Adjusting Column Widths in a Datasheet	Click in the column in a datasheet that contains the field value you want to locate and use the Find command to move to all occurrences of the text entered in the *Find What* text box.
	Use the Replace command to find all occurrences of an entry and replace the field value with new text.
	Activate any cell in a column for which the width needs to be adjusted, click the More button in the Records group on the Home tab, click *Field Width*, and then enter the desired width or click the Best Fit button.
	The **Best Fit** option adjusts the width of the column to accommodate the longest entry in the field.
12.6 Sorting and Filtering Records	Initially, a table is arranged alphanumerically by the **primary key** field values. A primary key is a field in the table that uniquely identifies each record, such as *StudentID*.
	To sort by a field other than the primary key, click in the field by which to sort and then click the Ascending button or Descending button in the Sort & Filter group on the Home tab.
	Filter a datasheet by clearing check boxes for items you do not want to view in the *Sort & Filter* list box accessed from the filter arrow next to the field name.
	Use the Toggle Filter button in the Sort & Filter group to redisplay all records in a filtered datasheet.
12.7 Creating a Query Using the Simple Query Wizard	Queries extract information from one or more tables in a single datasheet.
	The **Simple Query Wizard** helps you build a query by making selections in three dialog boxes.
	In the first Simple Query Wizard dialog box, choose each table or query and the fields in the order that you want them in the query results datasheet.
	In the second Simple Query Wizard dialog box, choose a detail or summary query.
	Assign a name to the query in the third Simple Query Wizard dialog box.
12.8 Creating a Query Using Design View	Every object in Access has at least two views. Opening an object from the Navigation pane opens the table, query, form, or report in the view that displays the object with table data.
	Design view is used to set up or define the structure or layout of an object.
	Design view for a query presents a blank grid of columns in which you add the fields in the order you want them in the query results datasheet.
	Add table field list boxes to the query from the Show Table dialog box by selecting the table names and clicking the Add button. Close the Show Table dialog box when all tables have been added.
	Double-click field names in the table field list boxes in the order you want the columns in the query results datasheet. Each field is added to the next available column in the query design grid.
	The **Run button** is used after building a query in Design view to instruct Access to generate the query and display the query results datasheet.

continued…

Topic	Key Concepts
12.9 Entering Criteria to Select Records in a Query	A query that displays only those records that meet one or more conditions is called a **select query**.
	Use the View button in the Views group on the Home tab to switch between Datasheet view and Design view in a query.
	Type the criterion by which you want records selected in the *Criteria* box of the column by which records are to be selected.
	In a field that displays check boxes, the criterion is either *Yes* or *No*.
	A date added as a criterion is displayed in the format *#m/d/yyyy#*. Use date keywords *Between* and *And* to select records based on a range of dates.
12.10 Entering Multiple Criteria to Select Records and Sorting a Query	More than one criterion entered in the same *Criteria* row in the query design grid is an *AND* statement, which means each criterion must be met for the record to be selected.
	More than one criterion entered in *Criteria* rows one below the other is an *OR* statement, which means that any condition can be met for the record to be selected.
	Choose *Ascending* or *Descending* from the *Sort* option box arrow for the column by which to sort query results in Design view.
	Access sorts a query by column left to right. If necessary, position the field to be sorted first to the left of another field that is to be sorted.
12.11 Modifying a Query, Calculating in a Query, and Previewing a Datasheet	A calculated field can be created in a query that generates values using a mathematical expression.
	Use the Delete Columns and Insert Columns buttons in the Query Setup group on the Query Tools Design tab to remove or add new columns in a query.
	A calculated column is created by typing in the *Field* box a column heading, a colon (:), and then the mathematical expression.
	Type a field name in a mathematical expression within square brackets.
	Open the Property Sheet task pane to change the format of a calculated field.
	A table or query results datasheet should be previewed before printing to make adjustments to page orientation and/or margins.

 Topics Review

Chapter 13

Creating a Table, Form, and Report in Access

Planning a new database involves understanding the purpose of the database and the information each database user will need. Prior to starting Access and creating a new database file, the database designer carefully analyzes the data to be collected and decides the best way to define and group the data elements into logical units. Tables are created first because they are the basis for all other objects. Next, tables that need to be connected for queries, forms, or reports are joined in a relationship. Objects such as queries, forms, and reports are created after the tables and relationships are defined.

In Chapter 12, you examined an existing database and added and edited data in a table and form. You also created queries to select records for a variety of purposes. Now that you have seen how Access data interacts with objects, you are ready to build a new database on your own. In this chapter, you will learn to create a new database, create a new table, assign a primary key, modify field properties, edit relationships, create a form, create a report, compact and repair a database, and create a backup copy of a database.

Learning Objectives

13.1 Create a new database and describe guidelines for designing tables

13.2 Create a new table using Datasheet view and assign a caption to a field

13.3 Create a new table using Design view and assign a primary key

13.4 Add a field to a table

13.5 Change the field size and add a default value for a field using Design view

13.6 Create a lookup list for a field

13.7 Identify a one-to-one relationship and a one-to-many relationship, and edit a relationship

13.8 Create and edit a form

13.9 Create, edit, and view a report

13.10 Compact and repair, and back up a database

Read & Learn

Content Online

The online course includes additional training and assessment resources.

13.1 Creating a New Database File and Understanding Table Design Guidelines

The first step in creating a database is to assign a name and storage location for the new database file. Because Access saves records automatically as data is added to a table, the file name and storage location are required in advance. Once the file is created, Access displays a blank table. Before you create a new table, you must carefully plan the fields and field names and identify a primary key. The tables you will create in this chapter have already been planned. The guidelines in Table 13.1 provide you with an overview of the table design process to understand how the tables you create were structured.

Watch & Learn

skills

Create a new database file

Table 13.1 Guidelines for Planning a New Table

Guideline	Description
Divide data into the smallest possible units	A field should be segmented into the smallest units of information to facilitate sorting and filtering. For example, a person's name could be split into three fields: first name, middle name, and last name.
Assign each field a name	Up to 64 characters can be used in a field name with a combination of letters, numbers, spaces, and some symbols. Database programmers prefer short field names with no spaces. A field to store a person's last name could be assigned the name *LName*, *Last*, *LastName*, or *Last_Name*. Short names are preferred because Access provides the ability to enter a longer descriptive title for column headings in datasheets, forms, and reports that is separate from the field name.
Assign each field a data type	*Data type* refers to the type of information that will be entered as field values. Look at examples of data to help you determine the data type. By assigning the most appropriate data type, Access can verify data as it is being entered for the correct format or type of characters. For example, a field defined as a Number field will cause Access to reject alphabetic letters typed into the field. The most common data types are Short Text, Number, Currency, Date/Time, and Yes/No. Data types are described in Table 13.2 in the next topic.
Decide the field to be used as a primary key	Each table should have one field that uniquely identifies a record, such as a student number, receipt number, or email address. Access creates an ID field automatically in a blank datasheet that can be used if the table data does not have a unique identifier. In some cases, a combination of two or more fields is used as a primary key.
Include a common identifier field in a table that will be joined to another table	Data should not be duplicated in a database. For example, a book title would not be stored in both the Books table and the Sales table. Instead, the book title is stored in the Books table only, and a book ID field in the Sales table is used to join the two tables in a relationship. Relationships will be explained in a later topic.

1 Start Access.

2 Click *Blank database* on the Access Start screen.

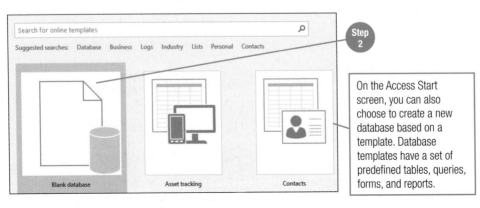

Step 2

On the Access Start screen, you can also choose to create a new database based on a template. Database templates have a set of predefined tables, queries, forms, and reports.

Tutorial

Opening a Blank Database

③ With the current text in the *File Name* text box already selected, type UsedBooks -YourName and then click the Browse button (file folder icon).

④ In the File New Database dialog box, navigate to the CompletedTopics folder on your storage medium, create a new folder named *Ch13*, double-click to open the Ch13 folder, and then click OK.

⑤ Click the Create button.

Access creates the database file and opens a new table datasheet named *Table1* in the work area, as shown in Figure 13.1.

•————— quick steps

Create a New Database
1. Start Access.
2. Click *Blank database*.
3. Type file name.
4. Click Browse button.
5. Navigate to drive and/ or folder location.
6. Click OK.
7. Click Create.

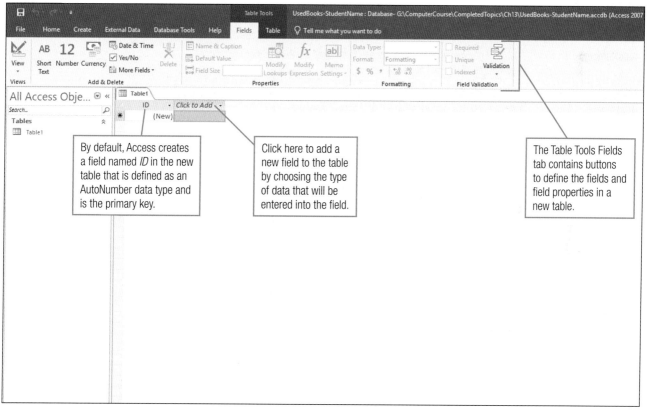

By default, Access creates a field named *ID* in the new table that is defined as an AutoNumber data type and is the primary key.

Click here to add a new field to the table by choosing the type of data that will be entered into the field.

The Table Tools Fields tab contains buttons to define the fields and field properties in a new table.

Figure 13.1

Access creates a blank table datasheet, like the one shown here, in a new database file.

⑥ Leave the blank table datasheet open for the next topic.

Each table in a database should contain information about one subject only. In this chapter, you will create tables for a used-textbook database that a student organization may use to keep track of students, textbooks, and sales. The three tables you will create in this chapter are described as follows:

Books: shows the title, author, condition, and asking price for each book

Sales: tracks each sale with the date, amount, and payment method

Students: shows information about each student who has textbooks for sale

13.2 Creating a New Table Using a Datasheet

Create a new table in a blank datasheet in Datasheet view by adding a column for each field. Begin by specifying the data type for a field and then typing the field name. Data types are described in Table 13.2. Once the fields have been defined, use the Save button on the Quick Access Toolbar to assign the table a name.

Watch & Learn

Hands On Activity

▬ ▬ ▬ ▬ ▬ ▬ ▬ Skills

Create a new table using a datasheet

Add a caption for a field

Table 13.2 Field Data Types

Data Type	Use for This Type of Field Value
Short Text	Alphanumeric text up to 255 characters for names, identification numbers, telephone numbers, or other similar data
Number	Numeric data other than monetary values
Currency	Monetary values such as sales, costs, or wages
Date & Time or Date/Time	Dates or times that you want to verify, sort, select, or calculate
Yes/No	Data that can only be Yes or No, or True or False
Lookup & Relationship or Lookup Wizard	Option list with field values from another table, or from a predefined list of options (items)
Long Text or Rich Text	Alphanumeric text of more than 255 characters; Rich Text enables formatting options such as font, font color, bold, and italic in the field values
AutoNumber	Unique number generated by Access to be used as an identifier field; Access generates sequential numbers starting from 1
Hyperlink	Stores web addresses
Attachment	A file such as a picture attached to a field in a record
Calculated Field	Formula that calculates the field value using data in other fields

1 With the **UsedBooks –YourName** database open and with the blank datasheet for Table1 open, click the Date & Time button in the Add & Delete group on the Table Tools Fields tab.

Tutorial

Creating a Table in Datasheet View

Choosing the most appropriate data type for a field is important for sorting, calculating, and verifying data. Access expects dates to be entered in the format *m/d/y* unless the region setting in the Control Panel is changed to another format.

2 With *Field1* selected in the field name box for the new column, type SaleDate and then press Enter.

The *Click to Add* column opens the Data Type option list for the next new field. Add a new field using either the *Click to Add* option list or the buttons in the Add & Delete group on the Table Tools Fields tab.

3 Click *Short Text* in the *Click to Add* option list.

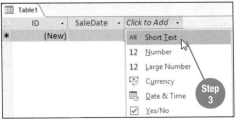

▬ ▬ ▬ ▬ ▬ ▬ app tip

Access displays the field name as the column title in a datasheet unless an entry exists in the Caption property, in which case the caption text becomes the column title. (See Step 8.)

④ Type BookID as the field name and then press Enter.

⑤ Click *Currency* in the *Click to Add* option list, type Amount, and then press Enter.

⑥ Click *Short Text*, type PayMethod, and then press Enter.

⑦ Double-click the *SaleDate* field name to select the field.

⑧ Click the Name & Caption button in the Properties group on the Table Tools Fields tab.

The **Caption property** is used to type a descriptive title for a field that includes spaces between words or the full text of an abbreviated field name.

⑨ Click in the *Caption* text box, type Sale Date, and then press Enter or click OK in the Enter Field Properties dialog box.

⑩ Click to select the *Amount* field, click the Name & Caption button, click in the *Caption* text box, type Sale Amount, and then press Enter or click OK.

⑪ Drag the right column boundary of the *Sale Amount* column until the entire column heading is visible, if necessary.

⑫ Click to select the *PayMethod* field, click the Name & Caption button, click in the *Caption* text box, type Payment Method, and then press Enter or click OK.

⑬ Double-click the right column boundary of the *Payment Method* column.

Double-clicking the right column boundary of a field sets the column width to the Best Fit option—the length of the longest entry in the column.

⑭ Click the Save button on the Quick Access Toolbar.

⑮ Type Sales in the *Table Name* text box in the Save As dialog box and then press Enter or click OK.

completed Sales table datasheet

⑯ Close the Sales table. Leave the database open for the next topic.

13.3 Creating a New Table Using Design View and Assigning a Primary Key

A new table can be created in Design view in which fields are defined in rows in the top half of the work area. In the previous topic, the Sales table, created in a blank datasheet, had an ID field automatically created and designated as the primary key. In Design view, an ID field is not created for you. After creating the fields in the Design view window, assign the primary key to the field that will uniquely identify each record and then save the table.

1 With the **UsedBooks-YourName** database open, click the Create tab.

2 Click the Table Design button in the Tables group. Close the Property Sheet task pane if the task pane opens at the right side of the window.

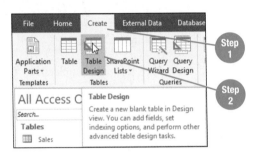

3 With the insertion point positioned in the first row in the *Field Name* column, type StudentID and then press Enter.

4 With *Short Text* in the *Data Type* column, press Enter to accept the default data type.

5 Press Enter to move past the *Description* column and move down to the next row to start a new field.

Descriptions are optional entries. A description is used to add information about a field or to enter instructions to end users who see the description in the Status bar of a datasheet when the field is active.

Press Enter at Step 5 to move past the optional *Description* entry.

6 Type LName in the *Field Name* column in the second row and then press Enter three times to move to the *Field Name* column in the third row.

7 Enter the remaining fields as shown in the image below.

☁ **Watch & Learn**

☁ **Hands On Activity**

●——————— Skills

Create a new table using Design view

Assign a primary key

☁ **Tutorials**

Creating a Table in Design View

Setting the Primary Key Field

Managing Fields in Design View

●——————— app tip

You can also use the Tab key to move to the next column in Design view.

⑧ Click to place an insertion point within the *StudentID* field name.

⑨ Click the Primary Key button in the Tools group on the Table Tools Design tab.

A key icon in the field selector bar (gray bar along left edge of *Field Name* column) indicates the field is designated as the primary key for the table.

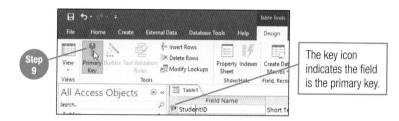

The key icon indicates the field is the primary key.

⑩ Click the Save button on the Quick Access Toolbar, type Students in the *Table Name* text box in the Save As dialog box, and then press Enter or click OK.

⑪ Close the Students table.

⑫ Click the Create tab and then click the Table Design button.

⑬ Create the first five fields in the new table using the default Short Text data type and without descriptions as follows:

> *BookID*
> *StudentID*
> *Title*
> *Author*
> *Condition*

⑭ Type AskPrice in the *Field Name* column in the sixth row and then press Enter.

⑮ Click the *Data Type* option box arrow and then click *Currency*.

⑯ Click to place an insertion point within the *BookID* field name and then click the Primary Key button.

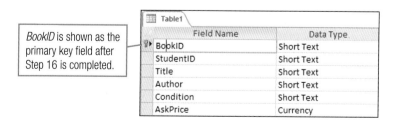

BookID is shown as the primary key field after Step 16 is completed.

⑰ Click the Save button on the Quick Access Toolbar, type Books, and then press Enter or click OK.

⑱ Close the Books table. Leave the database open for the next topic.

quick steps

Create a Table in Design View
1. Click Create tab.
2. Click Table Design button.
3. Type field name.
4. Press Enter.
5. If necessary, change data type.
6. Press Enter until new row is active.
7. Repeat Steps 3–6 until finished.
8. Assign primary key.
9. Save table.

Assign a Primary Key
1. If necessary, open table in Design view.
2. Click to place an insertion point in primary key field name.
3. Click Primary Key button.
4. Save table.

app tip

Access will not allow field values to be duplicated in a primary key—always choose a primary key field that you are sure will never have field values that repeat.

13.4 Adding Fields to an Existing Table

Open a table in Datasheet view and use the *Click to Add* column to add a new field, or make active a field in the datasheet and use the buttons on the Table Tools Fields tab to add a new field after the active field.

1 With the **UsedBooks-YourName** database open, double-click the Books table to open the table.

2 Click the *Click to Add* column heading and then click *Currency*.

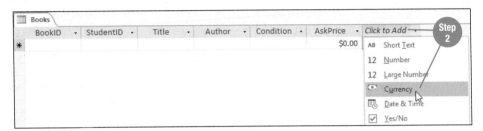

3 Type StopPrice as the field name and then press Enter.

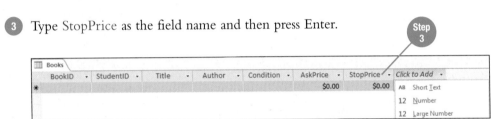

4 Click the top part of the View button in the Views group on the Table Tools Fields tab to switch to Design view.

5 Click in the *Description* column in the *StopPrice* field row and then type Do not sell for lower than the student's stop price value.

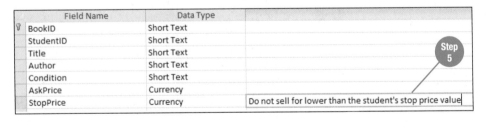

6 Save and then close the Books table.

7 Double-click to open the Students table.

8 Click the *Phone* field name to select the column.

9 Click the Table Tools Fields tab and then click the Yes/No button in the Add & Delete group to add the new field in the column to the right of the *Phone* field.

Watch & Learn

Hands On Activity

- - - - - - - - - Skills

Add a field to a table

Tutorials

Managing Fields in Datasheet View

Formatting Table Data

10 Type DirectDeposit as the field name and then press Enter.

11 Double-click the right column boundary of the *DirectDeposit* field to best fit the column width.

Steps
10-11

12 Save and then close the Students table.

13 Open the Books table.

14 Click the *StopPrice* field name to select the column.

15 Look at the message *Do not sell for lower than the student's stop price value* that displays in the Status bar.

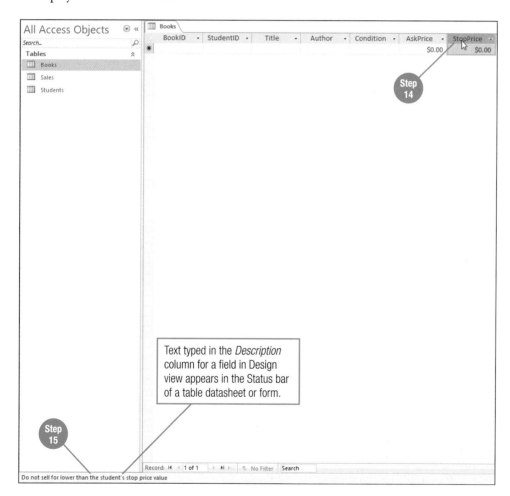

quick steps

Add a Field
1. Open table.
2. Click *Click to Add* column.
3. Click required data type.
4. Type field name.
5. Press Enter.
6. Save table.
OR
1. Open table.
2. Click field name to select column left of where you want the new field located.
3. Click the required data type button.
4. Type field name.
5. Press Enter.
6. Save table.

In this topic, you added a new field using the table datasheet. A field can also be added to a table using Design view. Open a table, switch to Design view, and then type the new field name and select the data type in the next available row. To add a new field positioned elsewhere, click in the field name row *below* the position you want the new field to be placed, and then click the Insert Rows button in the Tools group on the Table Tools Design tab.

16 Close the Books table. Leave the database open for the next topic.

13.5 Modifying Field Properties Using Design View

Each field in a table has a set of field properties associated with the field. A **field property** is a single characteristic or attribute of a field. For example, the field name is a field property, and the data type is another field property. The properties in each field can be modified to customize, format, or otherwise change the behavior of a field. The lower half of the work area of a table in Design view contains the **Field Properties pane** that is used to modify properties other than the field name, data type, and description.

1 With the **UsedBooks-YourName** database open, right-click the *Students* table name in the Navigation pane and then click *Design View.*

2 Click in the *StateOrProv* field name to select the field and display the associated field properties in the Field Properties pane.

Options displayed in the Field Properties pane vary by the field data type. For example, a Date & Time field does not have a Field Size property.

3 Double-click *255* or drag to select *255* in the *Field Size* property box in the Field Properties pane, type 2, and then press Enter.

Setting a field size for a state or province field ensures that all new field values use the two-character abbreviation for addressing letters or creating labels from the database.

4 Click in the *Default Value* property box, type MI, and then press Enter.

Access automatically adds quotation marks to the text in a *Default Value* property box. The text entered into a *Default Value* property box is automatically entered as the field value in new records; the end user presses Enter to accept the value or types an alternative entry. Adding a default value entry not only saves time when a new record is being added to the table, but it also makes sure that the field value is entered consistently and with correct spelling. Use the property whenever a field is likely to have several records with the same entry.

5 Click in the *Caption* property box and then type State or Province.

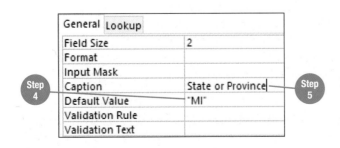

Watch & Learn

Hands On Activity

------- Skills

Change the field size

Add a default value

Add a caption in Design view

Tutorials

Modifying Field Properties in Design View

Applying a Validation Rule in Design View

•------- app tip

Buttons on the Table Tools Fields tab are available for changing the most common field properties in Datasheet view.

6 Click in the *StudentID* field name to select the field, click in the *Caption* property box in the Field Properties pane, type Student ID, and then press Enter.

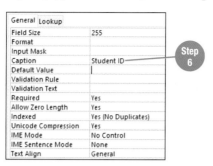

quick steps

Modify a Field Property
1. Open table in Design view.
2. Click in field name in top half of work area.
3. Click in property box or select current value in property box.
4. Type entry or select option from option list.
5. Save table.

7 Add the following caption properties like you did for Step 6.

Field Name	Caption
LName	Last Name
FName	First Name
Street	Street Address
ZIPOrPC	ZIP or Postal Code
Phone	Telephone
DirectDeposit	Direct Deposit
Email	Email Address

8 Save the table.

9 Click the top part of the View button in the Views group to switch to Datasheet view.

10 Double-click the right column boundary of column headings that are not entirely visible to best fit the column widths.

Notice that *MI* appears in the *State or Province* column by default.

11 Click in the *Student ID* column to place an insertion point, type 999, and then press Tab.

12 Type your name and a fictitious address in the remaining fields similar to the data shown in the image below. Adjust column widths as needed to view all data.

13 Close the table. Click Yes to save changes to the table layout. Leave the database open for the next topic.

See Table 13.3 for a description of additional field properties that are often used.

Table 13.3 Additional Field Properties and Examples

Field Property	Description	Example
Format	Modify this property to change the display of data entered into the field from the default format.	A field for storing dollar values can be formatted to show commas in thousands and a dollar symbol.
Validation Rule and Validation Text	An expression in the Validation Rule property is checked as data is entered; invalid data is not saved. The Validation Text entry displays a message to the user when a rule is in effect.	The expression >=5 in a numeric field ensures values less than 5 are rejected. A *Validation Text* entry such as *Please enter a value over 5* displays on the screen when a field value is rejected.
Required	A *Yes* in this property ensures that the field is not left blank in a new record.	This is used often for a *ZIP or PostalCode* field to make sure each record has a valid mailing code.

13.6 Creating a Lookup List

A **lookup list** presents a list of field values when a lookup field is made active while new records are added in a datasheet or form. The list entries can be a fixed list of options created for the field, or the list can present field values that exist in a field in another table that is linked to the lookup field. A lookup list has many advantages, including consistency, accuracy, and efficiency when adding data in new records. Access provides the **Lookup Wizard** to assist with creating field properties in which the user chooses options and types values in dialog boxes.

 Watch & Learn

Hands On
Activity

●------- Skills

Create a lookup list for
a field

Tutorial
Creating a Lookup
Field

1. With the **UsedBooks-YourName** database open, right-click the *Books* table name in the Navigation pane and then click *Design View*.

2. Click in the *Condition* field name to select the field.

3. Click in the *Data Type* box, click the option box arrow that appears, and then click *Lookup Wizard*.

4. Click *I will type in the values that I want.* in the first Lookup Wizard dialog box and then click Next.

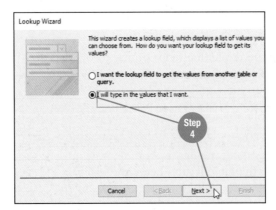

●------- app tip

To create a lookup list
that presents field values
from a field in another
table, select the option
*I want the lookup field
to get the values from
another table or query.*
In the subsequent dialog
boxes, select the table
or query name and
the field(s) that have
the values you want to
display in the list, select
a field to sort the list
entries, and then specify
the field value to store
if more than one field is
displayed in the list.

5. Click in the first blank row below *Col1* in the second Lookup Wizard dialog box and then type Excellent - No wear or markings.

6. Drag the *Col1* right column boundary to the right to increase the column width as shown in the image below.

⑦ Click in the second row and then type Very Good – Minor wear on cover.

⑧ Type the remaining entries in the list as shown in the image below.

You can also use the Down Arrow key to move to the next row in the column.

⑨ Click Next.

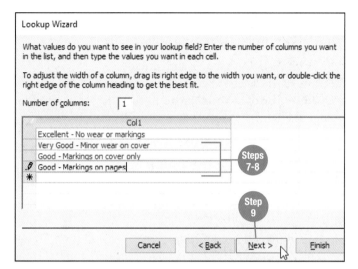

⑩ Click Finish in the last Lookup Wizard dialog box.

⑪ Click the Lookup tab in the Field Properties pane and review the entries made to each lookup property by the Lookup Wizard.

The entries typed in Steps 5 to 8 appear in the Row Source property. If you made a typing mistake while typing the list items, you can correct the error by clicking in the *Row Source* property box and inserting or deleting text as needed. Be cautious not to modify or delete syntax (quotations or semicolons) while correcting typing errors. If desired, you can limit field values in new records to only those items in the list by changing the Limit To List property to *Yes*.

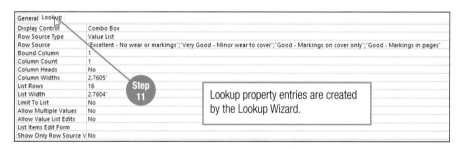

Lookup property entries are created by the Lookup Wizard.

⑫ Save the table and then click the top part of the View button to switch to Datasheet view.

⑬ Type the data in a new record as shown in the image below. In the *Condition* field, click the option box arrow that appears and click *Good – Markings on pages*.

⑭ Adjust column widths as needed to show all data in each column.

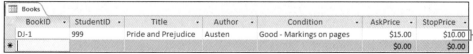

⑮ Save the table layout changes and then close the table.

⑯ Close the database.

quick steps

Create a Lookup List
1. Open table in Design view.
2. Click *Data Type* option box arrow for field.
3. Click *Lookup Wizard*.
4. Click *I will type in the values that I want*.
5. Click Next.
6. Type list entries in *Col1* column and adjust column width.
7. Click Next.
8. Click Finish.
9. Save table.

Oops!

Pressed Enter by mistake while typing a list entry in the second Lookup Wizard dialog box? Click the Back button to return to the list if you did not finish typing all the entries in Step 8.

13.7 Displaying and Editing a Relationship

A relationship allows you to create queries, forms, or reports with fields from two tables by connecting the two tables on a common field. Joining two tables in a relationship allows data to be reused, which prevents duplication and ensures consistency in records. For example, an ID, name, or title of a book can be looked up in one table rather than repeating the information in another table.

1. Open the database **UsedTextbooks** from the Ch13 folder in StudentDataFiles.

2. Click the File tab and then click *Save As*. With *Save Database As* and *Access Database (*.accdb)* already selected in the Save As backstage area, click the Save As button. Save a copy of the database as **UsedTextbooks-YourName** in the Ch13 folder in CompletedTopics on your storage medium.

3. Click the Enable Content button in the security warning message bar.

This file is similar to the database you have been working on in this chapter but with the Books table modified, additional lookup lists, and with 10 records added to each table.

4. Open the Books table, review the datasheet, and then close the table.

5. Open the Sales table, review the datasheet, and then close the table.

6. Open the Students table and then change *Doe* in the last record in the *Last Name* column to your last name.

7. Change *Jane* in the last record in the *First Name* column to your first name and then close the table.

8. Click the Database Tools tab and then click the Relationships button in the Relationships group.

A field list box for each table displays in the Relationships window. A black join line connecting two table field list boxes indicates a relationship has been created between the two tables. Observe that each join line connects the tables on the same field name in each table field list box.

9. Click to select the black join line that connects the Books table field list box to the Sales table field list box, and then click the Edit Relationships button in the Tools group on the Relationship Tools Design tab.

In the Edit Relationships dialog box that appears, *One-To-One* is shown in the *Relationship Type* section. A **one-to-one relationship** means that the two tables are joined on the primary key in each table. (*BookID* displays a key icon next to the field

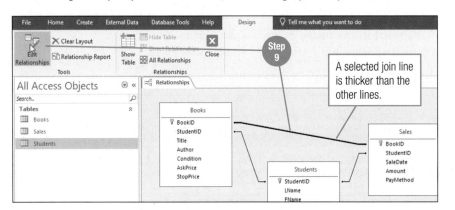

A selected join line is thicker than the other lines.

name in each table field list box.) In this type of relationship, only one record can exist for a *BookID* in each table.

10 Click to insert a check mark in the *Enforce Referential Integrity* check box and then click OK.

In a one-to-one relationship, the tables are joined on the primary key field in each table.

Turning on **Enforce Referential Integrity** means that a record in Books is entered first before a record with a matching *BookID* is entered in Sales. Notice in the screen image at the right, Books is the left table name below *Table/Query*, and Sales is the right table name below *Related Table/Query*. The table identified below *Table/Query* (in this case the Books table) is the one for which referential integrity is applied—the table in which new records are entered first. The table shown at the left is also referred to as the **primary table**.

11 Click to select the black join line that connects the Books table field list box to the Students table field list box and then click the Edit Relationships button.

12 Click to insert a check mark in the *Enforce Referential Integrity* check box and then click OK.

In a one-to-many relationship, the field joining the two tables is the primary key in one table and the foreign key in the other table.

A **one-to-many relationship** occurs when the common field used to join the two tables is the primary key in only one table (the primary table). *One* student can have *many* textbooks for sale. In this instance, a record must first be entered into Students (primary table) before a record with a matching student ID can be entered into Books (related table). A field added to a related table that is not a primary key and is included for the purpose of creating a relationship is called a **foreign key**. A one-to-many relationship is the most common type of relationship in a database.

13 Click the Close button in the Relationships group. Click Yes if prompted to save changes to the layout of the relationships, and leave the database open for the next topic.

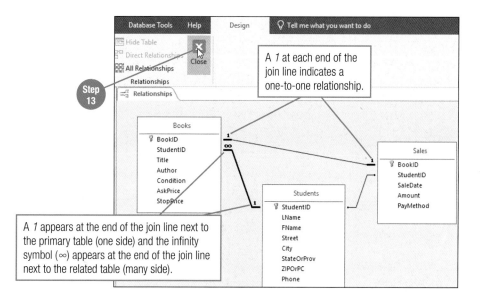

A *1* at each end of the join line indicates a one-to-one relationship.

A *1* appears at the end of the join line next to the primary table (one side) and the infinity symbol (∞) appears at the end of the join line next to the related table (many side).

quick steps

Display Relationships
1. Click Database Tools tab.
2. Click Relationships button.

Enforce Referential Integrity
1. Display Relationships.
2. Click to select black join line.
3. Click Edit Relationships button.
4. Click *Enforce Referential Integrity* check box.
5. Click OK.

app tip

To create a new relationship, drag the common field name in the primary table field list box to the same field in the related table field list box and then release the mouse. Change options as necessary and then click the Create button in the Edit Relationships dialog box that opens when the mouse is released.

13.8 Creating and Editing a Form

The Forms group on the Create tab includes buttons to create a variety of forms. A form can be as simple as all fields in a selected table arranged in a single column, to a complex form with fields from multiple tables and with some arranged in a subform within a form. Once created, a form can be modified using buttons on the Form Layout Tools Design, Arrange, and Format tabs.

1 With the **UsedTextbooks-YourName** database open, click to select the *Books* table name in the Navigation pane.

2 Click the Create tab.

3 Click the Form button in the Forms group.

A form is created with all the fields in the selected table arranged in a vertical layout and displayed in Layout view, as shown in Figure 13.2. **Layout view** is the view in which you edit a report or form structure and appearance. **Form view** is the view in which data is viewed, entered, and updated and is the view in which a form is opened when you double-click the form name in the Navigation pane.

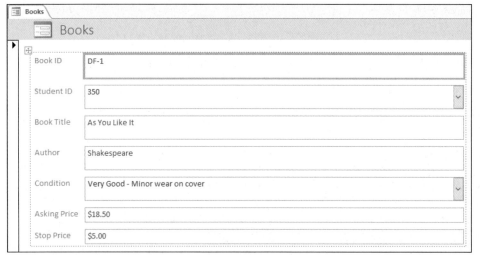

Figure 13.2
Shown is the Books form created using the Form button in Step 3.

4 Click the Themes button in the Themes group on the Form Layout Tools Design tab.

A theme sets the color scheme and fonts used on a form or report.

5 Click *Slice* in the *Office* section.

Watch & Learn

Hands On Activity

------- skills

Create a form

Apply a theme

Add and format an image on a form

Format the form title

------- app tip

Buttons to switch between views are at the right end of the Status bar.

Tutorials

Creating a Form Using the Form Button

Managing Control Objects in a Form

6 Click the Logo button in the Header/ Footer group.

7 In the Insert Picture dialog box, navigate to the Ch13 folder in StudentDataFiles and then double-click the file *Textbooks.jpg*.

The image is inserted into a selected logo **control object** near the top left of the form. A control object is a rectangular content placeholder in a form or report used to place images, text, field names, and field values. Each item on a form is placed in a control object. Each control object can be selected and edited to modify the appearance or other properties for the content.

8 With the logo control object still selected, click the Property Sheet button in the Tools group.

The Property Sheet task pane opens at the right side of the window and displays all the properties available for the selected control object.

9 Click the Format tab in the Property Sheet task pane, click in the *Size Mode* property box, click the option box arrow that appears, and then click *Zoom*.

The *Zoom* option for the Size Mode property fits the image to the control object placeholder size, maintaining the image proportions.

10 Select the current value in the *Width* property box and then type 1.75.

11 Select the current value in the *Height* property box, type 1.25, and then press Enter.

12 Close the Property Sheet task pane.

13 Click on the *Books* title to select the form title control object.

An orange border around the control object indicates the object is selected.

14 Click the Form Layout Tools Format tab.

15 Click the *Font Size* option box arrow and then click *48*.

16 Click the Save button on the Quick Access Toolbar and then click OK in the Save As dialog box to accept the default form name *Books*.

17 Close the Books form.

18 Double-click the *Books* form name in the Navigation pane to reopen the form, scroll through a few records, and then close the form. Leave the database open for the next topic.

13.9 Creating, Editing, and Viewing a Report

Create a report using techniques similar to those used to create a form. The Reports group on the Create tab has a Report tool similar to the Form tool. Other buttons in the Reports group include options to design a report from a blank page, create a report using the Report Wizard, or generate mailing labels using the Label Wizard. Modify a report with buttons on the Report Layout Tools tabs. Change the page layout options for printing purposes with buttons on the Report Layout Tools Page Setup tab.

1 With the **UsedTextbooks-YourName** database open, click to select the *Sales* table name in the Navigation pane.

2 Click the Create tab and then click the Report button in the Reports group.

A report is created with all the fields in the Sales table arranged in a tabular layout. By default, Access includes the current date and time, page numbering, and totals for numeric fields in all reports. Reports use the same theme as forms so that all objects have a consistent appearance.

3 Click the Logo button in the Header/Footer group on the Report Layout Tools Design tab and then double-click the file ***Textbooks.jpg***.

4 With the logo image control object still selected, open the Property Sheet task pane; change the Size Mode, Width, and Height properties to the same settings that you applied to the image in the previous topic; and then close the Property Sheet task pane. If necessary, refer to Steps 8 to 12 in Topic 13.8.

5 Click the *Sales* title to select the report title control object, click the Report Layout Tools Format tab, click the *Font Size* option box arrow, and then click *48*.

6 Click to select the current date control object near the top right of the report.

7 Drag the right border of the control object to the left until the control ends just left of the vertical dashed line that extends the height of the report. If pound symbols display after resizing the control, drag the left border of the control object towards the left margin until the date displays again.

The vertical dashed line indicates a page break. Resize control objects so that all objects are to the left of the vertical dashed line to fit on one page.

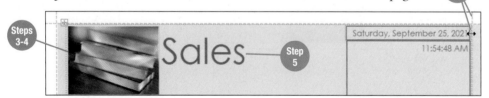

8 Click to select the *Book ID* column heading control object.

9 Drag the right border of the control object left about one-half inch to resize it to the approximate width shown in the image at right.

☁ **Watch & Learn**

☁ **Hands On Activity**

●──────── Skills

Create a report

Resize control objects

☁ **Tutorials**
Creating a Report
Formatting a Report

●────── Oops!

Textbooks image not shown? Access defaults to the last folder used in the Insert Picture dialog box. If necessary, navigate to the Ch13 folder in StudentDataFiles.

●────── app tip

A control object is filled with pound symbols (#) if the object is made too narrow for the content to be fully displayed. In that case, increase the width of the control object until the content redisplays.

Notice that resizing a column heading control object resizes the entire column.

(10) Click to select the *Page 1 of 1* control object and resize the control until the right border is just left of the vertical dashed line.

(11) Click to select the control object with the total at the bottom of the *Sale Amount* column and then drag the bottom border of the control down until the value is entirely visible within the object.

page number control resized to end left of the page break in Step 10

(12) Click the Report Layout Tools Design tab, click the View button arrow in the Views group, and then click *Print Preview*. Compare your report with the one shown in Figure 13.3. If necessary, switch to Layout view, resize control objects, and then switch back to Print Preview.

Buttons to switch views are also available at the right end of the Status bar.

● – – – – quick steps

Create a Report
1. Click to select table or query name in Navigation pane.
2. Click Create tab.
3. Click Report button.
4. Modify report as required.
5. Click Save button.
6. Type report name.
7. Click OK.

Tutorials

Managing Control Objects in a Report

Customizing a Report in Print Preview

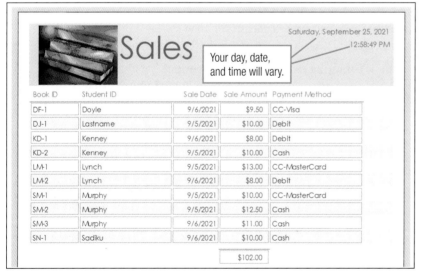

Figure 13.3

Shown is the Sales report for Topic 13.9 displayed in Print Preview.

(13) Click the Close Print Preview button in the Close Preview group.

(14) Click the View button arrow and then click *Report View*.

Report view is the view in which a report opens from the Navigation pane. Report view is used to view data on the screen instead of printing a hard copy. A report cannot be edited in Report view.

(15) Close the Sales report, saving changes to the report design and accepting the default report name of *Sales*. Leave the database open for the next topic.

13.10 Compacting, Repairing, and Backing Up a Database

A database file becomes larger and fragmented over time as new records are added, edited, and deleted. The file size for the database may become larger than is necessary if the space previously used by records that have since been deleted is not compacted. Access provides a **Compact & Repair Database button** that eliminates unused space and reduces the file size.

Backing up a database file should be done regularly for record keeping and data-loss prevention purposes. In most businesses, backing up of a database is a scheduled activity that occurs automatically, with some parts of the database backed up hourly. A database administrator is responsible for scheduling the backup routines. In this topic, you will perform a manual backup procedure, which can be done at any time a backup is deemed necessary.

1. With the **UsedTextbooks-YourName** database open, click the File tab.
2. Click the Compact & Repair Database button in the Info backstage area.

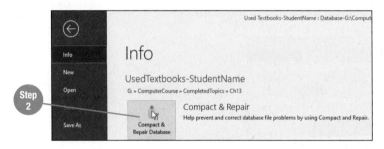

Access closes all objects and the Navigation pane during a compact and repair routine. The Navigation pane redisplays when the compacting and repairing is complete. For a large database file, compacting and repairing the database file may take a few moments to process.

If a database is shared, make sure no one else is using the database before starting a compact and repair operation.

3. Click the File tab and then click *Options*.

In the Access Options dialog box, a database file can be set to compact and repair each time the file is closed.

4. Click *Current Database* in the left pane of the Access Options dialog box.
5. Click to insert a check mark in the *Compact on Close* check box in the *Application Options* section.

Watch & Learn

Hands On Activity

○―――――――― Skills

Compact and repair a database

Create a backup copy of a database

Tutorial

Compacting and Repairing a Database

⑥ Click OK to close the Access Options dialog box.

⑦ Click OK in the message box that says the database must be closed and reopened for the option to take effect.

⑧ Click the File tab and then click *Save As*.

⑨ In the Save As backstage area, click *Back Up Database* in the *Advanced* section in the Save Database As panel.

⑩ Click the Save As button.

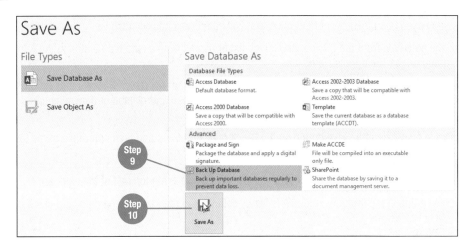

⑪ Click the Save button in the Save As dialog box.

By default, the backup copy of the database is saved in the same folder as the current database and the file name is the same database file name with the current date added after an underscore at the end of the name, for example, UsedTextbooks -YourName_*currentdate*.

A backup copy of a database is normally saved on another storage medium, such as a server connected to the PC housed in another building, or on a storage device at a cloud service provider, such as OneDrive. By saving a backup copy of a database to an offsite location, the data can be restored in the event of a fire, theft, or other loss of the PC on which the original database is stored.

⑫ Close the database.

● — — — quick steps

Compact and Repair a Database
1. Click File tab.
2. Click Compact & Repair Database button.

Turn on Compact on Close
1. Click File tab.
2. Click *Options*.
3. Click *Current Database*.
4. Click *Compact on Close*.
5. Click OK twice.

Back Up a Database
1. Click FIle tab.
2. Click *Save As*.
3. Click *Back Up Database*.
4. Click Save As button.
5. Click Save.

Topics Review

Topic	Key Concepts
13.1 Creating a New Database File and Understanding Table Design Guidelines	Access requires the name and file storage location before creating a new database because Access saves changes automatically as you work with data.
	Planning a new table involves several steps, some of which include dividing the data into fields, assigning each field a name, assigning each field a data type, deciding the field that will be the primary key, and including a common field to join a table to another table if necessary.
	To create a new database file, choose *Blank database* on the Access Start screen, type the file name, browse to the desired drive and/or folder, and then click the Create button.
	When a new database is created, Access displays a blank table datasheet.
13.2 Creating a New Table Using a Datasheet	Begin a new field in a table datasheet by first selecting the data type and then typing the field name.
	Several data types are available, such as Short Text, Number, Currency, and Date & Time. A data type is selected based upon the type of field value that will be entered into records.
	Choose the data type from the *Click to Add* option list or by choosing a data type button in the Add & Delete group on the Table Tools Fields tab.
	An entry in the **Caption property** is used as a descriptive title that becomes the column heading for a field in a datasheet. Use a caption if the field name has been abbreviated or has no spaces between words.
	Save a table by clicking the Save button on the Quick Access Toolbar and then entering a name for the table.
13.3 Creating a New Table Using Design View and Assigning a Primary Key	In Design view, a new table is created by defining fields in rows in the top half of the work area.
	Type a field name in the first row in the *Field Name* column and then specify the data type using the *Data Type* option list.
	An optional description can be added for a field, with additional information about the purpose of the field or with instructions on what to type into the field.
	Once the fields are defined, assign the primary key by placing an insertion point anywhere within the field name and then clicking the Primary Key button in the Tools group on the Table Tools Design tab.
13.4 Adding Fields to an Existing Table	Open a table and use the *Click to Add* column to add a new field to the end of an existing table datasheet.
	Select a column in a datasheet and use the buttons in the Add & Delete group on the Table Tools Fields tab to add a new field at the right of the selected field.
	A new field can be added in Design view by typing the new field name and specifying the data type in the next available row, or by selecting a field below the desired position and clicking the Insert Rows button in the Tools group on the Table Tools Design tab.
13.5 Modifying Field Properties Using Design View	A **field property** is a single characteristic or attribute of a field that customizes, formats, or changes the behavior of the field. Each field in a table has a set of associated field properties.
	The lower half of the Design view window is the **Field Properties pane** in which properties for a selected field are modified.
	The Field Size property is used to limit the number of characters that can be entered into a field.
	The Default Value property is used to specify a field value that is automatically entered in the field in new records.
	Other field properties that are often modified are the Format, Validation Rule, Validation Text, and Required field properties.

continued...

Topic	Key Concepts
13.6 Creating a Lookup List	A **lookup list** is a list of field values that displays when a field is made active in a datasheet or form.
	Items in the lookup list can be predefined or extracted from one or more fields in another table.
	The **Lookup Wizard** presents a series of dialog boxes to help create the field properties for a lookup list field.
	Create a custom list of predefined entries by choosing *I will type in the values that I want.* in the first Lookup Wizard dialog box.
	Type the list entries in the *Col1* column and adjust the column width in the second Lookup Wizard dialog box. Click Finish in the third dialog box.
	List entries and list options can be edited using the Lookup tab in the Field Properties pane.
13.7 Displaying and Editing a Relationship	A relationship is when two tables are joined together on a common field.
	Black join lines connecting a common field between two table field list boxes indicates a relationship has been created.
	A **one-to-one relationship** means that the two tables are joined on the primary key in each table.
	Enforce Referential Integrity causes Access to check that new records are entered into the primary table first before records with a matching field value are entered into the related table.
	A **primary table** is the table in which the common field is the primary key and into which new records are entered first. The primary table name is the table name at the left below *Table/Query* in the Edit Relationships dialog box.
	In a **one-to-many relationship**, the common field used to join the tables is the primary key in only one table (the primary table).
	A field added to a table that is not a primary key and is added for the purpose of creating a relationship is called a **foreign key**.
13.8 Creating and Editing a Form	The Form button in the Forms group on the Create tab creates a new form with all fields in the selected table or query arranged in a columnar layout.
	Layout view is the view in which you modify a report or form structure and appearance using buttons on the three Form Layout Tools tabs: Design, Arrange, and Format.
	Form view is the view in which a form is displayed when opened from the Navigation pane and is the view used to add, edit, and delete data.
	The Themes button on the Form Layout Tools Design tab is used to change the color scheme and fonts for a form.
	Use the Logo button to choose an image to display near the upper left of a form.
	A **control object** is a rectangular placeholder for content placed in a form or report. Each item on a form or report is placed in a control object.
	Each control object can be selected and modified to change the appearance or properties of the content.
	Open the Property Sheet task pane to make changes to a control object properties.
	Change the Size Mode property of an image to *Zoom* to fit the content to the object size with the height and width proportions maintained.
	A control object can be resized by changing the values for the *Width* and *Height* in the Property Sheet task pane.

continued...

Topic	Key Concepts
13.9 Creating, Editing, and Viewing a Report	The Report tool in the Reports group on the Create tab creates a report with all the fields in the selected table or query in a tabular arrangement.
	Access creates a current date and time control, a page number control, and a total control for each numeric column in a new report.
	The vertical dashed line in a report indicates a page break.
	Resizing a column heading control object resizes the entire column.
	Buttons on the Report Layout Tools Page Setup tab are used to change page layout options for printing purposes.
	Report view is the view in which a report is displayed when opened from the Navigation pane and is the view that displays the data in the report.
13.10 Compacting, Repairing, and Backing Up a Database	The compact and repair process eliminates unused space in the database file.
	Use the **Compact & Repair Database button** in the Info backstage area to perform a compact and repair operation.
	During the compact and repair routine, Access closes all objects and the Navigation pane.
	Turn on the *Compact on Close* option in the Access Options dialog box with the Current Database pane active to instruct Access to perform a compact and repair operation each time the database is closed.
	Display the Save As backstage area and choose *Back Up Database* in the *Advanced* section to create a backup copy of the current database.
	Access adds the current date after an underscore character to the end of the current database file name when a backup is created.
	A backup copy of a database is normally saved to an offsite storage location, such as a server in another building or a cloud provider, so data can be restored in the event of fire, theft, or other loss.

 Topics Review

Integrating Word, Excel, PowerPoint, and Access Content

Chapter **14**

The Office suite is designed to easily share and integrate data or objects among the applications or to other resources, such as a web page. For some tasks, you may have portions of a project distributed across more than one application. For example, you may have a chart in Excel and a list in Access that you want to add into a report in Word. The ability to integrate data from one application to another allows you to use the application that best fits each task and to assemble a comprehensive product without duplicating the of project contributors. In other cases, you may want to distribute content created in a format not native to the source application.

In Chapter 3, you used the Copy and Paste buttons in the Clipboard group to copy text, an image, and a chart between Word, Excel, and PowerPoint. Copy and paste is the best method for situations when the data to be shared is not large and is not likely to need updating. You also learned in Chapter 3 how to publish a document as a PDF, which makes a copy of the document in a format that can be viewed in a browser or PDF reader app. In this chapter, you will learn other methods for integrating and distributing data and objects that include importing, exporting, embedding, and linking. These methods allow greater automation and collaboration to aid in content management. For example, if you update a native chart file it automatically updates in other linked files. This can save a lot of content management time—something employers value.

 Read & Learn

Learning Objectives

14.1 Import Excel worksheet data into a table in Access

14.2 Export an Access query to Excel

14.3 Embed an Excel chart into a Word document

14.4 Embed Excel data into a PowerPoint presentation and edit the embedded data

14.5 Link an Excel chart with a PowerPoint presentation, edit the chart, and update the link

14.6 Create slides from a Word outline

14.7 Export a PowerPoint presentation as a video

 Content Online

The online course includes additional training and assessment resources.

14.1 Importing Excel Worksheet Data into Access

A new Access table can be created from data in an Excel worksheet, or Excel data can be appended to the bottom of an existing Access table. Because an Excel worksheet and an Access datasheet use the same column-and-row structure, the two applications are often used to interchange data. To facilitate the import, the Excel worksheet should be set up like an Access datasheet, with the field names in the first row and with no blank rows or columns within the data. The **Import Spreadsheet Wizard** in Access is used to facilitate the import operation by providing a series of dialog boxes that prompt the user through the steps to create the table or add data to the bottom of an existing datasheet.

1. Start Access and open the **Parking** database from the Ch14 folder in StudentDataFiles.

2. Use Save As to save a copy of the database as **Parking-YourName** in a new folder, *Ch14*, within CompletedTopics on your storage medium. Accept the default options *Save Database As* and *Access Database* in the Save As backstage area.

3. Click the Enable Content button in the security warning message bar.

4. Click the External Data tab.

5. Click the New Data Source button in the Import & Link group, point to *From File*, and then click *Excel*.

6. Click the Browse button in the Get External Data – Excel Spreadsheet dialog box.

7. Navigate to the Ch14 folder in StudentDataFiles in the File Open dialog box and then double-click *ParkingRecords*.

8. Click OK to accept the selected option *Import the source data into a new table in the current database*. Click Open if a Microsoft Access Security Notice message box appears warning you that a potential security concern has been identified.

Use the *Append* option if the table already exists in the database and you want to add new records from an Excel worksheet to the end of the existing datasheet table.

9 In the first Import Spreadsheet Wizard dialog box, Click Next to accept the worksheet *Student Parking Records*.

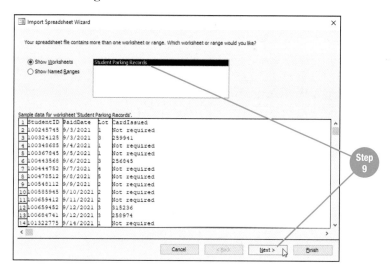

10 In the second Import Spreadsheet Wizard dialog box, click Next with a check mark already inserted in the *First Row Contains Column Headings* check box.

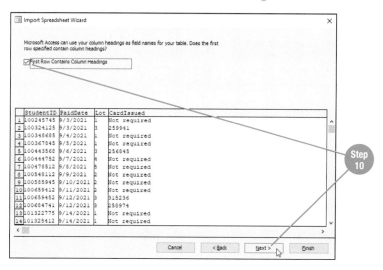

11 In the third Import Spreadsheet Wizard dialog box, click the *PaidDate* column heading and look at the option selected in the *Data Type* option box.

Notice that Access has correctly identified the data as a Date field. In this dialog box, you can review each column and modify the options in the *Field Options* section as needed, or you can elect to make changes in Design view after the import is completed. If a column exists in the Excel worksheet that you do not wish to import into the table, select the column and insert a check mark in the *Do not import field (Skip)* check box.

12 Click Next.

⑬ In the fourth Import Spreadsheet Wizard dialog box, click *Choose my own primary key*.

Access inserts the *StudentID* field name in the primary key option box (the first column in the worksheet).

⑭ Click Next.

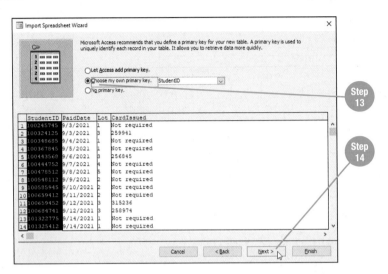

⑮ Type ParkingSales in the *Import to Table* text box and then click Finish in the last Import Spreadsheet Wizard dialog box.

⑯ Click Close to finish the import without saving the import steps in the Get External Data – Excel Spreadsheet dialog box.

For situations in which you frequently import from Excel to Access, you can save the import specifications and repeat the import later using the same settings.

app tip

You can import text into a Word document from another source by using the Open dialog box. Word will attempt to convert text from another file type into a new Word document. Word successfully imports text from text files, rich text format files, OpenDocument text files, and WordPerfect files. You can even open a PDF document in Word, and Word converts the PDF file into an editable Word document.

(17) Open the ParkingSales table from the Navigation pane and review the datasheet.

StudentID	PaidDate	Lot	CardIssued	Click to Add
100245745	9/3/2021	1	Not required	
100324125	9/3/2021	3	259941	
100348685	9/4/2021	1	Not required	
100367845	9/5/2021	1	Not required	
100443568	9/6/2021	3	256845	
100444752	9/7/2021	4	Not required	
100478512	9/8/2021	5	Not required	
100548112	9/9/2021	2	Not required	
100585945	9/10/2021	2	Not required	
100659412	9/11/2021	2	Not required	
100659452	9/12/2021	3	315236	
100684741	9/12/2021	3	258974	
101322775	9/14/2021	1	Not required	
101325412	9/14/2021	1	Not required	
101325685	9/14/2021	4	Not required	
101332486	9/17/2021	3	315235	
101334745	9/17/2021	2	Not required	
101334799	9/19/2021	1	Not required	
101348863	9/21/2021	5	Not required	
101352658	9/21/2021	3	248975	
101455623	9/21/2021	2	Not required	
101658235	9/21/2021	5	Not required	
101745866	9/22/2021	1	Not required	
104875111	9/22/2021	2	Not required	
110542642	9/22/2021	3	289456	

Datasheet view for table created from imported Excel worksheet data

quick steps

Import Worksheet Data into Access
1. Open database.
2. Click External Data tab.
3. Click New Data Source button in Import & Link group, point to *From File*, and click *Excel*.
4. Click Browse.
5. Navigate to and double-click Excel file.
6. Click OK.
7. Click Next with worksheet selected.
8. Click Next with *First Row Contains Column Headings* selected.
9. Change *Field Options* for columns, if desired, and click Next.
10. Choose primary key field and click Next.
11. Type table name and click Finish.
12. Click Close.

(18) Click the Home tab, click the top part of the View button in the Views group to switch to Design view, and then review the field names and data types for the new table.

(19) Click the *Data Type* option box arrow for the *Lot* field name and then click *Short Text*.

In the Parking database, the *Lot* field should be defined as Short Text, because lot numbers are not field values that you would add or subtract in a calculation. When Access imported the Excel worksheet data, the *Lot* column contained all numeric values, so Access assigned the field the Number data type option. In a database, a numeric data type option is used for those fields that will be calculated or totaled in queries, forms, and reports.

ParkingSales

Field Name	Data Type
StudentID	Short Text
PaidDate	Date/Time
Lot	Short Text
CardIssued	Short Text

Step 19

(20) Save and then close the table. Leave the database open for the next topic.

14.2 Exporting an Access Query to Excel

Watch & Learn

------ Skills

Export an Access query
to Excel

Tutorials

Exporting Access
Data to Excel

Exporting Access
Data to Word

Access table data can be exported to Excel for situations where you want to use the mathematical analysis tools in Excel. Access creates a copy of the selected table or query data in an Excel worksheet file in a drive and folder that you specify. Buttons in the Export group on the External Data tab provide options to send a copy of Access data in a variety of file formats.

1 With the **Parking-YourName** database open, click the Create tab and then click the Query Design button.

2 In the Show Table dialog box, double-click each of the four table names to add all four table field list boxes to the query, and then click the Close button.

When a table is created by importing, a relationship will not exist between the new table and other tables in the database. All tables in a query should be joined so that records are not duplicated in the query results datasheet. When a relationship is necessary (such as in a query), you can join the tables by dragging the common field name from one table field list box to the same field in the other table field list box.

3 Drag the *StudentID* field name in the ParkingSales field list box to *StudentID* in the Students field list box.

A black join line appears next to the *StudentID* field name between the table field list boxes when you release the mouse, as shown in the image at the right.

------ app tip

Create relationships
in the Relationships
window if the tables to
be joined will be used
together in other objects,
such as a form or report.

4 Drag the *Lot* field name in the ParkingSales field list box to *LotNo* in the ParkingLots field list box.

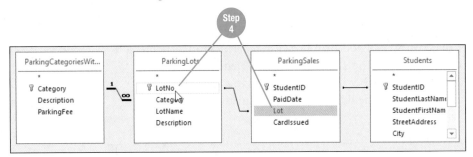

5 Double-click the following fields to add the fields to the query design grid. (Note that you are selecting fields in all four table field list boxes.)

Field Name	Table Name
StudentID	ParkingSales
StudentFirstName	Students
StudentLastName	Students
PaidDate	ParkingSales
Lot	Parking Sales
Description	ParkingLots
ParkingFee	ParkingCategoriesWithFees

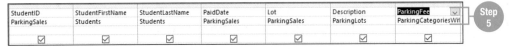

6 Click the Run button in the Results group on the Query Tools Design tab.

⑦ Save the query as **ParkingSales2021** and then close the query.

⑧ Click to select the *ParkingSales2021* query name in the Navigation pane.

⑨ Click the External Data tab and then click the Excel button in the Export group.

quick steps

Export a Query to Excel
1. Open database.
2. Select query name.
3. Click External Data tab.
4. Click Excel button in Export group.
5. Click Browse button.
6. Type file name and navigate to destination folder.
7. Click Save.
8. Specify export options.
9. Click OK.
10. If Excel opened, review worksheet and close Excel.
11. Click Close.

⑩ In the Export – Excel Spreadsheet dialog box, click the Browse button, type ParkingSales-YourName in the *File name* text box, navigate to the Ch14 folder in CompletedTopics on your storage medium, and then click Save.

⑪ Click to insert a check mark in the *Export data with formatting and layout.* check box and in the *Open the destination file after the export operation is complete* check box.

⑫ Click OK.

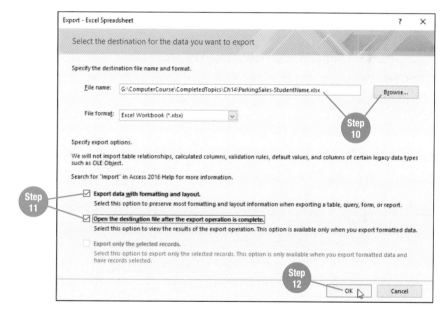

Excel is started automatically with the data from the query results datasheet shown in a worksheet. Notice the first row contains the field names from the query, and the worksheet tab is renamed to the query name.

	A	B	C	D	E	F	G
1	StudentID	StudentFirstName	StudentLastName	PaidDate	Lot	Description	Parking Fee
2	100245745	Anna	Takacis	9/3/2021	1	Main campus north of Administration building	$250.00
3	100324125	Jose	Ramirez	9/3/2021	3	Main campus south of Technology wing	$200.00
4	100348685	Celine	Gauthier	9/4/2021	1	Main campus north of Administration building	$250.00
5	100367845	Sara	Blewett	9/5/2021	1	Main campus north of Administration building	$250.00
6	100443568	Dwayne	Kenney	9/6/2021	3	Main campus south of Technology wing	$200.00

first six rows in Excel after query is exported

Green triangles display next to data in the *StudentID* and *Lot* columns because the data is numeric but was exported from Access as text. Green triangles in Excel flag data that is a potential error. You can ignore the error flags here.

⑬ Close Excel to return to Access.

⑭ Click Close in the Export - Excel Spreadsheet dialog box to finish the export without saving the export steps.

⑮ Close the database and then close Access.

14.3 Embedding an Excel Chart into a Word Document

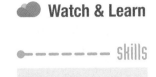

Watch & Learn

In Chapter 3, you used Copy and Paste features to duplicate text and a chart between applications. Another way to duplicate content between applications is to paste copied data as an **embedded object**. Embedding, like copying and pasting, inserts a duplicate of the selected text or object at the desired location. The application in which the data originally resides is called the **source application**, and the data that is copied is referred to as the **source data**. Using a similar naming scheme, the application in which the data is embedded is referred to as the **destination application**, and the document, worksheet, or presentation into which the embedded object is placed is referred to as the **destination document**.

●——————— skills

Embed an Excel chart into a document

Tutorial

Copying and Pasting Data between Programs

1. Start Excel and then open **SocialMediaStats** from the Ch14 folder in StudentDataFiles. If necessary, click the Enable Editing button.

2. Start Word and then open **SocialMediaProject** from the Ch14 folder in StudentDataFiles. If necessary, click the Enable Editing button.

3. Use Save As to save a copy of the Word document as **SocialMediaProject -YourName** in the Ch14 folder within CompletedTopics.

4. Click the Excel button on the taskbar to switch to Excel and then click to select the pie chart with the title *Global Market Share*.

5. Click the Home tab if Home is not the active tab.

6. Click the Copy button in the Clipboard group. Do *not* click the arrow on the button.

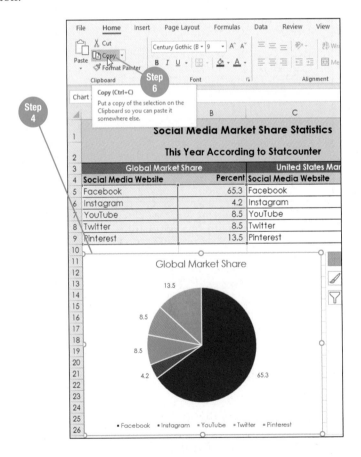

7. Click the Word button on the taskbar to switch to Word and then click to position the insertion point at the left margin on the blank line two line spaces below the first table.

8 Click the Paste button arrow and then click *Use Destination Theme & Embed Workbook* (first button in *Paste Options* section).

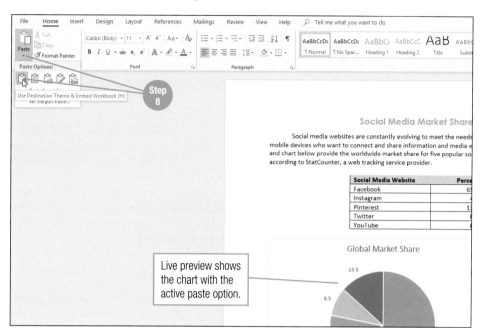

Live preview shows the chart with the active paste option.

quick steps

Embed an Excel Chart into Word
1. Open worksheet in Excel.
2. Open document in Word.
3. Make Excel active, select and copy chart.
4. Switch to Word.
5. Position insertion point.
6. Click Paste button arrow.
7. Click *Use Destination Theme & Embed Workbook*.

☁ **Tutorial**

Embedding an Object

9 Click to select the chart object in the document and then click the Center button in the Paragraph group on the Home tab.

The Chart feature is standardized in Word, Excel, and PowerPoint. A chart embedded within any of the three applications offers the Chart Tools tabs and three chart-editing buttons with which the chart can be modified after being embedded.

10 Click the Chart Elements button (plus symbol), point to *Legend* (right-pointing arrow appears), click the right-pointing arrow, and then click *Right*. Click in the document away from the chart to deselect the chart object.

11 Click the Excel button on the taskbar, click the pie chart with the title *United States Market Share*, and then click the Copy button.

12 Click the Word button on the taskbar. Click to position the insertion point at the bottom of the document, and then embed, center, and format the pie chart by completing steps similar to Steps 8 through 10.

13 Save the revised document using the same name (**SocialMediaProject -YourName**) and then close Word. Leave Excel and the **SocialMediaStats** workbook open for the next topic.

14.4 Embedding Excel Data into PowerPoint and Editing the Embedded Data

Embedding text or worksheet data follows the same process as for embedding a chart. Double-click an embedded object to edit text or worksheet data in the destination location. Embedded text or cell data is edited using the tools on the ribbon from the source application. Click outside an embedded object to end editing and to restore the ribbon of the destination application.

● **Watch & Learn**

●—————— Skills

Embed Excel data into a presentation

Edit an embedded table

● **Tutorial**

Embedding Objects

1. With Excel active and the **SocialMediaStats** workbook open, select A3:B9 and then click the Copy button.

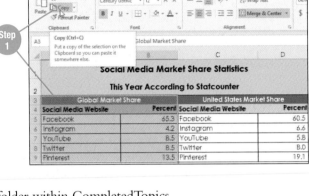

2. Start PowerPoint and open **SocialMediaPres** from the Ch14 folder in StudentDataFiles.

3. Use Save As to save a copy of the presentation as **SocialMediaPres –YourName** in the Ch14 folder within CompletedTopics.

4. Make Slide 3 the active slide.

5. Click the Paste button arrow.

6. Click *Embed* (third option in *Paste Options* section).

7. Click the Drawing Tools Format tab, click the Shape Fill button in the Shape Styles group, and then click *White, Text 1* (second option in *Theme Colors* section).

8. Resize and position the embedded object to the approximate size and position shown in the image below.

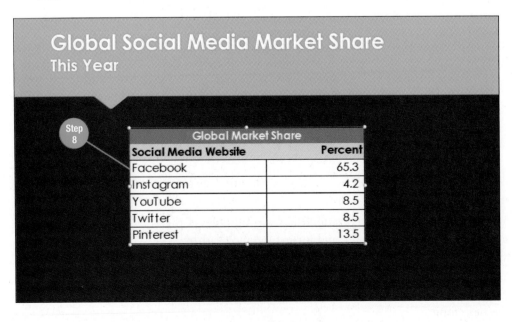

(9) Double-click anywhere over the cells to open the embedded object for editing.

Notice the embedded cells open in an Excel worksheet and the ribbon changes to Excel's ribbon.

(10) Select B5:B9 and then click the Decrease Decimal button in the Number group on the Home tab.

● – – – – quick steps

Edit an Embedded Object
1. Double-click embed-
   ded object.
2. Make desired changes.
3. Click outside object.

(11) Click on the slide away from the embedded object to end editing and restore the PowerPoint ribbon.

(12) Click the Excel button on the taskbar, select C3:D9, and then click the Copy button.

(13) Click the PowerPoint button on the taskbar. Make Slide 4 the active slide, and embed, format, resize, and position the copied cells by completing steps similar to those in Steps 5 through 11.

(14) Save the revised presentation using the same name (**SocialMediaPres -YourName**) and then close PowerPoint. Leave Excel and the **SocialMediaStats** workbook open for the next topic.

14.5 Linking an Excel Chart with a Presentation and Updating the Link

Watch & Learn

●------- Skills

Link an Excel chart with
a presentation

Turn on automatic link
updates

Edit a linked chart

Update links

Tutorial
  Linking Objects

If the data that you want to integrate between two applications is continuously updated, copy and link the data instead of copying and pasting or embedding. When copied data is linked, changes made to the source data can be automatically updated in any other document, worksheet, or presentation to which the data is linked. Linking avoids duplicating work and ensures that errors are not made when the same data is changed in more than one location. Linked objects are managed using the **Links dialog box**, where a link can be set to update automatically, a link can be broken, or the source location for a linked object can be changed.

1. With Excel active and the **SocialMediaStats** workbook open, use Save As to save a copy of the workbook as **LinkedSocialMediaStats-YourName** in the Ch14 folder within CompletedTopics.

2. Start PowerPoint and then open **SocialMediaPres**.

3. Use Save As to save a copy of the presentation as **LinkedSocialMediaPres -YourName** in the Ch14 folder within CompletedTopics.

4. Click the Excel button on the taskbar, click to select the *Global Market Share* pie chart, and then click the Copy button.

5. Click the PowerPoint button on the taskbar and then make Slide 3 the active slide.

6. Click the Paste button arrow.

7. Click *Use Destination Theme & Link Data* (third option in *Paste Options* section). If the Design Ideas task pane appears at the right side of the window, close the task pane.

8. Resize and move the chart to the approximate size and position shown in the image below.

9. Click the Excel button on the taskbar, select the *United States Market Share* pie chart, and then click the Copy button.

●---- in the know

Linking is not just for
integrating data between
two different applica-
tions; you can link two
documents in Word, two
worksheets in Excel, or
two tables in Access.

10 Click the PowerPoint button on the taskbar. Make Slide 4 the active slide and then link, resize, and move the chart by completing steps similar to those in Steps 6 through 8.

11 Click the File tab and then click *Edit Links to Files* in the *Related Documents* section at the bottom of the Properties panel (right panel) in the Info backstage area.

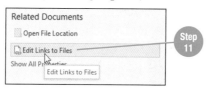

12 In the Links dialog box, click to select the first link in the *Links* list box and then click to insert a check mark in the *Automatic Update* check box.

13 Click to select the second link and then click to insert a check mark in the *Automatic Update* check box.

14 Click the Close button in the Links dialog box.

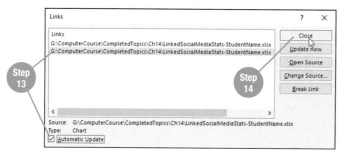

app tip

Open the Links dialog box to update the location of the source data if the source data file has been moved to another drive or folder or to break a link. Click the link and then click the Change Source button to browse to the new file location or click the Break Link button to remove the link to the content.

15 Click the Back button to exit the Info backstage area and return to the presentation.

16 Save the revised presentation using the same name (**LinkedSocialMediaPres -YourName**) and then close the presentation. Leave PowerPoint open for a task at Step 22.

17 Click the Excel button on the taskbar.

18 Change the value in D9 from *19.1* to *26.1*.

19 Change the value in D6 from *6.6* to *1.6*.

20 Change the value in D5 from *60.5* to *58.5*.

Notice the pie chart updated after each change in value. The revised chart is noticeably different from the original pie chart.

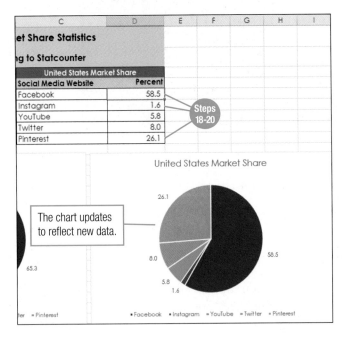

21 Save the revised worksheet using the same name (**LinkedSocialMediaStats -YourName**) and then close Excel.

22 Switch to PowerPoint, if PowerPoint is not already active, and then open **LinkedSocialMediaPres-YourName**.

Because the presentation contains linked data that is set to automatically update, you are prompted to update links. A dialog box with a security notice and the **Update Links button** appears when you open a file that has links to objects outside the document, worksheet, or presentation.

23 Click the Update Links button in the Microsoft PowerPoint Security Notice dialog box.

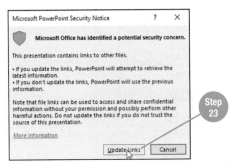

●------- **app tip**

If the source and destination files are both open at the same time, changes made to the source reflect in the destination file immediately.

In this instance, clicking the Update Links button is safe from a security standpoint because you are working with files that you have opened and edited. However, if you receive a dialog box like the one you saw in Step 23 for a file that you did not create, exercise caution before updating links. Take a moment to consider where the linked object originated and whether you are sure the source application and data are from a trusted source. Malware is sometimes circulated in Office documents, and updating a link to an infected file could spread malware to your device. If in doubt, the best option is to click the Cancel button and contact the source data creator for more information.

24 Make Slide 4 the active slide. Notice that the chart is updated to reflect the same data as the revised Excel chart.

quick steps

Link Data
1. Open source application and file.
2. Open destination application and file.
3. Activate source application, select and copy data.
4. Switch to destination application.
5. Activate desired slide or cell or position insertion point where linked data is to be pasted.
6. Click Paste button arrow.
7. Click *Use Destination Theme & Link Data*.

Turn on Automatic Link Updates
1. Make destination file active.
2. Click File tab.
3. Click *Edit Links to Files*.
4. Select link.
5. Click *Automatic Update* check box.
6. Click Close.

US Social Media Market Share
This Year

United States Market Share

The linked chart updates to reflect new data.

25 Make Slide 3 the active slide and then delete the title inside the chart above the pie.

26 Make Slide 4 the active slide and then delete the title inside the chart above the pie.

Global Social Media Market Share
This Year

US Social Media Market Share
This Year

Slide 3 and Slide 4 with the chart titles deleted after completing Steps 25 and 26

27 Save the revised presentation using the same name (**LinkedSocialMediaPres -YourName**) and then close PowerPoint.

14.6 Creating Slides from a Word Outline

Watch & Learn

──────── Skills

Create PowerPoint slides
from a Word document

The text for a presentation can be typed in a Word document as an outline and then imported into PowerPoint to create new slides. In the Word document, apply heading styles to control how the text will be formatted on a slide. A paragraph formatted with the *Heading 1* style becomes the slide title for a new slide. Similarly, a paragraph formatted with the *Heading 2* style becomes a level one bulleted list entry. Each subsequent heading style moves the text to the next bulleted list level.

Tutorial

Importing a Word
Outline

1. Start Word and then open **AutonomousObjects** from the Ch14 folder in StudentDataFiles.

2. Use Save As to save a copy of the document as **AutonomousObjects –YourName** in the Ch14 folder in CompletedTopics.

3. Examine the document, noting that all text is formatted as a *Heading 1* style, a *Heading 2* style, or a *Heading 3* style.

4. Click to position the insertion point at the end of the sentence *Amazon and others are developing delivery drones for the US market* and press Enter to start a new line.

5. Type Drone taxis are being developed by several companies and then press Enter.

6. Type Uber, in partnership with NASA, is planning to test drone taxi service in two US cities in 2020.

Autonomous Drones
The military has been using drones for many years in military operations
Commercial companies are now using drones for delivery purposes
In Rwanda, Zipline is using autonomous drones to deliver blood supplies to remote areas
Amazon and others are developing delivery drones for the US market
Drone taxis are being developed by several companies

Uber, in partnership with NASA, is planning to test drone taxi service in two US cities in 2020

Step 5
Step 6

7. Click to position the insertion point in the sentence *Drone taxis are being developed by several companies* and then click the *Heading 2* style option in the Styles group on the Home tab.

8. Click to position the insertion point in the sentence *Uber, in partnership with NASA, is planning to test drone taxi service in two US cities in 2020* and then click the *Heading 3* style option.

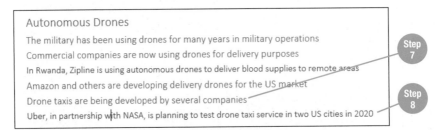

Autonomous Drones
The military has been using drones for many years in military operations
Commercial companies are now using drones for delivery purposes
In Rwanda, Zipline is using autonomous drones to deliver blood supplies to remote areas
Amazon and others are developing delivery drones for the US market
Drone taxis are being developed by several companies
Uber, in partnership with NASA, is planning to test drone taxi service in two US cities in 2020

Step 7
Step 8

9. Save the revised document using the same name (**AutonomousObjects –YourName**) and then close Word.

10. Start PowerPoint and then open the presentation **AutonomousObjectsPres** from the Ch14 folder in StudentDataFiles.

11. Use Save As to save the presentation as **AutonomousObjectsPres–YourName** in the Ch14 folder within CompletedTopics.

⑫ Click the New Slide button arrow in the Slides group on the Home tab and then click *Slides from Outline*.

⑬ In the Insert Outline dialog box, if necessary, navigate to the Ch14 folder in CompletedTopics and then double-click ***AutonomousObjects-YourName***.

PowerPoint converts the Word document text into slides. A progress message displays on the Status bar, and the slides appear when the conversion is done. A document formatted with a theme different from the theme for the presentation may need to have the presentation slides reset after importing the text. Resetting the imported slides reformats all slides to the presentation theme.

⑭ Click each slide in the presentation to view how the document was converted.

⑮ Click Slide 2 in the slide thumbnails pane. Hold down the Shift key and then click Slide 5 in the slide thumbnails pane.

This action selects Slide 2 through Slide 5.

⑯ Click the Reset button in the Slides group on the Home tab.

⑰ Click each slide in the presentation to view the changes.

Resetting the slides that were imported from Word caused the new slides to format according to the presentation theme (Circuit) instead of the Word document theme (Office).

⑱ Save the revised presentation using the same name (**AutonomousObjectsPres -YourName**). Leave the presentation open for the next topic.

Slide 2 to Slide 5 selected in the slide thumbnails pane after completing Step 15

14.7 Exporting a Presentation as a Video

After you have completed a presentation, you can export the presentation in a video format to share the content with others. PowerPoint includes options to create a video from the slides at various file sizes and qualities. You can export the presentation with preprogrammed transitions and animations in effect, or you can export the video using a set number of seconds for each slide. Once the video is created, the file can be shared by linking to the video file on a web page or by publishing the video to YouTube or other media-sharing websites.

☁ **Watch & Learn**

● ─ ─ ─ ─ ─ ─ ─ SKILLS

Export a presentation as a video

☁ **Tutorials**

Exporting Presentations

Saving a Presentation in a Different Format

1. With the **AutonomousObjectsPres-YourName** presentation open, click Slide 1 in the slide thumbnails pane if Slide 1 is not the active slide, and then click the Transitions tab.

2. Click the *Wipe* option in the Transition to This Slide gallery and then click the Apply To All button in the Timing group.

3. Select the current entry in the *After* text box in the Timing group, type 0:10, and then press Enter.

4. Make Slide 2 the active slide, select the entry in the *After* text box, type 0:15 and then press Enter.

5. Change the *After* time for Slide 3, Slide 4, and Slide 5 to 0:25 by completing a step similar to Step 4.

6. Make Slide 2 the active slide, click the View tab, and then click the Slide Master button.

7. Click to select the border of the title placeholder on the slide master.

8. Click the Animations tab.

9. Click the *Float In* option in the Animation gallery.

10. Click to select the border of the bulleted list content placeholder and then click the *Random Bars* option in the Animation gallery.

11. Click the *Start* option box arrow (displays *On Click*) in the Timing group and then click *After Previous*.

12. Select the current entry in the *Duration* text box, type 3.0, and then press Enter.

13. Click the Slide Master tab and then click the Close Master View button.

14. Make Slide 1 the active slide, run through the presentation in a slide show to view the transition and animation effects, and then return to Normal view.

15. Save the revised presentation using the same name (**AutonomousObjectsPres -YourName**).

16. Click the File tab and then click *Export*.
17. Click *Create a Video* in the Export backstage area.
18. With the *Full HD (1080p)* and *Use Recorded Timings and Narrations* options already selected in the Create a Video panel, click the Create Video button.

quick steps

Export a Presentation as a Video
1. Open presentation file in PowerPoint.
2. Add desired transition, animation, and timing options.
3. Click File tab.
4. Click *Export*.
5. Click *Create a Video*.
6. If necessary, change video options.
7. Click Create Video button.
8. Navigate to desired drive and folder and change file name if necessary.
9. Click Save button.

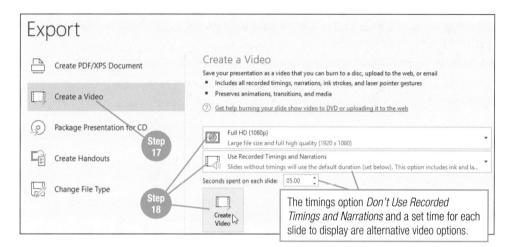

19. Click the Save button in the Save As dialog box with the file name *AutonomousObjectsPres-YourName* in the *File name* text box and with the *Save as type* option set to MPEG-4 Video (*.mp4).

PowerPoint displays a progress message on the Status bar as the video file is created. The video creation process can take from a few minutes to a few hours depending on the number of slides in the presentation and the complexity of the content, transition, and animation effects.

20. When the video creation is complete (watch progress message on Status bar), close PowerPoint.
21. Click the File Explorer button on the taskbar.
22. Navigate to the Ch14 folder in CompletedTopics on your storage medium and then double-click the video file ***AutonomousObjectsPres-YourName***.
23. Watch the video in the default media player app on your PC (or other video app that you prefer) and then close the window when the video is complete.

app tip

Video quality options include: *Full HD (1080p)* high quality and large file size, *Ultra HD (4K)* best quality and largest file size, *HD (720p)* moderate quality and medium file size, and *Standard (480p)* smallest file size and lowest quality.

video in default Windows 10 media player window (Movies & TV)

app tip

Click the *Create PDF/XPS Document* option in the Export backstage area to publish your presentation in a document with each slide as a page in landscape orientation. The PDF document can be shared via a link to the document on a web page or as an emailed file attachment.

24. Close the File Explorer window.

Topics Review

Topic	Key Concepts
14.1 Importing Excel Worksheet Data into Access	In Access, the **Import Spreadsheet Wizard** starts when you choose an Excel workbook from the New Data Source option in the Import & Link group on the External Data tab.
	Five dialog boxes in the Import Spreadsheet Wizard guide you through the steps to create a new table using data in an Excel worksheet.
	You can save the Excel import settings to repeat the import later using the same settings.
	Open an imported table in Access in Design view to modify the table design after the import is complete.
14.2 Exporting an Access Query to Excel	Export Access table or query data to Excel using the Excel button in the Export group on the External Data tab.
	Specify the file name, drive and folder, and export options in the Export – Excel Spreadsheet dialog box.
	You can elect to export the data with formatting and layout options in the datasheet, and to automatically open Excel with the worksheet displayed when the export is complete.
	Export specifications can be saved to repeat the export later.
14.3 Embedding an Excel Chart into a Word Document	An **embedded object** is data that has been copied from a document, worksheet, or presentation and pasted as an object in another application.
	The application from which data is copied is called the **source application**. The data that is copied is referred to as the **source data**.
	The **destination application** is the application that receives the copied data. The **destination document** refers to the document, worksheet, or presentation into which copied data is pasted as an object.
	Click the Paste button arrow and then choose the desired embed option to embed copied data as an object in the destination document.
14.4 Embedding Excel Data into PowerPoint and Editing the Embedded Data	Double-click an embedded object to open the object data for editing using the source application ribbon and tools.
	Click outside the embedded object to end editing and restore the destination application ribbon.
14.5 Linking an Excel Chart with a Presentation and Updating the Link	Source data that is continuously updated should be linked (instead of copied and pasted or copied and embedded) to avoid duplication of work and to reduce errors made when data is entered more than once.
	Click the Paste button arrow in the destination document and then choose the desired link option to link copied data.
	Click *Edit Links to Files* in the Properties panel in the Info backstage area to open the Links dialog box in which you manage links to source data.
	Select a link in the **Links dialog box** and insert a check mark in the *Automatic Update* check box to turn on automatic updates for the link.
	Click the **Update Links button** in the security warning dialog box that appears when you open a file with a linked object to update data from the source.
	Exercise caution when updating links to source data that you did not create yourself.

continued...

Topic	Key Concepts
14.6 Creating Slides from a Word Outline	Text typed in a Word document as an outline can be imported into PowerPoint to create new slides.
	Text formatted in the document with the *Heading 1* style becomes a new slide title and text formatted with the *Heading 2* style becomes a first level bulleted list entry.
	Click the New Slide button arrow in the Slides group on the Home tab and then click *Slides from Outline* to import text in a Word document into PowerPoint.
	The imported new slides may need to be reset in PowerPoint to apply the presentation theme formatting if the document theme is different than the presentation theme.
	Select the slides to be reset and then click the Reset button in the Slides group on the Home tab.
14.7 Exporting a Presentation as a Video	Export a presentation as a video to share the content with others by linking to the video file on a web page or by publishing the video to a media sharing website, such as YouTube.
	Apply the desired transition, animation, and timing options to the slides before exporting.
	When the presentation is complete, click the File tab, click *Export*, and then click the *Create a Video* option.
	Change the video quality, file size, and timings options, if necessary, and then click the Create Video button in the Create a Video panel. Navigate to the drive and folder where you want to save the video, change the file name if desired, and then click the Save button.
	When the video is completed, open a File Explorer window, navigate to the drive and folder, and then double-click the video file name to watch the video in the default media player app on your device.

 Topics Review

Using Office Online and OneDrive

Office Online includes the web-based version of Word, Excel, and PowerPoint, which can be accessed from OneDrive. Computing, software, and storage services accessed entirely from the web is called **cloud computing**. With cloud computing, all you need is a computer with a web browser to create and edit a document, worksheet, or presentation. With cloud computing technology, you do not need to install software on your PC or mobile device, because all software and storage of documents is online. Microsoft offers its web-based productivity apps free to Microsoft account holders.

In Chapter 3, you learned how to save a presentation to OneDrive within PowerPoint. In this chapter, you will learn to create and edit files using Office Online from OneDrive and upload, download, and share files in OneDrive.

Learning Objectives

15.1 Create a document in Word Online

15.2 Create a worksheet in Excel Online

15.3 Create a presentation in PowerPoint Online

15.4 Edit a presentation in PowerPoint Online

15.5 Upload and download files to and from OneDrive

15.6 Share a document in OneDrive

Read & Learn

Content Online

The online course includes additional training and assessment resources.

15.1 Creating a Document Using Word Online

Word Online is similar to the desktop version of Word that you used in Chapters 6 and 7; however, Word Online has fewer features than the desktop version. The program looks similar, but you will notice that for some features, functionality within a browser environment is different than the desktop version. As you work in Word Online, the document is saved automatically as soon as you make changes. A document created in Word Online is saved in the same file format as the desktop version of Word, which means documents are transferable between editions, desktops, and online.

1 Open a browser window.

2 With the insertion point positioned in a blank Address bar, type https:// onedrive.live.com and then press Enter.

3 If necessary, click *Sign in*, type the email address or phone number for your Microsoft account and click Next, type your password and click the Sign in button on the second sign-in screen. Skip this step if you are already signed in to OneDrive, which occurs with the Microsoft Edge browser when you are already signed in to your Microsoft Account for Windows.

Once signed in, the OneDrive window appears similar to the one shown in Figure 15.1.

Watch & Learn

———————— skills

Create a document in Word Online

Tutorial

Signing In to and Out of OneDrive

●——————— Oops!

Don't know your Microsoft account? If you have a hotmail.com, live.com, or outlook .com email address, your email login is your Microsoft account; otherwise, click the link to create a new account.

Figure 15.1

The OneDrive window initially shows the *Files* list in the Content pane for the signed-in user.

④ Click the App launcher in the upper left of the screen next to OneDrive (displays as a waffle icon and is sometimes called *the waffle button*) and then click the Word tile.

⑤ Click *Got it!* if a screen displays with information about new features in Office Online; this message appears the first time you use Office Online and when changes have been made to the software.

⑥ Click <u>New blank document</u> on the Word Online Start screen.

Word Online launches, as shown in Figure 15.2. By default, the **Simplified Ribbon** displays, with one row of buttons and without the group names.

● – – – – – go online

**https://CA3
.ParadigmEducation
.com/Office**

Go here to start Word Online without first starting OneDrive. You can access all the same web-based apps from https://www.office.com/. Click the desired tile and then sign in with a Microsoft account or a school account.

☁ **Tutorial**
Creating a New Document in an Office Online App

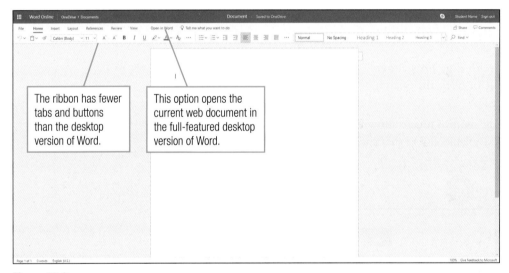

The ribbon has fewer tabs and buttons than the desktop version of Word.

This option opens the current web document in the full-featured desktop version of Word.

Figure 15.2
The Word Online new document window with the Simplified Ribbon is shown.

⑦ Type the following text in the document window, using all the default settings:

What Is Green Computing?

Green computing refers to the use of computers and other electronic devices in an environmentally responsible manner. Green computing can encompass new or modified computing practices, policies, and procedures. This trend is growing with more individuals and businesses adopting green computing strategies every year.

Strategies include the reduction of energy consumption by computers and other devices; reduction in use of paper, ink, and toner; and reuse, recycling, or proper disposal of electronic waste.

⑧ Proofread carefully and correct any typing errors that you find. If necessary, use the Spelling & Grammar button on the Review tab to spell check the document.

9. Click to place the insertion point within the title *What Is Green Computing?* and then click the Align Center button on the Home tab.

10. Select all the text in the document and then change the font size to 12 using the *Font Size* option box arrow.

11. Select the two paragraphs of text below the title, click the More Paragraph Options button (displays as three dots), point to *Line Spacing*, and then click *1.5*.

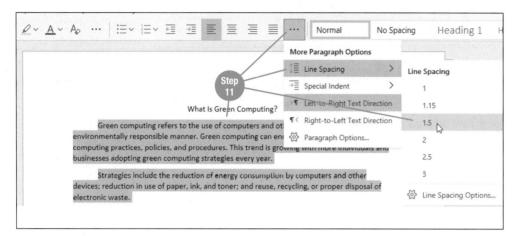

12. Click at the end of the last paragraph to position the insertion point and then press Enter to create a new line.

13. Click the Insert tab, click the Picture button, and then click *Bing*.

14. Type recycling in the *Search Bing Images* text box and then press Enter or click the Search button (magnifying glass).

15. Click the green recycling symbol image shown below and then click Insert. If the image shown is not available, insert the image using the student data file **recyclinglogo.jpg**.

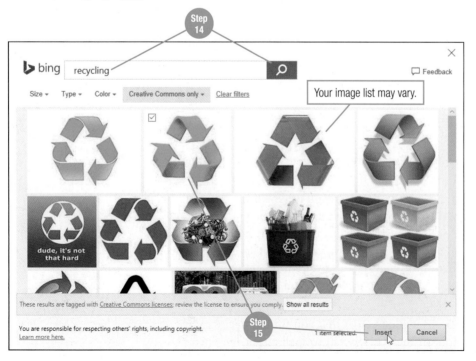

16. With the image selected, drag the lower right corner selection handle upward and left until the image is the approximate size shown in the image below.

17. With the image still selected, click the Home tab and then click the Align Center button.

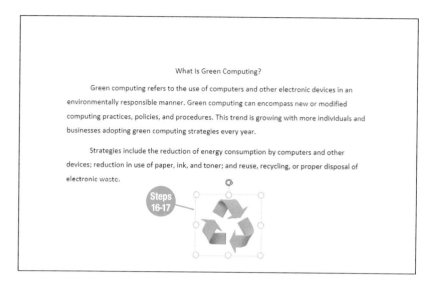

18. Click within the document text to deselect the image.

19. Click the File tab and then click *Save As*.

20. Click *Rename* in the Save As panel in the backstage area.

21. Type GreenComputing-YourName in the *Enter a name for this file* text box in the Rename dialog box and then press Enter or click OK.

22. Close the document browser tab.

23. Click the Documents folder in the <u>Files</u> list in the OneDrive Content pane. Notice the Word document thumbnail for the **GreenComputing-YourName** document. Notice also the file management options on the bar below the OneDrive banner. Leave OneDrive open for the next topic.

The document thumbnail is shown in the *Files > Documents* list.

15.5 Downloading Files from and Uploading Files to OneDrive

Watch & Learn

●------- skills

Download files from OneDrive

Upload files to OneDrive

Move files to a folder on OneDrive

Although you can work in Office applications with OneDrive as the default storage location, many people prefer to store files on a storage medium (such as their hard disk drive or a USB flash drive). In that case, OneDrive is used as a backup storage receptacle or to make a file accessible on multiple devices without having to copy the file to each PC. A file is also copied to OneDrive to share the file with other people. Similarly, you can download a file from OneDrive to your local PC or mobile device to view or edit the file offline.

1. With OneDrive open, click to clear the check mark in the check circle for the **GreenComputingPres-YourName** thumbnail and then click to insert a check mark in the check circle for the **GreenComputing-YourName** Word document.

2. Click <u>Download</u> in the bar along the top of the OneDrive window.

3. Click the Save button in the pop-up message at the bottom of Microsoft Edge with the options to Open

●------- Oops!

No check circle visible on thumbnail? Move the mouse over the thumbnail and a selection circle will appear.

or Save downloads and then click the *Dismiss* option (displays as ✕) when the message displays that the file finished downloading. Skip these steps if you are using a different browser and the messages shown do not display.

●------ app tip

You can copy and paste files to and from OneDrive from a File Explorer window. OneDrive is shown in the File Explorer Navigation pane above This PC.

By default, files downloaded from OneDrive are saved in the Downloads folder for the signed in user when you are using OneDrive in the Microsoft Edge browser. Another browser may display a Save As dialog box when you click the Download option. In that case you can select to save the file in the Downloads folder on your computer.

4. Click to clear the check mark in the check circle for the **GreenComputing -YourName** thumbnail.

5. Select and download the **EnergySavings-YourName** workbook to the Downloads folder by completing steps similar to those in Steps 1 through 3.

6. Clear the check mark for the **EnergySavings-YourName** thumbnail and then select and download the **GreenComputingPres-YourName** presentation to the Downloads folder by completing steps similar to those in Steps 1 through 3.

☁ **Tutorial**

Downloading Files from OneDrive

You can select and download multiple files in one operation instead of doing each file individually. OneDrive creates a zipped folder when more than one file is selected to download. Files in a zipped folder should be extracted after downloading.

7. Click the File Explorer button on the taskbar to open File Explorer.

8. Click *Downloads* in the Navigation pane.

The three files downloaded from OneDrive are shown in the Content pane, as seen in the image at the right.

9 Select and copy the three downloaded files to a new folder named *Ch15* in the CompletedTopics folder on your storage medium. Refer to Chapter 1, Topic 1.9 if you need assistance with this step.

10 Close the File Explorer window to return to the browser window with OneDrive active. Clear the check mark in the check circle for the **GreenComputingPres-YourName** thumbnail if the file is still selected.

Content pane with files downloaded in this topic. Your list may show additional files in the Content pane for the Downloads folder.

In the next steps you will copy three images from your storage medium to your account storage at OneDrive.

11 Click Upload in the bar along the top of the OneDrive window, and then click Files.

12 In the Open dialog box, navigate to the Ch15 folder in StudentDataFiles on your storage medium, select the three files in the folder whose names begin with **PaintedBunting**, and then click Open.

The three files are uploaded to the current folder in your account storage in OneDrive. Thumbnails appear for uploaded files when the upload is complete.

13 Click to insert a check mark in the check circle for each of the three painted bunting image thumbnails and then click Move to in the bar along the top of the window.

14 Click *Pictures* in the Move items to panel at the right side of the window and then click Move at the top of the panel. Leave OneDrive open for the next topic.

Files are uploaded to the active folder in OneDrive. An alternative way to complete this topic would be to first display the Pictures folder in the Content pane and then upload the three image files instead of uploading and then moving the files as you did in Steps 11 to 14.

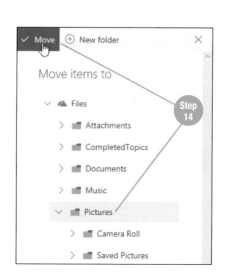

quick steps

Download a File from OneDrive
1. Sign in to OneDrive.
2. Select file.
3. Click Download.
4. Click *Save*, then *Dismiss* option.
5. Open File Explorer.
6. Display Downloads folder in Content pane.
7. Select, copy, and paste downloaded file to desired location.

Upload a File to OneDrive
1. Sign in to OneDrive.
2. Click Upload, then Files.
3. Navigate to drive and folder.
4. Select file(s) to upload.
5. Click Open.
6. If necessary, move files to desired destination folder.

Tutorial
Uploading Files

15.6 Sharing a File on OneDrive

OneDrive is an excellent tool for collaborating on documents when working with a team. A team leader can create or upload documents to OneDrive and then share the files with the team members who need them. An individual with shared access to a document receives an email with a link to the file. Changes to the file are made to the copy in OneDrive so that only one document, worksheet, or presentation has to be managed. Collaborating by sharing a file on OneDrive is less cumbersome than sending a file as an email attachment and then trying to manage multiple versions of the same document.

Note: In this topic, you will share a Word Online document with a classmate. Check with your instructor for instructions on with whom you should share the Word document. If necessary, share the document with yourself by using an email address other than your Microsoft account.

1. With OneDrive open, select the **GreenComputing-YourName** document.

2. Click <u>Share</u> in the bar along the top of the window.

3. If a message box pops up with an *Expiring links* message and a Get Premium button, click the close button (displays as ×).

4. Click <u>Email</u> in the Share *GreenComputing-YourName* option box.

5. Click in the *Enter a name or email address* text box and type the email address for a classmate.

More than one email address can be entered in the text box by typing a semicolon to separate email addresses.

6. Click in the *Add a message here* text box and then type Please make your changes to the file accessed from this link.

7. Click <u>Share</u>.

A message displays in the notifications area when the file is successfully shared.

 Watch & Learn

------- Skills

Share a file on OneDrive

 Tutorials

Sharing a File on OneDrive

Sharing a Folder from OneDrive

------- app tip

You can share files with anyone with a valid email address—the recipient does not have to have a Microsoft account.

8　Click the App launcher and then click the Mail tile. Click *Got it!* if a message displays with information about changes made to the Mail application in OneDrive.

9　With *Inbox* the active mail folder, click the message header for the message received from a classmate with the subject line informing you the **GreenComputing-StudentName.docx** file has been shared with you in OneDrive to view the message in the message pane.

10　Click the View in OneDrive button in the message window to open the document in Word Online. Notice the *Edit Document* option in the bar along the top of the window.

●- - - - **quick steps**

Share a File on OneDrive
1. Sign in to OneDrive.
2. Select file.
3. Click Share, then Email.
4. Click in email address text box and type recipient email address(es).
5. Click in message text box and type message.
6. Click Share.

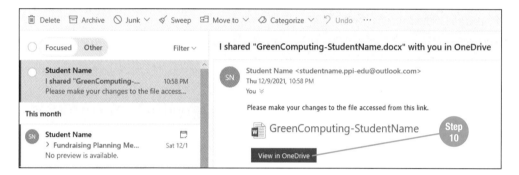

11　Close the document tab and close the Mail tab to return to the OneDrive window.

12　Click Shared in the Navigation pane to view the file details of files shared by you and with you in the Content pane.

You will have two entries in the Shared panel if you shared the document with a classmate and a classmate shared his or her document with you.

13　Click the *Account* option that displays your account picture or the generic user silhouette at the right end of the OneDrive bar to view the My accounts pane.

14　Click Sign out.

●- - - - - - **Oops!**

No message? Check the email address that the classmate used to ensure the correct address was typed. If an address other than Outlook, Hotmail, or Live was used, you need to go to another mail program to find the message with the link. In that case, sign out of OneDrive, launch your other mail program, and complete Steps 9 and 10. Note also that some mail programs may flag the message as junk mail. Check your Junk Mail folder if the message is not in your Inbox.

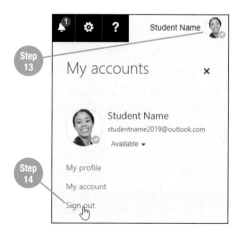

15　Close the browser window.

Topics Review

Topic	Key Concepts
15.1 Creating a Document Using Word Online	**Cloud computing** is a service in which computing resources, software, and storage are provided online, accessed via a web browser.
	Word Online is the web-based version of Word accessed from OneDrive. The application has fewer ribbon tabs and options than the desktop version of Word, and the functions of some features may vary.
	Documents created in Word Online are saved automatically in the same file format as the desktop version of Word, meaning files can be transferred between editions.
	Sign in to OneDrive with a Microsoft account, click the App launcher, click the Word tile, and then click New blank document to start a new document.
	Word Online starts with the **Simplified Ribbon** displayed by default that shows only one row of buttons and without group names.
	Use the Save As backstage area to rename the document saved automatically by Word Online.
15.2 Creating a Worksheet Using Excel Online	**Excel Online** is best suited for basic worksheets; use the desktop version of Excel for worksheets that need advanced formulas or editing.
	Worksheets created in Excel Online are saved in the same file format as the desktop version of Excel, meaning files can be transferred between editions.
	Like Word Online, Excel Online has fewer features than the desktop version, and some functionality may vary.
15.3 Creating a Presentation Using PowerPoint Online	Use **PowerPoint Online** to create a presentation that does not need charts, audio, advanced animation or transition effects, or advanced slide show setup options.
	Presentations created in PowerPoint Online are saved in the same file format as the desktop version of PowerPoint, meaning files can be transferred between editions.
15.4 Editing a Presentation in PowerPoint Online	Select a presentation file thumbnail, click Open and then click the Open in PowerPoint Online option in OneDrive to open a presentation in Editing view.
	View the slide show for a presentation in PowerPoint Online by clicking the Slide Show button at the right end of the Status bar.
15.5 Downloading Files from and Uploading Files to OneDrive	A check mark in the check circle at the top right of a file thumbnail indicates the file is selected.
	Click Download to copy a selected file from OneDrive to the Downloads folder on your computer. Open a File Explorer window to copy and paste the file to the desired location.
	Click Upload to select and copy a file from your computer to your OneDrive storage.
	A file is uploaded to the active folder in OneDrive. Use the Move to option to move a file to a folder other than the active folder after the file is uploaded.
15.6 Sharing a File on OneDrive	OneDrive can be used to collaborate with team members by sharing one copy of a file among several users.
	Select a file and choose Share to distribute a shared file via email or by a link to the shared file.
	When sharing via email, type the email address of individual(s) who will be allowed to view and edit the file and include a brief message to the recipient(s).
	Click Shared in the OneDrive Navigation pane to view files that you have shared and files that have been shared with you by others.

Topics Review

Glossary/Index

A

absolute address Excel address with a dollar symbol before the column letter and/or row number so that the address will not change when the formula is copied to another column or row, 204

Accept button used to send a message to a meeting organizer indicating acceptance of a meeting request, 115

Access 2019 database management application in Microsoft Office suite used to organize, store, and manage related data such as customers, vendors, employees, or products, 60, 277–301, 305–325
 Best Fit in, 289
 color scheme in, 60
 columns
  adjusting widths, 289
  inserting and deleting, 300–301
 control objects in, 321
 database in
  closing, 281
  compacting, repairing and backing up, 324–325
  creating new, 306–307
  opening, 278
 data in
  finding and replacing, 288–289
  importing Excel worksheet into, 330–333
 datasheets in
  adding records using, 282–283
  editing and deleting records in, 284–285
  previewing, 300–301
  printing, 301
 data types in, 308
 Design view in, 294
  creating new tables in, 310–311
  creating queries using, 294–295
  modifying field properties in, 314–315
 Enforce Referential Integrity in, 319
 field properties in, 314
  formatting and data validation, 315
  modifying, in Design View, 314–315
 Field Properties pane in, 314
 fields in, 279
  adding, to existing tables, 312–313
  sorting by more than one, 290–291
 field values in, 279–280
  creating lookup list with, in another table, 316
 files in, creating new, 306–307
 finding and replacing data and adjusting

column widths in, 288–289
 foreign key in, 319
 forms in, 278, 280–281
  adding, editing and deleting records in, 286–287
  creating, using the Form Wizard, 321
  creating and editing, 320–321
 Form view in, 320
 identifying database objects, 278–279, 278—279
 Layout View in, 320
 lookup list in, 316–317
 Lookup Wizard in, 316–317
 opening, 60
 primary key in, 290
  assigning, 310–311
 primary tables in, 319
 queries in, 278, 281
  calculated field in, 300–301
  Design view in creating, 294–295
  entering criteria to select records in, 296–297
  entering multiple to sort, 298–299
  exporting to Excel, 334–335
  Simple Query Wizard in creating, 292–293
 records in, 279–280
  adding, editing, and deleting in a form, 286–287
  best practices for deleting, 285
  datasheets in adding, 282–283
  editing and deleting using datasheets, 284–285
  entering criteria to select, in queries, 296–297
  entering multiple criteria to select, 298–299
  sorting and filtering, 290–291
  using find to move to, 288, 289
 relationships in
  creating, 319
  displaying and editing, 318–319
  one-to-many, 319
  one-to-one, 318–319
 reports in, 278, 280
  creating, editing, and viewing, 322–323
 Simple Query Wizard in, creating queries using, 292–293
 tables in, 278, 279
  adding fields to existing, 312–313
  creating lookup list with field values in, 316
  creating new, 308–309
  in Design View, 310–311

planning new, 206, 306–307
  primary, 319
  terminology in, 278–281

Accounting Number Format option in the Number group on the Home tab in Excel adds a dollar symbol, a comma in the thousands place, and displays two digits after the decimal point, 181–182

Action Center panel in Windows 10 opened from the Notification icon on the taskbar that displays notifications from settings, apps, applications, and connected accounts and shows quick action tiles to perform system changes, 15

active cell the cell with the green border around its edges and in which the next entry will be stored or that will be affected by a command, 176

Add Contact Picture dialog box, 116–117
adding
 in Access
  records in forms, 286–287
 in Outlook
  contacts in, 116–117
  tasks in, 118–119

Address bar the area in a web browser in which the web address (also called a URL) for a web page is viewed or typed, 38, 40

Adobe Flash Media, 264
advanced search options, 49–50
Alarms & Clock windows, 12–13

Align Left paragraph alignment in which lines of text are aligned at the left margin; left edge of page appears even, 137
alignment
 in Excel
  cells, 185
  indenting cells, 197

Align Right paragraph alignment in which text is aligned at the right margin; right edge of page appears even, 137

alignment guide colored vertical and/or horizontal line that appears while dragging an object to help you align and place the object; also called smart guides, 71, 239

Alt Text button, 150

Angle Counterclockwise option from Orientation button in Alignment group of Home tab in Excel that rotates text within the cell boundaries by 45 degrees, 199

animation involves adding a special effect to an object on a slide that causes the

G

press and hold, 5
slide, 5
swipe, 5
tap or double-tap, 5
zoom in, 5
zoom out, 5
Google, as search engine, 48
Google Chrome, navigating Web using
   advanced search options, 49–50
   bookmarking pages in, 45–46
   displaying web pages with, 44–45
     multiple, 45–46
   finding text on web page, 47
   searching Web from address bar, 46–47
   starting, 44
Go To feature to move active cell to a
   specific location in the worksheet, 198
Go To Date feature in Outlook with
   which you go directly to a specific date
   to display in the Appointment area of the
   Calendar, 110
Go To Special dialog box with options
   for moving the active cell by various cell
   attributes, 198
grammar check in Word, 130–131

H

hanging indent a paragraph in which the
   first line remains at the left margin but
   subsequent lines are indented, 138
hard page break a page break that you
   insert before the maximum number of
   lines that can fit on the page has been
   reached, 161
HD file, 347
header text that appears at the top of each
   page, 162
   in Excel, 220–221
   in PowerPoint, 249
   in Word, 162–163
help, in Office program, 76–77
hidden formatting in Word, 134
Highlight button button that allows you
   to highlight text, 90
home page the first page that displays for
   an organization when the user navigates
   to the web address of the organization, 41
Home tab, 61
horizontal scroll bar
   in Excel, 176, 177
   using, 80–81
hyperlink (link) text, image, or other
   object on a web page that when clicked
   takes you to a related Web page, 38
Hypertext Transfer Protocol, 39

I

I-beam pointer in Word, 126, 127
IF function, 210–211
images, editing, in PowerPoint presentation,
   255
Import Spreadsheet Wizard Access
   wizard used to perform an import of

Excel data into a new table in Access,
   or to append data to the bottom of an
   existing Access table, 330
   using, 330–333
Inbox Outlook mail folder into which
   received email messages are placed and
   is the active folder displayed by default
   when you start Outlook, 103
Increase Decimal button button used in
   Excel to add one decimal place to each
   selected value each time the button is
   clicked, 182
Increase Indent button button that
   moves a paragraph away from the left
   margin in a document or left edge of a
   cell in a worksheet each time the button
   is clicked, 138, 197
Increase List Level button button used
   to move text right to the next indent
   position within a bullet list placeholder in
   PowerPoint, 236
information, using search engine, to locate
   on the Web, 48–49
inline reply typing a reply to the sender of
   an email message from the Reading pane
   in Outlook, 104
Insert button button in Cells group on
   Home tab of Excel ribbon used to insert
   new cells, rows, or columns, 190
Insert Caption feature used to add text
   above or below an image to label the
   image or add other descriptive text, 151
inserting
   in Access
     columns, 300–301
   in Excel
     columns, 190–191
     commands, 222–223
     header and footer, 220–221
     rows, 190–191
     worksheets, 196–197
   in PowerPoint
     pictures, 254–255
     slides, 232–233
     SmartArt graphics, 256–257
     tables, 234–235
     WordArt, 258–259
   in Word
     caption with picture in documents,
      151
     citations in research paper formatting,
      164–165
     columns and rows in tables, 157
     pictures from computer in
      documents, 150
     pictures from online sources, 148–149
     table, 154–155
insertion point in Word, 126, 127, 129
Insert Options button button that
   appears in worksheet area after a new row
   or column has been inserted with options
   for formatting the new row or column,
   191

Insert Printout from PDF button
   used to insert an image, a file as an icon
   linked to the source document, or a file
   embedded on a page, 93
Insert Picture dialog box, 52
Instant search a search text box at the top
   of Mail, Calendar, People, and Tasks in
   which you search for an Outlook item by
   typing a keyword or phrase, 120–121
International Standards Organization (ISO)
   date format, 209
internet (net) a global network that links
   other networks such as government
   departments, businesses, nonprofit
   organizations, educational and research
   institutions, and individuals, 38
internet protocol (IP) address a unique
   name for every device connected to the
   internet for devices and computers to link
   to, 38
internet service provider (ISP) a
   company that provides access to the
   internet's infrastructure for a fee, 38

J

Justify paragraph alignment in which extra
   space is added between words so that the
   text is evenly distributed between the left
   and right margins; both sides of the page
   appear even with this alignment, 137

K

keyboard. *See also* touch keyboard
   navigating Windows 10 with, 7
keyboard command a key or
   combination of keys (such as Ctrl plus a
   letter) that performs a command, 7
   basics for Window 10, 7
   copy, 28
   cut, 30
   in Excel
     editing cell, 179
     selecting cells, 180
   paste, 28
   Word
     page breaks, 161
     paragraph alignment, 137
kiosk show, setting up, in PowerPoint
   presentation, 272–273

L

landscape layout orientation in which
   the text is rotated to the wider side of
   the page with a 9-inch line length at the
   default margin setting, 160, 194
Layout Options button gallery that
   provides options to control how an image
   and surrounding text interact with each
   other, 148
Layout view Access view in which you
   edit the structure and appearance of a
   form or report, 320
Line and Paragraph Spacing button

Image Credits

Microsoft images used with permission from Microsoft.

Chapter 1 4: Used with permission from Microsoft.; 6: istockphoto.com/Pen Wu, istockphoto.com/Malgorzata Beldowska, istockphoto.com/Kamil Krawczyk; 22: Used with permission from Microsoft.

Chapter 2 39: Courtesy of NASA.; 41: Courtesy of the NPS., Courtesy of the NPS., Courtesy of the NPS., Courtesy of the NPS., Courtesy of the Library of Congress.; 49: Used with permission from Duck Duck Go.

Chapter 5 115: Image from D. Roseneau, U.S. Fish and Wildlife Service, NIST

Chapter 7 157: ©shutterstock/onilmilk; 158: Courtesy of Wikimedia Commons/Memorial_Building_Whitman_College.jpg

Chapter 11 254: Painted bunting courtesy of NPS.; 255: Flickr/Dan Pancamo, Wikimedia/Unknown author; 265: Courtesy of: Julio C. Rios, Port St Lucie, Florida via Vimeo.com

Chapter 13 328: © Royalty-Free/CORBIS;

Chapter 15 357: CC License/Courtesy of Falls Church Times.;